EVENT MANAGEMENT

FOR TOURISM, CULTURAL, BUSINESS AND SPORTING EVENTS

OMAGH COLLEGE

D1428818

Pearson Education Australia
Unit 4, Level 2
14 Aquatic Drive
Frenchs Forest NSW 2086

www.pearsoned.com.au

Acquisitions Editor: Matthew Coxhill
Project Editor: Rebecca Pomponio
Copy Editor: Kathryn Lamberton
Proofreader: Kathryn Lamberton
Permissions Coordinator: Louise Burke
Cover and internal design by Natalie Bowra
Cover photo of ARIA Awards setup by Annabel Moeller/EventPix. Event produced by Republic
    Events (Melbourne).
Typeset by Midland Typesetters, Maryborough, Vic.

Printed in Malaysia, PP

5 09 08 07 06

    Van der Wagen, Lynn.
    Event management for tourism, cultural, business and
    sporting events.

    2nd ed.
    Bibliography.
    Includes index.
    For TAFE students.
    ISBN 1 86250 535 7.

    1. Entertainment events - Planning. 2. Entertainment
    events - Management. 3. Special events - Management. 4.
    Special events - Planning. 5. Tourism. I. Title.

    394.2068

PEARSON
Hospitality
Press

An imprint of Pearson Education Australia
(a division of Pearson Australia Group Pty Ltd)

Contents

Preface   viii

PART 1   **STRATEGIC MANAGEMENT**   **1**

Chapter 1   **Introduction to Event Management**   3
Size of events   5
Types of events   8
The event team   12
Event technology   12
Event management associations and resources   13
Ethical issues   14
Updating industry knowledge   15

Chapter 2   **Event Concept Development**   18
Developing the concept   19
Analysing the concept   24
Designing the event   26
Logistics of the concept   29

Chapter 3   **Feasibility of Event Projects**   31
Keys to success   31
The SWOT analysis   41
Project planning   41
Models of financial performance   41

Chapter 4   **Event Venue and Site Selection**   45
Analysing venue and site requirements   47
Confirming venue arrangements   54
Drafting scale maps   56

Chapter 5	**Legal Compliance**	**59**
	Updating legal knowledge	60
	Sources of law	60
	Legislation relevant to events	63
	Insurance	68
	Stakeholders and official bodies	71
	Contracts	71
	Policies, procedures and staff training	73

Chapter 6	**Business and Client Relationships**	**75**
	Who is the client?	76
	Analysing the needs of client populations	76
	Types of market segmentation	78
	Why is market segmentation necessary?	79
	Pros and cons of primary and secondary research	80
	Business relationships	82
	Evaluating client service relationships	84

Chapter 7	**Event Marketing**	**86**
	Nature of event marketing	87
	Process of event marketing	89
	The marketing mix	93
	Sponsorship	95
	Developing a marketing plan	97

Chapter 8	**Event Sponsorship**	**108**
	Motives for sponsorship	111
	Event categories for business sponsorship	112
	Types of sponsorship	113
	Sponsorship implementation	113
	Sponsorship evaluation	116
	Merchandising and other forms of income generation	118

Chapter 9	**Financial Management**	**121**
	The budget	123
	Budgeting process	124
	Break-even point	128
	Income strategy	128
	Cash flow analysis	129
	Account codes and prefixes	130
	Profit and loss statement	131
	Balance sheet	132
	Financial control systems	132
	Panic payments	133
	Post-event reporting	133

Chapter 10   **Risk Management**   **141**

What is risk?   142

Strategic risk management   145

Developing a risk management policy   153

Implementing and monitoring risk management strategies   154

Crisis management   154

Chapter 11   **Event Proposals and Bids**   **157**

Bidding, tendering and applying for grants   159

Interpreting the event brief   160

Researching information for a bid or tender   160

Addressing the criteria in the bid   161

Types of bids   165

Bid detail   166

Presentation of the bid document   166

PART 2   **OPERATIONAL PLANNING**   **169**

Chapter 12   **Event Project Management**   **171**

Develop a mission/purpose statement   172

Establish the aims of the event   173

Establish the objectives   174

Prepare an event proposal   175

Make use of planning tools   176

Facilitate communication   183

Chapter 13   **Event Promotion**   **186**

Image/branding   187

Promotional activities   187

Public relations and publicity   194

Promotional action plans   198

Chapter 14   **Staging Management**   **202**

Choosing the event site   203

Developing the theme   206

Conducting rehearsals   211

Providing services   212

Working with contractors   214

Arranging catering   215

Organising accommodation   216

Managing the environment   217

Chapter 15   **Staffing and Volunteer Management**   **220**

Developing organisation charts   221

Preparing job descriptions   221

Recruitment and selection ... 224
Drawing up rosters ... 229
Training ... 229
Managing legal requirements ... 232
Preparing staffing policies ... 233
Developing recognition strategies ... 233
Managing volunteers ... 234

Chapter 16   **People Performance Management** ... **239**
Developing leadership skills ... 240
Managing temporary and diverse teams ... 244
Motivation theories ... 245
Group development ... 248
Improving communication ... 249
Time management ... 250
Planning and managing meetings ... 251

Chapter 17   **On-site Management** ... **253**
Planning logistics ... 254
Developing operational policies and procedures ... 258
Establishing performance standards ... 258
Functional areas ... 259
Managing staff, volunteers and contractors ... 263

Chapter 18   **Safety and Security** ... **266**
Security ... 267
Occupational health and safety ... 269
Risk management ... 274
Process of risk management ... 274
Health and safety training and meetings ... 277
Incident reporting ... 278
Safety at outdoor events ... 280

Chapter 19   **Spectator Management** ... **284**
Spectator management plan ... 284
Risk management plan ... 287
Emergency planning ... 289
Implementing emergency procedures ... 291

Chapter 20   **Event Protocol** ... **296**
Order of precedence ... 297
Titles ... 297
Styles of address ... 299
Dress for formal occasions ... 300
Protocol for speakers ... 300
Seating plans for formal occasions ... 300

	Welcome to country	300
	Religious and cultural protocol	301
	Protocol for sporting ceremonies	304
	Rules of flag flying	305

Chapter 21	**Event Catering**	**308**
	Catering responsibilities	309
	Food preparation and service	313
	Beverage service	315
	Negotiating catering contracts	316
	Implementing the catering plan	317
	Food safety planning	317
	Waste management	320

Chapter 22	**Waste and Environmental Management**	**322**
	Planning a 'Waste Wise' event	323
	Logistics of waste management	324
	Communicating the waste management message	324
	Planning sanitary facilities	329
	General cleaning	330

Chapter 23	**Event Impact and Evaluation**	**332**
	Monitoring and control systems	333
	Operational monitoring and control	335
	Event evaluation	337
	Sponsorship evaluation	340
	Broader impact of events	340

Chapter 24	**Careers in a Changing Environment**	**346**
	Job opportunities	347
	Keeping up to date	350

Appendix A	Integrated Assessment — Event Proposal	355
Appendix B	Event Observation and Analysis Questionnaire	361
Appendix C	Heritage Festival — Edmonton 2003 Annual Report	363
Appendix D	Supplementary Internet Links	379

| Bibliography | | 382 |
| Index | | 385 |

Preface

As a professional field of practice, event management requires sophisticated skills in strategic planning, risk analysis, marketing, budgeting, cash flow planning and human resource management. There are chapters on all these topics and many others in this book. Indeed, more and more public events, such as the National Folk Festival illustrated in Chapter 9, are appointing professionally trained staff to senior positions. The project nature of events, as well as the range of risks they carry (including financial risk), ensures that skilled and knowledgeable management staff are required in the industry. Indeed, many major projects in today's corporate world are one-off events requiring these skills.

Event management, as a diploma or degree program, is a business course with a strong project focus. Topics covered include marketing, accounting and legal compliance. A small event planning team can explode to a workforce of several hundred for the short period of an event, thus providing significant challenges for human resource management. The skills and knowledge gained in the study of event management can be used in a diverse range of contexts. Event management can cover a wide range of interest areas including business, sport and the arts. Most significantly, governments and local councils are developing extensive policies and procedures supported by legislation, making legal compliance and risk management important roles for the professional event manager. The tourism impact of events is increasingly attracting the interest of governments seeking to maximise domestic and international tourism revenues. All these trends work towards the development of event management as a professional practice.

Having taught in the field of event management at Northern Beaches TAFE for the past five years, I can say that this is the most exciting environment in which one could hope to work. Students emerge with business and project management skills of the highest order, ready to face any business challenge. They can confidently apply for a wide range of positions (few are titled event manager) for which this type of training has prepared them. Indeed, recognising the project orientation and customer responsiveness of most modern organisations, students are confident that they are developing skills for the future. Many events are also community focused and this has particular appeal for many entrants to these positions.

There are several people who played a direct role in the writing of this book. Ron Beeldman read the proofs and provided feedback. Warwick Hamilton of Events Unlimited contributed many ideas and useful information included in the text. Peter Wilson provided advice on accounting (sorely needed). Nerolli Cassidy offered valuable feedback on several chapters and ongoing moral support!

This text is based on the Tourism & Hospitality and Sport & Recreation Training packages, copyright Australian National Training Authority, ANTA. Training packages comprise nationally endorsed standards and qualifications for assessing and recognising people's skills. In order to accurately reflect the nationally agreed guidelines, a number of headings, paragraphs and lists from the training packages have been integrated into the text and the author hereby acknowledges the use of this copyright material.

Many organisations made invaluable contributions by providing case studies, diagrams, photographs and discussion material. They include Adelaide Festival Centre; Arts Victoria; Australian Blues Music Festival; Australian Bomb Data Centre; Australian Bureau of Statistics; Australian Government National Capital Authority; Blue Mountains City Council; Cairns Convention Centre; Campbelltown Council; Clean Up Australia; Disability Services Commission, WA; EcoRecycle; Edinburgh Festival; Edmonton Festival; Eventscorp WA; Exhibition Hire Service; ICMS; ISES; Food Safety Victoria; Maleny Scarecrow Festival; Medinet; Melbourne Comedy Festival; Mosman Council; Mt Isa Rodeo; Musicological Society of Australia; National Folk Festival; New Mardi Gras; New Zealand Festival; New Zealand Royal Easter Show; Quantum Market Research; The SheppARTon Festival; Singapore Jazz Festival; Staging Connections; Standards Australia; Summernats; *Sun-Herald*; Suntec Singapore; *Sydney Morning Herald*; Tourism Training Australia; Tourism Victoria; Toyota Muster; TravelSmart; Waste Wise Events; Woodford Folk Festival; Worksafe Western Australia.

Thanks also to Jennifer Anson, Ellen Connolly, Ashlee Critchley, Stephen Dabkowski, Geesche Jacobsen, Maria Ligerakis, Max Mosley, Kirsty Needham, Mike Tauber, Danielle Teutsch, and the Grand Prix Girls.

Kathryn Lamberton has edited all my books. It has always been a pleasure working with her and with my publishers, Pearson Education Australia. To my loyal readers, students everywhere, thank you for your feedback. May all your events be successful!

Lynn Van Der Wagen

PART ONE

STRATEGIC MANAGEMENT

E vent management is particularly challenging from an operational viewpoint. In many cases events are staged on sites where everything has been set up over a 24-hour period, with all elements carefully synchronised. In contrast, many events are years in the planning: large convention bids are often won five years before the event is held. For the very competitive bidding process, budgets need to be developed and prices quoted, requiring a good understanding of market, economic and political trends, as well as consumer choices. This long-term view is the basis of strategic management, which is covered in Part 1, and focuses on the event concept, feasibility of the event, legal compliance and financial management. Marketing is a critical success factor and another important topic of this first section, many events (sporting, cultural and arts) involving long-term sponsorship arrangements with key industry players. Relationship building is particularly challenging since there are so many stakeholders involved in events, including government agencies at many levels. Part 1 will look at all these aspects, including strategic risk, before moving on to the second part where operational planning and implementation will be covered in detail.

COMPETENCIES

Chapter 1	Event Industry Knowledge	THTFME03A	Develop and update industry knowledge
Chapter 2	Event Concept Development	THTFME04A	Develop an event concept
Chapter 3	Feasibility of Event Projects	THHGGA09B Element 01	Manage projects
Chapter 4	Event Venue and Site Selection	THTFME05A	Select event venues and sites
Chapter 5	Legal compliance	SRXINU004A	Promote compliance with laws and legal principles

		THHGLE20B	Develop and update the legal knowledge required for business compliance
Chapter 6	Business and Client Relationships	SRXGCSS07A	Determine needs of client populations
		THHGCS08B	Establish and conduct business relationships
Chapter 7	Event Marketing	BSBMGT501A	Market services and concepts to internal customers
Chapter 8	Event Sponsorship	THTPPD10B	Develop and implement sponsorship plans
Chapter 9	Financial Management	THHGLE14B	Prepare and monitor budgets
Chapter 10	Risk Management	THHGLE22A	Manage risk
Chapter 11	Event Proposals and Bids	THTPPD08B	Plan and develop event proposals and bids

CHAPTER ONE

INTRODUCTION TO

EVENT MANAGEMENT

ON COMPLETION OF THIS CHAPTER YOU WILL BE ABLE TO:

- explain the structure and operation of the event industry
- classify and describe events according to size and type
- discuss relationships between event managers and other stakeholders
- discuss some of the ethical and legal issues relevant to event management
- update event industry knowledge.

As the massive storm bore down on the 1998 Sydney to Hobart fleet, the Cruising Yacht Club of Australia 'abdicated its responsibility to manage the race', the State Coroner found yesterday. In a damning indictment of the club, Mr John Abernethy said in his report: 'From what I have read and heard it is clear to me that during this crucial time the race management team played the role of observers rather than managers and that was simply not good enough'.

The roles assigned to individual members of the race management team had been so ill-defined as to be 'practically useless' and the team was organised in a way that made it, in a crisis, 'to all intents and purposes, valueless'.

SYDNEY MORNING HERALD, 13 DECEMBER 2000

The aim of this book is to assist you in your training to become an event manager of the highest calibre. Many of us have observed events, most of us have participated in events, but few of us have managed events. As an event manager, you are there to do far more than just observe. You are there to ensure the smooth running of the event, to minimise the risks and to maximise the enjoyment of the event audience. The demands on an event manager are far greater than one would expect.

Many events carry a significant risk to the safety of participants. The above example focuses on just one of the many safety risks and indicates what can happen when the management team plays the role of 'observers rather than managers'.

Financial risk is also an important concern of the event manager. Events are generally extremely expensive, with high expenditure required over a very short period of time, and there are far higher levels of uncertainty about revenue and profit than there are with the average business.

In the case of voluntary and charitable events, of which there are many in every community, the risk is that the time invested by individuals will be wasted and their objectives will not be achieved.

Finally, one of the most important things about an event is that it is often a highlight of a person's life. This is not to be taken lightly. A significant birthday, a wedding or a christening is so important to the main participants that nothing must go wrong. If something does go wrong, it cannot be easily rectified. A wedding at which the power fails due to overloading of the electrical supply cannot be repeated. The offer to 'come back again at our expense' just doesn't work! The event manager therefore carries overall responsibility for ensuring that the event, however large or small, is a success as there is often only one chance to get it right.

The Rugby World Cup in 2003 was certainly a 'once in a lifetime' experience.

From what we have discussed so far, events are characterised by the following:
- They are often 'once in a lifetime' experiences for the participants.
- They are generally expensive to stage.
- They usually take place over a short time span.
- They require long and careful planning.
- They generally take place once only. (However, many are held annually, usually at the same time every year.)
- They carry a high level of risk, including financial risk and safety risk.
- There is often a lot at stake for those involved, including the event management team.

This last characteristic is crucial, since every performer, whether athlete or entertainer, wants to deliver their best performance. The bride wants the day to be perfect in every way. The marketing manager and the design team want the new product to be seen in the best possible light. Consider for a moment how much easier it is to run a restaurant (where you spread your risk over a number of days and a number of customers) than it is to run a one-off, big-budget product launch — particularly if this launch has 500 key industry players and the media in attendance, and is taking place at a unique location with unusual demands for logistics, lighting, sound and special effects.

Having pointed out the level of demand on the event manger and thus the possible downside of the profession, it is important also to point out that the event industry is one in which people (the event audience) tend to have the time of their lives. Making this possible and sharing this with them is extremely gratifying. The work is demanding, exciting and challenging, requiring a finely tuned balance between task management and people management. As the newspaper article illustrates, an event manager must bring together a team with clearly defined responsibilities for all aspects of the event, including unexpected crises. The team needs to be both organised and flexible. Events can be unpredictable and do require quick thinking, based on a sound knowledge of procedures and alternatives. Decision-making is one of the most important skills of the event manager, and those with first-class analytical skills are highly sought after by most industries.

Professor Donald Getz (1997), a well-known writer in the field of event management, defines special events from two perspectives, that of the customer and that of the event manager, as follows:

- *A special event is a one-time or infrequently occurring event outside normal programs or activities of the sponsoring or organizing body.*
- *To the customer or guest, a special event is an opportunity for a leisure, social or cultural experience outside the normal range of choices or beyond everyday experience.*

Another well-known author, Dr J Goldblatt (1997), defines special events as 'A unique moment in time celebrated with ceremony and ritual to satisfy specific needs'.

In this book, the emphasis is on a wide range of events, including 'special events', as defined above, and more common events such as sporting events, meetings, parties, carnivals and prize-giving ceremonies, which may not meet the definition 'outside the normal range of choices'.

SIZE OF EVENTS

Classification of events can be done on the basis of size or type, as follows.

Mega-events

The largest events are called mega-events and these are generally targeted at international markets. The Olympic Games, Commonwealth Games, World Cup Soccer and Superbowl are good examples. The Superbowl, for which in 1967 there were 30 000 tickets unsold, now sells out before the tickets have been printed and attracts 100 000 visitors to the host city. It is televised to an audience of 800 million and adds US$300 million to the local economy.

All such events have a specific yield in terms of increased tourism, media coverage and economic impact. While some cities are continuing to meet a legacy of debt after hosting an Olympic Games, Sydney was fortunate in meeting its budget due to a last-minute surge in ticket and merchandise sales, returning $10 million to taxpayers. However, as with all events of this size, it is difficult to calculate the costs accurately with so many stakeholders (mainly government) involved. The budget for the Athens Olympic Games did not include a new tram network and a suburban rail line, which were both funded by the European Union's Third Community Support Framework.

While the size of the Olympic Games in terms of expenditure, sponsorship, economic impact and worldwide audience would undoubtedly put it in the category of mega-event, it is worth comparing its size with, for example, that of the Maha Kumbh Mela ('Grand Pitcher Festival'), the largest religious gathering in history. During 2001, approximately 70 million Hindu pilgrims converged on the Holy River Ganges for a sacred bathing ritual. The gathering takes place every 12 years and the 1989 Maha Kumbh Mela in Allahabad was attended by 15 million devotees. The 2001 festival will no doubt hold the record as the world's largest assembly of people for some time to come.

World's largest assembly of people.

Photo: Mike Tauber with permission

Hallmark events

Hallmark events are designed to increase the appeal of a specific tourism destination or region. The Tamworth Country Music Festival, the Melbourne Cup and the Adelaide Festival of Arts are all examples of tourist destinations achieving market positioning for both domestic and international tourism markets through their annual events. The annual Floriade in Canberra also fits into this category. Internationally, the Edinburgh Military Tattoo and the Carnaval Rio are international festivals with significant event tourism impact. In fact, Edinburgh has 16 key festivals that form the basis of their event tourism calendar. The events and their host cities become inseparable in the minds of consumers.

Major events

These events attract significant local interest and large numbers of participants, as well as generating significant tourism revenue. The Robbie Williams *Live Summer 2003* concert attracted a record audience in the UK of 375 000 people over five days. In Australia, 100 000 fans enjoyed his two performances. The Australian Open, Gold Coast Marathon, Royal Easter Show and the National Multicultural Festival in Canberra all fall into this category. Chinese New Year celebrations are held in most capital cities. The three-week festival in Sydney includes market stalls, food stalls, exhibitions, street entertainment, parades and dragon boat races. Friends and relatives of the Chinese community often visit at this time.

ICMS Australia, an event management organisation, has an outstanding reputation for management of such events, as indicated by the extent of commitment of ICMS and their clients:

9th World Congress of Gastroenterology
7600 delegates
ICMS commitment — six years

19th World Congress of Dermatology
6700 delegates
ICMS commitment — seven years

20th World Congress of Chemotherapy
4000 delegates
ICMS commitment — five years

ICACI 2000 (International Congress of Allergology & Clinical Immunology)
5000 delegates
ICMS commitment — seven years

14th World Congress of Cardiology
14 000 delegates
ICMS commitment — twelve years

International Congress of Human Genetics
4000 delegates
ICMS commitment — eleven years

The Sydney to Hobart yacht race mentioned at the start of this chapter also falls into this category, as would many other sporting and cultural events. The biannual World Solar Challenge is held in October in the Darwin area, while Perth promotes the Hopman Cup and the Whitbread Round the World Race.

Minor events

Most events fall into this last category, and it is here that most event managers gain their experience. Almost every town and city in Australia runs annual events. For example, the Broome area promotes the Pearl Festival, the Battle of Broome and the Mango Festival. A count of special events and festivals meticulously researched for the *Reader's Digest Book of the Road* reveals that nearly 2000 festival-type annual events are held around Australia. In addition to annual events, there are many one-off events, including historical, cultural, musical and dance performances. At one such event, parents were proudly watching their tap-dancing offspring performing in their expensive, colourful velvet outfits. Their proud expressions turned to dismay when several dancers landed on their rear ends having slipped on the stage. Quick-thinking organisers covered the stage in a mixture of soft drink and cleaning powder — all in a day's work for the event team!

Meetings, parties, celebrations, award ceremonies, sporting finals, and many other community and social events fit into this category.

TYPES OF EVENTS

In terms of type, events may be categorised as follows.

Sporting

The success of the Rugby World Cup (2003), following the success of the Olympic Games (2000) has established Australia as one of the world's leading event destinations. The professional image of the country's event organisers is firmly established following flawless planning and implementation of these and other mega-events. *The Times* special correspondent and author Bill Bryson was, like many other overseas correspondents, lavish in his praise of the Olympic Games organisation: 'I don't wish in my giddiness to overstate matters, but I invite you to suggest a more successful event anywhere in the peacetime history of mankind' (*Sydney Morning Herald*, 5 October 2000). Similar praise was heaped on organisers of the Rugby World Cup. Australian Rugby Union (ARU) chief executive John O'Neill said that revenue had also exceeded expectations and eclipsed past tournaments, with $80 million divided between the Australian Rugby Union and the world body.

Sporting events are held in all states and territories and they attract international sports men and women at the highest levels. Tennis, golf, rugby and car racing are just a few examples.

These major events are matched at the local level by sporting competitions for players at all levels. For example, the Pro Am, held annually at most golf courses, allows members to play with professional golfers. This event is usually the highlight of the golfing calendar and requires considerable effort by the team supporting it, including the PGA, the club committee, the club manager, the club professional, ground staff, club administration and catering.

The number of adults who attended a sporting event increased from 6.5 million in 1999 to 7 million in 2002 according to figures released by the Australian Bureau of Statistics. This represented an increase from 46 per cent to 48 per cent of the population aged 18 years and over. The main sport attended was Australian Rules Football (17 per cent), followed by horse racing (13 per cent) and motor sports (10 per cent) (ABS cat. no. 4174.0).

Two very different types of sporting events: race day on Sydney Harbour and the Pacific School Games 2000.

Entertainment, arts and cultural festivals

Entertainment events are well known for their ability to attract large audiences. In some cases, the concerts are extremely viable from a financial point of view; in others, financial problems can quickly escalate when ticket sales do not reach targets. Timing and ticket pricing are critical to the financial success of such events.

A survey of festivals conducted by the Australia Council showed that over half the attendances were at main arts festivals, followed by popular music festivals, and that females were more likely than males to have attended a festival. Of all international visitors aged 15 years and over, 14 per cent visited museums or art galleries (Bureau of Tourism Research, 1998).

Wine and food festivals are becoming increasingly popular nowadays, providing a particular region the opportunity to showcase its products. Small towns such as Tumbarumba in New South Wales and Mornington in Victoria attract interest with their food and wine festivals. Many wine regions hold festivals, often in combination with musical events, such as Jazz or Opera in the Vineyard. Religious festivals fall into this category, too, and Australia's multicultural community provides rich opportunities for a wide range of festivals. Chinese New Year and Carols in the Domain are good examples.

About 300 festivals devoted solely, or partly, to cultural activities are staged every year in Australia. Among the biggest are Adelaide's biennial arts festival and the annual arts festivals held in Sydney, Melbourne and Perth. Each lasts several weeks and attracts many visitors.

A balloon artist captivating a child at an Irish festival.

Commercial, marketing and promotional events

Promotional events tend to have high budgets and high profiles. Most frequently they involve product launches, often for computer hardware or software, perfume, alcohol or motor cars. One such marketing activity dazzled attendees with its new launch motorbikes riding overhead on tightropes, with special effect lighting.

The aim of promotional events is generally to differentiate the product from its competitors and to ensure that it is memorable. The audience for a promotional activity might be sales staff, such as travel agents, who would promote the particular tour to their clients or potential purchasers. The media are usually invited to these events so that both the impact and the risk are high. Success is vital.

Meetings, conventions and exhibitions

The meetings and conventions sector is highly competitive, as is the exhibitions sector. Known as MICE (Meetings, Incentives, Conferences and Exhibitions), these sectors are aligned under the

MICE banner with an associated bi-monthly journal. They can be more simply labelled as 'Business Events'. Many conventions attract 3000 or more people, while some meetings include only a handful of high-profile participants. Australia's worldwide popularity as a holiday destination has had a positive effect on its capacity for winning convention bids and attracting delegates. In the year ending June 2000, there were a total of 118 558 visitors to Australia for the purpose of attending a convention or conference, which was an increase of 8.8 per cent on the previous 12 months. Australia was ranked fourth in the world for the number of international conventions and business meetings held each year, up from seventh in 1999 according to this research. Australia hosted a record 152 meetings in 2000, outclassing destinations such as Spain, France and Italy. The number of international conventions in Australia rose by 37 per cent on the 1999 figures, boosted by Olympics exposure. Four Australian cities ranked among the top 51 convention destinations worldwide, with Sydney fifth, Melbourne fifteenth, Adelaide thirty-third and Brisbane fifty-first (Australian Tourist Commission, 2001).

The meetings category covers a wide variety, including:
- academic conferences (papers presented along a common theme by industry experts and academics are generally held on a one-off or annual basis)
- corporate meetings (large assemblies of staff and/or clients meet a range of informational and social needs, providing product updates and networking opportunities)
- association meetings (businesses belonging to a particular association, such as a wine growers association, may meet to discuss marketplace trends, consumption and other topical issues)
- government meetings (eductional forums within government departments or similar forums to which the public are invited to participate and comment)
- incentive meetings and travel (workers who meet their sales targets or who are being rewarded for their productivity are invited on incentive travel programs, which generally include a conference and leisure activities).

Exhibitions and trade shows are another special area, with annual shows featuring travel products; motor cars; agricultural equipment; craft supplies; giftware, etc. These may be open to the public as exhibitions or open only to members of the particular trade (for example, hairdressers).

Family events

Weddings, christenings, bar mitzvahs and, these days, divorces and funerals all provide opportunities for families to gather. Funerals are increasingly becoming big events with non-traditional coffins, speeches and even entertainment. It is important for the event manager to keep track of these changing social trends. For example, Asian tourists are a big market for the wedding industry, with many couples having a traditional ceremony at home and a Western wedding overseas. Australia and New Zealand compete with destinations such as Hawaii for this market.

Fundraising

Fetes and fairs are common in most communities, and are frequently run by enthusiastic local committees. The effort and organisation required for these events is often underestimated. As their general aim is raising funds, it is important that children's rides and other such contracted activities contribute to, rather than reduce, revenue. Sometimes the revenue gained from these operations is limited. There is also the risk that attendees will spend all their money on these activities and ignore those which are more profitable to the charitable cause. A number of legal requirements must be met by the charitable fundraiser and these are covered in Chapter 5.

Miscellaneous events

Some events defy categorisation. Potatoes, walnuts, wildflowers, roses, working dogs, horses, teddy bears and ducks all provide the focus for an event somewhere in Australia. The following list of some of the events held in Queensland demonstrates how varied these can be in terms of size and type (some falling into previous categories but others quite unique):

Allora Bush Christmas
Allora Celtic Concert
Almaden Races
Ambiwerra Wine, Food and All That Jazz Festival
American Independence Day
Andrew Fisher Day at Gympie
Anglican Spring Fair
Annual Australian Heritage Festival
Annual Drovers Reunion Festival
Annual Old Station Fly-in and Air Show
Anzac Day Celebrations at Proserpine
Asia Pacific Masters Games
Atherton Tableland Agricultural Show
Australia Day Awards and Citizenship Ceremony at Logan
Australian College of Tropical Agriculture Open Day
Australian Festival of Chamber Music
Australian International Movie Convention
Australian Italian Festival
Australian National Skydiving Championships
Australian Small Winemakers Show
Australian Surf Rowers League Convention
Autumn Gourmet Weekend
Back to the Bush Weekend
Back to the 60s Weekend
Bat out of Hell Raceday
Bayside Art and Craft Spectacular
Big Boys Toys Expo
Birdsville Races
Brass Monkey Season
Bribie Island Apex Mullet Festival
Bundy in Bloom Spring Festival
Burdekin Centenary of Federation Festival

It has to be said that the most common events are community related, and are run on a fairly small scale with voluntary support and sponsorship. These events provide the potential event manager with invaluable experience, as well as the opportunity to contribute to their community. Every event has a purpose and the theme is generally linked to the purpose. Analysis of even the smallest event can provide valuable insight into the general principles that apply to managing all events.

THE EVENT TEAM

An event manager is generally supported by a team which grows exponentially as the event draws near. A planning team of 12 that works together for a year can explode into a team of 500 for the short period of the event. This phenomenon has been termed the 'pulsing organization' by Alvin Toffler (1980), who coined the term to describe organisations that expand and contract in size. This is particularly appropriate for organisations such as the Australian Open Tennis Championships, as they surge in numbers for a short period every year.

Having just mentioned contractors, it is important to note that the event manager typically works with a number of contractors. These could include any or all of the following:

- venue managers
- stage managers
- lighting, audio and video companies
- decorators and florists
- entertainers
- employment agencies
- rental companies
- public relations and marketing consultants
- security companies
- catering companies
- cleaning companies
- ticketing operations
- printers.

For most events, the manager is also required to liaise with government agencies at a range of levels, from local government through to federal government. Local councils deal with event planning and approval; state governments provide approvals for traffic and policing; and the federal government gives advice on protocol for international dignitaries. These relationships will be explored further when looking in more detail at the planning and staging of an event (Chapters 12 and 14).

Fig. 1.1 illustrates the various relationships that exist within the event business, although this is very hard to characterise due to the diversity of events and the functional responsibilities required to stage them.

EVENT TECHNOLOGY

The scope of technology used for events is diverse, ranging from generic project management software to specialised logistics systems. Security systems are becoming increasingly complex, and even banquet chefs employ computerised cooking and refrigeration processes.

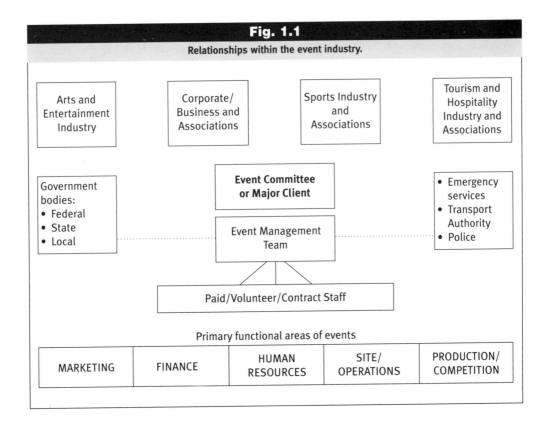

Fig. 1.1

Relationships within the event industry.

| Arts and Entertainment Industry | Corporate/ Business and Associations | Sports Industry and Associations | Tourism and Hospitality Industry and Associations |

Government bodies:
• Federal
• State
• Local

Event Committee or Major Client

Event Management Team

• Emergency services
• Transport Authority
• Police

Paid/Volunteer/Contract Staff

Primary functional areas of events

| MARKETING | FINANCE | HUMAN RESOURCES | SITE/ OPERATIONS | PRODUCTION/ COMPETITION |

The main technology solutions used by the industry include:

- project planning software (Gannt charts and PERT charts used for critical path analysis)
- venue booking systems (for leasing and contracting venues and services)
- audience reservation and registration systems (used for concert ticketing, conference bookings, races and competitions)
- identification and accreditation systems (to capture data about individuals attending exhibitions or race officials working in the field of play)
- employee records and police checks
- security systems (for managing assets, checking inventory, monitoring crowd movements)
- CAD systems (for designing stages, stands and venues)
- timing and scoring sytems
- broadcasting systems (for example, big screen replays, closed circuit for judging)
- communications systems (for example, radio)

Given the wide range of applications used at a major event, a sophisticated IT team is needed for installation of computer networks, customisation of software and integration of the tasks performed by the software packages.

EVENT MANAGEMENT ASSOCIATIONS AND RESOURCES

There are many event management associations that suppport the industry. The primary associations are listed below but there are others listed in Appendix D:

AEIA

Australian Entertainment Industry Association, the peak employer body in the arts and entertainment industry, has been registered with the Australian Industrial Relations Commission since 1917.

EEAA

Exhibition & Events Association of Australia primarily focuses on the exhibition industry.

EIA (WA)

The Events Industry Association (WA) is the peak events organisation in Western Australia.

FEA

The Festivals & Events Association members work primarily on public events.

IFEA

International Festivals & Events Association

ISES Sydney/ISES Melbourne

The International Special Events Society represents the interests of event producers, managers and suppliers working primarily in the corporate sector.

ISES (US)

The International Special Events Society's US headquarters site features a searchable database of ISES members worldwide.

MIAA

The Meetings Industry Association of Australia covers the conference industry.

VMA

Venue Management Association

ETHICAL ISSUES

As with all modern professions, the presence of a code of ethics can enhance the reputations of those involved, and can assist the customer to feel confident in their choice of event manager, supplier or contractor. Ethical issues for the event business that may emerge include gifts or kickbacks associated with commission procedures, bookings at venues and subcontracting. Other issues of concern include confidentiality of information, including client databases and information about celebrities, overbooking and overpricing.

The International Special Events Society (ISES) has the following code of ethics:

- *Promote and encourage the highest level of ethics within the profession of the special events industry while maintaining the highest standards of professional conduct.*
- *Strive for excellence in all aspects of our profession by performing consistently at or above acceptable industry standards.*
- *Use only legal and ethical means in all industry negotiations and activities.*
- *Protect the public against fraud and unfair practices and promote all practices which bring credit to the profession.*
- *Maintain adequate and appropriate insurance coverage for all business activities.*
- *Maintain industry standard of safety and sanitation.*
- *Provide truthful and accurate information with respect to the performance of duties. Use a written contract stating all changes, services, products, performance expectations and other essential information.*

- *Commit to increase professional growth and knowledge, to attend educational programs and to personally contribute expertise to meetings and journals.*
- *Strive to co-operate with colleagues, suppliers, employees/employers and all persons supervised, in order to provide the highest quality service at every level.*
- *Subscribe to the ISES Principles of Professional Conduct and Ethics, and abide by ISES By-laws and Policies.*

UPDATING INDUSTRY KNOWLEDGE

By staying up to date with industry trends, you can take advantage of new technologies, stay abreast of legislative changes and monitor consumer trends. Legal issues that concern professionals working in the industry relate to public liability, duty of care, licensing, risk management, and occupational health and safety. All of these are newsworthy issues, with case studies emerging almost daily.

Staying up to date can be done by:
- reading newspapers
- attending industry seminars
- participating in training seminars
- upgrading and extending qualifications
- joining relevant associations
- participating in industry association activities
- networking with colleagues
- reading industry journals
- subscribing to industry magazines (for example, *MiceNet*)
- web research.

Careers in the event business are extremely varied, few having the title Event Manager. As the last chapter in this book shows, there are many and varied event position titles, including Catering Sales Manager, Logistics Co-ordinator, Sponsorship Manager, Race Director, Production Manager and so on. Conventions, exhibitions, sports competitions, product launches, charity gala dinners, incentive tours and music performances all come under the umbrella of event management. The skills required are largely in the area of project management, covering the full range of traditional business skills, but applied in a more challenging, dynamic and deadline driven environment. Continued research and reading will enable you, the reader, to develop a better understanding of this evolving professional field and the many players involved, ranging from government to business and community groups.

Changing technology and its application to the event environment is one such consideration. For example, audiences at music performances are now able to purchase a CD of the performance as they leave. This techological solution to music pirating and copyright infringement serves to satisfy the event audience by providing a lasting memory of an enjoyable performance. Such value-adding also contributes to increased merchandise sales.

More detailed information is given on all the topics we have introduced here in the chapters that follow.

A group of university students decided to hold a rave party in the mountains in December, and advertised it on the Internet. Three bands attended the three-day party and there was 24-hour music. One young girl described it as living hell, although why she stayed is unfathomable. 'The dance area was in a valley and to get a drink of water you had to climb a steep hill. Even then, the water was dirty and brown. The toilets were so far away that nobody bothered to use them. The music pounded all night and the floor vibrated so you couldn't sleep. My friend was unwell and there was no medical help. The organisers didn't have a clue. They just wanted to make a fast buck.'

- What are some of the things that could go wrong, or have gone wrong, at similar events?
- List three ways in which the organisers were negligent.
- List three ways in which the event could have been improved.
- This event was described to the authorities as a cultural festival. Do you think it belongs in that category?
- The legal compliance issues of such an event will be covered in Chapter 5. However, what are some of the ethical issues involved in this and other events?

ACTIVITY

Investigate two events (ideally two that are quite different) and describe them in detail. You might like to do your research on the Internet, starting with one of the state or territory tourism web pages such as <www.tourism.nsw.gov.au> or <www.cyberlink.com.au/events/vic-events.htm>, or you could visit your local council. If you are attending an event, use the questions in Appendix B to guide you.

LINKS

Department of Industry, Tourism and Resources, Sport and Tourism Division
www.tourism.gov.au

ICMS Australia
www.icmsaust.com.au

International Special Events Society
www.ises.com

International Special Events Society, Australia
www.ises.org.au

Maha Kumbh Mela Festival
www.kumbhmela.net

Queensland events
www.qldevents.com.au

SUMMARY

In this chapter we have introduced you to some of the unique characteristics of events, one being that they are often one-off or annual occurrences, thus creating a high level of risk. This means that the event team has only one opportunity to get everything right. Most events take months or even years to plan, depending on the type and size of the event. And their focus varies, from the strictly commercial product launch to the school fete which aims to raise funds with the help of the local community. There are numerous stakeholders involved and each event has its unique character. The issues facing the event manager are mainly legal, logistical and financial. The job is also challenging from a people management point of view as it includes liaison with clients, government bodies, support services, contractors, volunteers and paid staff. Keeping up to date with your knowledge of the event industry, particularly technology and legal compliance, underpins effective performance in all organisational and management roles.

CHAPTER TWO

EVENT

CONCEPT DEVELOPMENT

ON COMPLETION OF THIS CHAPTER YOU WILL BE ABLE TO:

- establish the purpose/objectives of an event
- develop a theme and format that is consistent with the purpose
- analyse the needs of the event audience
- review financial and other resources
- identify an appropriate venue to suit the purpose of an event
- establish the timing and duration of an event
- review the logistical requirements of an event.

Steeped in over 40 years of history, The Mount Isa Rotary Rodeo (as it was first known) was born out of a desire by a young service club to 'think big'. The first Rotary Club in Mount Isa had been in operation for some months and had successfully completed a number of small community service projects. However, the Community Service Director felt the club needed to tackle a big project, one which would put Mount Isa on the map. And so the idea of staging a rodeo was unanimously and enthusiastically adopted, despite the fact that none of the club members had ever been involved in organising one before. Only a couple of members had even seen a rodeo! With no ground, no stock and no experience, a rodeo organising committee was formed and set about the task of staging the first ever Mount Isa Rotary Rodeo in 1959. Since its inception, the Mount Isa Rotary Rodeo has donated in excess of $2.5 million to charitable, community, cultural, sporting and service organisations. As accommodation outlets report a 100 per cent occupancy rate during the rodeo period, additional temporary camping facilities are created within the city, simply to cater for the Rodeo overflow.

MOUNT ISA ROTARY RODEO

V olunteerism and community support are the backbone of this successful event that injects $7 million into the region's economy. The rodeo is held in August and includes bareback bronc-riding, bull-riding, steer-wrestling and the much-loved rodeo clowns. The support of over 50 sponsors also contributes to the execution of this event and its long-standing success.

It is an excellent example of a concept that has worked and continues to work. Research undertaken by Molloy (2002) indicates a positive correlation between community support and community isolation in that the further a community lies from large metropolitan centres, the stronger is the level of community support.

In this chapter we will look at event concept and design — the creative element that inspires many to embark on careers in event management. While it is absolutely essential to be creatively inspired, it is also essential to understand that innovative ideas must also be reasonably practical owing to the limitations of cost, venue and safety. The other limitation on creativity is the taste of the client. In some cases, the client needs to be carefully guided in their choice of venue and theme, and both the event organiser and the client must have a clear idea of the event's purpose. Volunteer support, as illustrated by the Mt Isa Rotary Rodeo, is essential for community based projects.

Bareback bronc-riding at the rodeo.

© Kenyon Sports

Let's look first at the elements of an event that have an impact on the development of the overall concept.

DEVELOPING THE CONCEPT

There are numerous elements which need to be considered in developing an event concept. They include the purpose/objectives of the event, the event theme, the venue, the audience, available resources, the timing of the event and the skills of the team. The most important of these is the purpose, although the purpose is strongly linked to both the theme and the venue.

Purpose of the event

The purpose of the event should drive all the planning. For example, if you were running a conference for financial planners, there could be two quite different purposes:

1 To facilitate an exchange of information, bringing participants up to date with the latest changes in financial planning software products.

2 To achieve a memorable out-of-body experience for financial planners in order to develop a positive association with a new software product.

To achieve the first purpose would be quite straightforward, as this would require a fairly standard meeting or convention. Fulfilling the second purpose, however, would be more difficult. For this unforgettable experience you would need a unique venue and carefully planned activities that the participants would enjoy. At the same time, the product would need to be reinforced constantly so that attendees would leave with an inescapable association with it. To have the fun without the positive association would defeat the purpose.

The focus of the first of these purposes is **information**, while that of the second is **entertainment**.

While for many events the main purpose is making a **profit**, for many it is not. The mission statement of the Maleny Scarecrow Carnival is an excellent example of an event with a **community** purpose.

Maleny Scarecrow Carnival

Mission Statement

To make this unique event an annual celebration of Maleny's rich cultural and social diversity. To present an opportunity for the community to unite and share creative energy, spirit and pride.

Background

The aim of the celebration is to enrich the social and cultural fabric of our community. Since ancient times, scarecrows have been used by almost every culture in a rural context; in most instances, in the belief that their presence would increase fertility and enrich the harvest.

The Maleny Scarecrow Carnival began in 1998 with the concept of a cultural event that would enhance Maleny's distinctive rural qualities and offer a unique opportunity for the local and wider communities to express their creativity. It is difficult to imagine a more perfect setting for hundreds of artistic and whimsical scarecrows than the rolling emerald green hills of Maleny. The event is based on the creation and display of scarecrows throughout the Sunshine Coast hinterland. It is comprised of four major facets:

- Scarecrow Masquerade
- Scarecrow Contest
- Scarecrow Discovery Trail
- Scarecrow Fiesta.

The Carnival coincides with the September school holidays to maximise the opportunity for families, the local community and visitors to participate in a wide range of activities.

The Maleny Scarecrow Carnival provides broad-based regional economic benefits consistent with community values and encourages involvement from all sectors of the community. In doing so, it heightens community awareness of various local groups and services as well as providing the opportunity for entertainers and artisans to showcase their creative skills. Most importantly, the Carnival is based on whole family participation, from toddlers right through to grandparents. Following on from the overwhelming success of the inaugural event in 1998, the organisers are building on the framework already in place. Interactive skill development workshops will add a new dimension and greater opportunities for members of the community to participate.

People involved included community and support groups, hospitals, libraries, Chambers of Commerce, schools, preschools and kindergartens, tour groups, garden clubs, retirement villages, businesses, sporting clubs, service groups and, of course, individuals. It is most interesting to note that 14 towns outside Maleny participated in the Scarecrow Contest; many well beyond the Sunshine Coast hinterland. We even received international involvement, including 30 miniature scarecrows sent by the children of the Australian International School in Singapore.

We have initiated relationships with other Scarecrow festivals throughout the world, including Japan, Canada, USA and Europe, and our aim in the future is to seek international participation, with a view to expanding the cross-cultural elements available to the community.

<www.maleny.net.au/scarecrow>

Theme of the event

The theme of the event should be linked to the purpose. It should be completely compatible with guest needs and consistent in all respects. Most events adopt a colour scheme that is repeated on all items produced for the event, such as tickets, programs, uniforms, décor, posters and merchandise. This helps attendees to identify with the theme.

There is an endless number of potential themes, limited only by your imagination and the customer's pocket. Some examples include:

- historical
- geographical and cultural
- sporting
- film, music and entertainment
- artistic
- food
- objects (for example, scarecrows, CDs, boats).

When coming up with ideas for a theme, it is most important to consider the range of suitable venues available, keeping in mind the constraints of budget and other considerations.

A hall transformed into an underwater world.

© Annabel Moeller

Venue for the event

The event manager needs to carefully consider the planning implications of choosing an unusual venue in preference to a standard venue requiring decoration only to match the theme. Lighting, sound and catering also provide challenges in unusual settings. This will become more evident in the logistics section later in this chapter and in Chapter 3.

The following are examples of unusual venues:

- demolition site
- parking lot
- tunnel
- museum
- research facility
- amusement park
- orchard
- vineyard
- aquarium.

The remaking of the Australian Open is an example of a fully integrated event venue and theme. The Australian Open is the only sporting event in the world boasting two retractable roofs at its venue. When not in use for tennis, retractable seating moves away to reveal a velodrome which is used for cycling events.

A number of Internet links to event venues, including small meeting rooms and large convention centres, are provided at the end of this chapter. Many of these venues provide enormous flexibility and can be readily transformed to meet the requirements of the theme. The range is extremely wide — from hotel banquet rooms to theatres to sporting venues.

When considering the choice of venue, the event organiser needs to look at a number of factors, including:

- potential to fulfil the purpose of the event
- ambience
- location
- access by public transport
- parking
- seating capacity
- built features (such as stages)
- cost of decoration, sound and lighting
- cost of labour
- logistics of setting up
- food and beverage facilities
- safety.

There are many, many factors that need to be taken into account in selecting an event venue, but the overall strategy should be to aim for the best possible fit with the client's and the audience's needs at the lowest possible cost. If all stages, props, carpets, seating, portable kitchens and refrigerators, and so on have to be hired, the cost will be very hard to justify — even if the venue seems perfect in other ways.

Event audience

When organising an event, the needs of **all** participants must be considered before finalising the concept. When one of Australia's best known athletes was invited to give a presentation at an event attended by approximately 200 people, the rental agency said that they were unable to provide a ramp to the stage for her wheelchair and wanted to compromise by asking members of the audience to lift her chair onto the stage. This was clearly unacceptable. In this situation, the response from the event co-ordinator is 'Find one!'.

In the example of the entertainment based event held for the financial planners (conservative stereotype!), an organiser would be wise to challenge normal behaviour and encourage participation in unusual activities. However, great care would need to be taken to ensure that such an audience were not pushed beyond its conservative limits. At a similar event, an event co-ordinator found that persuading the audience to wear unusual hats was all that it took to break them out of their normal patterns of interaction. Of course, every audience is different, and the event manager needs to go with the flow and direct the event to meet audience response. This can involve sudden changes in plan.

Financial considerations

The topic of financial management will be covered in detail in Chapter 7. However, it is an important consideration at this early stage of event concept and design. Initial financial estimates can get out of control very easily, and the choice of event concept can certainly contribute to this. Otherwise good ideas should be knocked on the head at an early stage if they do not appear financially viable as it is possible to come up with concepts that are startling in their simplicity and also cost effective. This is where the creative and rational aspects of the event manager's abilities can come into conflict. Very often the creative aspect wins — sometimes at the expense of the company's profit on the event.

Timing of the event

The timing of an event is often linked to the season or weather. For example, a food and wine festival would be better programmed for early autumn than for mid-summer when the heat would be intolerable for both the audience and the stall-holders. And mid-winter is certainly not the time to hold a flower show. While this might seem obvious, it is surprising how often events are programmed to occur at very unsuitable times. The timing of sporting events is, of course, limited by the sporting season and their traditional competitions. Broadcast to international audiences is another consideration. Who could forget the proposal on the ABC TV show, *The Games*, to run the key athletic events at the Sydney 2000 Olympic Games at 5 am so that they could be seen on prime-time US television? Television schedules for local and international events are tightly managed, and live television broadcasts need to be carefully planned and managed. Not every sporting enthusiast is keen to stay up all night for a delayed broadcast.

Evaluation of an event concept must take into account the following four time-related factors:
1 season
2 day of the week
3 time of day
4 duration.

Generally, mid-winter events are poorly attended, while event audiences are faced with an oversupply of events in Spring.

Closely linked to this concept of timing (in the sense of scheduling on the event calendar) is the topic of lead time. This is the time available for planning and implementation. Last minute requests are very difficult to manage. For the event manager, a long lead time is preferable, allowing adequate time to develop the event specifications and commence contract negotiation with suppliers and other contractors.

The duration of the event is another consideration, with multiple day events providing the biggest challenges as the venue has to be cleared, cleaned and restocked between sessions. The case study at the end of the chapter illustrates an event that was timed badly and lasted too long.

Event team, contractors and other stakeholders

The skills of the event team and, just as importantly, the contractors, such as lighting technicians and catering staff, are an important consideration in terms of concept development. Staff working at most events have very limited opportunity for training, making job breakdowns and task sheets essential aspects of planning. In addition, stakeholders such as the waterways police, the Environmental Protection Agency and the transport authority have all sorts of requirements that could challenge the feasibility of an event, and these must be investigated.

The following list of stakeholders is not exhaustive but provides an idea of the many people involved in staging an event:
- event principal/client
- talent/performer/team and manager
- cast and crew
- local community
- organising committee
- local and government authorities
- emergency services
- customers
- colleagues
- contractors.

ANALYSING THE CONCEPT

The following elements will be covered only briefly here since they are revisited in a number of later chapters. The aim of introducing them in this chapter is to raise awareness of the problems and pitfalls that can occur if they are not considered at this early stage of concept development. In addition, if not dealt with, they can have a negative impact on the event planner's creativity.

Competition

Prior to involvement in any event, it is essential to conduct an analysis of your competition. This involves looking at the timing and duration of other events, even if they are unrelated. People have limited disposable income and festivals and events tend to be non-essential items in most family and tourist budgets. A wider study would include an analysis of the political, environmental, social and technological impacts, known as environmental scanning. This would place the event in a broader context.

Regulations

A wide range of laws and regulations have an impact on the staging of events and these can severely limit creativity. As a simple example, releasing balloons into the atmosphere is considered environmentally unfriendly. Parking, traffic and neighbourhood impact, especially in terms of timing and noise, are all aspects that require the event manager's liaison with local or state government.

Marketing

How to sell an event is a very important part of the initial planning, the timing of your marketing efforts being crucial. Do you advertise months beforehand or the day or week before? Will the audience turn up on the day? How can you encourage them to do so? Should you sell tickets in advance? (Many events actually have no advance ticket sales.) All these questions require the decision-making skills of the event manager or the event management team.

Community impact

The impact of an event on the local or wider community and others is a major consideration of the planning stage. Local traders and other lobby groups can raise hell for the unprepared event organiser, so it is absolutely essential that community benefits are explained and other impacts considered as part of the event proposal.

Risk

At this point you must be aware that for most events the weather is the greatest risk to attendance, enjoyment and success. (You will be reminded of this at several points throughout this book.) Drought-breaking storms forced the evacuation of 400 campers at the 2004 Tamworth Country Music Festival, creating a muddy mess reminiscent of Woodstock at the Brisbane Big Day Out. However, participants were excited to see the rain at these events, which were both scheduled at times when heavy rain was least unexpected. Measures to counteract the impact of the weather are essential aspects of event feasibility planning. You must also be aware that insurance premiums will be linked to the perceived risk to the safety of participants.

There are many risks associated with events and Chapter 10 covers this topic in detail. They may include, amongst many others:
- cancellation by a key performer
- non-arrival of equipment
- technical failure
- transportation crisis
- accidents.

Revenue and expenditure

Finally, losing money is the fastest way to get out of the event business. For this reason, the event concept (and the investment in event design) needs very careful analysis. So too does the topic of cash flow. In almost every case, contractors for catering, security and other services require deposits and payment in full prior to the event, which can cause cash flow problems if there are no advance ticket sales.

DESIGNING THE EVENT

Consistency and links to the purpose of the event are all essential parts of the creative process in designing an event. The following are the main creative elements that must be considered.

Theme

As Goldblatt (1997) points out, the theme should ideally appeal to all senses: tactile, smell, taste, visual and auditory. If the aim of the event is to transport the audience, appeal to all the senses will contribute positively to the outcome. Keep in mind, once again, the needs of the audience when planning, for example, what music will be played. As we all know, taste in music and desirable sound level vary enormously from one audience to another.

Layout

This creative element is so often given far too little consideration. Consider events that you have attended in which you have felt socially uncomfortable. Your discomfort was generally the result of too much open space, too much light or the limited opportunity for people to mix. The worst scenario is being seated at a long, wide table where you are too far away to talk to those opposite and are stuck with people you have little in common with on your left and right. And to add insult to injury the venue is ablaze with light. Worse still is the cocktail party in a huge ballroom where a small circle develops in the centre — not small enough, though, for everyone to talk. The audience needs to comfortably fill the venue to create a positive ambience.

Décor

Fabrics, decorative items, stage props, drapes and table settings can all be hired and it is generally worthwhile investigating these options before settling on the event theme as hiring items can reduce costs enormously. Floral arrangements need to be ordered from florists experienced in larger events. Australian native plants, some of them up to 2 metres high, can produce a stunning effect. In many ballrooms the floral arrangements are elevated above the table, on tall stands, so that guests can talk to each other more easily. The effect is quite dramatic, with the floral arrangements dominating the décor.

The décor has to be carefully considered for a special dinner event.

Suppliers

Good relationships with suppliers of all commodities will ensure that only quality products will be received, including the freshest flowers and the best produce the markets can supply. During most large events, suppliers are pressed for the best quality from all their customers at a time when volumes are much larger than usual. This is when a good long-standing relationship with a supplier is invaluable. It was reported that at Atlanta during the 1996 Olympic Games you could not buy tissues or towels anywhere. The success of the Olympic Games in Australia was due to early planning (especially of menus), allowing farmers and other suppliers to sign contracts well in advance. Consider for a moment that some of the flowers had to be planted years before the event! So, too, some of the fruit and vegetables, which were in good supply despite it being the off-season.

Technical requirements

Few people would have attended an event or meeting where there wasn't a single technical glitch. Speakers put their notes on the laptop and the screen starts changing at a phenomenal rate. Screensavers come on when the speaker goes on too long, the presentation is halted and file names appear on the screen. While none of these problems are caused by technical support, there are ways in which they can be reduced. Technical glitches by the contracted company are unacceptable. Microphones must have back-ups, the power supply must be assured, stages and video screens must be visible to all in the audience. There is no substitute for wide-ranging experience and this is a key attribute that should be sought when choosing technical contractors. New technology, especially anything used to demonstrate new products, needs to be tested thoroughly, through many rehearsals. A back-up system is essential.

There are times when an event concept should remain just that because it is technically impossible.

Staging

The following case studies provided by well-known staging contractor, Staging Connections, illustrate the challenges created by staging requirements.

CASE STUDY 1

The Man from Snowy River Arena Spectacular
Set Type: Entertainment

In August 2002, we were approached by the Jacobsen Entertainment Group and David Atkins to construct The Man from Snowy River Arena Spectacular set. The lead time was tight and our construction schedule was nearing capacity.

After locating additional building/warehouse space and gathering an additional team of experienced tradespeople from our database, the job was off and running. Elements of the stage and set included a life-sized homestead with mechanical removable roof for live entertainment, a moving windmill, a horse corral, fencing allowing for stunt performances, a portable campfire and the Aussie outback 'dunny'.

The Man From Snowy River set.
Courtesy of Staging Rentals

Mercedes Australian Fashion Week

Event Type: Fashion Parade

For the past six years, we have been working with Spin Events to provide staging and set construction services for Mercedes Australian Fashion Week. Each year ready-to-wear collections are paraded in addition to designer collections, such as Paablo Nevada in 2002.

The stage and set requirements for the Paablo Nevada Show were unique: real turf, football posts, a 'football' compere box. The challenge each year is to turn around the room for the next designer who is probably not going to need real turf for their show! With real turf laid out as a football field, the unique Australian comedians Roy and HG compered from their commentary box elevated above the action.

The construction of a set and stage can take many forms as Mercedes Australian Fashion Week demonstrates.

Australian Fashion Week Catwalk
Courtesy of Staging Connections

Entertainment

For some events, entertainment is central; for others, it is peripheral. The most important thing is that the entertainment should suit the purpose of the event, not detract from it. The needs of the event audience must be carefully considered when making this decision.

A clown creating balloon art is something one would consider for a children's party. However, the same idea (with different designs) could also work extremely well at a wedding reception while guests are waiting for the photography session to finish.

Talent

Closely allied to the previous point, talent may come in the form of musical performers, dancers, athletes, golfers, conference speakers, etc. When the 'talent' is the focal point for an event, management of the talent is exceptionally important. This includes meeting their essential needs as well as their many personal preferences for hotel rooms and unique foods! Most performers and top sports men and women have very clear requirements that must be obtained well in advance, particularly if there are staging needs for which equipment is specialised and perhaps not readily available.

Catering

Nothing makes participants at an event more frustrated than delays in service and poor quality food — except, perhaps, lack of toilet facilities! While guests may have patience with other delays, they will become very agitated if hours are spent in queues, especially if these are away from the action. Food quality and selection are notoriously bad, and outrageously expensive, at many events and planning must take this into account. These days an espresso coffee cart can be found every few metres at most events, reflecting changes in the expectations of the audience and event managers' response to this. Creative event planning frequently requires unique or unusual food and beverage products and these can take time to find. They may even need to be imported. Time means money, as does importing, and both can contribute to an escalation in costs.

LOGISTICS OF THE CONCEPT

The following logistical elements must be taken into account when considering an event concept:

- Access to the site (For example, can vehicles come close enough for off-loading or to park?)
- Physical limitations (Will the size or shape of the stairs make it impossible to move heavy equipment?)
- Dimensions of the site (Is it too high, too low, too narrow?)
- Refrigerated storage (Is it sufficient?)
- Physical space for food preparation (Is it too small?)
- Toilet facilities (Are they fixed or portable?)
- Cleaning (Is it contracted?)
- Catering (Will there be any physical problems with transporting, storing and serving food?)
- Safety (Are patrols, exits, fire procedures, first aid, etc. all in place?)
- Potential damage to the site (Is there a danger of flowerbeds being trampled?)
- Provision of basic services (Are water and electricity laid on?)

This chapter illustrates the careful balance required between the creative and rational aspects of decision-making when considering an event concept. Brainstorming by the planning team will generate ideas but these then need to be considered as to their feasibility in terms of the issues raised in this and subsequent chapters.

CASE STUDY 3

I was asked to plan a woman's 40th birthday party with a difference. The woman's husband was thrilled with the idea of a lunchtime harbour cruise as it would be a good way of surprising his wife. (Holding a party at home is usually impossible to keep secret.) I was to arrange the boat hire and catering, and to decorate the boat on the morning of the party.

As it turned out there were three complications. The first was the weather. It rained, and we could not use the top deck which was wonderful, but only on a sunny day. This meant that the downstairs area became quite crowded. The harbour was also quite choppy and a few people felt seasick because of the small swell.

The thing I really hadn't thought through carefully enough was the needs of the children who accompanied their parents. The older ones were just bored, not difficult to manage. The toddlers were a disaster. Mothers were on the trot all afternoon since they seemed to want nothing more than to climb over the rails (the children, that is). But by the end of the afternoon the mothers were ready to throw themselves over!

Finally, we were out on the water too long — long enough for some of the party to drink too much and long enough for others to get desperate for dry land and peace and quiet.

CASE STUDY *cont.*

It was a real lesson for me in planning for the audience (everyone who came), in selecting the venue and in timing. An evening party would have ensured that at least the toddlers would have been left at home.

- What were the three complications?
- How could these problems have been avoided?
- What would you suggest for a family party for a 40th birthday?
- List the types of events affected by weather.
- What are some general suggestions for avoiding weather problems?
- How can you keep young children amused when they are part of an event?
- What would have happened if one of the guests invited to the cruise had been in a wheelchair and there was no access ramp to the boat?

ACTIVITY

Start a collection of images that will inspire future event designs. These may come from a range of sources, including magazines, gift wrapping, table napkins, cards and posters. All will give you ideas for themes and colour schemes. You may also like to begin to investigate colours and textures by looking at fabric samples.

LINKS

Links to venues, florists, entertainers, fireworks, furniture, etc.
www.specialevents.com.au/directory/index.html

Mt Isa Rotary Rodeo
www.isarodeo.com.au/default.htm

Staging Rentals
www.stagingrentals.com.au

SUMMARY

In this chapter we have looked in detail at the event concept because it is essential that this be workable right from the start. We have stressed the importance of determining the purpose/objectives of the event in conjunction with all stakeholders. Early in the process it is also necessary to identify the potential audience as well as the financial and other resources required to support the event. The event concept can then be further developed to include the theme and the décor, and a suitable venue can be selected. We also pointed out that any logistical requirements of the event must be identified early in the planning process. The purpose, theme, audience and venue need to be compatible elements for the event concept to be successful.

CHAPTER THREE

FEASIBILITY

OF EVENT PROJECTS

ON COMPLETION OF THIS CHAPTER YOU WILL BE ABLE TO:

- discuss the feasibility of event concepts
- analyse the factors that contribute to feasibility
- look at infrastructure and other event requirements that have an impact on feasibility
- look at a range of risk factors that could have an impact on feasibility
- identify ways in which risk can be minimised.

Fireworks supremo Mr Syd Howard had been dumped from London's New Year's Eve celebrations after London's Lord Mayor cancelled the evening's festivities over transport and security concerns. A dispute erupted between transport organisers, police and the office of the Mayor, which was co-ordinating operations. A director of Howard Fireworks, Mr Garry Suprain, said it had been an 'unfortunate incident'. 'We're philosophical about it but it's a shame for London because they could have had the biggest and the best New Year's Eve [but] they were scared of "could have's" and "mights".'

SYDNEY MORNING HERALD, 5 DECEMBER 2000

This article clearly illustrates the issues associated with feasibility and risk. There are many events worldwide that are cancelled as a result of risk, not least financial risk. Careful analysis of feasibility and detailed analysis of potential risks are essential when looking at the feasibility of an event. Anticipating risk and planning preventive measures can reduce the liability of the event management company. In the end, however, the event should not go ahead unless there is an unequivocal 'Yes' to the question 'Is this event feasible?'.

KEYS TO SUCCESS

The following keys to success were developed by Ernst and Young, advisers to the Olympic Games, the Emmy Awards and the PGA Tours (adapted from Catherwood and Kirk, 1992):

1 Is the event a good idea?

2 Do we have the skills required to plan and run the event?

3 Is the host community supportive?

4 Do we have the infrastructure in the community?

5 Can we get a venue at a price we can afford?

6 Will the event attract an audience?

7 Will it attract media support?

8 Is it financially viable?

9 Are the success criteria reasonable?

These questions will be used in this chapter to look at the topic of feasibility. In addition to the nine questions listed, we will ask one final question, 'What are the risks?'.

Risk management is one of the most important concerns for the event manager. As mentioned in the first chapter, events can go spectacularly right, but they can also go spectacularly wrong. For an event manager involved in an event that goes wrong, it is not career limiting, it is catastrophic. The opportunity to run another event will not occur and an alternative, vastly different career will need to be considered. This is particularly the case if people are injured or if the event proves to be a financial failure. As mentioned earlier, risk for most business operations is spread more evenly than it is for the event manager or the event management organisation. A bad day's trading for a company that trades all year is not as problematic as a bad day's trading for a one-day event!

In order to consider the questions posed by Ernst and Young, we will focus on three very different examples: a computer gaming competition during each school holiday period for up to 200 teenagers (LAN nights); a monthly organic food market; and a concert raising awareness of youth suicide prevention with an audience of 10 000 (the Life Concert).

1. Is the event a good idea?

In the case of the **organic food market**, the organisers must first determine the purpose of the event. To raise the profile of the area and its products? To raise funds for charity? Or is it a straightforward commercial venture? Most markets charge the stalls a rental fee to cover management and venue expenses. In this case, sale of organic produce arriving direct from the farm is consistent with trends towards healthier lifestyles. Major considerations for this event would be competition from any other markets in the region and certification that products are indeed organic.

Main purpose for organiser/s: commercial venture allied with a personal interest in health issues.

The **Life Concert** to raise awareness for youth suicide prevention could be a success, depending on the support of volunteers and performers being persuaded to appear at no cost to the organisers. A high profile celebrity band would certainly attract an audience. Ticketing would be a major consideration for this event — advance ticketing would be costly (commissions). A small entry fee on arrival would be more palatable for the event audience. With a low budget and charitable/community outcome, the expenses, sponsorship and VIK (value in kind) for this event would have to be worked through very carefully indeed.

Main purpose for organiser/s: community benefit, cause related.

A youth concert.

LAN nights (local area network gaming events) are not new. These computer gaming meetings are commonplace but usually managed informally, with all attendees bringing their own computer equipment and expertise. This concept would formalise these meetings, enabling parents to leave younger teenagers (aged 13–16) under supervision and provided with a range of services such as network support, security and catering. The program would run over three nights (2 pm to midnight) and would be aimed at families staying in major tourist cities, allowing parents to visit attractions, eat out or just relax while 'the kids are at play'. This event could therefore have a significant tourism impact. It could also attract sponsors keen to reach this target market.

Main purpose for organiser/s: commercial, including merchandise sales and tourism impact.

The logistics of this computer gaming event are challenging.

Regardless of whether the organisers think their idea is good or not, the organising committee must consider their answer carefully by asking the questions below.

2. Do we have the skills?

The skills required to run an **organic food market** are largely administrative. If, however, the concept were developed as a charitable fundraising event, it would be necessary to carefully consider the ongoing time and commitment required by the volunteers to sustain the event on a monthly basis. If an ongoing event, it would certainly need to be managed by paid staff.

The organic food market got it together, but there were a few hiccups along the way.

Staging a **concert** is a challenge indeed, requiring extensive equipment and technical support. In many cases, the band's management and road crew can support the staging and music performance. This being the case, other event operations would need to be managed by the organiser or committee, including ticketing, perimeter fencing, security, safety, toilet facilities, catering, cleaning, etc. Professional skills in lighting, sound and other technical requirements would be essential to the success of the event. Ticket sales, donations and other income would need to be channelled into professional staging and security, the two main skill considerations.

The technical expertise of the organisers of the **LAN** event would be the key to a successful outcome. This event would place all sorts of demands for networking skills, customisation, specific hardware and software knowledge, venue planning, power supply, etc. If all attendees were to bring their own computers or laptops, connecting them all to the network and loading software onto machines with different specifications would be extremely challenging. This would be a significant risk factor for this event, minimised by providing a room already set up, with all equipment provided, which of course would add to the cost of the event.

3. Is the host community supportive?

A monthly **organic food market** would probably generate little opposition from residents unless stall holders were noisy when setting up early in the morning. However, local food retail stores might be quite antagonistic since the market would not be faced with the same overheads and could thus provide competition through lower pricing. On the other hand, the market could attract visitors from outlying areas and a few tourists, which could lead to increased trade for the retail outlets. Most studies show, however, that tourists visiting festivals and markets tend to do so on impulse so it would not make sense to base planning on the tourism potential of such markets.

Since the **concert** would support a good cause the host community would be far more likely to be supportive than if it were a commercial production. Local councils would be likely to provide permission; however, there would be a long lead time for this event, given the size and profile of the celebrities. Publicity would be a key element and a good relationship with local media would be essential. If church and other community groups were involved, this would provide a solid base of volunteers, free promotional opportunities and expertise which would otherwise be costly.

The **LAN nights** concept should be discussed with the local tourism or events corporation as it would be necessary to ensure that it did not clash with other events on the calendar. The proposed event would also have to fit with plans for marketing the city as a tourism destination.

4. Do we have the infrastructure in the community?

Transport and parking are generally important considerations. However, in the case of the **organic food market**, these would not be problems if held in a country town. If the market were held close to a railway station and timing were matched with peak arrivals and departures, this could in fact be advantageous.

Transport and parking for the **concert** would be a significant consideration. Advice would be needed from the local council and the roads and traffic authority. Since most attendees would be transported by parents, drive and drop areas and public transport would be priorities. Canberra would be well located for the **LAN nights** event since it is midway between major cities and accessible from many country areas. There are also many other attractions for the rest of the family, including the Australian National Gallery.

5. Can we get a venue at a price we can afford?

For most event organisers, the cost of venue rental is a key consideration. Many are tempted to save money by hiring marquees and using temporary accommodation, but this can prove a false saving since the cost of décor, lighting, catering and the like is generally more expensive and more risky. The benefits of function rooms include tried and tested facilities, safety plans and insurance, as well as numerous other features. The expertise of venue managers cannot be underestimated and this can contribute to the technical success of an event. With an entertainment event, the location and cost of the venue can have a critical impact on pricing and promotion.

The cost of the venue is also dependent on the time for which it is required. In some cases, the time needed for 'bump in' and 'bump out' (setting up and dismantling) is quite long, necessitating higher than expected rental costs. Motor car and boat shows are good examples, with huge demands on the logistics of setting up. Goldblatt (1997) refers to these as time/space/tempo laws, pointing out that the actual physical space governs the time required. He cites the example of a Superbowl at which 88 pianos had to be moved onto the field during half-time. Loading area access and storage are other considerations. And security is of particular concern because high-priced items can go missing: it was reported that a new model car disappeared from the floor of the 2001 Sydney Motor Show and was taken for a 600 kilometre joyride!

The costs incurred by an **organic food market** for its venue would be minimal compared with the enormous cost of purpose-built venues suitable for major events. Nevertheless, these costs are just as important a consideration for the markets as they are for the organisers of larger events since they are generally a proportion of income earned.

If it is assumed that the **concert** is being held outdoors, the venue cost would not be high if it were held on council property. The cost of a stadium or covered venue would be insurmountable. Venue issues would relate mainly to placement and cost of temporary structures.

As mentioned above, the most sensible venue for the **LAN nights** to minimise technical problems would be a room or rooms already set up with computers, although the cost of this could be prohibitive.

6. Will the event attract an audience?

The location of the event venue or site is crucial for attracting the numbers you require to make the event successful. In the case study at the end of this chapter, you are given a list of potential events and you are asked to rank them in terms of their feasibility. All are located in different towns and cities and a study will have to be made of the local population, as well as domestic and international visitors who may be attracted to the event. Identifying the audience is a key issue for event managers in planning an event.

Market research into current trends is essential for event feasibility planning. An extensive range of reports is available from tourism authorities, at both state and federal level. For example, findings from a report on the seniors market (Golik, 2003) show that this age group is a tourism market segment with significant potential. These statistics, combined with Australian Bureau of Statistics reports on the changing demographics (including age groups) of the Australian population, clearly point to the size of this market now and its potential in the future (ABS, cat. no. 3101.0). In the next 10 years the seniors population will swell from 3 to 4 million, while the 15 to 45 age group will experience zero growth (ABS, cat. no. 3222.0). Seniors from Australia, as well as from international source countries, are living longer than ever before. According to the above research, then, the feasibility of an annual event with seniors as a target market would seem to be far higher than one planned for the zero growth age group.

Returning to the example of the **organic food market**, this concept could be expanded to include the whole spectrum of health products and so become a highly feasible event targeted specifically at seniors. The location would need to be in an area in which this demographic group was large and continuing to grow, and the venue would need to have facilities that catered for seniors. Most councils and the Australian Bureau of Statistics can provide this type of information.

Figs 3.1, 3.2 and 3.3 illustrate the demographics of Warringah Council in Sydney. As is apparent from Fig. 3.1, Warringah's population is ageing in comparison with that of the broader areas of Sydney and New South Wales. It has a higher than average number of people in the age 55 and over demographic. At the other end of the age scale (Figs 3.2 and 3.3), the percentage of people in the 0–11 and 12–24 year demographics in Warringah is lower than those of the Sydney and New South Wales areas.

Fig. 3.1

Percentage of older people in the population of Warringah Council compared with Northern Beaches, Sydney and New South Wales.

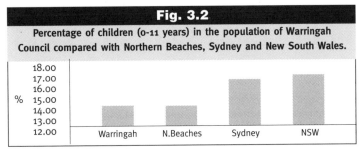

Courtesy: Warringah Council

Fig. 3.2

Percentage of children (0-11 years) in the population of Warringah Council compared with Northern Beaches, Sydney and New South Wales.

Courtesy: Warringah Council

Fig. 3.3

Percentage of young people (12-24 yrs) in the population of Warringah Council compared with Northern Beaches, Sydney and New South Wales.

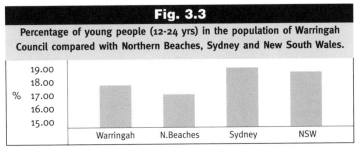

Courtesy: Warringah Council

In view of these statistics, a strategic 10-year plan for an annual event would target the age group showing the highest growth rate in Warringah, in this case people aged 55 and over. Targeting a declining age group would reduce the feasibility of the event in the long term.

Fig. 3.4 on page 38 shows the population distribution by suburb in the Warringah area and this information could be used effectively to indicate the feasibility of an event designed to attract a local audience. Dee Why and Frenchs Forest are Warringah's most populous suburbs and would thus appear to be the best locations for an event of this nature.

The demographic profile of teenagers attending the **Life Concert** would be a significant consideration, especially if planning an alcohol-free event. The promotional material would need to indicate the target age group, and if a tween market (between child and teenager), it would need to address the safety concerns of parents. If targeting an older age group, this concept would have less appeal since the entertainment alternatives for older teenagers are far more extensive. Peer group pressure needs to be considered, with careful market research to evaluate the messages developed for promotional literature. Small mistakes can turn the audience away very quickly or alienate the parent group who is giving permission and providing the entry fee and spending

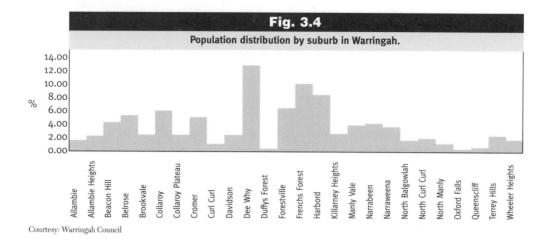

Fig. 3.4

Population distribution by suburb in Warringah.

Courtesy: Warringah Council

money. Mixed messages are required here — the audience wants a rave, the parents want a playground with supervision and perhaps a little low-key entertainment.

The audience for the **LAN nights** concept would be boys at high school since studies of computer game users show a largely male demographic and the aim is to attract the whole family to the city, leaving the teenagers at this event to play and participate. The organisers would need to ensure that the age group was targeted carefully. As with the concert for young teenagers, it would be important that the audience not be 'contaminated' by older, more sophisticated (or badly behaved) visitors/gatecrashers. This brings to mind the complaints about older men being attracted to schoolies week (end of school celebrations) and spoiling the fun.

7. Will the event attract media support?

Media support is essential. An event can be ruined by negative press. Media support for a new product launch, for example, is one of the main criteria by which the event is judged successful.

In the case of the **organic food market**, it would be best to approach local newspapers to seek their support. Stories and images, with a focus on the value to the community and the management of risks, would need to be provided to stimulate both media and community interest in the event. A special feature, including advertisements by exhibitors, would be the type of proposal that would be well received at local level.

Community media, such as local press and radio, are generally supportive of cause-related events such as the **concert** proposed. However, this would be a one-off event with limited exposure. Posters and word of mouth would be the most effective way of promoting this event. Schools and churches could be contacted for their support.

Since **LAN nights** is a commercial venture, only limited media support could be expected. The audience for this event would be more likely to hear about it via chat groups, bulletin boards and email.

8. Is the event financially viable?

An event that is financially viable and brings benefits to the community can defeat any objections. One that is not viable will have a short life span. The **organic food market** would be unlikely to make huge profits or generate substantial charitable funds, but it might contribute to community spirit and provide intangible benefits to the local population. For example, it might enhance the reputation of local agricultural products, thus attracting investment in the organic concept. Fees charged to stall holders would need to cover all expenses associated with the event since there would be no charge to visitors. It would appear that this concept is viable with long-term potential, however the margins would be very low.

The **concert** needs to break even in terms of operating costs and raising funds for suicide prevention. Depending on the range of donations, sponsors and VIK support, this could be achieved. However, it would be dangerous to underestimate the time and effort needed to get this level of support. A modest entry fee could help this event to break even, but the weather and other factors would make it hard to estimate gate revenues. Cash flow would be another major consideration.

For most events, the decision on the price to be charged to visitors or spectators, and when this price decision is made, is critical. Tickets cannot go on sale the day after an event is over, nor can the merchandise produced for the event. If T-shirts, caps and CDs are not sold, this too will mean lost revenue. Even the concession outlets that sell food and beverages do not get a second chance at sales. For these reasons, the decision on price — and the timing of this decision — are extremely important in ensuring that the event audience reaches a viable level.

In Chapter 9, on financial management, the concept of a break-even point will be discussed. For the event manager, careful attention to budgeting will provide a reasonably accurate idea of the costs involved in running the event, and this is essential in making a decision as to what to charge for tickets. This judgement is also informed by knowledge of the consumer market and likely perceptions regarding value for money.

However, not all events are ticketed. An exhibition, for example, involves renting stands to exhibitors, and the price charged for exhibiting is based on the cost of staging the exhibition and the likely number of exhibitors. For non-profit events, financial decisions involve keeping within the budget, which may be established by another body (for example, the local council). Where a client is paying for the staging of an event, the event management company would develop a budget for the event based on very clear expectations from the client as to the benefits expected from the event. Often the event management company earns a fee and the client is ultimately responsible for the cost of the budgeted items and any variations.

The viability of the **LAN nights** concept is most questionable in this regard, since the ticket sales for three-night attendance at this event would be unlikely to cover the venue and IT related costs. This audience, being young, would be unlikely to have any income, other than pocket money, and parents would have to carry the cost. A high price, even if the event were packaged with accommodation, would probably be too much for this family market to bear. The only way in which this concept could be feasible would be if extensive sponsor support could be obtained. The sponsors, including computer hardware and software companies, might well wish to make in-roads into this market by providing software and hardware for the event audience to sample. Developing brand loyalty at a young age is a priority for IT suppliers. However, in the view of the author, this event has little merit because of the major technical risks, and so could well be a bad financial risk too. Imagine all the network switches causing the LAN to collapse regularly, crashing games and leading to demands for money back!

9. Are the success criteria reasonable?

The **organic food market** could encourage local growers to develop entrepreneurial skills and to produce and market a differentiated product. This has already been done by many regional wine growers, such as the wine growers from Mudgee, who now hold an annual promotional event at Balmoral Beach in Sydney. Change in consumers' perception of a region's products is difficult to measure, as is the increased confidence of the local producers. These are known as intangible outcomes and seldom form part of the success criteria, which tend to be more tangible results, such as improved sales.

The **concert's** success would be measured largely against community related objectives while the **LAN nights** concept would be measured against commercial objectives for event organisers (ticket and merchandise sales) and sponsor (product) sales.

The criteria for success need to be established before the event takes place, as it is against these that the feasibility of the event is analysed.

10. What are the risks?

This final question is the most important of all because failure, and even fiasco, are always possible.

Brainstorming, in order to reveal all of the possible risks associated with an event, and then ranking them, is the first step. Risks may include:

- heavy weather, wind and/or rain
- flooding
- fire
- collapse of buildings or temporary structures
- accidents involving workers and/or the event audience
- crowd control
- security of participants and VIPs
- food poisoning
- breakdown in water or power supply.

Contingency planning, in order to deal with potential risks, is the next step. And thirdly, policies and procedures must be put in place to deal with every possible eventuality. In Chapter 10 we will discuss risk management in more detail, with particular focus on priorities and operational plans designed to minimise risk.

The IACC (International Association of Conference Centres) has set international standards for operations, facilities, equipment and management for small- to medium-sized conference centres (20–50 people), and conference venues around Australia are adopting these as a benchmark. This type of accreditation is reassuring for the event organiser and an excellent method of reducing many of the most common risks. Links to this association are listed at the end of the chapter.

To summarise, the aim of the event organiser is to improve feasibility and reduce risk (see Fig. 3.5).

The potential risks listed above could be used for a risk analysis for each of the three proposed events (although the process is described in more detail in Chapter 10). However, at first glance it would appear that the **organic food market** would have long-term potential but would generate a small profit margin. The **concert** has potential to achieve its purpose, which is to raise awareness

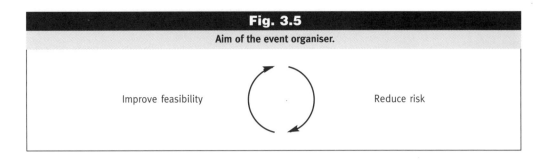

Fig. 3.5

Aim of the event organiser.

Improve feasibility   Reduce risk

of youth suicide prevention initiatives, particularly if it attracted extensive community support. The final event, **LAN nights**, carries far too many technical and financial risks to make it feasible even though the concept would be sure to excite the target audience for whom there are few suitable events of this nature.

THE SWOT ANALYSIS

It is traditional, and important, to do a SWOT analysis for every event. This involves analysing the strengths, weaknesses, opportunities and threats of the event or event concept.

S **Strengths** are the internal strengths of the organisation, for example, the enthusiasm and commitment of volunteers, the specialist knowledge of the lighting engineer or the wide range of products available for planning themes and décor.

W **Weaknesses** are the internal weaknesses of the organisation, for example, the skills and knowledge of the management committee or their lack of availability for meetings.

O **Opportunities** are the external favourable things that may occur, such as new sponsorships or unexpected positive publicity.

T **Threats** are also external: competition, poor publicity and poor crowd behaviour would all be classified as threats.

Essentially, the idea of improving the feasibility of an event is to improve the strengths of the organisation (and the concept) and to maximise the opportunities. Likewise, acknowledging potential weaknesses and dealing with them will minimise the risks. Assessing potential threats and introducing contingency plans to circumvent them will also improve the feasibility of an event.

PROJECT PLANNING

Project management principles form the basis for most event planning at both strategic and operational levels. For example, critical path analysis, an aspect of project management, is common to many occupations, including computer systems development. The key steps involved in the early event planning stages (Fig. 3.6) broadly cover the project scope, objectives, financial viability and project milestones. The more detailed implementation phases will be covered in Part 2 of this text where the focus is on operational planning.

MODELS OF FINANCIAL PERFORMANCE

Once an event concept is agreed, it is then possible to create a number of financial models. In the example in Fig. 3.7 there are two models, one in which the main source of income is

---

Fig. 3.6

Project planning.

Develop the objectives and scope of the project

⇓

Determine and develop a resource strategy for the project

⇓

Evaluate the financial viability of the project through analysis of key factors

⇓

Plan and create an administrative structure for the project

⇓

Allocate project responsibilities in agreement with others

⇓

Plan internal and external communications and public relations and marketing strategies

⇓

Reach agreement on suitable project evaluation methods

⇓

Develop an overall project management plan

⇓

Identify key project milestones and communicate these to persons involved

---

ticket sales and the other in which ticket sales projections drop from 66 per cent of income to 42 per cent of income. In Model B, there is a much stronger push for sponsorship and fundraising is abandoned. However, as a result, the festival is in a loss situation. Given the difficulty associated with raising sponsorship, the first model would appear to be the best. These models are simplified and do not take merchandise or fixed and variable costs into account (more on this in Chapter 9). However, for this purpose, they illustrate the value of modelling techniques.

Another form of modelling, based on historical data, is very useful for annual events, or those that are reasonably predicatable in terms of demand. Differential ticket pricing is based on a concept of revenue management initially popular in the airline industry and now used widely in many other service industries. Using information systems, it is possible to allocate different prices for different shows, seats, sessions and market segments. It is also possible to monitor advance sales and offer special deals. For example, if it is anticipated that an event is going to be a sell-out, then more tickets can be sold at A prices than for a match that is unlikely to fill the stadium. In the case of mega-events, many tickets are allocated to overseas bodies or sold as part of tour packages. Consequently, these tickets may return unsold at the very last minute, causing much consternation when some of the best seats come onto the market very close to the event. To manage differential pricing well, historical data is required to predict demand.

McMahon-Beattie & Yeoman (2004, p. 202) describe this well:

Revenue management (RM) or yield management marries the issues of supply, demand and price, and is considered to be a method of managing capacity profitably.

Fig. 3.7
Financial modelling

Income	Model A	% of Income	Model B	% of Income
Ticket sales	$175 758	66%	$102 301	42%
Memberships	$12 036	4%	$25 123	10%
Sponsorship	$10 230	3½%	$52 146	22%
Grants	$32 156	12%	$32 513	14%
Donations	$12 351	5%	$12 351	5%
Fundraising events	$9 856	3½%	$0	0%
Stall rentals	$15 623	6%	$15 623	7%
Total Income	**$268 010**		**$240,057**	
Expenses		% of Expenses		% of Expenses
Artist performance contracts	$68 952	28%	$68 952	28%
Festival production	$35 612	15%	$35 612	15%
Marketing and fundraising	$22 613	9%	$22 613	9%
Salaries and wages	$62 133	26%	$62 133	26%
Office and related	$22 613	9%	$22 613	9%
Postage	$5 021	2%	$5 021	2%
Other	$27 591	11%	$27 591	11%
Total Expenses	**$244 535**		**$244 535**	
Net Income	**$23 475**		**−$4 478**	

CASE STUDY

Use the questions provided in this chapter and any other relevant ideas or information to discuss the feasibility of the following event concepts. Then rank them in order, from most to least feasible.

- Agricultural Show in June in the town of Nerang, Queensland
- Flower Show in Renmark, South Australia, in August
- Wedding on an island in Sydney Harbour in January (with marquee)
- Red Earth Arts Festival in Alice Springs, Northern Territory, in February
- Aboriginal Dance Festival at Cooktown, Queensland, in January
- Marathon in Hobart in July
- Food and Wine Festival in Geelong, Victoria, in June
- Wildflower Show in Albany, Western Australia, over the Easter weekend
- School-leavers Celebration at Merimbula on the New South Wales coast in December.

ACTIVITY

List the advantages and disadvantages (and thus the feasibility) of the following event durations:

- *one session on one day*
- *multiple days*
- *annual.*

Use an example for each in your discussion, which should be based on some of the concepts in this chapter and Chapter 2.

LINKS

Department of Families, Youth and Community Services
www.families.qld.gov.au/seniors

International Association of Conference Centres
www.iacconline.com
www.iaccaustralia.org

International Congress & Convention Association
www.iccaworld.com

SUMMARY

In this chapter we have compared three very different types of events and in the process have shown that asking simple questions can help you to determine the feasibility of an event concept. Questions need to be asked about the financial viability of the concept, the demographics of the audience, the infrastructure required to stage the event and, very importantly, the potential risks. We have also discussed the contribution of community and media support to the success of an event. An evaluation of an event's success or otherwise, based on criteria established in the planning stages, should be carried out after the event. Some events are measured by profits, others by their social impact and the level of community support they attract.

CHAPTER FOUR

EVENT

VENUE AND SITE SELECTION

ON COMPLETION OF THIS CHAPTER YOU WILL BE ABLE TO:

- analyse venue or site requirements
- source event venues or sites
- conduct a site inspection
- confirm venue or site arrangements.

The Disability Discrimination Act (1992) requires that people with disabilities are able to access and use places open to the public and to access any services and facilities provided in those buildings. People with disabilities can face barriers to attending and participating in public functions in a variety of ways. They may experience difficulty hearing what is said, seeing small print on an invitation, climbing steps to the venue, understanding signage or using a rest room in the building. Public events need to be planned to ensure they are accessible to all members of the community. Consideration of aspects such as the venue, continuous accessible path to the venue, invitations, and hearing augmentation are important.

www.dsc.wa.gov.au/content/Access/conducting_events_meetings.asp

The terms 'venue' and 'site' are used almost interchangeably by event managers, with 'venue' used mainly for built structures and 'site' for outdoor spaces. 'Site' has more general use for a range of locations, which in turn can be transformed into event venues. Events are also held at convention centres, hotels, clubs, restaurants and many other places. The term 'facility' is also used extensively, particularly in North America in the context of a 'sports facility' or 'convention facility'.

In this chapter the various attributes of event sites will be considered, particularly for outdoor events where all infrastructure has to be brought in and erected on site. This chapter will also look at disability access, since best practice in this area is likely to meet the needs of all visitors, particularly in the areas of signage, lighting, pathways and emergency exits.

As the earlier quote from the Western Australian Disability Services Commission illustrates, many requirements need to be fulfilled to meet legal obligations on access to public places. Building codes ensure that most modern buildings comply with disability specifications, for example, that doorways are wide enough for wheelchair access. For the event manager considering an established venue, a site inspection would determine whether the venue is suitable for the planned event, particularly from a functional perspective. When planning an outdoor event the onus is on the management team to ensure that the infrastructure meets the needs of everyone in the event audience.

When evaluating the suitability of a venue or site, there are two main considerations: the functionality of the venue and the suitability of the site for its creative purpose. Natural features of some sites lend themselves well to creating an extraordinary event experience. Concerts held in caves and natural amphitheatres are good examples. In such situations, however, the event manager would need to be mindful of the costs of using unusual, untested sites and the functional problems inherent in using such sites.

The size and scope of major events are considerations when looking for appropriate cities and venues for staging such events. When a major event is planned, such as the Soccer World Cup, various cities bid for the event. During this process, the city presents the infrastructure available for the event, not only specific competition venues but also descriptions of transportation, accommodation, etc. The city must demonstrate that it has the full range of physical and human resources to support the bid, as well as the financial resources for the event to succeed. In bids for international events such as the Olympic Games, Commonwealth Games and the Soccer World Cup, the infrastructure is promised but in some cases not delivered. For example, the steel and glass roof for the Athens Olympic Games swimming centre could not be finished in time for the Games. Bids also need to address the issue of accessibility for both athletes and audience. This topic is covered briefly in this chapter. The challenge of providing accessible public spaces is fairly easily met when the venues and transport networks are new; however, it is much more difficult when the event is held in an ancient city like Athens.

> A top inspector from the International Olympic Committee (IOC) said Beijing has done a 'perfect' job in venue construction for the 2008 Olympic Games on February 23.
>
> 'We're extremely pleased to see how fast the work has been advanced', said Hein Verbruggen, chairman of the IOC's Coordination Commission for the 2008 Olympic Games. Verbruggen made the remarks after an inspection tour of the construction site of the National Stadium and the National Swimming Center, two major venues for the 2008 Games, in north Beijing. The Chinese capital has promised to finish construction of its sporting facilities for the 2008 Games at least a year ahead of time so test events can be held during 2007.
>
> <http://english.people.com.cn/200402/24/eng20040224_135663.shtml>

When bidding for a large conference of, say, medical professionals, the bid would again cover the city, its accommodation, entertainment options and attractions. Indeed, conference centres in Singapore and Melbourne would differ little in what they could provide as regards the conference venue and meeting rooms. Delegates arriving at the conference are more interested in the city that hosts the event and the attractions it has to offer.

The role of the event manager as a walking, talking checklist will become clear in this chapter with its focus on site specifications.

ANALYSING VENUE AND SITE REQUIREMENTS

In Chapter 3 we looked in some detail at analysing the feasibility of event concepts, with the assistance of three case studies. Now we will consider the aspects of an event that must be taken into account when developing venue or site specifications. These include:

- creative theme or image required
- estimated numbers
- audience composition
- facilities and services to be provided
- staging/competition requirements
- budget parameters
- location
- capacity of site or venue
- timing (including availability and access for set-up and breakdown)
- accessibility.

The requirements of all stakeholders also need to be considered when developing site specifications. Such stakeholders may include:

- attendees/delegates/guests/spectators
- host organisation
- sponsors
- contractors
- emergency services
- regulatory authorities.

Imagine, for example, that a client has requested a small event, the purpose of which is to introduce newly appointed executive staff (and their partners) following a merger of two banks. The client wants to 'break the ice' and for this reason wants something a bit different from a conventional dinner with more of a team focus. However, it cannot be a tacky team building theme or an outdoor activity. Pretending to be spiders in a web, walking over logs, or something similar is absolutely out of the question.

This elegant solution could well meet the needs of this client:

A chef's table dinner in a five-star commercial kitchen where guests, guided by the executive chef, 'prepare' the food. A chef's table is usually located inside a commercial kitchen, providing a unique venue, surrounded by glimmering stainless steel and professional cooking equipment. Usually the chef invites selected people to dine at the chef's table and this is a privilege few enjoy. The food is generally unsurpassed in quality and creativity. This concept is unique in that guests at an event would never normally get their hands dirty. Guests would arrive expecting a conventional dinner, be surprised by the location, and further surprised when given a large apron and asked to assist. Since all ingredients would already be prepared, as on a television cooking show, none of the guests would find the situation daunting. Each guest would be involved, with movement around the kitchen and the table, observation, questions, congratulations and so on. No time for embarrassing conversational lapses when discussing the jobs people have lost in the merger process! Rather, an unforgettable dining experience that would really 'break the ice'!

The number of guests that needed to be invited would be the major consideration when sourcing the venue. Only five star commercial kitchens would be suitable and the size of the chef's table would be limited by the space available in the kitchen. The dining area would also need to be a distance away from the heat and flames! One solution would be a banquet table in a function room outside the kitchen but this would destroy the energy and creativity of the concept. For the concept to work, a dining table in the kitchen would be essential. Such a space could well be available in a convention centre on a Saturday night, but would be hard to find in a busy five star hotel conducting normal peak business.

As this example illustrates, décor, availability, capacity, safety and access issues are all relevant when selecting an appropriate venue.

Venue information sources

When looking for a venue, there are various sources that can be utilised:

- local/regional/state tourism organisations
- convention and visitor bureaus
- venue publications and directories
- destination brochures
- trade journals
- Internet searches.

In conducting such a search, it is useful to compare services and specifications. Some venues have interactive websites that allow you to configure function rooms, depending on whether the event is a cocktail party, meeting or dinner function. These CAD designs are most useful in showing the space available (not forgetting any space needed for a stage and possibly wheelchair access). Clear communication of requirements is essential, particularly if the event is so large that it will be sent out to tender.

Site inspection — conference

Figure 4.1 on page 49 provides a checklist of the technical requirements for a small conference, as this is the most important consideration for an event of this nature. A more detailed analysis of the site for the conference would cover other fundamentals such as parking, public transport, accessibility and smoking areas, as well as registration, seating and catering.

All elements of an event need to be itemised to ensure that even the smallest detail is given attention. For an outdoor music concert, for example, the site inspection checklist would run to many pages, including site elements such as perimeter fencing, lighting, signage, pathways, parking and so on.

Fig. 4.1
Conference technical requirements.

Registration desks	Lecterns
Display screens	Speakers
Staging	Audio equipment
Data projector	Video projectors
VHS video	Laptop with presentation software
Remote controls	Sufficient power supply
Overhead projector	Accessible power outlets
Extra lenses and bulbs	Extension cords
Laser pointers	Lighting effects (including dimmer)
Projection screens	Microphones and stands
Projector trolleys	Radio microphones (hand held and lapel)
Whiteboards	Technician on site
Flipcharts	

Site inspection — accessibility

The Western Australian Disability Services Commission mentioned earlier in the chapter provides a checklist for creating accessible events, which is reproduced on pages 50 and 51. This covers invitations and promotional materials, external access, internal access, communication and function space requirements. A more detailed planning approach to a major event might cover these elements and more:

- way-finding
- signage
- transport
- parking
- footpaths
- ramps
- stairways
- lifts
- surfaces and finishes
- entries and exits
- doorways and doors
- toilet facilities
- emergency provisions (must comply with Australian Standards).

Site inspections — outdoor events

For an outdoor event significant considerations would include:

- access for emergency services
- public access

DISABILITY
SERVICES
COMMISSION
making a difference

Checklist for creating accessible events

External environment

People with disabilities require a continuous, even, accessible path of travel. An accessible path of travel means there are no obstacles in the internal or external environment such as revolving doors, kerbs or steps.

Location of the nearest:

Bus stop: _____

Train station: _____

	Yes	No
Accessible parking bays		
Does the venue have an accessible parking bay?	☐	☐
Is the accessible parking bay/s identified by the international symbol of access?	☐	☐
Raised sign	☐	☐
Ground markings	☐	☐
If the accessible parking is undercover is the roof a minimum of 2500 mm in height to allow the use of a car top hoist?	☐	☐
Is the distance from the car park to entrance less than 40 m?	☐	☐
Continuous accessible path of travel		
Is there a continuous accessible path of travel, including kerb ramps, to the building from the:		
Accessible parking bay/s?	☐	☐
Set down area?	☐	☐
If there are steps to the building:		
Is there a ramp available for wheelchair users?	☐	☐
Do all steps have handrails?	☐	☐
Is there a contrasting strip on step edges?	☐	☐
If there is a ramp to the building:		
Is the gradient no steeper than 1:14?	☐	☐
Does the ramp lead to the main entrance?	☐	☐

The building
Entrance

	Yes	No
Is the entrance threshold level?	☐	☐
If there is a step/s at the entrance of the doorway:		
Is there a ramp of not more than 450 mm in length and with a gradient of 1 in 8?	☐	☐
Is the entrance door easy to open?	☐	☐
Is the clear door space 800 mm (preferred)?	☐	☐

	Yes	No
Internal environment		
Is the inquiry or reception counter low enough for a wheelchair user?	☐	☐
Does the venue have an accessible path of travel from the front entrance to all areas guests will use?	☐	☐
If there are internal steps:		
Do all steps have handrails?	☐	☐
Is there a contrasting strip on step edges?	☐	☐
If there are ramps:		
Are they no steeper than 1:14?	☐	☐
Do they have handrails?	☐	☐
Do all doors have a clear space 760 mm (essential) or 800 mm (preferred)?	☐	☐
If there is only a side approach to the door, is there 1200 mm clear space in front of the door?	☐	☐
Does the venue have a non-slip floor surface or carpets with a firm low pile of 6 mm or less?	☐	☐
Visibility		
Are facilities in the venue clearly signed?	☐	☐
Is the venue well lit?	☐	☐
Are there any areas of high reflection or glare?	☐	☐
Toilets		
Does the venue have a unisex accessible toilet?	☐	☐
Is the toilet situated on the same floor as the function?	☐	☐
Does the door have a clear space of 800 mm (preferred)?	☐	☐
If there is only a side approach to the door, is there 1200 mm clear space in front of the door?	☐	☐
If the door of the toilet opens inwards, is the space large enough for the person in a wheelchair to shut the door once inside?	☐	☐
Is there 950 mm space at one side of the toilet pan?	☐	☐
Is there a grab rail next to the toilet at 800 mm – 810 mm high, preferably in an 'L' shape?	☐	☐
Signage		
Does the venue have clear, directional signage to:		
The function room?	☐	☐
The toilets?	☐	☐

Please note that disabled facilities in older buildings will only have a clear space of 760 mm. The standard has now been revised to a clear space of 800 mm.

<www.dsc.wa.gov.au/content/access/documents/CreatingAccessibleEvents.rtf>

- service access and loading docks
- parking
- public transport
- power supply
- potable water (cold)
- sanitation.

Set up for a marathon start.

For a sporting competition considerations would include:
- competition area cleanliness, maintenance and safety
- competition area clearly marked
- adequate lighting for competition area
- spectator area cleanliness, maintenance and safety
- marked out-of-bounds area
- perimeter fencing
- buffer between spectators and competitors
- competitor change rooms
- sports equipment of appropriate standard
- all areas clear of non-essential equipment
- exits and entrances clearly marked and unobstructed
- electrical systems in good condition
- waste containers provided
- walkways clean and well-maintained
- stairs non-slip
- wheelchair access to all areas
- compliance with fire safety regulations in all aspects.

The checklists could be endless, including also loading docks, storage areas, access, refrigeration space, etc. In particular, the special requirements of large items such as stages and athletics equipment need to be considered to ensure that they can be brought into the event area, otherwise known as loading restrictions. The logistics of boat shows and car shows are complex and have to be linked to both space and scheduling, making sure that items arrive in an orderly and timely way.

The Adelaide Festival Centre
Access Details

Vehicle access

Passenger vehicle access is via Festival Drive (off King William Street).

Height clearance is 2.1 metres.

Heavy vehicle access to dock is from North Terrace down ramp (in front of Casino).

Height clearance is 4.5 metres.

Loading dock

A 'Cab Over' prime mover is essential when manoeuvring a semi-trailer flush against the dock.

The Space, Dunstan Playhouse and STC Workshop, share a common dock. The dock is an 'end loading' facility service, one vehicle only at any time.

There is a 1500 kg capacity hydraulic lift platform from ground level to dock floor immediately in front of the dock. This lift platform is 2.75 metres wide x 1.5 metres deep.

The dock door is 3.15 metres high x 2.75 metres wide.

Scenery and equipment must be moved from the dock to the Space stage via a 4355 kg capacity hydraulic lift 7.3 metres long x 2.4 metres wide x 2.75 metres high. Scenery must then travel through the STC Workshop and onto the Space stage. The door from the STC Workshop into the Space is 3 metres wide x 5.5 metres high and provides full acoustic isolation.

The Adelaide Festival Centre

Fit with audience profile

An overriding consideration in the choice of an event venue is the fit with audience needs. It is easy for an event manager to lose sight of this when inspired by a concept and unusual location or bogged down with checklists. Will the event audience travel to the venue? Will the venue provide too little or too much space for the number of people? This psychological factor contributes a great deal to the event experience. What is the event purpose? Being constantly mindful of the event purpose and the needs of the event audience is necessary throughout the venue selection process. Being able to think three-dimensionally in terms of height and décor is another beneficial attribute for an event manager.

Venue safety

The subject of venue safety has been mentioned several times and will be covered in more detail in Chapters 10 and 18. There are several examples of structural failure at events that have led to fatalities and two stage failures are described in the following article:

On the same day and within minutes of the Justin Timberlake rig crashing to the floor at Atlantic City due to failure of the venue mothergrid, another catastrophic failure hit in Nebraska. Once again no one was injured, but as with the Timberlake show, the potential for mass death and injury is massive when a concert roof falls.

CXWeb, 28 April 2004

Staging an event at a modern, state-of-the-art stadium, using the best known contractors is a low-risk option from a safety point of view. Running a conference in a purpose-built conference centre is also a low-risk option. Outdoor events using hire equipment present a much higher level of risk. Checking engineering and other certification, as well as contractor references, can reduce this risk. There are no short cuts or savings in the area of venue safety — old buildings may not meet fire safety standards — and attention to detail is essential.

CONFIRMING VENUE ARRANGEMENTS

A contract must be negotiated for venue hire. Most venues have a standard contract and this must be read carefully. It is essential that all parties meet their legal obligations. Insurance is an important consideration which will be covered, with various legal topics, in the next chapter.

Under the contract in Fig. 4.2, the venue management will provide a fire safety officer (on an hourly basis) for the duration of the event.

The pre-event (immediately before bump-in) and the post-event (after bump-out) checklists are most important. The pre-event checklist ensures that any damage to the venue that had not been noticed before hiring is pointed out before the event. At the end of the event, it is essential that the venue is left in a safe condition, with all ovens, grills and other equipment turned off.

Fig. 4.2

Sample venue contract.

CONDITIONS OF HIRE AGREEMENT

Between the VENUE MANAGEMENT and the hirer.

BOOKING PROCEDURE: Every person applying to hire the VENUE must provide a permanent address and contact details. This booking is unconfirmed until such time as a signed copy of the Conditions of Hire Agreement has been returned to us together with payment of the required deposit and other actions as specified within this and supporting document(s). Our return of this countersigned agreement with deposit receipt will provide formal acceptance of your confirmed Hire Contract.

CANCELLATION: Any cancellation after confirmation of this agreement, or part thereof, will result in forfeiture of the total deposit value, plus any other costs incurred.

SET-UP AND BREAKDOWN: Set-up and Breakdown (bump-in and bump-out) shall be agreed and stated within the Conditions of Hire Agreement. In the event of any performance or use continuing beyond these times, the Tenant shall pay to VENUE MANAGEMENT such further sum or sums as is specified in the Venue Rental Schedule. The keys of the Building shall be kept by the Caretaker or nominated deputy. Labour costs for access outside normal operating hours shall be payable by the Tenant.

SUBLETTING: The Tenant may not sublet the venue or any part thereof.

Fig. 4.2 CONTINUED

Sample venue contract.

DEPOSIT: On the signing of this Conditions of Hire Agreement and receipt of the deposit invoice, the sum shall be payable to secure confirmation of this document.

The balance of the account as invoiced by VENUE MANAGEMENT shall be payable within seven days of the event date.

CATERING: VENUE MANAGEMENT, through their in-house caterers, retain sole and exclusive right to supply to persons attending the premises, or surrounding car parking, wines, spirits and other drinks, food, confectionery, cigars, cigarettes, or other articles excluding programs. A separate catering deposit may be required should there be any pre/post-performance catering required by the Tenant. Numbers and menu confirmation must be made not less than 72 hours (3 days) prior to the function date.

SMOKING: Smoking shall not be permitted in any part of the building. The Tenant shall be liable for any damages or costs should any person smoke within the venue.

FURNITURE AND EQUIPMENT: The Tenant shall be accountable for the replacement of all furniture and equipment to where it came from at the conclusion of the event unless set-up and dismantling fees are being paid as detailed in this agreement. The Tenant shall be accountable for damages or breakages. At the conclusion of the event, the Tenant shall be responsible for removing any furniture, equipment items or decorations introduced to the venue at that time, unless alternative arrangements have been made with VENUE MANAGEMENT.

LABOUR: VENUE MANAGEMENT can provide labour for the set-up and dismantling of your event. This is charged out at a $30.00 per hour per person (normal working hours) and $35.00 per hour per person (after hours). This does not include technical staff.

CLEANING: The Tenant is expected to leave the facilities in the condition they were found. If this is not so, additional cleaning charges will be incurred and charged on the final invoice. The final decision will be made by VENUE MANAGEMENT.

NOISE LEVELS: These shall be restricted to a maximum of 100 decibels within the venue, or less if determined by VENUE MANAGEMENT.

FIRE ALARMS: The Promoter/Tenant shall be liable for any charges incurred due to the activation of the fire alarm by 'false alarm' during the hire period.

EVACUATION PROCEDURE: As a requirement of the Fire Safety Regulations, the Tenant and their staff should familiarise themselves with the Venue Evacuation Procedure, copies of which are on display in all areas of the venue. If the Tenant and their staff are unsure of any part of the procedure please contact the Caretaker.

THE TENANT covenants with VENUE MANAGEMENT as follows:
(a) Not to infringe or breach, or permit to be infringed or breached, any copyright, performing right or other protected right by or in the conduct of any performance.
(b) Shall make no alteration to the structure, fittings, decorations or furnishings of the buildings without previous written permission of the Caretaker and shall after each performance or user leave the building in as good a condition as they were in before any permitted alteration to the satisfaction of the Caretaker. Any damages or costs associated with alterations, or other activities, shall be made right, with the full cost met by the Tenant.

Fig. 4.2 CONTINUED

Sample venue contract.

(c) Shall not introduce, display, attach or suspend any equipment, fittings or furniture without previous written permission from VENUE MANAGEMENT.

(d) Shall meet all Australian standards in the use of electrical equipment.

(e) Shall pay the cost of any special electrical equipment installation or fittings which may be required for the purpose of the Tenant's event, and shall obtain written permission prior to any such work from VENUE MANAGEMENT.

(f) Shall permit the VENUE MANAGEMENT (or Caretaker) to visit at any time all parts of the premises.

(g) Shall ensure that they operate with current policies as required under the Occupational Health & Safety Act, Australian Standards for building evacuation and any other Acts or local by-laws as may be relevant. The Tenant will accept total liability, as the lessee of the facilities, for adhering to these laws.

(h) Shall provide certificate of currency for Public Liability Insurance Policy and Workers Compensation Insurance. Shall do likewise if subcontractors are employed.

VENUE MANAGEMENT agrees as follows:

(a) Shall provide such staff, equipment and services as are specified at the full cost to the Tenant, or as included within Venue Rental as determined within the Venue Rental Schedule.

(b) The Fire Safety Officer is a separate charge to the Tenant, to be present in the venue one hour before the doors are due to open, through until the building is vacated at the conclusion of the performance or use.

(c) Shall reserve the right to revise fees and charges from time to time as may be found necessary.

(d) Shall reserve the right of entry to any of our venues for our staff members or management at no charge.

(e) Shall have complete supervision and control over admission of the public, the Tenant or subcontractors.

(f) VENUE MANAGEMENT shall not be responsible for the loss or damage to any article of any kind brought to or left in the building.

DRAFTING SCALE MAPS

The usefulness of CAD drawings was mentioned earlier in the chapter. Once the event venue or site has been selected, the process of drafting the physical dimensions of the event becomes necessary in order to develop more detailed equipment specifications. A map, plan or CAD drawing of the event and two- or even three-dimensional models helps to achieve the outcomes intended and clarify expectations to all stakeholders. Many events are set up at the last minute and the most difficult thing for all concerned is visualising the event and the work environment. Maps and diagrams must be drawn to scale. Always check them or you may not hire enough carpet!

The CAD drawing on the following page shows an island sometimes used for events. As this map illustrates, there are few amenities provided, other than water taps and barbeques. For an event to be held on this site, all equipment (including generators) would need to be brought across by boat. There is limited shelter and only a small paved area. The prospect of holding an event on this site would no doubt be appealing, but the logistics would need to be carefully considered.

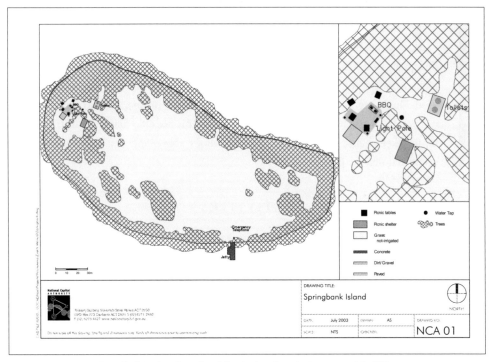

Sample CAD drawing of an island, showing picnic area and facilities.

Springbank Island, National Capital Events <http://www.nationalcapital.gov.au/EVENTS/maps/Springbank.pdf>. © Commonwealth of Australia. Reproduced with permission.

Features of an outdoor event map include:

- parking
- public transport
- entrance
- exit
- emergency access
- disability access
- information booth/s
- toilet facilities
- stages, fields, function rooms
- food stands/catering/food and beverage
- lost and found
- first aid
- emergency and venue control centre
- zones for public access
- out-of-bounds areas — limited access
- service roads.

A map showing the final layout of the event, including all temporary facilities, is needed to guide the bump-in process and inform the public attending the event.

The Brisbane Convention and Exhibition Centre provides detailed specifications and guidelines for events held at the centre. These can be found at <www.bcec.com.au/downloads/Guidelines.PDF>. Any other large venue would do equally well. Use the information on the website to prepare a scale map for the LAN nights concept considered in Chapter 3 to see how well the function space could be used. Don't forget that chill-out and catering areas will be needed, and each participant will need a workstation area for their computer. It is possible that several attendees will be in wheelchairs. Read the general guidelines above and discuss elements of this event that may be problematic.

ACTIVITIES

1. *Visit a large convention centre in your state or territory (see links in Appendix D) and look at the facilities available. Find scale diagrams of meeting and function rooms and check the suitability of the convention centre for a two-day conference for 200 delegates, including a gala dinner.*
2. *Develop your own site inspection checklist and visit a public site often used for big events to look at disability access. Evaluate the site.*

LINKS

Disability Services Commission, Western Australia
www.dsc.wa.gov.au/content/Access/conducting_events_meetings.asp

Right of Access, Villamanta Publishing Services, 1997
www.villamanta.org.au/publish/index.htm

SUMMARY

The creativity of an event concept is often tempered by the suitability and availability of venues or sites to stage the event. Of course, many venues and sites can be totally transformed if there are unlimited funds available to the event manager! As this is not the case in most instances, choosing the right venue for an event is crucial to its success. In this chapter we have covered what you need to know to develop accurate site specifications for different types of events and how to source suitable venues or sites. For the event manager, there are many aspects to consider when preparing site specifications, not least of which is safety. We have also stressed the importance of confirming venue arrangements in writing and reviewing and signing a venue contract for which an example has been provided.

CHAPTER FIVE

LEGAL

COMPLIANCE

ON COMPLETION OF THIS CHAPTER YOU WILL BE ABLE TO:

- explain the laws and regulations that may have an impact on event planning
- identify the bodies from whom approval is required, or support is needed, to stage a particular event
- explain the legal compliance requirements of an event
- identify insurance premiums and fees that need to be paid
- describe the contracts required between event organisers and other parties, including subcontractors
- update legal knowledge.

While the press reports would lead one to believe that the party was a disorganised, feral bunch of teenagers running an illegal rave party at which drug dealing was rife, this was not the case. The party had been carefully planned with approvals sought from police and council and had met requirements for liquor licensing, security and amenities. Showers, water and first aid were all provided. The event was supported by a range of sponsors and had taken two years of planning. Recreational drug use is widespread and difficult to control, although it is illegal.

EVENT ORGANISER

This case study clearly illustrates the dilemmas faced by event organisers of dance parties, whether at fixed or open venues. In this case, the organisers had sought all approvals and had the support of the police and St John Ambulance's first aid services. It is easy to see, then, why event organisers must ensure that they comply with the relevant legislation. For example, if you were organising a music event, it would be necessary, amongst other things, to contact the two bodies responsible for music licensing and to pay fees to satisfy copyright agreements with all artists.

This chapter will cover all the necessary requirements, such as music licensing, food hygiene plans, the building of temporary structures, entertainment in public places and road closures.

UPDATING LEGAL KNOWLEDGE

It is unnecessary, and indeed almost impossible, for event managers to fully understand all laws pertinent to their industry and all their ramifications. For professional legal advice, most managers would contact their professional association (meetings, event, exhibition, venue association) or their organisation's own solicitors. The key issue for managers in the industry is knowing when to seek professional legal advice.

In order to be able to make such a judgement, the event manager must remain abreast of general changes to legislation that could have an impact on daily operations. For example, public liability issues have recently brought about many legislative changes in the Australian states and territories, so anyone operating an event business needs to carefully research the implications of those changes. They would also need to seek advice from their insurance company, as well as from their solicitor, regarding appropriate indemnity forms that their customers may need to sign. Sudden increases in insurance premiums may be the stimulus needed to research this issue further.

The aims of this chapter are therefore to provide a general understanding of the legislation that could have an impact on event operations and to underline the importance of updating knowledge on any changes to this legislation. Creating the right environment to minimise litigation is every manager's and every supervisor's role. Indeed, every staff member has a part to play in this regard. Reporting safety issues, for example, can help prevent accidents, often the cause of customer complaint and, at times, legal action. It is therefore the responsibility of management to create awareness of legislative compliance requirements, to develop appropriate policies and procedures, to undertake induction and training of employees, and to provide leadership that motivates employees to meet the highest professional standards.

Up-to-date information can be obtained from:
- print and news media
- reference books
- Internet
- industry associations
- industry journals and magazines
- clients and suppliers
- legal experts.

Most event industry associations run seminars to update their members on any changes or trends and these are recommended to anyone working in the event business. Associations are listed in Appendix D.

SOURCES OF LAW

In Australia, the law consists of:
- Australian **common law**, which developed from English common law and is interpreted and modified by the **courts**
- **Acts** passed by the **Federal Parliament** within the scope of its powers under the Australian Constitution (Statutory Law)

- **Acts** passed by **State Parliaments** and the **Legislative Assemblies** of the Northern Territory, the Australian Capital Territory and Norfolk Island (Statutory Law).

The Australian Constitution does not allow the Commonwealth Parliament the power to make laws on all subjects. Instead, it lists the subjects about which the Commonwealth Parliament can make laws. These include taxation; defence; external affairs; interstate and international trade; foreign affairs, trading and financial corporations; marriage and divorce; immigration; bankruptcy; and interstate industrial arbitration. Economic considerations have resulted in income tax being imposed solely by the Commonwealth.

Although the State Parliaments can pass laws on a wider range of subjects than the Commonwealth Parliament, the Commonwealth is generally regarded as the more powerful partner in the federation. If a valid Commonwealth law is inconsistent with a law of a State Parliament, the Commonwealth law operates and the state law is invalid to the extent of the inconsistency.

The *Racial Discrimination Act 1975* is an example of a Commonwealth Act, and is an important Act for event managers to take into consideration. This is the principal Act and there have been numerous amendments. Section 9 of the Act states that:

This Act is not intended, and shall be deemed never to have been intended, to exclude or limit the operation of a law of a State or Territory that furthers the objects of the Convention and is capable of operating concurrently with this Act.

It states further that:

It is unlawful for a person to do any act involving a distinction, exclusion, restriction or preference based on race, colour, descent or national or ethnic origin which has the purpose or effect of nullifying or impairing the recognition, enjoyment or exercise, on an equal footing, of any human right or fundamental freedom in the political, economic, social, cultural or any other field of public life.

Related Acts have been passed in the states and territories, which cover a range of issues in more detail. Under the *Anti-Discrimination Act 1991 (QLD)*, for instance, it is discriminatory to refuse to allow a guide dog onto a premises.

Local governments have a range of **Regulations** under their jurisdiction. Examples of such Regulations are building codes, signage limitations, lighting, and noise restrictions, all of which are important considerations for the event co-ordinator. Local council offices generally give advice on all legal compliance and they will request the event organiser not only to comply with council requirements but also to contact the Police Service or the Environment Protection Authority, if applicable. Some local councils have event planning policies which include all relevant council Regulations, as well as higher level legal compliance requirements.

Links are provided at the end of this chapter to the Department of Local Government in New South Wales web page where a comprehensive document called 'A Guide to Major and Special Event Planning' can be located. Similar guides are available in other states and territories. In

Appendix A, the outline for an event proposal provides prompts for a range of legal requirements, some of which may not be applicable, for example, to the organisation of an indoor event. However, this general outline gives you the main cues for event planning, and for meeting legal obligations.

The three levels of government discussed above are illustrated in Fig. 5.1.

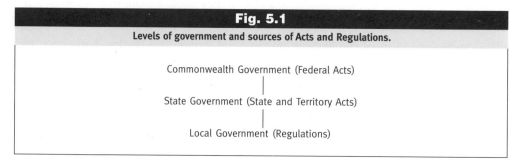

Fig. 5.1
Levels of government and sources of Acts and Regulations.

Commonwealth Government (Federal Acts)
|
State Government (State and Territory Acts)
|
Local Government (Regulations)

Common law

The third source of law in Australia, as mentioned above, is common law. Common law was introduced in the previous chapter with the illustration of the venue hire agreement/contract. For a contract to be valid there must be an offer, an acceptance and a consideration (an exchange for goods and services rendered). Where there is a dispute about a contract it is taken to court. In this circumstance, a judge needs to make a decision, largely based on precedent. One of the most fundamental areas of common law for event organisations is **duty of care**. Where lack of **reasonable** care can be shown in court, the resulting claim for negligence can lead to an award for damages being made by the judge. Accidents occurring at events are usually brought to court with the plaintiff arguing negligence. This argument could be made against the event organiser; the venue management; the security company; or the ride operator. In fact the claim might be

---

Fox Studios was ordered to improve its public safety yesterday after a coroner found the death of a nine-year-old boy was foreseeable and preventable.

David Selinger was crushed to death on January 15, 2001 when metal fence palings fell on him during a storm as he walked to the toilets. Despite an extensive search his body was not discovered until the next day.

The senior deputy state coroner, Jacqueline Milledge, found yesterday the failure of a site supervisor at Fox Studios to remove unsecured metal fencing, inadequate protocols for dealing with missing children, and poor lighting contributed to his death.

While she said there was no criminal negligence, she made nine recommendations, directing Fox Studios to improve its public safety by revising its protocols for dealing with lost children, establishing a storage area for fence panels, and appointing a person to oversee safety issues.

She said floodlighting should be available at the complex for use in emergencies, noting that inadequate lighting meant David's body lay under the fencing for 13 hours ...

Ms Milledge said the inexperience of Lisa Webb, site supervisor for the Fringe Festival, who left the unsecured fencing, was a contributing factor. Ms Webb testified that the panels were intended to be there briefly, and she had thought the fencing contractor would have dealt with them. Ms Milledge said Fox Studios should not have allowed the fencing to be stored in a public area near toilets.

Ellen Connolly, *Sydney Morning Herald*, 15 February 2003

made against all four, and it would be up to the courts to judge whether the defendants had shown the appropriate duty of care. Risk management strategies and contingency plans demonstrate that all reasonable steps have been taken to prevent an accident. A theme recurring through this book is therefore concern for the safety and welfare of everyone on the event site, with policies and procedures to reduce or eliminate risks where they are foreseen.

LEGISLATION RELEVANT TO EVENTS

The principles of the major Acts and Regulations relevant to event management are covered below, in general terms.

Local government Acts and Regulations

There are a number of local government Acts and Regulations that may apply to events. These vary considerably from one area to another. Some councils have detailed guidelines, while others have less formal requirements. The size of the event largely determines the detail required in the submission since smaller events tend to have a lower impact on the community.

If an event has already been held in one council area, with approval, it may still be necessary to obtain approval for a second similar event in another location. Likewise, if the event covers more than one jurisdiction, additional proposals may need to be submitted.

If the event requires the building of permanent structures, a development application would most likely be required, and this would link to the Local Environment Plan (LEP), which is the community's vision for the future of the area. Application for the use of the premises and property for entertainment may also be necessary. Plans would need to be developed for the erection of temporary structures and approval would need to be sought for them.

Approvals are required by most councils for:
- using loudspeakers or amplifiers in public spaces
- installing amusement devices
- singing or providing entertainment in public places (fees would also apply)
- using a building or structure for entertainment (change of approval classification)
- building a temporary structure.

Councils are also very concerned about cleaning programs during and after an event, noise and disturbance of local residents, and traffic management.

Business registration

Every business must be registered with an Australian Business Number (ABN) for taxation and Goods and Services Tax (GST) purposes. The name of the business must also be registered. A business can take the form of a sole trader, a partnership or a company.

A **sole trader** is an individual who is trading on their own. That person controls and manages the business. The income of the business is treated as the person's individual income, and they are solely responsible for any tax payable by the business.

For tax purposes, a **partnership** is an association of persons that carries on business as partners or receives income jointly.

A **company** is a legal entity separate from its shareholders. For tax purposes, a company is a body or association, incorporated or unincorporated, but does not include a partnership. Companies are regulated by the Australian Securities and Investments Commission (ASIC). New companies must be registered with ASIC. The first step in the registration process is to ensure that the proposed name is available for registration as a company. Contact details for the National Names Index are provided at the end of this chapter. The index can be used to check if a proposed company name is identical to another name already registered.

Taxation

For anyone running a commercial business (fee for service), compliance with taxation rules is essential. All businesses must be registered and this can be done by contacting the Australian Taxation Office (ATO). Advice will be provided on all types of taxation applicable, including deductions of PAYG for paid employees. Deductions for superannuation must also be made. All commercial businesses must pay GST, although charitable bodies and some educational institutions are exempt from GST.

Industrial relations

Employers and employees have certain obligations or duties to each other under common law. These obligations or duties are regarded as legal standards of behaviour in the employment relationship. Some rights and obligations of employers as interpreted and applied by the courts are to:

- pay wages
- reimburse employees for work-related expenses
- ensure a safe working environment suitable for the performance of the employee's duties
- not act in a way that may seriously damage an employee's reputation or cause mental distress or humiliation
- not act in a way that will damage the trust and confidence necessary for an employment relationship
- not provide a false or misleading reference (should one be provided)
- forward tax instalments to the Australian Taxation Office.

The employee's main obligations are to:

- obey the lawful and reasonable commands of the employer
- exercise due care in the performance of the work and to do it competently
- account to the employer for all moneys and property received while employed
- make available to the employer any process or product invented by the employee in the course of employment
- disclose to the employer information received by the employee relevant to the employer's business
- be faithful to the employer's interests, for example, by not passing on to a competitor information about the employer's business or denigrating the employer's products.

The employment relationship between employers and employees is also covered by legislation at Commonwealth and state/territory level. The legislation deals mainly with the framework for negotiating working conditions, including wages, holidays and other leave. In particular, employees may be paid under industrial awards (which tend to cover an industry or occupation, such as the catering industry) or workplace agreements (which cover a particular place of work). For more information regarding awards or agreements relevant to the event industry, the Wagenet website (for which details are provided at the end of this chapter) is a good starting point. Departments of Industrial Relations in the states and territories will also provide information relating to employment.

Entertainment industry legislation

Licences for the entertainment industry cover agents, managers and venue consultants. The disbursement of fees, as well as trust accounts for performers, are covered by this type of legislation. There is also a code of ethics. Entertainment industry legislation allows·for complaints to be heard and resolved regarding payments to performers, agents, managers and venue consultants.

Copyright

The right to use music in a business or commercial operation requires a licence from APRA (Australian Performing Rights Association) for the copyright in the song, composition or lyrics. A licence is also required from PPCA (Phonographic Performance Company of Australia), the association representing music publishers and record companies. Therefore, if a sound recording were to be played at an event, the event company would need to apply for licences from both APRA and PPCA. The fees, while nominal, recognise the copyright and commercial value of the music. They vary according to the use of the music (from background music, live performance, music played or sung at sporting venues or function centres, to karaoke).

To clarify, there are two copyrights in each recording: firstly, the copyright in the sound recording of the recorded performance and, secondly, the copyright in the song, composition or lyrics. There are usually at least three copyright issues in a music video clip, namely, copyright in the cinematographic film that embodies the recorded performance, copyright in the recorded performance itself and copyright in the song (i.e. composition or lyrics).

Copyright on text is generally held by the writer, artist or publisher, and permission is required from the copyright holder of any text or image that you wish to reproduce. In the same way, you hold the copyright in your own work. Logos and trademarks must be registered separately.

Liquor licensing

In general, this legislation covers the age of drinkers, the venues and the situations (for example, with meals) in which alcoholic drinks can be served, as well as the legal hours of alcohol service. Liquor must be correctly labelled and sold in legal measures. A sign must be displayed to say that ·it is an offence to sell or supply liquor to, or obtain liquor on behalf of, a person under the age of 18 years. The licensee must be able to show that reasonable steps (including requests for identification) have been taken to ensure that minors have not been served alcohol. Complaints about noise or indecorous behaviour can be made to the Licensing Board.

A liquor licence is required to serve alcohol.

Trade Practices

The Trade Practices Acts aim to ensure that advertised goods and services are provided in accordance with the advertising. For example, at one concert in Sydney featuring an overseas performer, the stage design was so poor that many members of the audience could neither see nor hear. As a result, the event management company was forced to refund the money paid for the tickets to those who had been affected. The staging problem was resolved to everyone's satisfaction before the next performance.

The Trade Practices Act (Commonwealth) and the various state Fair Trading Acts protect the consumer against misleading advertising and deceptive conduct. A consumer (or a client) can sue under common law, under the Trade Practices Act or under the relevant Fair Trading Act. This means that one cannot engage in conduct that is liable to mislead the public as to the nature, the characteristics, the suitability for the purpose or the quality of any services. The contract for services to be provided in the organisation of an event thus needs to be extremely explicit.

Privacy

Information kept on a database provided by a client, exhibitor or spectator can only be used for the purpose for which it was given, i.e. registration or ticketing. This data cannot be used for any other purpose, or used or sold to another business for direct marketing. The event business works closely with celebrity performers and athletes and a breach of confidentiality should never occur. Thus all employees should know that personal information should not be given to the media.

Anti-discrimination legislation

The Human Rights and Equal Opportunity Commission investigates discrimination on the grounds of race, colour or ethnic origin, racial vilification, sex, sexual harassment, marital status, pregnancy and disability. A case can be made for unlawful discrimination if management or staff refuses entry to a premises on the basis of any of the above factors. Equal employment opportunity legislation is a subset of anti-discrimination legislation referring specifically to workplace discrimination. It is unlawful to discriminate when advertising for new staff, when selecting new staff, when offering training opportunities, and when selecting staff for promotion and other career development opportunities.

Environmental protection legislation

This legislation aims to prevent pollution, including air and waterways pollution. Discharge of sewage, oil and other waste into water systems is illegal and our waterways are protected by a number of Acts of the various states and territories, all relating to protection of the environment. Noise is covered in this category. Noise is a troublesome problem for festivals and events since by their very nature they attract crowds, entertainment events being particularly problematic. It is therefore essential to check noise limitations in terms of allowable decibels and the times during which loud music is permitted.

Food safety

Food Acts provide guidelines for safe food handling. Every contract caterer is required to develop a food safety plan covering food safety at all stages of delivery, preparation and service. This is necessary to guard against bacteria which may develop if food is left standing after delivery, or during preparation and service, and not kept at an appropriate temperature. Buffets where food is left unrefrigerated are notorious for high bacteria levels. Generally, food needs to be kept cool or heated to a hot temperature. The mid-temperature range is the most dangerous. A qualified caterer should know all about food hygiene and should follow correct procedures to avoid contamination. A food safety plan should be part of any catering contract, which should also include menus and prices.

Safe plating of food. These trollies are designed to be stored in refrigerators.

Charitable fundraising legislation

The aims of this legislation are to:

1 promote proper management of fundraising appeals for charitable purposes
2 ensure proper record-keeping and auditing
3 prevent deception of members of the public who desire to support worthy causes.

A person who participates in a fundraising appeal which is conducted unlawfully is guilty of an offence. Authority is required to conduct a fundraising appeal and this is obtained by applying to the relevant body in your state or territory.

Security legislation

This legislation provides for the licensing and regulation of persons in the security industry, such as crowd controllers, bouncers, guards and operators of security equipment. In general, there are different levels of licences requiring different levels of training.

Summary Offences Act

Summary Offences legislation covers issues such as desecration of public and protected places, shrines, monuments, statues and war memorials.

Occupational health and safety

This legislation is designed to prevent workplace accidents and injuries. The legislation has specific requirements for employers to provide safe work places and safe work practices. This topic will be covered in detail in Chapter 18.

Workers compensation insurance

Workers compensation insurance, which is obligatory, covers treatment and rehabilitation of injured workers. There are penalties for businesses that do not insure their employees for work-related accidents and injuries. Through workers compensation schemes, claims may be made for medical expenses and time off work.

Where rehabilitation is necessary, redeployment to another role may occur until the person is fit to return to their original position. Employers have a responsibility to:

- register with WorkCover
- pay insurance levies by the due date
- send end-of-year reconciliation statements to WorkCover
- submit all claims for compensation on the prescribed forms
- assist with rehabilitation of injured workers.

When an event is organised, all contracting organisations on site (employers) should carry this type of insurance for their workers and a certificate of currency is generally required when negotiating such contracts with service suppliers of security, maintenance, staging, catering and so on.

Volunteers and spectators are covered, in most cases, by **public liability insurance** since they are not **paid workers**. In some cases, event organisations take out specific insurance for volunteers to cover accidents and injuries. In the absence of this type of cover, volunteers fall under the umbrella of public liability.

INSURANCE

The various different types of insurance are summarised below, some being obligatory, others voluntary.

Public liability insurance

The most important insurance required by an event management company is public liability insurance. This covers a business owner's legal liability to compensate any person who is not an employee or a family member (a third party) for injury, damage to property or death as a result of the business operations should the owner and/or employees/volunteers be shown to be negligent.

Claims against this insurance can be reduced by careful risk analysis and prevention strategies. One council requires a $10 million level of insurance for minor events and a $20 million level of insurance for major events. The average householder has a $1 million public liability insurance cover. As with most local government requirements, these may change from one council or municipality to another. Assets and motor vehicles also need to be insured.

The following disclaimer is aimed at reducing the liability of a race organiser:

1 *I, the undersigned, hereby waive any claim that I might have arising out of my participation in this event and fully accept all the risks involved.*

2 *This waiver shall operate separately in favour of all bodies involved in promoting or staging the event.*

3 *I hereby attest and verify that I am physically fit and have sufficiently trained for this event. I agree to be bound by the official rules and regulations of the event.*

4 *I hereby consent to receive medical treatment that may be deemed advisable in the event of injury or accident.*

Essentially, the person who signs this disclaimer is taking responsibility for his or her actions. However, from a legal point of view, there is nothing to stop the contestant from making a case for negligence against the race organiser. Clearly it would have to be shown that this negligence led directly to the injury, and the extent and impact of the negligence would then be investigated. In other words, an event organiser cannot avoid liability for negligence by having participants sign an indemnification agreement. The person has the right to sue in any circumstances and the case would be judged on its merit.

The following example is another indemnification agreement to which the above principles would still apply, despite the strong wording:

I understand that the event is held in primitive, dangerous and inaccessible wilderness areas where I will be exposed to hazards and conditions that may cause me serious injury, illness or death. I voluntarily accept these risks.

With this example, too, a fatal accident involving this event volunteer would be investigated by the coroner and the case would land up in court if the victim's family felt that the organisers had been negligent. That actions or omissions of the organiser had led directly to the accident would, however, have to be proven.

In addition to public liability insurance which must be taken out by the event management organisation, all contracts signed with subcontractors, such as a company that erects scaffolding, should also include a clause requiring the subcontractor to hold a current policy covering them against liability for incidents that may occur. As you can see, there are a number of different stakeholders who are potentially liable and the event organiser needs to limit their own liability by managing risk and ensuring that subcontractors are also insured.

In the following article, the honorary vice-president of Clowns International advised 70 members to take out insurance against potential claims for custard pie injuries!

Clowns gathered at a special Big Top conference last week — to discuss the legal risks of chucking pies. They got serious as they discussed whether circus audiences sitting in the front row were wilfully placing themselves in the line of fire. Clowns fear they could be liable for compensation if a member of the public got it in the face.

INTERNATIONAL EXPRESS, 10 APRIL 2001

Sports injury

This type of insurance provides injury protection during sanctioned practices, games and related travel that is approved and under the supervision of a proper authority. The policy can cover all participants, managers, coaches, trainers or officials, volunteers, auxiliary workers and employees.

Professional indemnity

Another policy which should be considered is professional indemnity insurance. This indemnifies the insured against any claim for breach of professional duty through any act, error or omission by them, their company or their employees. It is essential cover for lawyers and accountants who may be sued for their 'unprofessional' advice, as well as for anyone providing consultancy advice in the area of event safety, security and fire risk.

Product liability

Product liability is another type of insurance, essential if selling tangible products such as event merchandise, particularly toys, but not generally required as the event experience is intangible. With product liability insurance, damages arise out of product failure. However, should the scaffolding collapse, the event company would expect that the hire company and manufacturer of the scaffolding carry this insurance.

Superannuation

It is now compulsory to provide for employee superannuation.

Fire insurance

Fire insurance covers the building, contents and stock of the business against fire, lightning, storms, impact, malicious damage and explosion.

General insurance

General insurance covers property, including equipment, fixtures, fittings and miscellaneous property.

Business interruption or loss of profits insurance

This insurance provides cover if a business is interrupted through damage to property by fire or other insured perils. It ensures that a business's net profit projection is maintained and pays employee wages and additional working costs if alternative facilities have to be used.

Burglary insurance

Theft of property and damage caused by burglars breaking into property are covered by this type of insurance. It does not cover theft by shoplifters or staff.

Fidelity guarantee

Fidelity guarantee insurance covers losses resulting from misappropriation of goods or cash (i.e. embezzling or stealing).

Money in transit

This covers loss of money on the business premises or when being taken to and from the bank. It can be extended to cover money taken home overnight or deposited in a bank night safe. Responsibility for money in transit should be made very clear when negotiating with stall holders, concessions or merchandise outlets. Security organisations can provide cash management services, delivering change, receiving takings, transportation, counting and banking. The event organiser should make it clear to contractors that they should take out their own insurance for money in transit.

Machinery breakdown

Designed to cover breakdown of all mechanical and electrical plant and machinery at a work site, this type of policy can be extended to cover spoilage of foodstuffs consequent of such breakdown.

Cancellation or non-appearance (contingency insurance)

Where the cause is beyond control, such as the non-appearance of the main performer or abandonment by financial supporters of the event, this insurance would cover the costs incurred through cancellation of the event.

Weather

While insurance can be obtained for event cancellation due to weather conditions, this type of cover is extremely costly and claims are hard to fully substantiate.

STAKEHOLDERS AND OFFICIAL BODIES

Some of the following bodies may require detailed plans or briefings depending on the extent of their involvement in an event.

Transport Authority

Any impact on traffic because of an event must be discussed with the relevant authority, which is generally the Roads and Traffic Authority (RTA). The staging of an important party in Melbourne proved problematic when all the visitors arrived in limousines. The driveway was too small to accommodate them and the traffic backed up for miles, resulting in the event program being delayed. This had implications for the VIPs invited, including senior members of local and overseas governments, who missed flights and other engagements.

Police Service

Police patrols, if required, are charged to the user at an hourly rate, except in such circumstances as charitable fundraising events.

State Emergency Services and St John Ambulance

Both these bodies need to be briefed. St John Ambulance is staffed primarily by volunteers and they should be included in staff recognition programs in order to acknowledge their very important role.

CONTRACTS

This topic is the most important in this chapter and could become a book in its own right. The effectiveness of the contracts between the parties involved in an event is crucial. Specifications need to be incredibly detailed in order to avoid disputes. Clarity and agreement between all parties is essential. The contract provides the basis for variation in price every time the customer has new demands. For this reason, time invested in the writing of the contract will reap rewards and often resolve legal disputes. Professional legal advice is essential for a new event management business.

Many events involve a range of contractors for services such as catering, cleaning, sound, lighting and security. While it is tempting for an event organiser to take on all roles, the benefits of employing contractors are many. Specialist organisations generally have more expertise and better equipment, they generally carry their own insurance and they have a lot of experience in their particular field. By dealing with a range of contractors and using professionally prepared, well-negotiated contracts, the event organiser can dramatically reduce risk and liability. On the day, the main role of the event organiser is to monitor the implementation of the agreed contracts.

Content of Contract/Agreement

- parties to contract
- deadline and deposit
- specifications (for example, space booked, timing, food and beverage, accommodation)
- services to be provided
- special requirements
- schedule of payments
- insurance

- cancellation
- termination/non-performance
- contingency
- consumption
- confidentiality
- arbitration
- warranties
- signatories
- date

Many different types of contract are entered into by event organisers, including the implied conditions of a ticket held by the participant. Contracts are made between the event organiser and:
- participants (any member of the event audience, ticketed or registered)
- funding bodies (any donor, sponsor, contributor, bank or financing institution)
- employees (the employment relationship is a form of contract, with many elements determined in law)
- providers of goods and services (plumbers, scaffolding and staging suppliers; caterers; security companies, including preferred providers).

Contracts also cover:
- licences (music, liquor, rides, fireworks)
- trademarks/branding (logos, trademarks, images)
- transfers of contracts or rights (such as rights to a musical performance)
- franchises (operational guidelines, branding and marketing agreements).

Where there are chains of contracting parties, it is essential to identify who is acting as principal and as agents down the chain. The event organiser is potentially liable all the way down the chain and this is why insurance certification is advisable.

POLICIES, PROCEDURES AND STAFF TRAINING

As the previous discussions illustrate, events are a legal minefield! This is why industry professionals are highly sought after for their understanding of compliance issues and, more importantly, their understanding of the implications of the legislation for undertaking risk analysis and developing policies and procedures. In summary, compliance with legislation can be improved by:

- developing policies and procedures
- recruiting knowledgeable staff
- inducting and training new staff
- reinforcing legal responsibilities in meetings and in written communications
- conducting ongoing risk assessments in relation to non-compliance
- developing a culture of commitment by employees, volunteers, supervisors and managers.

CASE STUDY

You and your friends are planning to have a party to celebrate the end of the college year. Your plan is to hold the party at the local football oval, but if it rains you will hold it in your garage. Invitation has been informal and your whole year has been invited. Everyone will bring their own alcohol, although a few of the people will be under eighteen. A friend with a sound system is bringing it along and you have decided to charge everyone who attends $5 to cover your costs. Another friend who runs a catering company will do a spit roast and charge $2 for a beef roll.

- Is permission required to use the football oval? If so, from whom?
- What are the implications of charging an entry fee? Would you recommend this?
- Should the police be told about the party? (Is there any chance that uninvited people may turn up?)
- Do you need a liquor licence if alcohol is not sold?
- Who is responsible for underage drinking?
- What would happen if a fault in the wiring caused someone to be electrocuted?
- What are the limitations on the use of a sound system, either at home or at the football oval?

ACTIVITY

Investigate two venues that offer weddings and compare their advertised services/products, contracts and checklists from the point of view of the customer and the owner of the business. In addition, compare the contracts of the two venues in terms of the potential for misunderstandings to develop and legal disputes to follow.

LINKS

ASIC National Names Index
www.search.asic.gov.au/gns001.html

Australian Performing Rights Association
www.apra.com.au

Blue Mountains City Council, Guide for Youth Events
www.bmcc.nsw.gov.au/files%5CEventsYouthOutdoor.pdf

Department of Local Government, New South Wales
www.dlg.nsw.gov.au/97-65.pdf

Event planning (permits and other requirements)
www.alicesprings.nt.gov.au/tourism/pdf/Events_Starter_Pack_2003_MTC.pdf (Alice Springs, NT)
www.ballarat.com/events/organising_events.htm (Ballarat, Vic)
www.greaterdandenong.com/infopage.cfm?SubMenuId=173 (Greater Dandenong Council, SA)
www.shoalhaven.nsw.gov.au/council/forms/CEIK/Part5.pdf (District of Shoalhaven, NSW)

Phonographic Performance Company of Australia
www.ppca.com.au

Roads and Traffic Authority NSW
www.rta.nsw.gov.au/trafficinformation/downloads/tmc_specialevents_dI1.html

Wagenet (awards and agreements)
www.wagenet.gov.au

SUMMARY

This chapter dealt with legal and related issues that must be considered during the planning of an event, including licensing and approvals. Legal compliance is one of the major risk issues for organisers of an event and research into these requirements is essential. Tight contractual arrangements with the client and subcontractors are equally important as these can ensure the financial viability of an event or completely derail it. Insurances of various types are also required, including workers compensation and public liability, while workplace health and safety should be a major consideration of any event organiser.

CHAPTER SIX

BUSINESS AND
CLIENT RELATIONSHIPS

ON COMPLETION OF THIS CHAPTER YOU WILL BE ABLE TO:

- analyse the needs of client populations/market segments
- establish and conduct business and client relationships
- plan and develop client service
- conduct negotiations with clients
- make formal business agreements
- maintain business and client relationships
- evaluate client service relationships.

*The SheppARTon Festival focuses on **Raising Dreams** and the key to raising the dreams of the community, that is Shepparton and its visitors, is **participation**. Thanks to our many sponsors, we offer a program full of opportunity. There are opportunities for visual artists and those who appreciate the visual arts; opportunities to engage in and appreciate the performing arts of drama, comedy and music and opportunities to feast on wines and foods specific to our region and those that will expand our culinary horizons. The program is rich, but it needs YOU to participate. Accept the challenge and engage with all that the 2003 SheppARTon Festival has to offer.*

www.sheppartonfestival.net.au/

In the previous chapters we have discussed various different types of events; we have introduced the creative element of the event concept; and we have tempered enthusiasm for the event concept with legal and logistical issues that impact on the feasibility of an event. So far, the audience has not been mentioned, except indirectly.

This chapter looks at the event audience, the client population, the spectators, the customers, the delegates, the visitors and the attendees. The introductory paragraph invites the audience to visit the SheppARTon Festival, emphasising the word '**participation**' in bold. The organisers of this event have clearly developed a purpose for the event, a guiding vision that focuses on audience participation in a range of programmed activities. The profiles of these visitors will be discussed further later in this chapter.

In this chapter we also focus on building and maintaining business relationships with clients and suppliers.

WHO IS THE CLIENT?

As event managers, it is necessary to meet the needs of the 'client', the person paying for the event, as well as those of the 'audience', so it is essential to understand what both the client and the audience want to achieve. The two may have quite different expectations, providing a challenge for the event manager. For example, a client (a software company) may wish to profile a new product, say a stock control system for wineries. For the client, the desirable end result would be that everyone invited to the product launch leave with an in-depth understanding of the new system and the product attributes that make it better than any competitor's stock control system. For the owners of regional wineries who receive the invitation to the product launch, the main motivation may be to network with colleagues in the industry. In fact, many could see the launch as an opportunity to have a good time, to party, to indulge in some revelry. As this example illustrates, it is essential for the event organiser to research and understand the needs of all client populations involved in an event in order to maximise its effectiveness.

ANALYSING THE NEEDS OF CLIENT POPULATIONS

When you ask someone why they want to work in the event business, 'I like working with people' is pretty much the standard response. To be successful, however, an event organiser needs to do much more than like people. He or she must research and understand the characteristics of many different client populations, and this analytical process starts with formal and informal research.

Firstly, a diagram illustrating everyone involved is most useful and should include stakeholders and customers, as shown for a regional festival in Fig. 6.1.

Fig. 6.1
Stakeholders and customers for a regional festival.

Stakeholders		Customers/clients/consumers
Arts council		Local residents
Regional tourism body		Regional visitors
State tourism body	Event organiser	Capital city visitors
Major sponsors		Interstate visitors
Local council		International visitors

These lists are by no means exhaustive; however, they provide examples of the relationships that need to be managed to ensure a successful ongoing event. The needs and expectations of the customers, the event audience, must be met for the festival, or any event for that matter, to be called a success. In addition, all stakeholders must in turn be convinced that this was the case if they are to fund, sponsor or support the festival in the longer term. To do this, a post-event report analysing the audience provides the information necessary for evaluating the event and planning the next festival. Several such reports included on websites listed at the end of this chapter illustrate the value of ongoing research.

For the 2003 SheppARTon Festival the composition of the audience was surveyed to provide demographic profiles, as illustrated in Tables 6.1 and 6.2. This is known as primary research.

These statistics show that 70 per cent of the audience was female, and that the largest segment of attendees was in the 41–50 age bracket.

Patrons were also asked to indicate the town, state or country (if from overseas) they were from, most being local or from the local region (within a one-hour drive).

Clearly, the first time an event is organised demographic statistics and psychographics (interests) of the event audience are largely unknown. Even if the concept is a new one, sponsors and other stakeholders will want to know about the anticipated audience and this is where the research effort comes in. For the first time an event is held, the research is more likely to be secondary research. Secondary research describes information gathered from, for example, publications, broadcast media and government agencies. Over the years of event operation, primary research, such as the surveys for the SheppARTon Festival, can be used to further inform decisions. This is illustrated in Fig. 6.2.

Using marketing terminology, the event audience would be the **consumers**. There are several terms used to refer to the consumer in the event business but they all refer to the person or persons who consume the end product:

- audience
- spectator
- conference delegate
- visitor
- tourist
- customer
- buyer
- patron
- client
- participant.

Table 6.1

SheppARTon Festival, 2003
Demographics — gender and age of audience.

	Male	Female	Overall
Under 20	1%	4%	5%
21–30	3%	9%	12%
31–40	4%	13%	17%
41–50	7%	20%	27%
51–60	8%	15%	23%
60+	7%	9%	16%
Total	30%	70%	100%

<www.sheppartonfestival.net.au>

Table 6.2

SheppARTon Festival, 2003
Demographics — origin of audience.

Resident	48%
Local region	36%
Regional Victoria	8%
Melbourne	5%
Interstate	3%
Overseas	0%

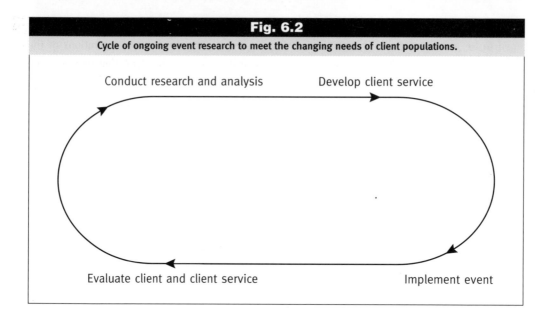

Fig. 6.2

Cycle of ongoing event research to meet the changing needs of client populations.

Conduct research and analysis   Develop client service

Evaluate client and client service   Implement event

In many cases, the consumer is also a participant. Anyone entering a bike race or fun run is both a consumer and a participant in the event.

When these consumers are grouped together as a target market, this grouping is referred to as a **market segment**.

It is not sufficient for the event organiser to assume that an event meets the needs of 'the public' since few events attract an even distribution of the public, whether of local or distant origin. A street festival will attract a lot of families, a rock concert mainly teenagers, opera an older age group. In developing a better understanding of the consumer it is essential to look at their demographic and psychographic profiles.

TYPES OF MARKET SEGMENTATION

Market segments can be defined in a number of ways. The most popular types of segmentation are described briefly below.

Demographics

Consumers can be grouped on the basis of characteristics such as age, sex, family size, occupation, life cycle, etc. This is easy to do and it is relatively easy to reach such segments through the media. The Australian Bureau of Statistics (ABS) is a valuable source of demographic data, particularly data projections such as the future age profiles of the population. Bodies such as the Australian Tourist Commission also provide detailed information on various tourism market segments, such as tourists typically visiting regional areas. Demographic segmentation is the most popular basis for segmenting consumer markets because consumer needs often vary closely with demographic variables and also because of the ease of measurement of these variables. Even when other bases are used for segmentation, demographic variables are still used in the description of the segments. For example, you may divide a state into northern, southern, eastern and western regions, but you may still describe each of the regions in terms of the demographics of the buyers living there, for example, by age, sex or family size.

Socioeconomic

Characteristics such as income, occupation and education can be used to determine segments that are easy to reach. Such segments are indicators of behaviour, such as lifestyle, price sensitivity and preferences. The liquor industry (sponsor of many events) conducts detailed ongoing market research to better understand the socioeconomic profiles of their consumers.

Psychographics

Personality, attitudes, opinions and lifestyles are often used as bases of segmentation. These characteristics have some relationship to behaviour and provide insight into how to communicate with chosen segments. They provide the data for dividing a market into leisure-seeking, work-oriented and family-oriented segments. Studies of attitudes towards sport, leisure and entertainment would clearly be useful here as they could be taken into account when developing an event concept and planning promotional activities.

Generation

Generation, or cohort, refers to people born in the same period of time. For example, the Baby Boomer generation can be defined as those people born between 1946 and 1955. Such cohorts share much in common, having experienced similar economic, cultural and political influences. A new term developed by the author, 'Moulds', describes middle-aged to older consumers who refuse to be categorised as 'old'. This is the youthful, red wine and blue cheese club. For this group, rugby events have particular appeal, as do performers (famous in the sixties) who have reached their use-by dates!

Geography/origin

Place of residence is often used for market segmentation in the event business, as illustrated in the arts festival example. Where the event has a tourism impact, it is important to know where people come from. In the example, there were no visitors from overseas in the sample surveyed. This does not mean that there were no international visitors at the event as the sample would not include everyone, but it would be safe to say for this festival that the international tourist is not a target market segment. Segmenting markets on the basis of geography involves dividing the market into different geographical units, for example, states, regions or countries, and the event management company will then focus on geographical differences in needs and wants.

Behaviour/product usage

Behaviour segmentation involves dividing consumers into groups based on their product knowledge, usage, attitudes or responses. Of particular importance is a powerful form of segmentation, benefit segmentation, which groups buyers according to the various benefits sought by them from the product class. Loyalty to different sporting codes or types of music would fit into this category.

WHY IS MARKET SEGMENTATION NECESSARY?

Market segmentation is necessary for a number of reasons. First and foremost, the product can be developed to best suit the needs of the most common market segments. An event experience is, in marketing terms, a **product**, something the consumer enjoys. The target market for a Family Fun Day is already described in the name of the event. This helps to communicate with this particular group and refine the product to suit its needs. In developing the Family Fun Day product, one would look at product attributes, such as the day and time the event would be held. This type of event would need to start early and finish in the late afternoon. Much of the event experience is intangible. For example, 'fun' is intangible, and is much more difficult to guarantee than a tasty hamburger.

Market segmentation also makes it easier to reach a particular market segment. In the above example, advertising to local play groups, kindergartens and schools would be more cost effective than blanket advertising on the radio or in a national newspaper. Since the market segment is also likely to live locally, this is another consideration when promoting the event.

Segmenting a market enables the event marketer to:

1 Describe the market more accurately. The more accurately the market can be segmented, the better its needs will be appreciated.

2 Increase the effectiveness of marketing. When the needs of the various segments have been described, their associated promotional activities will be more effective.

3 Spread the risk associated with producing a product (event) for only one segment of the market. When the marketer measures the relative size of each segment, they can determine the viability of targeting each segment.

4 Position a product in a market to target more profitable segments. When segment characteristics are known, the economics of each segment will allow profitable ones to be targeted (sometimes known as yield analysis).

5 Understand and assess competition. Segmenting the market helps focus promotional activity in a particular area in order to be more competitive.

6 Clearly define the customer. When the overall market for a commodity or service has been systematically analysed and segmented, the marketer not only has a better idea of how to influence the decisions of the customer, but also has a much clearer idea of who the customer really is.

PROS AND CONS OF PRIMARY AND SECONDARY RESEARCH

The following yearly market research for the Melbourne Comedy Festival provides primary data, which can be used by management to target its audience more effectively each year, and this, in turn, has been a major factor in the growth and success of this event.

The specific nature of this information is extremely advantageous for decision-making, but it is costly to conduct this type of research. Survey design and sampling are just two aspects of this research that are best managed by market research professionals.

As we have seen earlier in this chapter, secondary data is available from other sources, such as government bodies, journals and trade associations. This type of data can be obtained quickly and easily from the Australian Bureau of Statistics. Following is an example of secondary research on musical and opera attendance carried out by the ABS (cat. no. 4114.0):

Females were more likely to attend musicals and operas than males — the attendance rate for females was 22%, compared with 15% for males. Over one-fifth of people in each of the age groups 45–54 years and 55–64 years had been to a musical or opera in the 12 months before interview.

Market Research

Who came to the 2003 Melbourne International Comedy Festival?

GENDER

68% Female

32% Male

AGE

0–18 years 5%

18–24 years 22%

25–34 years 38%

35–44 years 22%

45–54 years 10%

55 plus years 3%

MARITAL STATUS*

51% Single

45% Married/De facto

4% Other

RESIDENCY

18% Inner City

68% Elsewhere in Melbourne

6% Elsewhere in Victoria

6% Interstate

2% International

EDUCATION LEVEL

22% Secondary School

3% Trade

15% Certificate/Diploma

36% University Degree

20% Post-Graduate

WORK STATUS

65% Full-time

21% Part-time

9% Student

2% Unemployed

2% Home Duties

1% Retired

PERSONAL WORK LEVEL*

5% Manual/Unskilled

24% Sales/Clerical/Administrative

12% Semi-skilled/Trade/Technical

53% Professional/Manager

6% CEO/Director/Senior Executive

PERSONAL INCOME*

19% Up to $20K per annum

38% Up to 49K per annum

27% Up to $99K per annum

6% Over $100K per annum

HIGH TECHNOLOGY USE

87% Personal computer ownership

93% Access e-mail

79% Use Internet at home

90% Use a mobile phone

* Figures have been rounded up.

Melbourne International Comedy Festival Report 2003, Quantum Market Research

The highest attendance rates for musicals and operas were recorded for people who:

- *were working part-time (24%)*
- *had graduate diplomas and certificates (36%), postgraduate degrees (35%), or bachelor degrees (32%)*
- *were in the highest equivalised household income quintile (31%).*

Secondary sources are accessible and a useful starting point; however the data may be limited in value, and certainly not as valuable as primary data in targeting audiences. Following is an example of secondary data that is too broad to allow accurate market segmentation:

According to information collected from the Population Survey Monitor, about 2.9 million Australians (22% of the population aged 18 years and over) attended at least one art and cultural festival in the 12 months prior to September 1996. These people accounted for 4.1 million attendances at festivals, an average of 1.4 attendances per person. Over half of attendances were at multi-arts festivals. The next most attended was popular music festivals (0.6 million attendances) and film/video festivals (0.3 million attendances). Attendance rates were highest amongst the younger age groups (31% of 18–24 year olds) and declined steadily with age (10% of persons aged 65 years and over).

Population Survey Monitor, November 1995 to September 1996,
Cultural Trends in Australia No. 6: Attendance at Festivals, Australia,
Department of Communications and the Arts.

This type of survey is done infrequently — while the most up to date available, it clearly has limited value for this reason as well.

In the next chapter we will cover the topic of market segmentation and marketing in further detail. Having looked at developing relationships with client populations, we will now look at the many business relationships that need to be fostered and maintained in the event industry.

BUSINESS RELATIONSHIPS

In many sectors of the event industry, the consumer or client is a large corporation, association or government body. A conference, exhibition or incentive event is usually the result of extensive negotiation with such an organisation. The following general guidelines are provided to aid event managers who may enter into detailed discussions with a client about the event concept, the parameters of the event and its feasibility.

In preparing for a business negotiation, it is necessary to understand the goals and positions of both parties, as these goals are often contradictory. Price is a good example. If price is being negotiated for a conference, the client will require the best outcomes for the lowest price while the event organiser (or professional conference organiser) will want the highest possible price or profit margin. Ultimately, it is necessary for both parties to identify their bottom line so that the process of negotiation can continue. Chapter 9 will deal with budgeting to inform this aspect of the negotiation.

It is also important to ensure that the appropriate people are conducting the negotiation. Ideally, the event organiser should negotiate with the owner or manager of the company or one person in the organisation with delegated authority. The event organiser should likewise have the authority to close the deal when the correct price and other conditions, such as conference specifications, have been agreed.

Communication tools and tactics in negotiation

Active listening and questioning are essential negotiation tools, particularly when used in conjunction with one or more persuasive negotiation tactics. Active listening involves confirming and clarifying what the person has said by paraphrasing and checking assumptions.

Negotiation techniques may include:
- preparatory research of the facts of the business situation or parties to the agreement
- identification of goals of the negotiation and limits to the discussion
- clarification of the needs of all parties, including third party stakeholders such as suppliers and contractors

- identification of points of agreement and points of difference
- active listening and questioning to clarify points of discussion
- non-verbal communication techniques to reinforce messages
- use of appropriate language, avoiding jargon, acronyms and colloquialisms
- bargaining strategies, including attempts to achieve win-win outcomes
- developing options and alternatives using brainstorming
- confirming agreements verbally and in writing
- using appropriate cultural behaviour.

Where those involved in the negotiation exhibit a wide range of individual differences, particularly in language or culture, some strategies can help to develop effective communication. These include identifying specific information needs of all participants in the negotiation; using plain English; developing sub-teams; using graphical information; and providing all individuals with opportunities to participate.

Fig. 6.3 outlines the five main steps in the negotiation process.

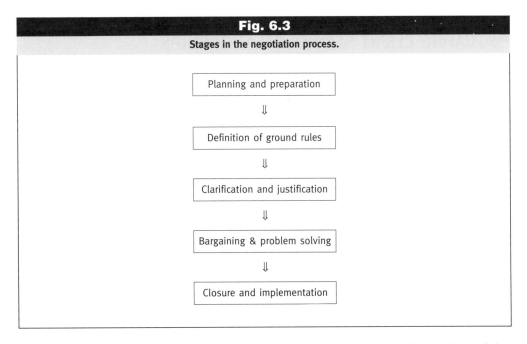

Fig. 6.3

Stages in the negotiation process.

Planning and preparation

⇓

Definition of ground rules

⇓

Clarification and justification

⇓

Bargaining & problem solving

⇓

Closure and implementation

Many books have been written on the many different types of strategies that can be used, but here we will outline just a few:
- We will beat our competitors. 'Name any price you have been given and we will beat it' is a common sales technique.
- Try it out. Once the customer or client has committed to trying a product (such as sampling the menu for a banquet), the deal is as good as done.
- Take it or leave it. Starting at a ridiculously low price, the aim is for the other party to feel that they have 'won' when the price is negotiated higher.
- Pressed for time. Creating pressure for a decision by creating an artificial deadline, 'by this date for this price', it is possible to force an early commitment.

- Worn out. Constant communication using different channels and reinforcing customer benefits can work in some situations.
- Compromise. The most common approach is to identify the extremes of, say, price and reach a mid-level compromise.

The above techniques work in some negotiating situations but not in others. For the most part, a successful negotiation is one in which both parties strive for a win-win outcome, with the aim of ensuring the long-term commitment of both parties to the business relationship.

Cultural sensitivity is also important. As mentioned earlier, different cultures approach bargaining and negotiation in different ways. In some cultures, the aim is to get straight to the point, while in others relationship building is seen as more important than the specifics of the final agreement. It is always best to negotiate face-to-face than indirectly over the telephone or via email.

Following agreement, the details should be confirmed in writing. Agreements should be monitored over a period of time, since it is much more difficult to find new customers than it is to retain existing ones. Existing customers or clients with whom relationships have been developed should also be closely monitored to gauge their satisfaction level with the products or services supplied.

EVALUATING CLIENT SERVICE RELATIONSHIPS

Having established the target market segments for an event, including clarifying their expectations, development of concepts can proceed to finalisation of plans, followed by implementation and evaluation. Chapter 23 will cover evaluation of events in detail; however, as this chapter has shown, evaluation can only be done if the event concept has been clearly defined and its feasibility tested. The evaluation report is written for the major clients, such as the business partners or sponsors involved in the event, thus fulfilling its role in closing the management cycle, starting with planning and finishing with evaluation. Operational aspects of implementation will be covered in Part 2.

CASE STUDY

As the newly appointed Film Festival co-ordinator, you will have the opportunity to screen 30 ten-minute films developed by graduates of the state's high profile Film and Television School. This event has attracted an enthusiastic audience in the past, has achieved media attention and has launched some young artists into stellar careers. Develop a diagram to illustrate all the parties involved including the 'consumers'. Using market segmentation analysis, describe the audience for this event, explaining your assumptions in doing so.

ACTIVITY

Explore the sponsorship of sports matches. This can be done by watching the sports channel! Briefly describe the primary target market for ten sponsors' products. Then visit the sponsors' websites to further investigate the product and its target market segment/s.

LINKS

Australian Bureau of Statistics
www.abs.gov.au

Comedy Festival
www.comedyfestival.com.au

Cultural industry publications
www.dcita.gov.au/Article/0..0_1-2_1-4_10025.00.html

SheppARTon Festival
www.sheppartonfestival.net.au

Tourism and local government
www.localtourism.com.au/Links/section1.asp

SUMMARY

Analysing the needs of client populations is the starting point for strategic planning. In doing so, the event manager or organiser identifies the business clients and associates as well as the event audience. There are numerous relationships developed during the planning of an event, with successful negotiation being essential for managing all these relationships. This is particularly the case where a range of clients are involved, all with possibly different objectives. Sponsors, in particular, can be very competitive. The final consumer of the event product can be described in terms of market segments, this concept being very useful for tailoring the event to meet the needs of those market segments most likely to attend the event, and to target these people in promotional efforts. Market segmentation can be achieved through both primary and secondary research and the advantages and disadvantages of both types of research have been outlined in this chapter.

CHAPTER SEVEN

EVENT

MARKETING

ON COMPLETION OF THIS CHAPTER YOU WILL BE ABLE TO:

- describe the features of event marketing
- establish the features of an event product
- understand market segmentation
- analyse consumer decision-making processes
- develop a marketing plan
- evaluate the marketing effort.

The Edinburgh International Festival was founded in 1947. It is now recognised as one of the most important celebrations of the arts in the world. The Festival brings to Edinburgh some of the best in international theatre, music, dance and opera and presents the arts in Scotland to the world. It is an annual event held over three weeks in late summer using all the major concert and theatre venues in the city. The 2003 Festival was comprised of 168 performances of 80 different productions and concerts including three world premieres featuring artists from around the world.

EDINBURGH INTERNATIONAL FESTIVAL <www.eif.co.uk>

Research has shown that over half the visitors to the Edinburgh International Festival have attended at least nine times before. Eighty per cent of visitors said that they came to Edinburgh either specifically for the International Festival or it was a very important part of their decision to visit Edinburgh, and the average stay was seven nights. This festival is a marketing success, with significant tourism impacts for the city. The reason for its success has a lot to do with marketing and what is known as the marketing mix — the combination of product, price, promotion and place. The consumer thinks about the cost and effort to attend and weighs these against the benefits of attending. An understanding of the decision-making processes of the audience is therefore essential for anyone planning and promoting an event.

The UK Chartered Institute of Marketing defines marketing as:

The management process responsible for identifying , anticipating and satisfying customer requirements profitably.

The American Marketing Association provides the following definition:

Marketing is the process of planning and executing the conception, pricing, promotion, and distribution of ideas, goods, and services to create exchanges that satisfy individual and organizational goals.

Another definition involves satisfying customer needs and wants through an exchange process. In this definition the concept of profit is not included, suiting many non-profit community events. Most people think that marketing is only about the advertising and/or personal selling of goods and services. Advertising and selling, however, are just two of the many marketing activities. Marketing activities are all those associated with identifying the particular wants and needs of a target market of customers, and then going about satisfying those customers better than the competitors. This involves doing market research in relation to customers, analysing their needs, and then making strategic decisions about product design, pricing, promotion and distribution.

NATURE OF EVENT MARKETING

When marketing something purely intangible, such as a performance, show, festival or contest, there is a large service component. In some respects it is far more difficult to market something that the customer cannot take home or physically consume. Thus promotional efforts might suggest that the audience will be entertained, have fun at a concert or learn from a conference presentation. Zeithaml and Bitner (1996) define services as 'deeds, processes and performances'. The definition suits the event business well, whether it refers to a conference, street parade or sporting contest, and clearly places event marketing in the field of services marketing.

The first feature of services marketing that makes it challenging is its **intangibility**. This highlights the fact that services are much more difficult to evaluate when they are intangible. 'Excitement' is very much a subjective perception and difficult to evaluate compared with a personal computer. Tangible goods which may be purchased include cars, food and household furniture. While many goods are sold in conjuction with services, there are some services with little or no 'goods' component. The intangibility of various event products is illustrated by the continuum in Fig. 7.1.

Fig. 7.1		
Continuum of intangibility in event products.		
Tangible (goods component)		
	organic fruit market	
	art and craft fair	
	food and wine festival	
	wedding	
	exhibition	
	conference	
	concert	
	consultancy service	
Intangible (services component)		

The service and the service provider are also distinguished by their **inseparability**. This means that as an event organiser you are very reliant on your staff, performers and athletes to meet the needs of the audience. You have far less quality control than you would over tangible goods (such as soft drinks) — unless your training is first rate. Interaction between the customer and the various service providers occurs at four stages:

1 **Pre-purchase**
   - interactive website
   - email
   - telephone enquiry
2 **Purchase/pre-event**
   - ticket sale
   - transportation
   - parking
   - queuing
   - entry
   - security check
3 **Event**
   - seat allocation/usher
   - food and beverage
   - entertainment
   - performance/participation (as in, for example, concert/fun run)
   - information
   - first aid
   - merchandise sales
   - lost and found
4 **Post-event**
   - exit
   - queue
   - transport
   - online results
   - photographs/memorabilia.

Another feature of services marketing is **variability**. This means that there is little consistency since the service performance is delivered by different people whose performance can vary from day to day, and indeed from customer to customer. The consumer is also involved in the service communication, thus influencing the transaction with the service provider.

In summary, the three features of services marketing are:
- Intangibility (such as fun, entertainment, information)
- Inseparability (such as the usher's service approach to the customer where product and provider are inseparable)
- Variability (such as different levels of service provided by different ushers or different responses from two or more customers to the same experience).

There is one final important consideration for the event marketer. A restaurant in a good location can rely on a level of passing trade. So, too, can a general store. This is not the case with an event, as the decision to attend or not attend is generally made shortly before the event and is irrevocable. If a customer decides not to attend, revenue to the event organiser is completely lost. This is not the case for the restaurant owner or shopkeeper who may see the customer at a later date.

An event, whether it is one-off or annual, is highly **perishable**. Unsold tickets cannot be put out on a rack at a reduced price!

Services provided at events, then, are intangible, inseparable, variable and perishable, presenting a number of marketing challenges as value for money is generally an issue for the consumer.

PROCESS OF EVENT MARKETING

The event marketing process is summarised in Fig. 7.2. Ultimately the aims are to enhance the profile of the event (and associated sponsors), to meet the needs of the event audience and, in most cases, to generate revenue. Some festivals are fully funded by government bodies, and although they are not expected to raise revenue, they aim to attract a high level of attendance or interest as a minimum expectation.

Fig. 7.2
Event marketing process.

Establish the features of the product

⇓

Identify customers (segmentation)

⇓

Plan to meet audience needs and wants

⇓

Analyse consumer decision-making process

⇓

Establish price and ticket program

⇓

Promote the event

⇓

Evaluate marketing efforts

Establish the features of the product

Each event offers a range of potential benefits to the event audience. These may include one or more of the following:

- a novel experience
- entertainment
- a learning experience
- an exciting result
- opportunity to meet others
- chance to purchase items

- dining and drinking
- inexpensive way to get out of the house
- chance to see something unique.

Many marketing experts are unable to see past the main motivating factor for the event, which may be the opportunity to watch an international cricket match. There may, however, be some members of the audience who have little interest in cricket, but are motivated by some of the other features of the product such as the opportunity to see and be seen. Generally, people attending an event see the product as a package of benefits. Convenience and good weather, for example, could be benefits associated with an event product. Most products also carry negative features. Like a pair of jeans that is just the right fit but not the perfect colour, the event may have features that are not desirable such as crowding, heat and long waiting times.

When marketing an event, therefore, alignment between the product benefits and the needs of the audience is necessary to guide the design of the event and the promotional effort. Pre-match and mid-match entertainment are good examples of adding value to the main benefit offered by a sporting event product.

Having fun and meeting friends are all part of the enjoyment of attending the Australian Grand Prix.

Identify customers

Market segmentation is the process of analysing your customers in groups. Some groups may enjoy a particular type of country and western music. Others may enjoy line dancing. Yet others may visit the music festival just for the excitement and the atmosphere. It is absolutely essential to analyse the different motivations of the event audience and to develop a profile for each of these groups.

As the Mayor of Tamworth, Warren Woodley, says about the festival audience at the Country Music Festival:

The festival is a cultural event the whole nation can be proud of. That's why tens of thousands of fans and families come here every year — the young, the old, the diehards and the curious.

It's a safe haven with a carnival atmosphere made even more enjoyable by the alcohol-free zone in the heart of the city.

Tamworth is an amazing soundscape of different styles: contemporary, traditional, acoustic, bush music, country rock, rockabilly, blue grass, western swing, blues, urban country, comedy and gospel — not to mention astonishingly popular bush poetry.

Plan to meet audience needs and wants

Once you have identified your customer groupings, it is then necessary to ensure that all their needs are met. With the Tamworth example, there may be a generation of older music enthusiasts who are looking for a certain type of entertainment as well as a younger group (say aged 10 to 14) which needs to be entertained, too, so that they can gain something from the experience. As another example, a Symphony under the Stars concert would attract many fans of classical music. However, many others would come 'for the atmosphere' and some just for the fireworks at the end. None of these customer segments' needs can be ignored. All audiences need food and facilities, but food and beverage may or may not be a high priority of a particular event audience. For some the fairy floss is the highlight; for others the food is unimportant.

Analyse consumer decision-making

The next step is to analyse the customer's decision-making process. Research conducted here will produce information which is very useful in guiding promotional efforts. There are many features of the event product, some valued by the audience more than others.

Competitive pressure (positioning)

Competition from other forms of entertainment for a person's disposable income would need to be considered. The economic environment would also need to be scanned in order to understand factors that might have an impact on discretionary spending on tickets, as well as possibly on travel and accommodation.

Motivation

Customer motivation has already been mentioned in Chapter 6. Potential customers may have positive responses to some aspects of an event and negative responses to others, such as the distance to be travelled, crowding and the risk of bad weather. Customers can be divided into decision-makers, followers, influencers and purchasers. While in most cases the person who decides to attend (and perhaps take his or her family or friends) is the one who makes the purchase, there are situations in which the decision to spend money on an event is influenced by others. For example, if a teenager wished to go to a concert, they might exert pressure on their parents to make the purchase on their behalf. In this case, both the needs of the teenager and those of the parents would need to be met. As teenagers would generally discourage their parents from attending, promotional efforts would need to ensure that parents perceived the concert to be a 'safe' environment. Those who tag along to an event are the followers. Each of these, the influencer, the decision-maker, the follower and the purchaser, would generally have different expectations of the event and would evaluate it differently.

Timing

This is the most important aspect of consumer decision-making since it has implications for the promotions budget. The issue is: when does the consumer make the decision to attend? If the decision will be made two months before the event, you need to deploy all promotional initiatives at that time. If, on the other hand, the decision will be made the week or the day before the event, this will have important implications as to how and when the advertising and promotions dollar will be spent.

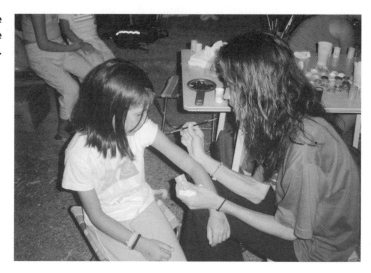

The decision to attend a fete or festival is often impulsive and made on the day.

Purchase or attendance

Finally, the desire to attend needs to be translated into a purchase action. If it is perceived that getting good tickets is going to be difficult, some consumers might not make the effort. In fact, for some festivals, there are no advance sales of tickets. This means that the decision to attend is considered impulsive and that it would generally be made on the day. Clearly, advance ticket selling means a better opportunity to plan for an event as well as a substantial boost to cash flow.

Establish price and ticket program

Sale and distribution of tickets have been mentioned briefly above. Now it is necessary to consider that event attendance could be tied in to tourist travel to a destination. If this were the case, it would involve negotiations with a tour wholesaler, extending the timeline for planning. Plans would need to be finalised long before the event, with price determined, brochures printed and advertising done (sometimes overseas) well in advance. This type of package tour might also include airfare and accommodation.

Promote the event

Having made the decision as to when it is best to promote the event, the next question is how to promote it.

Differentiation

An event, whether a concert, festival or surf carnival, needs to be differentiated from other related leisure options. The consumer needs to know why this event is special.

Packaging for effective communication

The messages used to promote an event are extremely important. Usually there is only limited advertorial space for convincing all market segments to attend. Thus the combination of text and images requires a lot of creative effort. If there is time and sufficient budget available, trialling the effectiveness of communication messages with consumers is recommended.

There are many forms of promotion, including personal selling; brochures; posters; banners; Internet advertising; news, radio and television advertising; and press releases. Balloons and crowd pleasers (people balloons with moving arms) are examples of eye-catching promotional strategies that you can use.

Evaluate marketing efforts

The effectiveness of all promotional efforts needs to be carefully monitored. With an annual event, for example, customer responses to the various types of promotion will guide promotional efforts in future years. Evaluation needs to be done systematically by asking questions such as 'Where did you find out about the event?' or 'When did you decide to attend this event?'

There are three stages at which research can be conducted: prior to the event, during the event and after the event. The research can be qualitative, such as focus groups and case studies, or quantitative. In the latter case, the research generates statistics such as customers' expenditure at the event.

THE MARKETING MIX

In the final analysis, the marketing efforts need to be analysed in terms of the marketing mix (see Fig. 7.3). In other words, was the event positioned well, priced well, promoted effectively and distributed through different channels efficiently. All these factors must work together if success is to be the outcome.

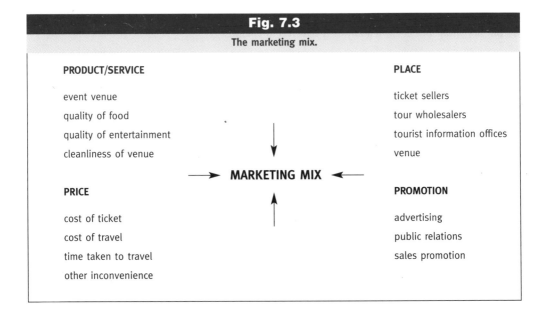

Fig. 7.3

The marketing mix.

PRODUCT/SERVICE

event venue
quality of food
quality of entertainment
cleanliness of venue

PLACE

ticket sellers
tour wholesalers
tourist information offices
venue

→ **MARKETING MIX** ←

PRICE

cost of ticket
cost of travel
time taken to travel
other inconvenience

PROMOTION

advertising
public relations
sales promotion

Product

Product features have already been discussed in this chapter. While the product/service may be intangible, it is not difficult to analyse some of these features from the consumer perspective. These can include the event 'performance' of, for example, the keynote speaker, entertainer, athlete or dancer. A street parade, exhibition, conference and competition all include elements of performance. Interestingly, the level of participation by the audience is a significant consideration: at an operatic concert the audience is largely passive, while at a mini-marathon the audience participates fully. The timing of this participation can be extended to include the build-up to the event, anticipation being an important element of the event product.

Prior to the 2003 Rugby World Cup, for example, many enthusiastic supporters visited the website daily. In this case, the website was a key element of the product, bordering on a virtual event (there are a few – such as virtual dating!). The ambience, food, lighting and many other features form part of the product. For a conference, the program of events or speakers is the main product. The members of the audience, and their behaviour, contribute to the audience perception of the product, albeit peripherally.

The event product is often positioned against competition for the audience's disposable income or time. The questions to ask are: 'Is the choice of event appropriate and is it positioned correctly in terms of competition?' For example, one would hesitate to run a food and wine festival in a small town when there was already a Spring Market Festival in a larger town nearby. Transportation, seating, cover against the elements, food and beverage, and other nearby tourism attractions are other potential features of the product.

Price

Pricing for an entertainment event is very tricky. It depends on the size of the potential audience and the selected venue. If the ticket price is too high, and the featured artist not as popular as expected, then the half empty venue will result in a dismal financial outcome. Pricing of food and beverage items is also an important consideration because customers become annoyed if mark-ups are excessive. For events involving travel, the price includes the cost of transportation and accommodation. Break-even analysis is covered in Chapter 9.

Promotion

Promotional activities need to be chosen carefully and timed effectively. Promotion is a costly exercise, radio and television advertising being two of the most expensive. Overall, the most cost-effective methods of promotion are feature articles in local newspapers and banners. Many events are promoted by tourism bodies and by tourism information offices at minimal cost. And increasingly, the Internet is being used as a source of information by the event audience.

Place/Distribution

Tickets can be distributed as part of package tours, through ticket sellers (who take commission) or at the venue. In many cases, the event product is produced, distributed and consumed at the venue. This contrasts, for example, with goods that are imported for sale and ultimately consumed by the customer at home. The effectiveness of the channels through which an event is promoted and sold is a crucial aspect of its success.

The event venue is the location at which the product is enjoyed, playing an important part in meeting the needs of the consumer. Easy parking, good seating, excellent visibility, cleanliness and provision of facilities are often determined by the physical location of the event.

An example of a motorshow below illustrates the four Ps for an exhibition of the latest wheels on the road:

Product
- featured motor vehicles (high-tech concept cars)
- number and variety of exhibitors/brands
- dates and hours of exhibition
- associated events (such as seminars)
- prizes (door prizes, competitions)
- entertainment
- décor, lighting, special effects
- staffing
- parking
- transportation.

Place
- city location (capital city, distance to travel)
- type of venue (and proximity)
- accommodation options (and proximity)
- tourist attractions (and proximity)
- ticket purchase (online, at venue, from dealers).

Price
- price of admission
- free tickets for sponsors and exhibitors.

Promotion
- website
- motor magazines
- print news (such as motoring supplements)
- direct mail.

SPONSORSHIP

Many events are substantially subsidised by sponsorship, with marketing plans closely linked to sponsorship. For example, Red Bull has created a niche for itself in the energy drink category by aligning with extreme sports and events. Exclusively produced in Austria and exported worldwide, the brand is wildly popular in 70 countries around the world.

While this topic will be covered in detail in the next chapter, it is worthwhile looking at some of the marketing issues associated with sponsorship.

The sponsor can have part or absolute control over the event and this will in turn influence marketing and operational planning. Sponsorship is one of the most common funding sources for staging an event. In some cases, the sponsor is happy to provide cash to support the event in exchange for increased profile and sales of their products. In other cases, the sponsor provides 'value in kind'. This means that the sponsor will provide free goods and services, again with the expectation that this will have a bottom line benefit. For example, a newspaper sponsor may provide free advertising space. Some sponsors use an event to promote a new product and, in this case, the whole event is aimed at developing customer awareness and loyalty. In all of these situations, the marketing messages must be consistent with the event and must be clear to the audience. An expensive party to celebrate the release of a new product is a waste of money if the audience cannot recall the name of the product a few weeks later, much less purchase it.

Essentially, the sponsor identifies with the event, mainly through the use of their name and logo, and expects a return on their investment. It is thus essential to evaluate both the sponsor profile and the sponsor's sales, or any other sponsorship objectives, after the event to ensure that the sponsorship has been successful and that the sponsor's relationship with the event will continue.

There are a number of questions to ask before approaching a potential sponsor.

The QANTAS and Coca-Cola logos are often seen at major events.

What are the benefits for the sponsor?

Can the sponsor's involvement lead to some benefit for them in terms of increased profile or increased sales? What other benefits are there? At what cost? Will it be time-consuming for their staff?

How long will the association last?

Is it possible to build a long-term alliance with the sponsor? Can an agreement be reached for perhaps a five-year sponsorship?

How much exposure will the sponsor achieve?

Will the sponsor's logo appear on all advertising? Will they have naming rights to the event or will specific prizes be awarded for particular events by their senior staff. Will the winning athlete wear one the sponsor's caps when interviewed by television crews? Will the sponsor be named in the prize-giving ceremony?

Will the sponsorship be exclusive?

Will this sponsor be the only one and thus clearly associated with the event? Or will there be a large number of sponsors?

Is there compatibility?

Have the potential sponsor's competitors agreed to provide sponsorship and will this lead to a conflict of interest? Is there compatibility between the sponsor's product and the event purpose (for example, if the purpose of the event was promoting a healthy lifestyle)?

Will there be ambush marketing?

Are there organisations which will attempt to gain advertising mileage and sales from the event, despite their lack of sponsorship or other commitment? Will competitors' products be on sale at the event or in a nearby area?

Ultimately, the most important question of all concerns the sponsor's benefit from their involvement in the event. This needs to be negotiated early in the arrangement and a process for measuring sponsor objectives, such as recognition or purchase of their products, needs to be put in place prior to, during and after the event. Where clearly audited records or professional surveys can demonstrate sponsorship outcomes, renegotiating sponsorship arrangements for subsequent events, or different events, will be much easier since success has been demonstrated in a tangible way. At the end of the day, the sponsor needs a report detailing all promotional efforts and the ensuing benefits, as well as photographs and success stories for post-event publicity.

DEVELOPING A MARKETING PLAN

With all this in mind, the process of developing and implementing a marketing plan can be initiated (see Fig. 7.4 on page 98). A marketing plan can be developed for an event business or for a single event. An event business might regularly organise several concurrent events and would thus develop a marketing plan in a traditional format with a focus on the business, its services and profile. Developing a marketing plan for a single event (whether annual or not) follows the same guidelines but in most cases the plan carries higher risks.

Analyse internal business environment

When developing a marketing plan for a specific type of event (such as conferences), a new business enterprise (a wedding planner) or a single event (such as a street parade), it is essential to analyse the internal business environment. The process of analysis is illustrated in Fig. 7.5 on page 98. Keep in mind that the focus is the internal business environment, as well as the strengths and weaknesses of that environment.

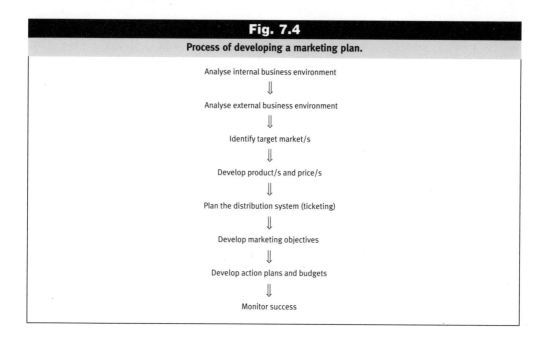

Fig. 7.4

Process of developing a marketing plan.

Analyse internal business environment
⇓
Analyse external business environment
⇓
Identify target market/s
⇓
Develop product/s and price/s
⇓
Plan the distribution system (ticketing)
⇓
Develop marketing objectives
⇓
Develop action plans and budgets
⇓
Monitor success

When analysing the strengths and weaknesses of the internal environment, there are a number of resources and capabilities that may need to be considered, depending on the particular business or event. Some of these are outlined below.

Fig. 7.5

Analysis of internal business environment.

Identify core activities, customer base, business values and current business direction
⇓
Analyse current and past marketing and its effectiveness
⇓
Review performance of the business to identify strengths, weaknesses and critical success factors
⇓
Identify current capabilities and resources, including the need for specialist assistance
⇓
Identify any underperforming products and services and analyse and report on reasons
for underperformance
⇓
Record and report information and develop marketing action plans

Location

For most event businesses, location is a key factor. The central business district is a good location for a Professional Conference Organiser (PCO). The organising body of most major events is generally close to or within the venue or general precinct.

Client base

An existing client base is a valuable resource for a new marketing initiative. It is also an important consideration when purchasing an existing business. In direct selling, the response rate from existing clients is likely to be higher than from a more generalised marketing campaign. For an existing business, a client base is useful only if customers are likely to return or to organise new events. If the majority of customers of a business are transient, and there is no likelihood of repeat business, then targeting a client list would be a waste of money. One would expect this to be the case with wedding planning!

Human resources

The existing staff of a business, from frontline service personnel to management, can be the key to its success. An excellent office administrator can be the making of an event business, encouraging loyalty among the existing clientele and attracting new customers. A reliable source of skilled labour is also an important factor when planning new events or expanding operations. For example, if expanding to include catering, an event business would need access to qualified chefs who may be in short supply.

Financial resources

The current and future financial performance of a business is critical, as significant budgets are required for new marketing initiatives. Reaching a target market can be very costly, with the visible return occurring over a lengthy period. Sometimes businesses simply do not have the cash flow to sustain involvement in new types of events and major advertising campaigns. Specialisation is a critical consideration, whether in the incentives market or the exhibitions sector. Arts festivals, in particular, tend to make five- to ten-year financial projections, sometimes expecting earlier losses to be made up over the long term.

Facility and equipment capacity

Access to a range of facilities is essential for most event managers as these are generally hired for the period of the event. The props and staging equipment are also hired. Few event businesses carry stock such as curtains, crockery, lighting or costumes. When these requirements are unique to an event and cannot be hired, the costs escalate quickly. If an outright purchase is made, the stock in hand is seldom used again, leading to issues of storage and disposal.

Hours of operation

Council regulations might limit hours of an event, while noise regulations might render a concert a non-event from a feasibility point of view.

Community profile

Most existing event businesses have ongoing communication with a wide range of customers, potential customers and suppliers. These networks and the community profile of the business are key factors in its success. Popular beaches, small towns and central parks generally have an existing calendar of events, making it difficult for the newcomer.

E-business capacity

Nearly every event or event business is listed on the web, with many offering online ticket sales or registration. The range in sophistication, and thus cost of e-business, can vary.

Analyse external business environment

The viability of a business is affected by any number of factors in the external business environment beyond the owner's or manager's control. For example, a decline in economic growth can have a negative impact on domestic tourism, while threats of terrorism overseas can boost this sector. Trends in international and domestic tourism can have a significant effect on events that attract tourists. Sports tourism is a growing field, with more and more spectators travelling the world to watch matches, with other attractions being secondary. England's Barmy Army started with 1000 enthusiastic cricket supporters in 1994–95 travelling to Australia to support their team. The group has grown rapidly since then, also supporting many international events in their thousands. The cessation of Ansett Airlines in 2001 and the SARS virus in 2003 had significant positive impacts on a range of local events.

It is therefore necessary to analyse all pertinent factors in the external business environment when developing a new marketing strategy. The steps to take are outlined in Fig. 7.6.

Fig. 7.6
Analysis of external business environment.

Identify and analyse information on expected market growth or decline and associated risk factors
⇓
Analyse projected changes in the labour force, population and economic activity
⇓
Gather and analyse comparative market information
⇓
Analyse industry and customer trends and developments, including emerging issues, fashion and technology
⇓
Analyse the legal, ethical and environmental constraints of the market and potential business impacts
⇓
Report information and develop action plans for marketing

The following are examples of trends and developments in the external business environment that could provide either opportunities or threats to a new enterprise or event or new marketing strategy.

The economy

Both the domestic economy and the international economy have a strong impact on the event business. For example, when these economies are strong, leisure travellers have access to a high disposable income and sports enthusiasts will travel vast distances to watch matches. Conversely, when they are in decline, tourism drops and event attendance by international visitors drops off, as does related expenditure in the event sector. During times of recession, companies spend very little on product launches, promotional events, sponsorship and company celebrations. Business during the Christmas season (with extravagant parties for clients) is highly dependent on the state of the economy.

Demographic changes

Any event business that does not pay attention to demographic change cannot plan strategically. Analysis of demographic change in Australia predicts that the age structure of the population will change noticeably by 2101. As can be seen from Fig. 7.7, there will be a heavier concentration of people in the ages from 50 years onwards

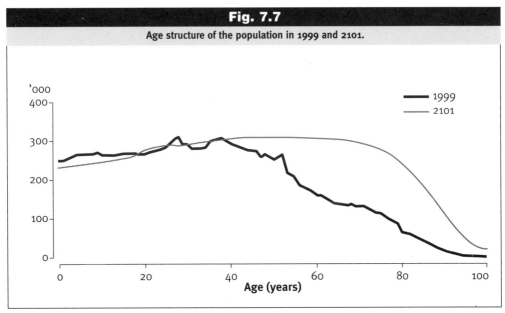

Fig. 7.7
Age structure of the population in 1999 and 2101.

Population Projections, Australia, 1999 to 2101 (ABS cat no. 3222.0); Population by Age and Sex (ABS cat. no. 3201.0)

The proportion of the population aged 65 years and over is expected to increase substantially, from 12 per cent in 1999 to between 24 and 27 per cent in 2051 and to between 25 and 28 per cent in 2101. The proportion aged 85 years and over is expected to almost quadruple, from 1.3 per cent in 1999 to around 5 per cent in 2051 and around 6 per cent in 2101. Meeting the needs of these market segments is a consideration for almost any event planner, whether thinking about a writers festival, outdoor opera or regional food and wine promotion.

Seasonal factors

Australia and New Zealand are fortunate in that most areas are suitable for tourism all year round, whereas in other parts of the world seasonal factors have a major impact on tourism, effectively closing some operations in mid winter. This is a positive factor for event planning in temperate climates with many good months for outdoor events. Sporting calendars are, however, more complex to manage with efforts needed to ensure that there is no clash between significant games. This is relevant for attendance and television broadcasts.

Government activities

Government plans, such as the *Medium to Long Term Strategy for Tourism* issued by the Australian Federal Government in 2003 (see web address at the end of this chapter), are useful sources of information when preparing a new event marketing strategy. Federal Government websites, as well as those of the states and territories, all provide short- and long-term plans for tourism, including priorities and general directions. The Australian Tourism Commission produces outstanding research data on international market segments to assist with the marketing of Australian events to these markets. Subsidies for the arts are government activities that underpin the running of many arts festivals. Government grants for a wide range of community events have a significant impact on event planning.

Tourism trends

Very often a target market can be identified using information on tourism trends. Tourism forecasts predict fluctuations in visitor numbers, both international and domestic. When a trend is clear (for example, an increase in visitors from China) then an event can be promoted to this market via tour wholesalers. Tourism bodies conduct regular research to monitor such trends.

Social and cultural change

Social change is reflected in the conceptualisation of new events. For example, a recent event was labelled as a 'grown up music concert with the vibe but without the mosh pits and porta loos'. This reflects the needs of a more sophisticated consumer who has enjoyed outdoor concerts as a teenager. The popularity of different music genres such as folk, country, blues, jazz, latin and world fusion, rap and hip hop follows fashion trends linked to social and cultural change. Short film festivals and outdoor cinema are reasonably new entertainment 'products'. Some products have a long life cycle (for example, Opera in the Park), while others might lose popularity quite quickly. Young children are a particularly fickle market, which depends on who is popular in current television programming.

Ecological and environmental factors

Developing community awareness of ecological and environmental issues has led to the creation of 'waste wise' events. Indeed, environmental awareness has led to the development of one of Australia's most famous events, Clean up Australia, which is now staged annually around the world.

Technological developments

Developments in technology have transformed the event environment in ways not generally envisaged even 20 years ago. The big screen is one of the industry's best innovations, extending the size of audiences dramatically. The Internet, of course, has had a major impact on how the event industry operates, with even the smallest event advertising on their website.

Industrial relations legislation

Many aspects of industrial relations legislation, such as pay provisions, have an impact on event operations, and must be taken into account during the planning phase. Initiatives such as enterprise bargaining also need to be considered for human resources planning, as these in turn can impact on the level of service and labour cost. And occupational health and safety is a major consideration for staff, contractors and volunteers.

Legal and ethical issues

A range of legal and ethical issues were covered in Chapter 5 from which it is possible to see that Laws and Regulations can place restrictions on business ideas and marketing strategies. Marketing departments need to be particularly aware of trade practices legislation to ensure that, for example, all products and services are accurately represented in the advertisements they create. The aim of a marketing campaign is to raise, meet or exceed customer expectations, but it is essential that expectations created in the consumer mind can be fulfilled. For example, tickets should not be oversold or overpriced. Public safety is a current concern with many outdoor events moving indoors to safer venues because insurance cannot be secured.

Competition

Whether running a single event or an event business the issue of competition is paramount. Finding a new niche is increasingly difficult. Sand sculpture competitions, mini marathons, food and wine festivals, and craft fairs are fairly commonplace. Party planners are a dime a dozen — everyone thinks that they can plan a good party! Exhibition companies are highly competitive. Research into current competitive companies and events is an essential element of marketing planning.

Identify target market/s

Planning is a cyclical process in which target market segments (customers) are identified, events are developed to suit their needs, and the event is competitively positioned. The aim is to develop a perception on the part of the customer that the event is desirable, indeed more desirable than the products and services of competing organisations. Fun runs and craft fairs, for example, attract completely different target markets.

Develop product/s and price/s

It should be clear by now that there is an important difference between marketing and selling. Selling is only one aspect of marketing and is primarily concerned with promoting the organisation's products and services through sales calls (personal and telephone) and direct communication with the customer by frontline staff. Marketing is a much broader concept, starting with an analysis of the internal and external environments, as we have discussed above, targeting specific markets and developing products that people will pay for. Briefly, marketing involves:
- ascertaining the needs and wants of the customer
- creating the appropriate product/service to satisfy the customer
- promoting and selling the product/service at a profitable level.

As discussed earlier in this chapter, one the most neglected market segments is the 60–80 year age group. Developing an event product that would suit this market would involve careful selection of the type of event. For example, it may be worth investigating the feasibility of an outdoor symphony. In this case, ease of access to the event site would be an important element of the product to consider and would be closely related to the choice of venue. A beach or outdoor venue would not provide the same level of comfort or accessibility for those in wheelchairs or with walking sticks. For this event, price sensitivity would be high since many of this age group would be pensioners with little disposable income, so obtaining sponsorship for the event would be worth considering to reduce the ticket price. Consideration would also need to be given to the cost of transport and food, and the choice of food available.

Plan the distribution system (ticketing)

Ticketing is a key consideration in event planning. If done through a conventional ticketing agency, commission would be payable on each ticket sold, and direct ticket sales are generally logistically impossible. In relation to the previous example and many other community events, online ticketing agencies and door sales are the best options.

Develop marketing objectives

Once the product, price and positioning have been decided, the next step in preparing a marketing plan is to determine the marketing objectives (see Fig. 7.8). These should be measurable and time related. This means that it should be possible to evaluate achievement of the stipulated targets within a given time frame. Developing specific marketing objectives, action plans and corresponding budgets are the steps involved in implementing marketing plans. Success must be monitored to identify whether the marketing plan is working, and modifications to the plan made if necessary.

Develop action plans and budgets

Promotion is essential in creating awareness of event products and occurs in a number of ways, including:
- advertising
- personal selling
- sales promotion
- merchandising
- public relations.

This applies to all types of events (such as sports and entertainment events) and event businesses (such as exhibition hire companies and conference organisers).

Budgets are an essential aspect of action planning, and these will be covered in Chapter 9.

Monitor success

Both formal and informal techniques can be used for the ongoing evaluation process. Informal staff meetings can be held to discuss customer satisfaction with the event product, while ongoing analysis of sales figures provides valuable financial data on the event business or event.

A market research company can be contracted to conduct formal field research, surveying event attendees using questionnaires. Sampling of the survey group is particularly important to ensure valid results. Statistical analysis and reporting are all part of the professional

Fig. 7.8

Simplified marketing plan for a launch of an alcoholic beverage.

Event Launch: Alcoholic Beverage

Target Audience

Direct target audience: 'A list' celebrities and key television media.

Indirect target audience: 20–30 year olds, mainly female, responding to associated promotion and publicity.

Marketing Objectives

- Achieve 80% attendance by invitation-only guests, VIPs and celebrities.
- Attract two of three key television channels for publicity purposes.
- Achieve $3000 publicity value in print media write up.
- Achieve 15% increase in retail and wholesale beverage sales within the first three months.
- Establish the brand as first choice for 5% of target market segment.
- Achieve 45% brand sampling or recognition by target audience.

Action Plan

- Conduct market research in February (pre-event).
- Plan launch and obtain budget approval by 31 March.
- Prepare promotional brief and objectives by 4 April.
- Employ PR company to achieve publicity objectives by 12 April.
- Finalise promotional campaign plans by 29 April.
- Approve promotional material, including advertising, invitations and guest list by 30 April.
- Issue invitations and press releases by 10 May.
- Implement promotional campaign as per schedule.
- Launch advertising campaign on 15 May.
- Follow up on RSVPs by personal calls by 25 May.
- Stage launch 31 May.
- Conduct market research (post event) in June.
- Media coverage final report due 3 July.

Event Marketing Budget

- Public relations campaign $95 000.
- Advertising campaign $250 000.
- Invitations — design, printing and postage $8000.
- Marketing staff and administration $60 000.

Monitoring and Evaluation

- Media monitoring done by PR company.
- Market research conducted pre- and post-launch.
- Value of retail and wholesale liquor sales monitored.
- Follow-up telephone survey of invited guests.

services provided by market research specialists. Consulting organisations can arrange mystery customer programs that will provide ongoing feedback on customer satisfaction. A focus group of clients is another technique for developing, reviewing and modifying products or improving service.

A Marketing Information System (MKIS) is a useful management tool that systematically gathers information about prospective and current customers to enhance marketing decision-making, providing both quantitative and qualitative information. This analysis should be systematic, and reports generated should be distributed to all involved, including frontline employees.

As mentioned previously, the event promotional campaign is carefully planned in collaboration with major sponsors. Approvals are needed from all sponsors when using their logos, developing promotional material and writing publicity material. These approvals must be obtained in writing. This is time consuming and must be written into the timeline. Events involving multiple sponsors are particularly challenging since all relevant groups and individuals must be involved at every stage of planning. A marketing risk analysis should be undertaken to look at potential situations such as the loss of a major sponsor, clash between sponsors, or ambush marketing by a competitor. The topic of risk management is covered in more detail in Chapter 10 and these methods can be used to analyse the level of risk and develop contingency plans.

CASE STUDY

Using the concepts in this chapter, develop a very brief marketing plan for two or three of the following events. When complete, analyse the differences in the approaches you have suggested.

1   Ballarat Winter Festival, Victoria
    Festival held each year to promote the arts, heritage, food and beverage, and recreation in Ballarat.
    http://winterfest.ballarat.net.au

2   Melbourne International Flower and Garden Show.
    Features displays designed and constructed by some of Australia's most talented landscape designers.
    www.melbflowershow.com.au

3   Melbourne International Comedy Festival
    Long-running annual festival of fun and laughter, rated as one of the world's three major comedy fests (with Edinburgh and Montreal).
    http://www.comedyfestival.com.au

4   Melbourne Writers' Festival
    Annual event featuring workshops and talks by both Australian and international writers.
    www.mwf.com.au

5   Moonlight Cinema
    Movies under the stars in Sydney, Melbourne and Adelaide.
    www.moonlight.com.au

CASE STUDY *cont.*

6 Perth International Arts Festival
Western Australia's leading cultural event.
www.perthfestival.com.au

7 Alice Springs Camel Cup
Event organised by Lions Club Alice Springs.
www.camelcup.com.au

8 Boulia Desert Sands, Queensland
Australia's Premier Camel Racing Festival.
www.camelraces.asn.au

LINKS

Australian Bureau of Statistics, *A century of population change: year book of Australia 2001*
www.abs.gov.au/ausstats/abs@.nsf/Lookup/NT0001768A

Department of Tourism, Industry and Resources
www.industry.gov.au

Tamworth Country Music Festival
www.tamworth.nsw.gov.au/tcc/cmf/index.html

SUMMARY

In this chapter we have discussed the marketing mix for event marketing, including product, price, promotion and place (distribution). Identification of consumer interest in the product and their decision-making processes form a key part of the planning of promotional efforts. Since most promotional budgets are limited, the expenditure must be timed carefully to ensure maximum impact. Sponsorship is one way of attracting funding or 'value in kind' and this is an important element of the marketing strategy. Evaluating the marketing effort is essential as it will facilitate planning of future events.

CHAPTER EIGHT

EVENT

SPONSORSHIP

ON COMPLETION OF THIS CHAPTER YOU WILL BE ABLE TO:

- identify sponsorship opportunities
- create and promote a sponsorship package
- implement sponsorship opportunities
- follow up with sponsors and conduct event sponsorship evaluations.

Capitalising on its sponsorship of the Australian Open tennis, Heineken has launched a new Palm PC-based guide to Melbourne. Heineken BarTrek, a software program for the Palm hand-held computer, provides visitors with details about the Australian Open schedule as well as information on Melbourne hot spots, restaurants, accommodation and events around the city.

'For people in Melbourne during the Australian Open, BarTrek will help them get a feel for the city and unwind with a cold Heineken beer in pleasant company and great surroundings', Heineken Australia managing director Hans Erik Tuijt said.

'Heineken will extend its high-visibility presence throughout the Australian Open venue with a beer garden, hospitality area and live entertainment.'

Tuijt described Heineken's sponsorship of the Australian Open, now in its fourth year, as a 'perfect fit'.

'Heineken's sponsorship of the Australian Open further strengthens our international association with the sport and enables us to market the Heineken brand on a global scale', he said.

MARIA LIGERAKIS, *B&T*, 24 JANUARY 2001
www.bandt.com.au

As this article illustrates, the 'fit' between a sponsor and an event is critical. A sponsor seldom commits to an event on purely altruistic grounds. There is generally a motive, such as developing brand awareness in association with a particular product.

For example, the sponsor will choose a sport that attracts an event audience that has the appropriate characteristics. This is why a beer company will select a sporting code (such as soccer) with a corresponding audience demographic and a car manufacturer will choose another sporting code (such as Rugby Union) with a different demographic. Most large organisations have long-term strategic plans for sponsorship that are closely linked with their marketing plans. This is again illustrated in the fit between sponsor and event for the Toyota National Country Music Muster.

TOYOTA NATIONAL COUNTRY MUSIC MUSTER

'A celebration of the rural spirit —
the quintessential Aussie event with good friends, good music
and good times in the Australian bush'

It is not only the diverse world-class entertainment program that draws fans from around Australia and overseas to the Toyota National Country Music Muster — the atmosphere is phenomenal; the beauty of the bushland setting; the warm glow of the campfires; starry nights; magical days; a musical feast in the company of old and new friends.

Twelve great on-site venues offer a musical smorgasbord, from the best in Country to Bush Poets, Bluegrass, Australia's richest Talent Search, Kids Country … kick up your heels line dancin', rock 'n' roll or clogging, catch your breath in the Lagoon Wine Bar/Restaurant or the Theatre. Party till late at the Crow Bar … there's something to please every musical taste! And the ever-popular blues venue, exploded this year to six whole days from Tuesday 26 to 31 August, will feature, among the greats, renowned international artist Eric Bibb. Amazingly, all this entertainment is included in your ticket price!

The Muster site, just 2 hours drive north of Brisbane, and 40 minutes from Noosa.

By pre-purchasing your tickets or accommodation packages, you will be in the draw to win a **Toyota Echo**. Ticket purchases made before 30 June 2003 receive discounts.

All proceeds raised are donated to worthy causes including the Toyota Muster's Rural Aid Appeal.

<www.muster.com.au/TheEvent/theevent_doc.html>

Many new event organisers assume that big companies will be generous with sponsorship for small events and often the first step suggested by the committee is to contact corporations. Unfortunately, this seldom works, because companies of this size already have well-established plans, with specific objectives to be achieved as part of their sponsorship deals. In fact, in most cases, the outcome is a joint marketing effort by the sponsor and the event organiser. Most large organisations also have policies with regard to sponsorship and for this reason will reject a request from a fringe arts festival, for example, if this is not consistent with their marketing plan and policy to support a sporting code.

If a straightforward donation, or patronage, is made to an event, without strings attached (no logo, publicity etc.), this is known as philanthropy. When seeking assistance for an event, it is important to identify whether the request is for a donation or a sponsorship arrangement. Sponsorship is defined as follows:

A 'partnership' between an organisation and another organisation or event in which the sponsor publicly endorses an activity and ties its reputation with that of the organisation or event being sponsored.

<www.murdoch.edu.au/cwisad/glossary.html>

Sponsorship is a business relationship between a provider of funds, resources or services and an individual, event or organisation which offers in return some rights and association that may be used for commercial advantage.

The key distinction between sponsorship and patronage is that no commercial advantage is sought or expected in return for the support of a patron.

<www.sponsorship.co.uk/sponsorship/main.htm>

With these definitions in mind, it is clear that any hint of poor media exposure (for example, drugs in sport or crowd safety issues) is likely to make the sponsor very edgy!

Potential sponsors may include:

- individuals
- private companies
- government agencies
- industry associations
- educational institutions.

Sponsorship may cover:

- naming rights for events or event venues (for example, Toyota National Country Music Muster)
- media coverage (for example, a particular channel always broadcasting a particular series or event creating viewer loyalty)
- staging or performances costs
- telecommunications expenses (for example, providing communications equipment and service for the event)
- IT support (for example, scoring, results processing)
- overall sponsorship of the event (for example, agricultural conference sponsorship)
- physical items (for example, satchels, prizes)

- food and beverage (for example, morning and afternoon teas)
- travel for performers, artists or athletes
- entertainment (for example, National Anthem, new talent)
- speaker sessions (for example, supporting topical research such as salinity)
- ongoing organisational activities (for example, annual publications)
- one-off promotional activities or projects.

MOTIVES FOR SPONSORSHIP

There are many different motives for sponsoring an event and these fit into five major categories. When approaching a potential sponsor it is essential to use these motivational factors to harness the sponsor organisation's interest, particularly when writing to them about sponsorship packages. Once the sponsor's motives are clarified, it is then a matter of developing (where possible) measurable objectives, so that when the event is over the benefits of the sponsorship arrangement can be demonstrated.

Broad corporate and social objectives

There are many broad objectives for an organisation participating in a sponsorship arrangement, including community involvement, promoting the organisation's image and linking the company's image to success. Any change in audience attitude to corporate and social objectives is hard to measure. Public perception of an organisation shifts very slowly and it is difficult to evaluate this shift over a short time span. Qantas, for example, promotes its corporate image by linking advertising to sporting achievement and national pride, thus cementing their image as the national carrier.

Product/brand-related objectives

Many sponsors use events to promote a product. Examples of products include airline travel, beer, wine and communications products. Examples of sponsoring organisations include Qantas, Heineken, Lion Nathan, Lindeman's and Telstra. They in turn may have a number of brands. For example, Lion Nathan has several brands in Australia: Toohey's New, XXXX Gold, Hahn Premium Light and Toohey's Extra Dry. The organisation may choose a specific event to promote one of their products. In many cases, the brand can be sampled at the event (especially beer at sporting matches) hopefully leading to higher brand awareness and strengthening brand preference.

Sales objectives

Sales objectives are far more specific, having to do with the sales force prospecting for new customers and strengthening relationships with current customers. Sales staff may circulate at an event. At one recent event a mobile telephone company built product awareness through personal selling. Roving sales staff took photos of spectators and then (with their permission) sent these photos to friends of the spectators using mobile phone technology.

Business to business relationships can result from networking between a number of sponsors for a particular event, in turn leading to long-term benefits to all sponsor organisations in the alliance. Events such as the Olympic Games offer exclusive rights and all sponsors must work inclusively with other sponsors, using only their products and services.

For sponsors signage is important.

Data capture is of significant benefit to sponsors of trade exhibitions and conferences because the contact information of all attendees is available to sponsors to be used at a future date for direct mail purposes.

Media coverage

Gaining media exposure is one of the most obvious objectives for sponsors. Who has not seen the winning captain put on a cap featuring the sponsor logo before being congratulated on prime time television and thanking the sponsor in view of hundreds of thousands of television viewers? There are many ways that the sponsor organisation can gain media coverage before, during and after the event. Outdoor advertising, publicity activities, branded clothing items and extensive signage are all part of this package.

Corporate hospitality

Hospitality (in the form of corporate boxes) is often a key element of a sponsorship package. The guests are generally old or prospective clients who are entertained during the event. In some cases, the hospitality is also provided to key staff as an incentive for good performance.

EVENT CATEGORIES FOR BUSINESS SPONSORSHIP

In 1996–97, businesses in Australia provided $467 million of sponsorship. Of this, $282 million went to sport, $29 million to art and cultural activities, $37 million to education, $50 million to trade shows and conferences, and $68 million to other activities (ABS cat. no. 4144.0). Released in 1999, these are the latest statistics available. While sponsorship for sporting events is clearly in a league of its own as far as dollars spent, as indicated above, some businesses do support important cultural areas such as the arts and education.

For example, Fujitsu is the national tour and technology partner of The Bell Shakespeare Company, Australia's only national touring Shakespearean theatre company. Both partners are committed to taking its productions and educational programs to audiences Australia-wide and internationally. In 2004 the main productions were *The Servant of Two Masters and Twelfth Night*.

As mentioned previously, some sponsors support events as part of their community profile. Every year, employees from BHP Steel take part in Clean Up Australia over three weeks. Hundreds of employees are involved, with the company contributing to cash prizes for participating teams.

TYPES OF SPONSORSHIP

Many different types of sponsorship are negotiated with companies by event organisers. These include sponsorship packages, value in kind sponsorship and naming rights.

Sponsorship packages

The example on pages 114–115 illustrates the ways in which sponsorship packages can be developed to meet the needs of different types of sponsor; in this case there were six levels of sponsorship: platinum, gold, silver, bronze, trade and special. Sponsorship was for a regional conference, co-hosted by the Australian and New Zealand Societies for Horticultural Science (AuSHS and NZSHS), on 'Harnessing the Potential of Horticulture in the Asia-Pacific Region'. It was held in conjunction with the Fifth International Strawberry Symposium.

For smaller events there is often only one type of sponsorship or one sponsor.

Value in kind sponsorship

In the examples illustrated so far, the sponsors have been asked to make a cash contribution. In many cases, however, sponsorship is provided as 'value in kind'. This means that the sponsor provides its goods and services free as part of the sponsorship arrangement. For example, air travel could be sponsored by Virgin Blue, vehicles provided by Holden and advertising could be underwritten by Fairfax Publications. A value is placed on this contribution and this value must be reflected in the event budget even though there is no cash contribution.

Naming rights

The primary sponsor of an event is often able to obtain naming rights, for example, Mercedes Fashion Week; Qantas Australian Motorcycle Grand Prix; Heineken Golf Classic; Billabong World Junior Championships; VB One Day International Cricket Series.

In some cases, sponsors negotiate naming rights for event venues or facilities, such as the ANZ Pavilion in Melbourne, Telstra Stadium in Sydney, First National Bank Stadium in Johannesburg and the Pepsi Center in Denver. These agreements are generally long-term strategic agreements with associated sponsor benefits such as tickets, hospitality, parking, etc. The exposure of the sponsor's name in all media communications in relation to the facility is the key element of this negotiation.

SPONSORSHIP IMPLEMENTATION

The timelines for sponsorship negotiation and event planning are significant. Three to five years should be allowed for locking in a major sponsor. Finalisation of sponsorship agreements has to occur before any of the following can be planned and implemented:

REGIONAL HORTICULTURAL CONFERENCE 2004
PROGRAM OUTLINE & SPONSORSHIP OPPORTUNITIES

The Regional Horticultural Conference 2004 is a joint initiative of the Australian and New Zealand Societies for Horticultural Science in association with the New Zealand Society for Plant Physiology, and is proudly supported by the Horticulture Australia Ltd, Department of Primary Industries, Queensland and the University of Queensland.

The event builds on the synergies across the Tasman and to develop an effective network of horticultural scientists across the Asia-Pacific Region. The Conference is being held in conjunction with the Board, Executive and Council meetings of the International Society for Horticultural Science and the Fifth International Strawberry Symposium, also being held at the Hyatt Regency Coolum in August to September 2004.

Program Outline

Details of the Conference program can be found on http://www.aushs.org.au/
The conference program is structured to provide for variety in presentation styles, including formal presentations, workshops and field activities:

Date	Program
Tuesday 31 Aug 2004	Arrival / Welcome Reception / Pre-conference technical tour
Wednesday 1 Sep	Official Opening / Speaker Program 'Achieving commercial potential – Case Studies from discovery through to commercialisation', 'Harvesting the genetic potential', and 'Reaching the potential for sustainable horticulture' – papers, case studies or workshops / Taste of Australia – horticultural delights and wine/ Aussie barbecue
Thursday 2 Sep	Speaker Program: 'Building Bridges – unlocking the potential for international collaboration', and 'Education and Training – training the potential horticulturists of the future' / Poster Session / Annual General Meetings / Conference dinner
Friday 3 Sep	Speaker Program: 'Enhancing Economic Potential by Innovative Production Systems', and 'Harnessing the potential of sensory and postharvest technologies' – papers, case studies or workshops.
Saturday 4 Sep	Technical Tour of horticultural enterprises on the Sunshine Coast / Departure

Sponsorship Opportunities

Attached for your information are details of the wide range of sponsorship opportunities available to your company. Should you require further details please do not hesitate to contact:
Australia: Jodie Campbell   e-mail Jodie.ac@bigpond.com.au
New Zealand: Jill Stanley

Sponsorship Registrations

We look forward to your early acceptance of this exceptional opportunity to capture high profile exposure for your goods and services. As they say, the 'early bird gets the worm'.

Jodie Campbell
Conference Secretariat

REGIONAL HORTICULTURAL CONFERENCE 2004
SPONSORSHIP ENTITLEMENTS and OPPORTUNITIES
'PLATINUM SPONSOR' – $20,000 *

We are proud to offer the following 'Platinum' sponsorship entitlements:

- **Exclusive category** representation on a first come, first served basis (eg. no other sponsor will be accepted if they directly compete in the same market with same or similar products or services).
- Prime location mega-display booth of 6 metres x 3 metres with high exposure to delegates during the conference.
- Acknowledgment as a 'Platinum Sponsor' in the pre-conference brochures, magazines, and other promotional materials.
- Opportunity to make a five minute presentation during the main conference program.
- Naming rights to conference dinner.
- Public acknowledgment of support at the beginning, during and at the end of the conference.
- Unlimited opportunity to include promotional materials in delegates conference kits.
- Opportunity to display signage on auditorium stage during conference.
- Frequently repeated exposure of individual corporate logo on sponsors' screen via electronic display during all sessions.
- Be provided with contact details of all conference participants for post conference service.
- Five complementary conference session registrations with a complementary table for ten at the conference dinner.
- Allocation as 'host' sponsor to a specific session or room for the Conference program.
- Identification of your organisation on the Conference www site for the world to see.

Pre-Conference Publicity

As part of your sponsorship, you will also receive complimentary editorials in any trade magazines promoting the conference. You will be individually contacted to maximise exposure of your organisation as the major sponsor of this conference.

Other Opportunities

- Additional trade display space by negotiation.
- Additional conference registrations are available at $350 per person.
- The complete conference proceedings will be printed as an issue of *Acta Horticulturae*, and able to be purchased from the International Society for Horticultural Science (ISHS).

*All prices are quoted inclusive of GST.

We are proud to offer the following 'Gold' sponsorship entitlements:

- Prominent display booth of 3 metres x 3 metres with high level access to all delegates during the conference.
- Acknowledgment as a 'Gold Sponsor' in the pre-conference brochures, magazines, and other promotional materials.
- Opportunity to make a five minute presentation during the conference.
- Naming rights to Welcome cocktails, Aussie Barbecue or wine-tasting event.
- Public acknowledgment of support at the beginning and at the end of conference.
- Opportunity to include multiple items of promotional materials in delegatesî conference kits.
- Frequently repeated exposure of individual corporate logo via electronic display during main sessions.
- Be provided with contact details of all conference participants for post conference service.
- Three free conference session registrations, and three additional conference dinner tickets.
- Allocation as 'host' sponsor to a specific presentation in the conference program.
- Identification of your organisation on the Conference www site for the world to see.

Pre-Conference Publicity

As part of your sponsorship, you will receive complimentary editorials in any trade magazines promoting the conference. You will be individually contacted to maximise exposure of your organisation as the major sponsor of this conference.

Other Opportunities
- Additional trade display space by negotiation.
- Additional conference registrations are available at $350 per person.
- The complete conference proceedings will be printed as an issue of *Acta Horticulturae*, and able to be purchased from the International Society for Horticultural Science (ISHS).

*All prices are quoted inclusive of GST.

We are proud to offer the following 'Silver' sponsorship entitlements:

- Display booth of 3 metres x 2.4 metres.
- Acknowledgment as a 'Silver Sponsor' in the pre-conference brochures, magazines, and other promotional materials.
- Opportunity to include two items of promotional materials in delegates' conference kits.
- Frequently repeated exposure of corporate logo via electronic display during concurrent sessions.
- Naming rights to a conference lunch.
- Opportunity to make a five minute presentation prior to lunch.
- Two free conference registrations, plus two additional conference dinner tickets.
- Identification of your organisation on the Conference www site for the world to see.

Pre-Conference Publicity

As part of your sponsorship, you will receive complimentary editorials in any trade magazines promoting the conference. You will be individually contacted to maximise exposure of your organisation as the major sponsor of this conference.

Other Opportunities
- Additional trade display space by negotiation.
- Additional conference registrations are available at $350 per person.
- The complete conference proceedings will be printed as an issue of *Acta Horticulturae*, and able to be purchased from the International Society for Horticultural Science (ISHS).

*All prices are quoted inclusive of GST.

- printing brochures and posters
- developing a website
- ticketing
- merchandising
- staff training
- signage
- catering and hospitality.

There are a number of sponsorship issues that can emerge during the implementation phase. These include ambush marketing; incompatibility between sponsors; and a sense of inequity in the profile achieved by other sponsors. In this last situation, one sponsor may feel that their company profile has been eclipsed by another who has achieved more air time or has superior signage. Sponsors can become quite competitive, insisting that one or other has been given higher exposure, a more prominent logo, a taller flag, and so on. Logos must be handled with care by the event co-ordinator with regard to correct reproduction in terms of colour and style, as there have been many occasions when a whole production run of T-shirts, banners and posters have had to be written off due to sponsor complaints. When sponsor logos are used in any public arena a sign-off by the sponsor is an essential procedure.

Sponsors are always concerned about ambush marketing, which as we have seen occurs when competitors muscle in on the media attention gained by the event. This generally occurs when T-shirts with a competitor's logos are distributed free or body paint is used to achieve similar exposure. Sponsors want exclusive rights and want a 'clean' event.

Incompatibility between sponsors is another issue, although it is fairly obvious that an approach would never be made to more than one organisation in a particular product category. For example, never two beer companies, two soft drink companies or two breakfast cereal brands. Since some of these organisations are major conglomerates with many products and many brands this can be a minefield only avoided if the organisation and its products are carefully researched prior to negotiations. 'Who are the other sponsors?' is one of the first questions asked of the event manager. Sponsors want to be associated with appropriate partners, and this includes the event company as well as other sponsors. Athletes, models, actors and performers also have their own sponsors and they may not be compatible with the sponsors of the event. Rules about exhibiting logos and promoting competing sponsors must be very clear. For example, a competitor logo cannot appear in the event precinct, particularly if worn by a high-profile celebrity. At a recent Mercedes Fashion Week event, a Volkswagen display car had to be hurriedly removed from the bar area following complaints by the main sponsor.

Finally, sponsors want to be associated with success. Any hint of failure in the press causes major consternation. This can result from cancellation of acts, ticketing problems, accidents on site and many other unforeseen problems that can crop up. For this reason, a risk management plan in relation to sponsorship is essential, with contingencies in place for every eventuality.

SPONSORSHIP EVALUATION

Evaluation is an essential component of the sponsorship arrangement. For a contract to be renewed there must be demonstrable gains made by the sponsorship organisation. These are measured in terms of the sponsorship objectives discussed earlier. The process illustrated in Fig. 8.1 shows the process cycle for sponsorship planning and evaluation. Unless evaluation in its various forms is carried out, it is impossible to demonstrate the success or otherwise of the sponsorship arrangement after the event. A warm glow is not enough to convince future sponsors that the event can produce tangible marketing benefits.

Fig. 8.1

Process of sponsorship planning and evaluation.

Plan the sponsorship program/target potential sponsors

⇓

Develop specific, measurable sponsorship objectives

⇓

Negotiate and finalise the sponsorship plan

⇓

Implement the sponsorship plan

⇓

Evaluate the success of the sponsorship plan

⇓

Provide feedback to the sponsor

There are numerous sponsorship evaluation methods, including:

- value of 'free' TV or radio exposure (measured as minutes x advertising rates)
- column centimetres in the press (publicity)
- geographic scope of media reach (number and location of media exposure, such as five country radio stations)
- consumption of sponsor's products at the event
- purchase of sponsor merchandise such as caps and T-shirts
- spectator figures
- spectator demographics
- sponsor name recall surveys
- product awareness surveys
- alliance with other sponsors (value of business generated)
- increased product sales post-event
- success of hospitality provided
- analysis of corporate image (need pre- and post-event surveys).

Sports merchandise goes on sale the next day.

Research is generally undertaken by a professional market research organisation in order to produce reliable and valid statistical information for reporting.

This chapter started by illustrating the 'fit' for the sponsorship of the Australian Open. The article that follows discusses Heineken's rationalisation of their sponsorship of this event. This is part of the planning and evaluation cycle for every sponsor and a reminder to event organisers that complacency has to be avoided in this critical area. Events, large and small, are often reliant on sponsorship (whether in cash or kind) and the contracts need to be negotiated very early.

Rethink by big sport backer jolts sponsorship market

The sponsorship industry has been rife with rumours about Heineken getting out of sport in Australia. There is some suggestion the company might direct funds into the arts and might also aim to cut back its budget after its major investment in the Rugby World Cup. Heineken has always been a classic case study in how the relatively cheap sports sponsorship deals available in Australia by international standards can be used as part of a global marketing strategy. Heineken always justified its multi-million-dollar investments in both the Australian Open and Heineken Classic on the basis that they reached massive overseas television audiences. It has often been speculated that Heineken might spend as much on sports sponsorship as it made in profits in Australia — a ridiculous concept except if the marketing budget has an international orientation.

If sport loses Heineken, the $10 million black hole that would open in the sponsorship market is a scary prospect for many sport organisers, especially the Heineken Classic.

Sweeney Sports, a marketing company that evaluates the impact of sponsorships, says that Heineken rates in the top 20 most recognised sponsors. Martin Hirons, a director of Sweeney Sports, says his company's surveys indicate that in the niche golf market, Heineken had become the most recognised sponsor of all. 'Heineken has invested millions of dollars in two particular sports — golf and tennis — which cater more, generally speaking, for higher income earners ... so you can understand their strategy', he said.

Stephen Dabkowski, The Age, 1 March 2003

In fact, since this article appeared in *The Age*, it has emerged that Dutch brewer Heineken declined to exercise its option on a deal estimated at more than $6 million a year. This left the Australian Open facing a big sponsorship search for an associate sponsor.

MERCHANDISING AND OTHER FORMS OF INCOME GENERATION

Merchandise is increasingly popular with event spectators and audiences. Big shows sell CDs, soft toys, caps, pens, posters, mouse pads and any number of other merchandising products. At sports events people buy hats, T-shirts, pins and stickers. The event audience wants a tangible reminder of their event experience.

Y ou have just been appointed as sponsorship manager of a four-wheel drive motor show. In addition to exhibitors, there is a range of other organisations that may wish to be associated with the show, such as camping, clothing and wine companies.

- Develop a sponsorship package for various types of sponsor.
- Identify 10 potential sponsors as targets.
- For each potential sponsor, explain why the sponsor may be motivated to enter into this arrangement.
- Write a letter of introduction to send with your sponsorship proposal.

ACTIVITIES

- *Visit the websites of two major organisations to find out about their sponsorship arrangements. Then explain how the sponsorship arrangements meet their corporate objectives.*
- *Visit a website that sells corporate merchandise and suggest which items would be suitable for a Jazz Festival on the beach.*

LINKS

Australasian Sponsorship Marketing Association
www.asma.com.au/

B&T online
www.bandt.com.au

BDS Sponsorship
www.sponsorship.co.uk

Smart Marketing (links)
www.smsw.com/links.htm

Sweeney Research (sports report)
www.sweeneyresearch.com.au/sports_sreport.asp

SUMMARY

Sponsorship is a partnership arrangement between the event organiser and the sponsor organisation. This is usually formalised in a legal contract. Developing marketing and publicity objectives as part of the sponsorship plan provides the opportunity to evaluate the success of the event from the sponsor's perspective. This is essential for maintaining ongoing relationships with primary and secondary sponsors from one event to the next. All parties have expectations of these relationships and they need to be clarified before operational planning begins. Staff need to be briefed about sponsorship arrangements and activities must be organised in accordance with sponsorship agreements (such as hospitality, signage, merchandising). Every opportunity to enhance the value to the sponsor/s should be taken and every effort must be made to keep sponsors involved and up to date with ongoing plans.

CHAPTER NINE

FINANCIAL

MANAGEMENT

ON COMPLETION OF THIS CHAPTER YOU WILL BE ABLE TO:

- develop an event budget, including income and expenditure
- identify the break-even point in order to make pricing decisions
- review and manage cash flow
- produce a simple profit and loss account
- develop control systems for managing finances within budget.

The Perth International Arts Festival has posted a deficit of $1.5 million, its main losses attributed to the failure of its extensive film program and newly located festival club, the Watershed.

Doran, who directs the next four Perth Festivals, said the event was conceived and curated as a four-year strategy, with public funds of $12 million from the State's Lotteries and $2 million from the University of Western Australia. The former director of the Belfast Festival was determined that his first festival would make its mark in spectacular fashion. In effect, the overall shortfall for the event was $2.6 million, but a meeting of the festival board last year approved $1.1 million to be amortised across the four festivals to support the new paradigm of the festival in terms of its different marketing, administrative and repositioning initiatives for its future development.

SYDNEY MORNING HERALD, 7 APRIL 2000

ong-term financial results are an important consideration in event management. In the above case, part of the shortfall for the first festival is being amortised (spread) across future festivals but, in general, the aim of financial management is for all expenses to be recouped at the time.

However, not all events are profit oriented. For example, a promotion for a new product, such as a new brand of perfume, would be part of a major marketing initiative, with the expectation being long-term return through sales. The perfume company would meet the expenses associated with staging the event. Similarly, a party or celebration is usually paid for by the client. Good financial management by the event company will ensure that the quote given to the client at the beginning will at least cover the expenses incurred in staging the party — and hopefully make a profit for the company! In other cases, ticket revenue and other sales (such as from merchandising) are expected to exceed the expenses, thus delivering a profit to the organisers or investors. This would certainly be the case for a major concert or sporting event.

According to Goldblatt (2002) there are three categories of event budgets:

- profit-oriented events where revenue exceeds expenses (for example, ticketed events)
- break-even events where revenue is equal to expenses (for example, community events)
- hosted events where the client meets the cost of the event (for example, product launch, celebration)

The first step in the financial management of an event is to ask the following questions.

Is the aim to make a profit?

There are many events that have a range of objectives that do not include making a profit. For example, street parades or music festivals may be offered to the public free of charge, the expenses being met by government agencies and/or sponsors. Often, goods and services are provided by businesses and individuals to assist in the running of an event, thus making it difficult to accurately estimate the actual costs. However, it is still essential that all other expenses are properly approved and documented.

Where the objective of an event is raising money for charity, a target needs to be set and, once again, both the expenses and the funds raised need to be accounted for correctly.

How much will the event cost?

In the example of the fundraising event above, as indeed for any non-profit event, it is important to estimate how much the event will cost as well as to keep track of the actual expenses incurred. With every event, money changing hands must be properly documented and, in most cases, the financial records should be audited. Expenses, or costs, include fees, hire costs, advertising, insurance, and so on.

What are the revenue sources?

Generally, revenue is raised by selling tickets or charging admission or registration fees. Merchandise sales also contribute to revenue. Merchandising items, such as T-shirts and caps, may be sold by the event organiser or under arrangement with the retailer whereby the event organiser earns a percentage of any sales. The same arrangement may occur with food and beverage sales.

How many tickets must be sold to break even?

This is a critical question. In essence, it relates to whether you decide on a large venue, large audience and low price or a small venue, small audience and high price? This will be discussed in more detail later in this chapter.

What is the cash flow situation?

Events are fairly unique in that, for many, revenue comes in only on the day of the event. This means that all costs, such as salaries, office expenses and fees, have to be met up-front from existing funds. When ticket sales occur long before an event is staged, as they do with major concerts, this puts the company in the enviable position of being able to pay for its expenses from revenue while also earning interest on this money until the remaining bills become due. Very few events fit this category. Cash flow planning is an essential part of the event planning process for the above-mentioned reasons.

What control systems are needed to avoid fraud?

All businesses are accountable and systems need to be put in place to ensure that moneys are accounted for. Systems and procedures are needed so that every transaction will be recorded and all expenditure approved, including payment of invoices, handling of cash, paying of tax and so on. Cash management systems for the day of the event are often lacking and it is not uncommon for registers to be left open, for staff to take handfuls of change without substituting notes and for bags of cash to be left lying around. This is clearly unsatisfactory.

How will legal and taxation obligations be met?

Employing the services of a properly qualified accountant will ensure that your organisation maintains accurate records and meets its legal obligations.

THE BUDGET

Preparing a budget is part of the initial planning stage. A budget includes projected revenue and expenditure from which an estimate of the net profit (or sometimes net loss) for the proposed event can be ascertained. It is a plan based on accurate quotes from all contractors and suppliers and careful research to ensure that no expenses have been overlooked. It provides guidelines for approving expenditure and ensuring that the financial aspects of the event remain on track. The budget is part of the event proposal or the basis of the quote by the event management company to the client.

Several sample budgets are provided in Figs 9.1 to 9.3 on pages 125–128. As you will see, they vary considerably in the number of expense and revenue items, though the general principles remain the same. Note the differences between fixed costs (these do not alter) and variable costs (these vary in accordance with the size of the event audience).

Management fees

In many cases, an event organiser charges a management fee to oversee an event. As a ballpark figure for planning purposes, this is generally in the region of 10–15 per cent of total costs. While an event might have a low budget, it might still require

Ten thousand emergency ponchos may be required for an outdoor event and should be included in the budget unless the supplier will take returns. If sold the margins could be high.

Equipment rental is a common expense item for events.

considerable time and effort in its organisation and the lower end of the range, 10 per cent, would simply not cover management costs. In this case, or in the case of smaller projects, clients can be billed on a per hour fee basis. In a fiercely competetitive environment, there may be situations in which the event planner may look at business as a short-term opportunity with long-term gain.

Prior to contracts being signed, the event organiser should work out the tasks involved in the event, allocate staff to the various roles and determine their pay rates in order to come up with a more accurate estimate of management costs and therefore the management fee to be charged. In some situations, the event organiser might wish to involve themselves in a collaborative entre-preneurial arrangement with the client whereby the management fee is based on income earned or sponsorship raised.

If a management fee is charged, the client is usually responsible for all pre-event payments to venues and subcontractors. The fee is for the management and co-ordination of the event by the event organisers, and for their expertise, from concept through to execution. By charging a management fee only (and not assuming financial risk), the event organiser is to some degree at 'arm's length'. This in turn is linked to other risks, such as public liability risk. Since many events are structured with cascading responsibility through many layers of client, contractor and subcontractor, it is essential that all these contractual relationships are clear, including financial and legal responsibilities at each level.

Contingencies

Most event budgets include a contingency for unexpected expenses. This ranges from 5 per cent of the costs (if the event organiser is confident that the costs are controllable) to 10 per cent (if there are a number of unknown variables or the costs are uncertain).

BUDGETING PROCESS

The budgeting process is as follows:

1 Draft the budget, based on analysis of all available information, ensuring that income and expenditure estimates are clearly identified and supported by valid, reliable and relevant information.
2 Analyse the internal and external environments for potential impacts on the budget.
3 Assess and present alternative approaches to the budget.
4 Ensure that the draft budget accurately reflects event/business objectives.

5   Circulate the draft budget to colleagues for comment and discussion.

6   Negotiate the budget with all relevant stakeholders, including the client where relevant.

7   Agree and incorporate modifications to the budget.

8   Complete the final budget in the required format within the designated time.

9   Inform colleagues of final budget decisions and ramifications in a timely manner.

10   Review budget regularly to assess performance against estimates.

11   Analyse and investigate deviations (variances).

12   Collect information for future budget preparation.

Fig. 9.1
Budget items for outdoor running event.

INCOME (inc. GST)

Entry — corporate 40 @ $

Stall rental

Merchandising

Raffle

Entry donation

Other donations

Total Income (inc. GST)

EXPENDITURE
Fixed Costs
Hire

Structures

50 team marquees 6 x 6 m
   (30 pax)

5 fete stalls (food)

3 fete stalls (merchandising)

1 officials structure (6 x 6 m)

6 marshall/official posts

1 children's marquee

50 m synthetic grass

Allowance for under panels for grass

Ticket barrel

3 flag poles

Glassware (4000 @ $0.25)

3 trestle tables

2 urns

5000 paper cups

Cartage

1 information booth 4.8 x 2.4 m

1 site office 6 x 2.4 m

Toilets

20 dual sex toilets — GP and runners

1 disabled toilet

Service attendants

5 hand basins

Equipment

Stage 6 x 3 m, 6 x 0.3 m

Stage roof 6 x 3 m

Lectern

850 metal racks

150 witches' hats

10 rolls safety marking tape

Cartage

3 x 9.5 cu m coolrooms — VIPs and runners

Govt Stamp Duty @ 2%

Control

Scoreboard

Scoreboard production

Timekeeping

Hire of PC and equipment

500 coded wristbands

Hire of 2 bar code readers

10 radio sets

4 phone lines

50 x 10 prs team numbers

70 marshalls/officials bibs @ $11

PA system for stage and area

Start/finish hooter gas

1 winner's shields @ $110

10 winners' medals with ribbon

500 competitors' medals with ribbon

Fig. 9.1 CONTINUED
Budget items for outdoor running event.

Staff

    MC/announcer

    Security

    20 control/carpark

    Labour, set-up/pull-down

    50 marshalls/race officials, incl. relief

    St John's first aid

    Photographer

Logistics

    Garbage bins

    Cleaning up and garbage removal

    Power

    Water

    Transport/cartage

    AJC staff

Promotion

    Printing

    Design/artwork

    500 entry forms

    10 000 flyers

    2000 programs

    50 corporate prospectus

    50 competitors' entry kit preparation

    Stationery

    1500 'show bags'

    Signage

    2 banners 6 x 3 m

    20 directional signs

    5 sponsor marquee signs

    50 team names for tents

    Advertising

    Marketing

    Media Launch

Administration

    Couriers, postage

    Phone, fax, email

    Insurance: 3rd party, property, volunteer

    Council permit

    Alcohol licence

    Children's amusements

    Raffle prizes

Management fee

    For collection of team monies and database management; media co-ord; production; co-ord and running of event, including budget

Total Fixed Costs

Variable Costs (based on 40 teams)

Food and beverage

    Catering 1200 @ $

    Buffet tables set-up

    Beverage (4 hr package) 1200 @ $

    Waiting staff 40 @ $

    Health drink for athletes

    Health food for athletes

Total Variable Costs

Contingency

Sub-total

10% GST

TOTAL EXPENDITURE

PROFIT

Fig. 9.2

Budget items for music event.

Fixed Costs

Venue hire

Artists

> Speaker
>
> Actor/scriptwriter
>
> Singer/composer
>
> Choreographer
>
> Technical director
>
> Set designer
>
> Make-up designer
>
> Props designer

Production Team

> Stage manager
>
> Asst stage manager
>
> Asst technical

Costumes

> T-shirts @ $ (+10% extreme sizes)

Sound

> Copyright
>
> Hire

Lights

Vision (for presentation and speaker)

> Based on powerpoint presentation and
> video
>
> Preparation of visuals

Staging

> Preparation of production detail
>
> Set backdrop, paints etc.
>
> Props materials
>
> Expendables
>
> Posters for theatre x 6
>
> Props
>
> Laptop and printer

Printing

> Individual group labels
>
> Invitations
>
> Programs — shell plus insert
>
> Reviews

Onsite staff (catering)

Other hire (catering)

Gifts

Photography (digital camera)

Video recording

> Video camera hire
>
> Tapes

Set-up/dismantle

Freight

Airfares

> SYD-AKL return x 1
>
> SYD-AKL return x 1 (bus.class)
>
> SYD-MEL return x 5 @ $

Transfers

> Airport
>
> Coach — Hotel-theatre-hotel
>
> Coach — Office-theatre-office
>
> Coach — Airport-theatre-hotel

Accommodation and meals

> AKL 2 x 2 days
>
> MEL 4 x 2 days, 1 x 1 day

Miscellaneous

> Phone, fax, courier estimate

Contingency

Management fee

Total Fixed Costs

Variable Costs

Catering

Coffee on arrival	@ $	
Morning tea with muffins	@ $	
Lunch — working type	@ $	
Afternoon tea	@ $	
Pre-show canapé and buffet dinner	@ $	
Beverage	@ $	
Total	**$**	**per head**
Breakfast for interstate arrivals 15	@ $	

Total Variable Costs

Total Each Location

10% GST

GRAND TOTAL

BREAK-EVEN POINT

To work out the break-even point, the event organiser has to estimate the number of tickets that need to be sold in order to meet expenses (see Fig. 9.4). These expenses include both fixed costs and variable costs. Fixed costs, such as licensing fees, insurance, administrative costs, rent of office space, advertising costs and fees paid to artists, generally do not vary if the size of the event audience increases and are often called overheads. Variable costs increase as the size of the audience increases. If food and beverage were part of, say, a conference package, clearly these costs would escalate if the numbers attending the conference increased. Once the total revenue is the same as the total expenditure (fixed and variable) then break-even point has been reached. Beyond it, the event is profitable.

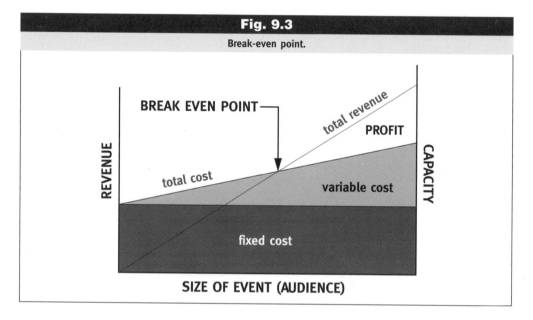

Fig. 9.3
Break-even point.

In the case of an exhibition, the organiser would be using the budget to establish how many exhibitors were needed to break even. The price charged for exhibiting could clearly be quite low if there were a lot of exhibitors; the price charged would have to be high if there were few exhibitors and if the aim were to meet the budget (particularly for fixed costs). However, this is not an altogether feasible way of setting prices or fees since there is a maximum price the market will bear and a minimum level at which the event becomes viable. This iterative process of analysing ticket prices or fees charged and the break-even point is part of the financial decision-making process.

INCOME STRATEGY

Income strategy is a most complex issue for both large and small events. Even the smallest school fete committee wonders whether to charge an entry fee at the gate, and how much, to meet all costs of those attending, or whether to allow stall holders and ride operators to charge individually and then to take a commission from these operators.

Event income can come from the following sources:

- entry tickets
- rental for stalls, stands and exhibitors
- merchandise sales (hats, CDs, etc.)
- licensing
- sale of programs
- sale of food and beverage
- sponsorship or grants
- parking fees.

Licensing the sale of products can be a major source of income. When, for example, there is significant demand for merchandise associated with a major event (such as the World Cup, Le Tour de France, *The Lion King*), an agreement may be reached with another organisation to manufacture and sell products such as toys, clothing, CDs, pins and souvenirs. This licensing arrangement will include a royalty for use of logos, names and images of the event on specific products, and the products will often be sold in retail outlets outside the event precinct, such as K-Mart, as well as at the event. Each item sold will attract a royalty payment for the event organising body.

Food and beverage items are often sold by concessionaires who pay a retainer to the event organiser or client to operate on the event premises and sell at the event. This arrangement is also common for bars and coffee stalls. In addition, well-recognised food chains sometimes have multiple stands throughout the event premises.

Ticket pricing

All sources of income must be factored in when making a decision on ticket prices. Clearly, the higher the level of sponsorship and other income, the lower the ticket price.

Ticket pricing decisions also need to reflect the anticipated size of the audience; the potential for different pricing levels (for example, seating allocations); the price the audience will bear; the opportunity for last minute discounting and many other factors. The logistics of ticketing include printing, distribution, collection and reconciliation, which all have implications for cash flow. A ticketing agency charges a commission on sales and distribution; however, pre-event ticketing does provide a source of cash when it is most needed.

Ticket sales and distribution on the day of an event can be problematic in terms of service and safety if not managed well — crowds forming at an entrance and long queues are to be avoided at all costs.

In addition to numbering of tickets and development of an interval pass system, the event organiser needs to consider the logistics of delivering cash for change and banking large amounts of money (often necessary when banks are shut) at the close of the event.

CASH FLOW ANALYSIS

Capital is required to set up any business and even more so in the event business as the planning phase can be quite long and the period for capturing revenue very short. For example, an event team may spend a year planning an event during which period costs will be incurred, all of which have to be paid long before there is an opportunity to recoup any money. Having spent a year planning, it is possible that tickets will be sold at the venue and all revenue will be collected on the one day. This is in contrast to an everyday business where there is a more even cash flow.

In instances where the client is paying for the event, a deposit is generally negotiated. However, payment of the balance may not be paid to the event management company until at least a month after the event. Ideally, complete upfront payment, or a significant establishment fee, should be negotiated to alleviate cash flow problems.

In summary, monthly expenses and projected revenue need to be entered into a spreadsheet to establish how cash flow can best be managed. A funding crisis, just days before an event, is not uncommon in this industry.

The illustration in Fig. 9.5 provides an example of an event held in September generating very little income until the month and days before the event. Only small amounts in the form of grants and sponsorships are shown as income during the planning phase in April, May and June. Meanwhile, expenses were incurred from the beginning of the planning process, peaking in July and August when suppliers were becoming demanding. Expenses include salaries for staff, office expenses, deposits and up-front payments to subcontractors for catering and equipment hire. The gap between expenditure and income is the cash shortfall, which in this example was particularly problematic in July and August.

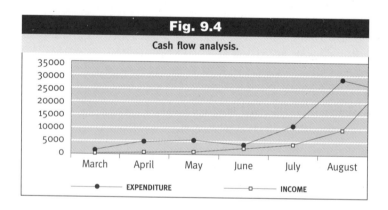

ACCOUNT CODES AND PREFIXES

Traditionally, accountants have allocated a code to each different type of expense. For example, in the hospitality industry there is a uniform system of accounts so that hotels can compare statistics more readily. In the absence of a similar system in the event business, the following system could be adopted:

Assets 100–199   Revenue 400–499
Liabilities 200–299   Expenses 500–599
Owner's equity 300–399

In addition, prefixes can be used to assign expenses to different 'departments' in order to measure individual performance. This is relevant for an event business, which may be running several events concurrently. In this case it would be necessary to separate staff expenses for one event from staff expenses for another. The prefix enables the business to do this and analyse each event separately. For example, ticket revenue for the Caribbean Festival below may be allocated 01400 — 01 being the festival prefix (in any other business the festival might be called a department). Ticket revenue for another event, the Water Wizard Show, would be coded 02400. When running a multi-venue event it may also be appropriate to look at the budget and profit and loss for each venue to analyse financial performance.

Very simply, the accounting of the two events mentioned above could yield comparative information as illustrated in Fig. 9.5.

Fig. 9.5

Comparative revenue and expenditure figures for two events.

	Caribbean Festival		Water Wizard Show	
		$		$
Revenue (400–499)				
Ticket sales	01400	993 000.00	02400	805 012.00
Expenses (500–599)				
Salaries and wages	01500	116 000.00	02500	104 901.00
Venue rental/fees	01501	21 900.00	02501	165 550.00
Performance contracts	01502	425 000.00	02502	179 000.00
Advertising	01503	11 205.00	02503	14 895.00
Cleaning costs	01504	12 000.00	02504	8 900.00
Printing and stationery	01505	29 000.00	02505	15 002.00
Plant and equipment hire	01506	5 000.00	02506	16 507.00
Etc.				

PROFIT AND LOSS STATEMENT

This is a list of an organisation's revenue, expenditure and net profit (or net loss) for a specific period. In many cases the profit and loss statement (or income statement) is prepared after the event.

In a perfect world, the profit and loss statement would match the budget. The budget is the plan, and if everything went to plan this would be reflected in the profit and loss statement. In the event industry, the budget is generally prepared before the event and the profit and loss statement afterwards, while in most ongoing business operations, budgets and profit and loss statements are done regularly and routinely. In an event management company, a profit and loss statement would be done for each event, as well as for the ongoing concern, the company itself. Alternatively, each event could be shown as a different cost centre.

On the profit and loss statement, the most important source of revenue, such as sales of tickets, appears as the first item. If the event is paid for by a single client, this will be the first item as it is the predominant source of revenue. Gross revenue is the total revenue before any costs have been deducted. This is a similar concept to gross (not unpleasant) wages, the amount you would receive if there weren't all sorts of deductions such as tax, superannuation and the like before it reached your pocket.

If you deduct the cost of goods sold (also known as direct costs) from the gross revenue, you get the gross profit. If the gross revenue from an event were $750 000 and direct costs of $520 000 were deducted, this would result in a gross profit of $230 000. Cost of goods sold covers those which relate directly to the revenue earned. They could include cost of venue hire, labour and equipment rental. After calculating the gross profit, you would then deduct your overhead costs, such as administration costs and rent, of $165 000 and you would be left with an operating profit of $65 000. Finally, your net profit is your profit after all other costs and tax have been deducted, in this case $41 000. This is illustrated in Fig. 9.7.

Fig. 9.6		
Profit and loss statement.		
Profit and Loss Statement as at 30 June 2001		
Gross revenue	$750 000.00	
Less cost of goods sold	$520 000.00	
Gross profit		**$230 000.00**
Less adminstrative and other overhead costs	$165 000.00	
Operating profit		**$65 000.00**
Less other income expenses (such as interest)	$6 000.00	
Profit before tax		$59 000.00
Less tax	$18 000.00	
Net profit for the year/event		**$41 000.00**

BALANCE SHEET

While the profit and loss statement captures results for a given period, such as a financial year, the balance sheet gives you an idea of what a business is worth at a certain point in time. Where the owners of the business have acquired assets, such as sound and lighting equipment, this becomes very relevant. Likewise if there were outstanding bills to be paid. The balance sheet shows what the result would be if all bills were paid and everything were sold (assets minus liabilities). This result is the owner's equity in the business. The problem for many event management companies is that many of their assets, such as their reputation, are intangible and difficult to value!

FINANCIAL CONTROL SYSTEMS

All purchases must be approved and usually a requisition form is used for this purpose. This means that the manager has the opportunity to approve costs incurred by employees. Once goods are ordered, or services provided, checks must be made that they meet specifications before the bills are paid. Fraud could occur if an employee had authority to make purchases, record and physically handle the goods, and pay the bills. This is why these roles are usually carried out by different people. In any case, the system should have checks and balances to make sure that:

- purchases or other expenses are approved
- goods and services meet specifications
- payment is approved
- accounts are paid
- incoming revenue is checked and banked
- revenue totals are recorded correctly
- debts are met
- all transactions are recorded and balanced
- taxation requirements are met
- financial matters are correctly reported to stakeholders.

The following article quoting Leo Schofield illustrates the Sydney Festival's aim of making a profit on box office events while ensuring that free outdoor events were well attended. This is a good example of a major event with several objectives which was successfully staged and financially well managed.

Thrilled by the festival's success, Mr Schofield yesterday said it had exceeded the $2 million box office target 'handsomely'. The number of people attending the festival had also been 'an extraordinary' success, he said. The surplus would be in addition to $500 000 which had been put aside as a 'war chest' to ensure future festivals were in good financial shape.

'When I came to the festival it was $500 000 in the red and I'm leaving it the same amount in the black', Mr Schofield said. 'This year we have done a significantly impressive box office … enormous considering the range, and in the end I'm a subscriber to the view that every artistic decision is a financial one. We've had no event falling below the projected box office.'

'The big free outdoor events characterising the festival this year have been stronger than they have ever been.' Symphony in the Domain, always popular, had drawn 120 000 last weekend while Jazz in the Domain attracted 105 000 people earlier in the festival.

DAILY TELEGRAPH, 24 JANUARY 2001

PANIC PAYMENTS

This unusual accounting term is not exclusive to the event industry, but this industry is one in which inflated panic prices are often paid. In an ideal world, the event manager has all quotes sewn up and the budget locked in long before the event. There should be few unforeseen contingencies — but don't forget this line in your budgets!

In reality, Murphy's law dictates that something will always go wrong. And the closer it is to the event, the more difficult it is to negotiate a reasonable price for what you require to put it right. In fact, if it is a last-minute crisis, it could easily lead to a price with a high premium — a panic payment. Essentially, the supplier has the event manager over a barrel. Careful planning, budgeting and detailed contracts negotiated well in advance can prevent this situation occurring (see Fig. 9.7).

POST-EVENT REPORTING

As we have mentioned in earlier chapters, post-event reporting is essential, and many public events make their annual reports public. One very good example is the National Folk Festival, held in

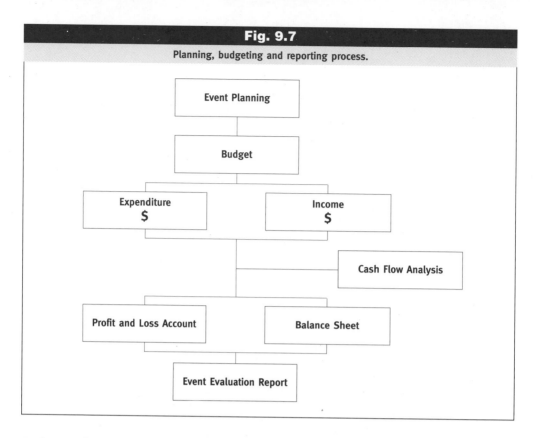

Fig. 9.7

Planning, budgeting and reporting process.

Event Planning

Budget

Expenditure
$

Income
$

Cash Flow Analysis

Profit and Loss Account

Balance Sheet

Event Evaluation Report

Canberra, which features all recent annual reports (and an earlier five-year report) on their website. The National Folk Festival has been presented annually since its inception as the Port Phillip Folk Festival in Melbourne in 1967. Until 1992 it was organised by the State Folk Federations on behalf of the Australian Folk Trust (AFT) on a rotating basis in the various major cities throughout Australia. The festival was highly successful in terms of attendance and community support. Nevertheless, heavy financial losses were sustained by organising groups between 1988 and 1992. In 1992 the AFT decided that the size and scope of the event had grown such that the festival needed a permanent home and a professional management team. Several cities were considered and, eventually, Canberra was chosen. In 1993 the festival established a company to operate the event and employed a full-time director.

The five-year report shows the following attendance figures:

1993   15 000   1996   31 600
1994   19 100   1997   38 000
1995   24 000   1998   42 000

From 1999 to 2002 attendances were fairly static, increasing to 51 000 per day in 2004 when the festival dates again coincided with school holidays. This festival has a strategic plan with measurable objectives linked to a diverse cultural program. The Annual Report for the festival held in 2002 is partially reproduced below and is particularly helpful as it attaches a narrative to the year's expenditures. A survey of festival participants is also included in the annual report. The financial statements show an excess of income over expenditure of $5752.

Annual Report
for
National Folk Festival,
28 March – 1 April 2002

Performers

Another 1100 performers were engaged in 206 acts to present many themes, but principally the major Outback theme. In recognition of the 11 September 2001 World Trade Centre terrorism the Opening Concert encompassed a Living Together theme, starting with Afghan Sitar player Kahlil Gudaz and compered by Ted Egan — a fitting start to four days of living together in an atmosphere of friendship and enjoyment. A survey about the need to increase performer payments (many act as volunteers in the way that their payment sometimes simply covers travel and living expenses) there were 64% that supported an increase and this will be attempted at the 2003 festival . . .

Publications

Following the 2001 festival comments about describing the fun of the event better in our publications, new wording was developed. Most were thrilled with the new designs and our thanks again go to Franki Sparke for the poster design. Images are now the subject of some suggestions, so new images are being explored for 2003.

Stall holders

For the first time all stall fees were collected prior to the festival and all had to co-operate with upgraded insurance requirements. Together with clothing, massage, palmistry, exceptional food, coffee, mediaeval wares and master instrument makers, these combine to make their own feature each festival.

Volunteers

We have not yet been able to work out how to gather all the names of the 900 volunteers in time for inclusion in the Final Program — maybe by the 40th celebrations in 2006. It's the 50 co-ordinators and their teams that put the festival together 'on the day'. These people therefore make a major contribution to the success of the festival. This year we are particularly indebted because of the way that all concerned adopted new policies and adapted to the changes brought on by new Risk Management and Access Plans. Thank you all.

Sound and PA systems

This year was the first that there were no reports of problems with sound spill, sound quality or electrical failures. In many ways it is an enormous task to not only put all the contracts together but for delivery of professional sound across 14 venues — for some 18 hours a day. The ability of sound operators to both listen and mix sounds for this length of time is a credit to all involved. Over the years a lot of energy has been invested in matching abilities to the needs of a large range of types of venues and we now seem to have achieved combinations that provide a great experience for a wide variety of sounds.

Site hire and cleaning

The EPIC site continues to offer a unique opportunity, so that only one of our amplified venues is not inside — it is a deliberate choice to provide the Piazza as an outdoor venue with all its attended benefits and weather susceptibility. The camping aspect is a unique use of how we package the event, and feedback has suggested that we need to apply more administration earlier than before. We entered this festival without a lease for 2003, and at the time of writing had not been advised of the formal approval of a new 10-year contract. Cleaning with street sweepers has become an issue in recent years and more resources early each day need to be found.

Car parking

After providing improved buses to ferry patrons from the top carpark to the entertainment precinct we seem to have now overcome any major problems that were associated with the establishment of new car parking areas, after being compelled to move these from the Flemington Road site. Volunteer teams have now adapted and signage is about the only item that needs fine-tuning.

Staffing

With increased risk and legal responsibilities, the provision of three full-time staff, two trainees and a part-time publicity officer, it is now essential to provide the managerial and operational basis of this large annual event — topped up with additional help nearer the event, some paid. Workloads have continued to grow and more resources are indicated for the servicing and maintenance of computers and associated technology — the office now has 15 computer terminals to cope with the necessary workstations for staff, volunteers and automatic management of intranet and databases.

Ticketing

In-house advance ticket sales increased these sales by the budgeted extra $50 000 income prior to the event. A major improvement at the festival was the responsibility of window cashiers to account for all their sales made during their respective shifts. This required investment in professional tellers to supervise this new process. Improvements point to not only maintenance of this initiative but spread of this across all areas of the festival — to enhance the attitude of sales personnel towards the need to account for all income.

Drink vouchers

As part of the need to improve service at bars and for the upgrading of risk management issues, drink vouchers were introduced for the sales of products across the Sessions and Guinness Bars. While initially there was some reluctance, it seems that with the same system now at many festivals it did not take long for acceptance to prevail. Some improvements are indicated, particularly as some operators could not assist with improving service. Movement to roles of tickets is indicated, as is greater attention to destruction of vouchers once used.

Blackboard venues and sessions

A unique part of this festival is the facilitation of jamming sessions throughout the site. The largest of these areas has always been the Sessions Bar, where up to 20 groups of musicians, dancers or singers can congregate, perform, play and just have fun — it is said that some just set themselves up in this area all weekend, sometimes never repeating a song. There is now a range of other informal areas around the site that are either planned or just happen. It is not unusual for these sessions to lead to the collaborative groupings, which can readily see a blackboard gig emerge. Demand at blackboard venues has increased and this is an area where various attempts have been made to provide more opportunities to get a gig on a daily basis. With the demand from booked and non-booked acts increasing, we need to find ways to spread the already considerable resources across more of these venues.

Annual financial outcomes

The annual Financial Statements for 2001/02 are attached. The accounts reflect an excess of income over expenditure of $5752.

Tax deductibility of donations

This tax deductibility drew donations totalling $6825 — a worthwhile contribution to operations.

The future

As reported by the President above, we are now facing a new era in festival activities. We need to take stock and introduce plans to attend to our sustainability. This will involve appropriate development and consultation about a Business Plan, to take us forward.

In the meantime, it is up to us all to continue to join together in supporting our Mission Statement:

The National Folk Festival will provide an annual celebration of Australian folk life emphasising the quality of our creativity and the diverse cultural heritage of all our Australian communities through showcasing a fun-filled community event, which features participation as an imperative.

NATIONAL FOLK FESTIVAL LTD ACN 058 761 274
TRADING AND SURPLUS & LOSS ACCOUNT
FOR THE YEAR ENDED 30 JUNE 2002

	2002 $	2001 $
INCOME		
Sales income	793.312	716.412
LESS COST OF GOODS SOLD		
Opening inventory	600	1075
Purchases	263,892	247,043
Other cost of goods sold	9.638	–
Less Closing inventory		600
Total Cost of Goods Sold	274,130	247,5183
GROSS PROFIT	519,182	514,097

	2002 $	2001 $
LESS EXPENSES		
Professional fees	139,391	126,762
Salaries & wages	116,000	104,799
Directors' emoluments	52,000	52,000
Printing & stationery	48,157	55,157
Hire of plant & equipment	43,021	46,061
Travelling expenses	40,276	29,149
Sundry expenses	27,479	30,318
Cleaning	18,632	16,617
Consultancy fees	18,502	14,738
Postage	16,724	15,637
Insurance	15,272	11,458
Bank charges	13,504	12,199
Telephone	13,437	16,720
Superannuation	12,894	10,520
Staff training & welfare	11,808	751
Electricity	11,297	10,332
Magazines, journals & periodicals	10,597	6,723
Rent	8,669	8,034
Operating expenses	7,828	5,386
Depreciation	7,309	8,030
Motor vehicle expenses	4,741	4,804
Security costs	3,942	3,997
Advertising	3,872	2,664
Long service leave	2,702	4,979
Computer expenses	2,322	3,807
Audit fees	2,250	3,320
Repairs & maintenance	2,048	5,838
Legal costs	1,025	77
Writedowns	996	(5,393)
Consumables	404	671
Accounting fees	350	2,249
Bad debts	100	440
Holiday pay	(3,287)	5,531
Other expenses	–	1,056

NATIONAL FOLK FESTIVAL LTD ACN 058 761 274
TRADING AND SURPLUS & LOSS ACCOUNT
FOR THE YEAR ENDED 30 JUNE 2002

	2002 $	2001 $
TOTAL EXPENSES	654,262	615,431
NET PROFIT	(135,080)	(101,334)
OTHER OPERATING INCOME		
Subsidies and grants	120,461	88,730

	2002 $	2001 $
Interest	12,531	12,086
Other income	8,267	3,224
Donations received	6,825	–
Fringe benefits tax contributions	1,300	750
Bad debts recovered	–	220
Total other operating income	149,384	105,010
OPERATING PROFIT	14,304	3,676
Less transfer to Self-Insurance Reserve	(8,652)	–
RETAINED PROFITS FOR YEAR	5,752	3,676

Courtesy National Folk Festival

CASE STUDY

Your event business, Rave Reviews, has the opportunity to quote for two major parties. Having experienced some financial difficulties in your first year of operation, you want to ensure that you choose the most feasible of these for which to prepare a proposal and produce the winning quote.

The first party is for a top celebrity and will be held at her waterside mansion. The party will be outdoors and the brief is to transform the garden through the use of a spectacular theme. The party will be attended by 350 guests and a lavish dinner is expected.

The second party is much larger, as 500–600 people will be invited. The company is giving the party to celebrate its 50th year of tractor and farming equipment operations. The party will be held in a large airport hangar in the country. Food will be pretty basic and alcohol will be very plentiful. Décor is not important, but entertainment is.

Discuss which of these two events you would choose in terms of its ease of financial management and its potential profitability.

ACTIVITY

Prepare a budget for the promotion of a local fundraising event. You can use any number of promotional strategies, including various forms of advertising. Make sure you include the time taken to prepare the communication messages and designs for these materials. In the case of brochures, there may be print costs as well as distribution costs. Your budget should comprehensively cover all activities and expenses associated with promotion, including any salaries or wages involved.

SUMMARY

This chapter has covered the important subject of financial management. We have learnt that the budget developed prior to an event must anticipate all revenue and expenditure and that steps should be taken to finalise contracts as early as possible to ensure that expenses do not exceed budget forecasts. The event manager also needs to take into account the cash flow situation in the lead-up to an event since most expenses occur early in the planning process while the bulk of the revenue is generally collected close to, or during, the event. We have touched on profit and loss statements and balance sheets and have emphasised the importance of financial control systems for managing expenditure and revenue from sales. Reporting systems need to be in place so that complete and accurate records are available for the final post-event report.

CHAPTER TEN

RISK

MANAGEMENT

ON COMPLETION OF THIS CHAPTER YOU WILL BE ABLE TO:

- identify the risks associated with an event
- assess and prioritise the risks
- manage the risks by prevention or contingency planning
- implement risk management strategies
- monitor risk management strategies.

Exhibition Park in Canberra is where street machine enthusiasts meet, display and strut their mechanical stuff. It's the place to find the most highly customised, modified and faithfully restored cars from early model street machines through to the cutting edge, late model, 'techno' cars.

Exhibition Park offers the opportunity to cruise the kilometres of roadways, and stretch performance to the maximum, in the outrageous Burnout and Go-Whoa competitions on the world's first and only purpose-built burn-out facility. Entrants' cars, tortured on the Chassis Dyno, search for the Summernats Horse-power Hero, while grass driving events provide the stage to demonstrate those proudly held driving abilities.

The Top 80 Show, Car Audio Sound Off, and Miss Summernats combine with entertainment and displays to bring Exhibition Park to life with a high-spirited, automotive, New Year atmosphere.

SUMMERNATS CAR FESTIVAL

While not everyone's choice of event, this car festival is extremely popular, attracting a crowd of enthusiastic rev heads to the world's only purpose-built burn-out facility. This crowd has been described as high spirited, so the organisers insist on the following rules in an effort to minimise risk: no alcohol to be brought in; no glass bottles; no pets; no fireworks; no weapons; and no illegal drugs.

All event organisers face a range of risks, and in this chapter we will look at ways in which these risks can be identified, analysed, prioritised, minimised and monitored. Firstly, however, we will look at the major risks an event organiser is likely to encounter.

WHAT IS RISK?

Risk is the chance that something will go wrong. Event organisers often think of risk in terms of safety and security, but risk is much broader than that. It may include a cash flow crisis, a staff strike, poor publicity or, of course, bad weather. The last of these is the event manager's greatest risk. Even if it does not have a direct impact on the event, poor weather will reduce the number of people attending an event unless adequate weather protection is provided. Rainy or stormy weather also has an impact on people's mood and motivation, making it a serious concern for which careful planning is required. **Risk management is the process of identifying such risks, assessing these risks and managing these risks.**

In the case of the Summernats Car Festival, the potential for bad crowd behaviour, and the negative publicity that could result, is no doubt the reason for the organisers establishing such strict rules of entry to this event. The organisers, in this instance, have adopted a risk prevention strategy. At a broader level, any negative behaviour and publicity could have a negative impact on the profile of Canberra, where the festival is held, as an event destination.

The following risks need to be considered if relevant to the event you are planning.

Natural disasters

Heavy rain is a disaster for an outdoor event, as too are hail, snow and extreme heat. Flooding can affect event venues, particularly temporary ones, and it can also cause damage to electrical wiring — potentially a very serious risk. Of course, fire is one of the risks most venue managers fear, and must plan for, since evacuation of large crowds is extremely difficult.

Financial risk

Financial risk may involve unforeseen costs, lower than expected revenue, high exchange rates, general decline in economic circumstances and disposable income, fraud, fines and cash flow problems.

Legal risk

Legal risks include disputes over contracts between the event organiser and the client and/or between the event organiser and a subcontractor. These can occur if expectations are unrealistic or if a gap develops between the expectations of the client and the product the event organiser can produce for the price negotiated. Disputes can also occur if the venue hired does not meet the required standards in terms of such things as reliable electricity supply and suitable access for delivery vehicles. Breach of legal requirements is another form of legal risk, an example being a venue losing its liquor licence for a violation of the liquor laws, such as selling alcohol to underage drinkers.

Technology-related risks

Technological failure is an increasing risk for high-profile events that are extremely reliant on computer programming and computer networks operating successfully. For example, a problem with guest registration at a trade exhibition would prevent the successful capture of attendee data, which is essential information for all stall holders. For the exhibition organiser, the attendance list (generated during registration) is their most valuable asset. It would be made available to current exhibitors wanting to follow up contacts, as well as being used by the event organiser in the advertising drive for the next event of a similar nature.

New Year's Eve fireworks displays are probably one of the events that are most reliant on highly sophisticated technology. No doubt pyrotechnics planners for major firework displays have many back-up systems. If an event is simulcast live around the world, preparation and planning have to be flawless. Every possible contingency has to be anticipated, such as a delay to the telecast or even cancellation of the event.

Technology-related risks of this magnitude are of increasing concern for the event management team.

Mismanagement

A successful event requires good management, detailed planning and sound interpersonal relationships at all levels. Mismanagement can prevent an event reaching its objectives, so too can people-related problems, such as disputes at top management level, leading to the dismissal of key personnel. Both are potentially serious risks.

Safety and security risk

Accidents, riots, terrorism and sabotage are all safety and security risks. Safety and security measures will be described in Chapter 18 in more detail.

Risk at sporting events

While the risks associated with most community, commercial and entertainment events are largely financial, with sporting events there is the additional risk of danger to the sports men and women involved and, in some cases, to the audience. For example, most bike and car races carry the risk of injury to both drivers and spectators, whether on the track or off-road. Bike races, and even fun runs, generally experience a number of medical emergencies and the occasional fatal heart attack.

The challenge for organisers of such events is to reduce risk to an acceptable level by careful planning and by introducing new procedures and technologies where available, as safety standards change over time. Working out the safety standards for a particular sporting event at a particular time involves looking at a number of factors:

• perceived level of acceptable risk for participants and audience

Bike races carry risk both for the competitors and the audience.

- current legislation and legal precedents
- availability of risk management solutions
- development and implementation of plans, procedures and control mechanisms.

The last of these is extremely important for event organisers, for if they could show that their procedures for managing risk were well considered and well implemented, this would stand them in good stead if a charge of negligence were laid.

From the following interview with Mr Max Mosley, President of the Federation Internationale de l'Automobile (FIA), reported on the Australian Grand Prix website <www.grandprix.com.au/cars/>, it is evident that the issue of risk is always on the agenda for the organisers of this race and that change is something that they have to deal with.

Q: Just going back to safety quickly … a couple of issues, separate, but possibly disastrous if combined. There are suggestions a number of teams have failed crash tests. That is the first part. The second part is: almost a quarter of the field will be made up of rookies this year. Are they concerns for you?

Mosley: The crash tests, that's very worrying for the team concerned, because when they fail, they have to do it again. But what is happening is that the teams want to build the chassis as light as they possibly can, but still pass the crash tests, and sometimes they overdo the lightness and then they have to strengthen it and come back and do the tests again. Inconvenient for them, but it isn't really an issue for us. The question of the rookies is always a slight problem, but don't forget that the great majority of these people have a huge fund of experience in other forms of racing, so it shouldn't present a problem. But inevitably, in any sport, you're going to have new people coming in all the time and at this level in Formula One we do have the safeguard of the lower formulae. But it is a process which is bound to happen and I think the experienced drivers will take account of this, and I hope the rookies will be very careful.

Another important risk issue for sporting event organisers concerns temporary fencing and seating. Recently, a theatre company was fined $40 000 for two breaches of the Occupational Health and Safety Act because a temporary seating stand collapsed at a play resulting in four people being hospitalised. According to *WorkCover News*, Issue 16, the judge determined that the theatre company had not obtained a report from a structural engineer and had not taken steps to ensure that correct safety standards had been met.

This sporting venue is well designed, not only for the comfort and convenience of the audience and the sportspeople, but also for the excellent facilities provided for the organisers and contractors. First-class facilities help to improve safety.

From the discussion of the types of risk the event organiser could face, it is clear that a first-rate risk management strategy is essential.

STRATEGIC RISK MANAGEMENT

Risk management is recognised as an integral part of good management practice. It is an iterative process consisting of steps which, when undertaken in sequence, enable continual improvement in decision-making. Risk management is the term applied to a logical and systematic method of identifying, analysing, evaluating, treating, monitoring and communicating risks associated with any activity, function or process in a way that will enable organisations to minimise losses and maximise opportunities. Risk management is as much about identifying opportunities as avoiding or mitigating losses.

AS/NZS 4360:1999 : Risk management

Strategic risk management is not only about dealing with threats it is also about dealing with opportunities. Both concepts were introduced in Chapter 3 and discussed in relation to marketing in Chapter 7.

There are many situations in which an event business may be poorly placed to capitalise on opportunities. Where, for example, an unexpectedly high number of people turn up for an event, this can have many repercussions. An annual show may expect approximately a million visitors over five days, and while it may be feasible to manage this number if the event audience is fairly evenly spread over this period, rainy weather for the first three days may see the attendance at a record low, followed by a huge surge on the fourth day. The venue may be stretched beyond capacity, leading to dissatisfaction on the part of those attending, long queues, delays and, in the worst case, risks to safety. Being unable to meet this demand can occur when tickets have been oversold or the organisers have not expected everyone to turn up at the same time. In the most serious of cases, spectators arriving for soccer matches have stormed the stadium leading to fatal crowd crush (see examples in Chapter 19).

The steps and terms used in the Australian and New Zealand Standard, Risk Management AS/NZS 4360:1999 (see Fig. 10.1), will be used to identify and analyse risks for events. This task is fundamental to the event manager's role. Indeed, the capacity to think strategically and to plan at a micro level is a valuable attribute for an event manager.

Fig. 10.1

Risk management model.

Establish the context

⇓

Identify the risk

⇓

Analyse the risk

⇓

Evaluate the risk

⇓

Treat the risk

Risk management strategies must be put in place during the following developmental phases of an event:

- development of concept and marketing strategy (identify strategic risk)
- logistics planning, for example, development of registration or ticketing policies (identify operational risk at macro level)
- equipment safety and food safety planning (identify operational risk at micro level).

The above risk management model will be used again in later operational chapters dealing with safety, security and spectator management.

Establishing the context

The process of establishing the context for the risk management process provides guidance for decision-makers, as well as establishing the scope for the development of risk management policies and plans.

Strategic context

The focus of the strategic context is on the external environment. For the event manager, this means looking at the global economy, the local economy, tourism trends, political initiatives, competitive forces and social trends. As the world becomes globally oriented, consideration must be given to scheduled competitive major events (particularly sport and entertainment).

Organisational context

The size of the event or event business and its dependence on market segments creates the organisational context. All factors involving markets, products and timing are part of the organisational context. For example, an event business that specialises in conference organisation for the accounting profession (with associated tours, entertainment, etc.) may find hat new probity guidelines will limit the scope of all future events and, in turn, have a major impact on profit margins. Reliance on any one market, including a particular source country for overseas tourists, is another aspect of organisational context that might need to be reviewed with a view to diversification. Extreme sports events clearly carry a higher risk than many others, as do some music concerts. However, these may be niche markets for a particular event company and they may need to accept (to some degree) the level of risk involved. Effort would be made to treat these risks, rather than avoid them by planning different types of events.

Risk management context

Specific security threats, such as terrorism, would be a significant factor in the risk context. Close liaison with relevant authorities and task forces would provide more specific information about the level of threat for different types of public event.

As a further example, a dramatic increase in insurance premiums may necessitate a review of all organisational and operational activities, the level and type of insurance coverage the organisation carries and the level of risk the organisation is prepared to carry. The issue for the organisation would be to decide on the appropriate level of insurance cover. This would mean looking at 'replacement costs' and policy limits. Insurers can provide quotes with specific attention given to:

- public liability, volunteer personal accident and weather cover for all community and corporate events
- prize indemnity: hole-in-one tournaments, sporting events and corporate promotions
- equipment cover for performers and artists, event organisers and promoters.

The different types of insurance were covered comprehensively in Chapter 5.

Identifying the risk

The process of identifying risk can be undertaken by brainstorming the following questions:

- What are the worst things that could happen?
- Where are we exposed?
- What are the best things that could happen?
- How would we cope?

There are a number of sources of risk. Table 10.1 on page 148 includes a framework for looking at the generic sources, together with specific examples from the event industry.

When considering generic sources of risk, an event organiser needs to look at a range of potential risk events which could conceivably impact on their specific operation. For example, a major breakdown of lighting equipment at an event could be nothing short of catastrophic. If preventative measures and contingency plans were in place, this risk could be minimised (as will be discussed later in the chapter).

Table 10.1

Generic sources of risk.

Source of strategic risk	Examples of event risk
Human behaviour	Celebrity endorses an event unexpectedly, resulting in wide positive media exposure and crowd crush.
	Security staff member critically injures fan.
	Senior management disguises significant losses.
Technology and technical issues	Video conferencing facility at conference centre fails during high-profile session with global audience.
	IT specialist leaves company.
	Lighting and sound systems are incompatible with local conditions.
Occupational health and safety	Passive smoking claims impact on compensation claims.
	Negative media exposure causes damage to reputation.
	Rides declared unsafe by authorities.
Economic	Decrease in family disposable income due to rapid increase in interest rates leads to lower patronage.
	Budget tightening results in cancellation or downsizing of all corporate Christmas functions.
Legal	Public liability costs lead to cancellation of a community festival.
	Contractual arrangements, such as naming rights, result in disputes between the organisers and competing sponsors.
Political	Emphasis and support for regional events in overseas advertising on Australian tourism has negative impact on capital city events.
	Funding sources for festivals and events dry up.
Financial/market	Economic recession in overseas source country impacts on a major inbound tourism market, impacting on ticket sales.
	Financial institution refuses to cover cash flow crisis.
Property and equipment	Gas supply fails over a sustained period rendering cooking equipment inoperable.
	Rented equipment does not meet safety standards.
Environmental	Fans damage the environment at the Botanic Gardens.
	The local community protests about the approved decibel level of a music concert.
Natural events	Constant rain during event leads to cancellation of performances/games.
	Cyclone devastates marquees and temporary buildings.
	Heat exhaustion causes problems for tennis players and spectators.

Analysing the risk

Risks need to be analysed from various viewpoints. First, what is the **consequence** or impact of the risk event likely to be? Second, what is the **likelihood** of the risk event occurring? Fires tend to have a major or even catastrophic impact, but they are extremely rare. A long, rainy holiday season could have a moderate financial impact, and in the life of certain event businesses the likelihood of this is almost certain. In Table 10.2 the qualitative measures of consequence or impact of an incident are provided, and the qualitative measures of the likelihood of an incident occurring are given in Table 10.3.

Table 10.2

Qualitative measures of consequence or impact of an incident.

Level	Descriptor	Example
1	Insignificant	No injuries, low financial loss
2	Minor	First aid treatment, on-site release, immediately contained, medium financial loss
3	Moderate	Medical treatment required, on-site release, contained with outside assistance, high financial loss
4	Major	Extensive injuries, loss of production capability, off-site release with no detrimental effects, major financial loss
5	Catastrophic	Death, toxic release off-site with detrimental effect, huge financial loss

Table 10.3

Qualitative measures of likelihood of an incident occurring.

Level	Descriptor	Description
A	Almost certain	Is expected to occur in most circumstances
B	Likely	Will probably occur in most circumstances
C	Possible	Might occur at some time
D	Unlikely	Could occur at some time
E	Rare	May occur, but only in exceptional circumstances

Once the consequence and likelihood have been evaluated, it is then necessary to look at the **level of risk** and decide which risks need treatment. Clearly a potentially catastrophic risk, such as fire, while having a low probability, would still be rated as a high-level risk. The level of risk is calculated by finding the intersection between the likelihood and the consequences (see Table 10.4 on page 150).

After the level of risk has been determined, it is then appropriate to develop a risk analysis form similar to that illustrated in Fig. 10.2 on page 151. The columns in this form that are most important are 'Prevention' and 'Contingency'. From this form it is evident that a number of risks can be expressed in generic terms.

An organisation can take steps to prevent a risk event. Such steps may be based on legal obligations, for example, the installation of a fire detection system.

Table 10.4
Level of risk.

LIKELIHOOD	Insignificant	Minor	Moderate	Major	Catastrophic
Almost certain	High	High	Extreme	Extreme	Extreme
Likely	Moderate	High	High	Extreme	Extreme
Possible	Low	Moderate	High	Extreme	Extreme
Unlikely	Low	Low	Moderate	High	Extreme
Rare	Low	Low	Moderate	High	High

Key:

Extreme An extreme risk requires immediate action as the potential could be devastating to the organisation.

High A high level of risk requires action, as it has the potential to be damaging to the organisation.

Moderate Allocate specific responsibility to a moderate risk and implement monitoring or response procedures.

Low Treat a low level of risk with routine procedures.

AS/NZS 4360:1999 : Risk Management

Contingency planning is necessary in case the risk event occurs. Fire fighting systems would be put in place for such contingency, as would evacuation procedures. Contingency plans need to be developed for all the following emergency situations:

* prohibited access to a facility or venue
* loss of electric power
* communication lines down
* ruptured gas mains
* water damage
* smoke damage
* structural damage
* air or water contamination
* explosion
* chemical release
* trapped persons.

Security risks could include:

* cash stolen in transit
* hold-up at ticket booth
* goods stolen from site
* illegal entry (for example, climbing fences)
* illegal entry to performance or VIP areas
* vandalism to facilities and equipment
* insufficient number of security on duty to control crowds
* untrained and unqualified security staff
* use of excessive force by security staff.

Fig. 10.2

Risk analysis form for an event management company.

Identified risk	Likelihood	Consequence	Level of risk	Prevention	Contingency
Main sponsor withdraws support	Possible	Major	Extreme	• sign long-term contracts with blue chip business partners • maintain ongoing business intelligence activities • maintain ongoing communication to develop business relationship with sponsor	• approach other sponsors • approach government bodies for assistance • take out a short-term loan • extend other sponsorship involvement • cancel the event
Cash flow crisis	Possible	Major	Extreme	• careful budgeting • short-term contracts • monitoring and control of expenses • review pricing • review promotional activities	• increase borrowings • search for new markets • extend promotion • discount tickets • find more sponsorship or funding
Major fatal accident	Rare	Major	High	• safety policies and procedures • staff training • insurance coverage • PR crisis plan	• implement crisis management plan • provide accurate information to the media
Maintenance systems failure	Rare	Major	High	• high calibre staging/engineering staff • systems and procedures for preventative maintenance • insurance	• contingency plans for breakdown of major plant or equipment

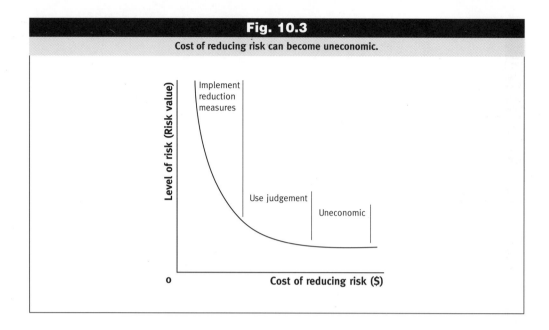

Fig. 10.3

Cost of reducing risk can become uneconomic.

Level of risk (Risk value)

Implement reduction measures

Use judgement

Uneconomic

0

Cost of reducing risk ($)

It must be stressed, however, that not all risks are physical or tangible. For any event risks need to be categorised and evaluated.

Evaluating the risk

The outcome of a risk analysis is a prioritised list of risks for further action. The cost of managing the risk needs to be commensurate with the benefits obtained. Often large benefits can be obtained for a reasonable cost, but to continue to strive for reduction incurs an escalating cost disproportionate to the result. This is called the Law of Diminishing Returns, and is illustrated above in Fig. 10.3.

Treating the risk

Risk treatment involves identifying the range of options for treating the risk, assessing those options and preparing risk treatment plans. There are a number of options for most risk events:

- Avoid the risk by abandoning the activity, for example, abandoning children's rides.
- Reduce the likelihood of the occurrence, for example, implementing prevention programs such as a maintenance program.
- Reduce the severity of the consequences, for example, contingency planning for first aid training.

Risk treatments are linked to the management functions of planning and control. Planning for prevention includes many of the processes described in this book, such as the development of sound contractual arrangements; inspection processes; training; supervision; technical controls and compliance programs. Contingency plans for emergency situations have likewise been discussed at length. And this chapter will close with a brief overview of crisis management planning, particularly in terms of damage control and public relations.

It is important to note that waivers do not release an organisation from its duty of care to the person who signs the waiver. They do not protect organisations which act negligently or fail to act when they should have. Disclaimers (statements that responsibility is not accepted for certain incidents) also do not exempt organisations from their duty of care.

Risk treatment generally identifies the following:

Source of risk	How can the risk arise?
Risk event	What can happen?
Priority	What priority does this risk have in relation to others?
Likelihood	Almost certain, likely, moderate, unlikely, rare?
Consequences	Insignificant, minor, moderate, major, catastrophic?
Level of risk	Extreme, high, moderate, low?
Risk treatment	What will be done to avoid the risk, control the risk, transfer the risk or retain the risk?
Responsibility	What is the name of the person who will implement the risk treatment option?
Resources required	What physical and human resources are needed to implement the risk treatment?
Performance measure	How will it be known that the risk treatment is working?
Timetable	When will the treatment option be implemented?

DEVELOPING A RISK MANAGEMENT POLICY

The Australian and New Zealand Standards bodies recommend the following steps in developing a risk management policy:

- Obtain the support of senior management for ongoing risk analysis, evaluation and treatment.
- Decide who is responsible for managing risks.
- Develop the required documentation.
- Develop a timeline for implementation and ongoing review of the policy.
- Integrate risk management with strategic and operational planning.
- Communicate with staff on an ongoing basis.
- Manage the program at each relevant level and integrate with all other management responsibilities.
- Monitor and review the policy, procedures and outcomes.

In the following situation a policy was developed to stop participants over the age of 50 from participating in an event. In light of the feedback obtained with regard to this policy, no doubt it will be reviewed.

Peter Biscoe reckoned he was in good shape for yesterday's Rough Water swim at Bondi Beach. But the former champion swimmer, lifesaver and water polo player didn't get his chance. He was among about 90 swimmers aged over 49 who were excluded from the 1-kilometre swim because of rough surf.

> *Organisers said they had made the decision based on the greater health risks —*
> *particularly of heart attacks — among older swimmers. It didn't sit well with Mr Biscoe.*
> *'[Age] is an extremely arbitrary and irrational basis on which to exclude people', he said.*
> *'Any of my children could go in the race, even though I am a much stronger swimmer*
> *than any of them.'*
>
> *Last night, the head of the Anti-Discrimination Board, Chris Puplick, said such a*
> *decision based on age, not fitness, might breach the state's discrimination laws.*
>
> Geesche Jacobsen, *Sydney Morning Herald*, 13 January 2003

IMPLEMENTING AND MONITORING RISK MANAGEMENT STRATEGIES

Risk management is an iterative, ongoing process. It occurs during the event planning phase but must also become part of the minute by minute management of an event. Activities must be monitored on an ongoing basis using an incident report form (illustrated in Chapter 18). These incidents must be analysed and 'near miss' incidents given special attention. Likewise any incidents that indicate a risk to health, safety and security should be given special attention and action taken immediately to reduce or eliminate the risk.

CRISIS MANAGEMENT

While most organisations cannot predict the exact nature of a crisis, it is useful to develop a communications strategy for each of the following scenarios:

- spontaneous and unexpected crisis (failure of water supply, cyclone, fire)
- slowly emerging crisis (doping issues)
- sustained crisis (airline failure and cancellation of flights).

A crisis protocol for what to do, what to say and who should say it needs to be developed. These steps are recommended:

- Notify senior management.
- Obtain information.
- Reach decisions on statements and actions.
- Set up a media centre.
- Send journalists' questions up the line to a spokesperson and respond promptly with a prepared response, not 'off the cuff'.
- Provide accurate, reliable information to the media.
- Brief and counsel employees.
- Maintain a watching brief as the issue emerges.
- Provide information to the public via the Internet or advertising.

Additionally, the spokesperson should:

- show deep concern
- avoid speculation
- avoid attributing blame, making excuses or passing the buck
- avoid providing information unless sure of the facts

Conduct a risk management analysis using a table format and appropriate headings (see Fig. 10.2 on page 151 as an example) for at least two of the following events:

- Outdoor launch of a soft drink product, with entertainment, for a target audience of children aged nine to fourteen.
- Minor/local surf carnival (run, swim, paddle) for all age groups, with a handicapping system based on heat times.
- Wedding ceremony on the beach followed by a reception at the local RSL Club.
- School swimming competition for high school students of the Asia-Pacific region.

- explain the steps to be taken.

ACTIVITY

Consider some of the social and legal issues relating to the use and abuse of alcohol and drugs at events. Identify some of the factors that increase the level of this risk for the event organiser. Identify ways in which this risk can be minimised and managed.

LINKS

Australian and New Zealand Standards for Risk Management
www.standards.com.au/catalogue/script/Details.asp?DocN=stds000023835

Australian Institute of Risk Management
www.airm.org.au/index.cfm?L1=1&L2=30&Item=15

Big Day Out event
www.bigdayout.com

Crowdsafe
www.crowdsafe.com

Insurance and Risk Management
http://203.32.220.220/docushare/dscgi/admin.py/View/Collection-79
Public Relations Society of America (crisis management)
www.prsa.org/_Resources/topic/crisis.asp?indent=topic34

Queensland Government (risk management)
www.riskmanagement.qld.gov.au/info/faq/faq_6.htm

SUMMARY

The event industry has experienced many downturns that have had a serious impact on business. The SARS epidemic caused cancellation of many conferences, meetings and exhibitions. Internal forces, such as destabilising and lengthy contract disputes or serious accidents, can also impact negatively on a business in this industry. For these reasons, this and other chapters in this book stress the value of risk management planning for all stages of event planning, from concept through to execution. Strategic and operational risk management can prevent damage to a company's financial status and/or reputation. This is achieved through contingency and crisis management planning, which assists in minimising losses and maximising benefits.

CHAPTER ELEVEN

EVENT

PROPOSALS AND BIDS

ON COMPLETION OF THIS CHAPTER YOU WILL BE ABLE TO:

- identify key event impacts
- interpret an event brief
- develop a bid proposal
- develop bid materials
- present a bid proposal.

Adelaide wins bid to host 2007 Games

South Australia expects to raise $30 million in revenue when it hosts the World Police and Fire Games in 2007. In excess of 15 000 competitors and supporters from around the world are expected to descend on Adelaide for 10 days of action at one of the world's biggest sporting events. South Australian Tourism Minister, Joan Hall, described Adelaide's winning bid as a coup for the tourism industry. The local industry is confident the Games will generate tourist dollars and interest in Australia as a tourist destination, in much the same vein as the Sydney 2000 Olympic Games. Staging the Games will cost South Australia $7.74 million, which includes a $4.75 million Games rights fee. The State Government will contribute $4.75 million to the event.

AUSTRALIAN TOURIST COMMISSION, 20 JANUARY 2003

www.atc.net.au/enews.asp?art=148

Many major events are subsidised by public funds since it is recognised that these events have a positive economic impact on the city and country in which they are held. For example, expenditure by event organisers can stimulate the local economy, producing increased demand for goods and services and higher levels of employment. As mentioned previously, an event might also have a significant tourism benefit, attracting both domestic and international visitors. The long-term impact can be significant if the event is given international exposure in the media, raising the city's tourist destination profile. This has certainly been the case for Barcelona, Sydney and Athens following Olympic Games exposure. All media attending a major event are issued with photographs of the city showing it in its best light, and it is common for visiting journalists to develop documentary material about the city and the country in the lead-up to the event. This media coverage (measured in minutes) is worth millions of dollars.

Media attention for events is highly valued.

Other events are designed for social impact. The Croc Festival™ is an innovative event that builds partnerships in regional and remote communities by celebrating youth culture. Involving young indigenous and non-indigenous Australians in visual and performing arts, sports clinics and careers markets in a 100 per cent drug and alcohol free environment, the festival promotes health, education and employment in a spirit of reconciliation. An evaluation of the festival demonstrated that 'there was an overwhelming consensus that The Croc Festival™ was beneficial for the participants, communities, and for Weipa as a town. The Croc has become a symbol for a host of activities conducted in schools and communities as far apart as Cairns and the islands of the Torres Strait.' (Allard et al., 2001) This evaluation illustrates the important link between the aims of the event and its outcomes, which are generally analysed in a post-event evaluation report. In Chapter 23 the subject of evaluation will be covered in more detail.

Planning and evaluation of events are linked, with most event organisations working hard to demonstrate their success in a measurable way.

The main topic for this chapter is bidding and tendering for events. However, bidding does not happen in a vacuum. When bidding, the event organisation must establish credibility using previous event evaluation reports and references to support the bid. Successful use of grant funds, charitable fundraising efforts and sponsor return on investment are all ways to demonstrate a solid reputation for planning, management and evaluation of events.

Table 11.1 provides a simplified outline of the potential impacts of an event and the basis on which they might be monitored. For a major event, a professional event evaluation report would be required, establishing measures for monitoring and reporting. Market research and testimonials would need to be included in the report.

With this wider focus on the potential impacts of an event, the event organisation is in a better

Table 11.1

Monitoring event impacts.

Impact	Monitoring
Social and cultural	Visitor surveys
	Audience participation
	Professional judging
	Media exposure, publicity
Economic	Expenditure by event organisers
	Infrastructure development
	Employment
Tourism	Visitor movements
	Visitor expenditure (event and non-event)
	Survey of destination awareness
	Return visits
	Media exposure, publicity
Environmental	Environmental impact analysis (noise, waste management, damage to natural environment, use of energy and water)

position to bid for larger events and compete with other organisations. A bid document for an event to be held in a park showing how environmental issues would be managed would be looked upon favourably by the potential client.

BIDDING, TENDERING AND APPLYING FOR GRANTS

While the concept of bidding is well known in the sporting event, meeting and convention arenas, it is now increasingly being used in the context of other events. A **bid** is generally a document covering the event concept and planning which is submitted to the organising committee. The submission is sometimes prepared collaboratively by a range of partners, which may include:

- sponsors
- donors
- providers of goods and services
- marketing company
- venue
- government bodies
- convention/event bureaus and associations
- tourism and hospitality partners (airlines, hotel companies)
- voluntary organisations.

The lengthy bidding process for summer and winter Olympic Games events is well known and the website for more information on this topic is provided at the end of this chapter. In the conference area, too, bids are called for long before the meetings are planned. A proposed annual conference with 5000 attendees may be planned 10 years ahead of time, and bids will be called for across the world. In most cases, the larger conventions like to move the event from one continent to another to provide interest and tourism opportunities for delegates.

In some cases, the event comes within the orbit of government, in which case there may be a **tendering** process. This means the same thing, although tendering usually involves only one provider and a procedurally specific and complex submission to the relevant government body. Probity is a significant concern in government tendering and it is essential that each tender document is carefully ranked against select criteria.

For a smaller event, an **expression of interest** (or quote) may be requested from several event companies. This is a more informal process with fewer objective criteria for success. While the cost may be an important factor, the client may be swayed by a highly creative concept.

A **grant** is a request for funding, which does not cover all costs associated with an event. The grant is usually one component of the event funding, in most cases supporting non-profit sporting event initiatives or artistic endeavours. However, grant applications are dealt with in very similar ways to bids with specific criteria to be met. Once the event is over the acquittal process will show how the grant money was spent.

In all cases, the general principles are the same, although the level of detail may differ widely depending on the size and scope of the planned event.

INTERPRETING THE EVENT BRIEF

When preparing a bid document, it is essential that the stated criteria remain the central focus of the bid, as it is against these criteria that the bid will be judged. In some cases, the criteria are listed in general terms; in others, each criterion is given a particular weighting. For example, as Table 11.2 shows, an application for a local council grant may have an assigned value for each section of the submission.

When interpreting the brief it may be necessary to clarify requirements. Following this, an action plan is necessary for preparing the bid. The deadlines for bids and tenders are immutable and for this reason all documents must be accurate and flawlessly presented on time.

RESEARCHING INFORMATION FOR A BID OR TENDER

When preparing a bid an extensive range of information may be required, including a review of current events on the event calendar where this is relevant, as well as a review of potential competitors. An analysis of the potential audience for the event, as described in Chapter 7 on 'Event Marketing', is also essential. This might include a detailed investigation of local demographics and tourism visitation to the region.

Most importantly, the client or bidding organisation needs to be investigated. Many local councils have a range of policies (such as the local environment plan) and community profiles and it is essential to fit within these guidelines. A corporate organisation may have a particular sponsorship policy and the bidder would not want to suggest a sponsor (or activity) that was inappropriate in terms of the organisation's community profile.

The event concept and plan, including the budget, play an important part in establishing

Table 11.2

Weighting of criteria for a grant application.

Criteria	Points
Fit with current event calendar — utilising date not currently being used	10
Innovative ideas and match with community profile, feasibility analysis	20
Event impacts, including social and environmental	10
Level of contribution to the event by other supporters:	
• sponsors	
• applicant	
• other grants or subsidies	10
Budget including cash flow	10
Planning, including business plan, marketing plan, timelines	20
Legal compliance, stakeholder consultation	10
Risk management plan	20
Potential value to the district economy	
$25 000 – $50 000	
$50 001 – $100 000	
$100 001 – $200 000	
Over $200 000	20
Tourism visitation to the region	
200–500	
500–1000	
1000–2500	20
Level of community support	20
Community legacy	10
Previous event reports, referees	20
TOTAL	

the credibility of the bidding event organisation. The professionalism of bids varies widely and the selection of the successful organisation is very easy when professional expertise is immediately apparent in a bid document. However, no amount of professionalism is going to allow a bid to be accepted if the criteria are not accurately addressed.

ADDRESSING THE CRITERIA IN THE BID

In the following two sections, the criteria that may need to be addressed when applying for an arts festival grant can be compared with those to be dealt with when applying for a grant for a sporting event. It is evident that the grounds on which the grant will be made in each case are quite different and need to be taken into account by the applicant. The first rule in bidding for events is to be mindful of the criteria!

The following brief by Arts Victoria provides specific funding guidelines that illustrate the criteria by which a bid for funding support for an arts festival may be judged. Their website is listed at the end of the chapter.

ARTS VICTORIA Victoria
The Place To Be

Purpose — Local Festivals Program

The Local Festivals Program aims to support a sustainable and diverse mix of local festivals in urban, regional and rural parts of Victoria that demonstrate a high level of innovative and professional arts programming, strong community participation and active audience engagement.

By supporting local festivals, access to the arts will become more widespread in Victoria. More Victorians will be able to celebrate local distinctiveness through the arts and will have greater potential to explore their artistic and creative interests in their local community.

Funding through this program is available to support festivals that are well managed, build on professional arts strengths, support innovative ideas and cultivate new talent, and have a high level of local involvement, including the support of appropriate agencies such as Local Government, tourism agencies and corporate supporters. Funding is for festivals occurring in Victoria within a localised environment and a discrete time frame.

Applicants must demonstrate a highly developed artistic rationale for the festival, strong partnerships with the local community, an ability to engage with new audiences and sound management.

Grants of up to $25 000 are available on a project basis for local arts festivals that have a sound track record for a minimum of two years. Support is provided for professional artist fees and marketing costs.

Aims and Objectives

The Local Festivals Program aims to:

- widen opportunities for all Victorians to access the arts
- increase participation and engagement in arts and cultural activities
- enhance community creativity and community well-being
- promote community cultural participation through volunteering.

Evaluation Criteria

Submissions will be evaluated against the following standards:

- Artistic merit — based on the festival's overall artistic framework/rationale, the extent to which the artistic program contributes to the evolution of the festival and introduces new ideas or experiences that might not otherwise happen, and the quality of the proposed artists.
- Community relationship — incorporates genuine community involvement in well-conceived artistic work delivered at a high standard. This includes partnerships with local business and local government and not-for-profit organisations and volunteers.
- Management plan — based on the festival management and budget plan being achievable and structured appropriately to the scale and complexity of the festival. The plan must incorporate suitable measures to ensure sustainability of the festival and mitigate risk.
- Marketing plan — demonstrates how the festival will broaden community participation in the arts as well as attract new audiences and increase existing audiences.
- Public outcome — based on the benefits and values that will accrue from the project for both the participating artist/s and the community.

Definitions

Professional artist — a practising artist who has specialised training in their field (not necessarily in academic institutions), is recognised by their peers (professional practitioners working in the art form area), is committed to devoting significant time to artistic activity and has a history of public presentation.

Community — a community may be defined culturally, geographically and/or by other distinguishing characteristics. It may also include specific communities — such as schools, prisons, universities and hospitals — and communities with specific interests such as the environment.

Public outcome — the tangible and intangible benefits to the public that accrue from a project. It can be defined in artistic terms but when linked to a community development context may also refer to cultural, social, economic and environmental outcomes.

Priorities

Priority will be given to funding Victorian artists' fees, however festivals applying for interstate or international artists' fees may be considered in instances where the applicant can demonstrate that the desired outcome cannot be achieved with Victorian artists.

Funding is provided for artists' fees, as part of the overall festival program, and/or marketing costs. The program will not fund the entire cost of a festival program and applicants are expected to have support from other sources, whether cash and/or in-kind. In general, the larger the funding requested the higher the level of support required from other sources. There is an expectation that the community or its representative body such as Local Government will contribute to other costs.

Eligibility

The proposal must involve professional artists. The program only accepts proposals from organisations for non-profit making activities and only the festival director/manager or festival organising body such as Local Government can apply for support. The program does not support competitions and eisteddfods, fund raising activity, film festivals or projects that will only benefit a discrete audience, to the exclusion of the broader community, e.g. clubs or schools.

Assessment Process

Local Festivals applications are assessed by a committee comprising external arts sector representatives and Arts Victoria staff. The committee formulates recommendations for final approval by the Minister for the Arts.

How to Apply

Note that it is important to explain how the festival's artistic program/or marketing will meet the stated aims, priorities and evaluation criteria for the Local Festivals Program ...

1. Festival Description

   Provide a short description of the Festival (maximum 25 words)

2. The Art

   Describe the professional arts content of the festival, including:
   * the artistic framework/rationale for the festival
   * how the proposed program fits within this framework/rationale
   * the creative personnel and artists involved and details of their professional arts experience
   * how the proposed program introduces new ideas into the local community and evolves the festival's development
   * how local identity is being expressed or reflected in the festival program
   * all applicants must attach a full draft artistic program for the festival as part of the support material.

3. The Community

Please describe community involvement and links with the community organisations including:

- partnerships that are being developed between artists in the festival, local artists and the community
- the partnerships with key local organisations such as the Local Government, community organisations and main street businesses
- volunteers that are involved in the management and the artistic programming of the festival.

4. The Audience

Please provide information on your audience, including the:

- target audience for the festival
- breakdown of where the festival audience comes from, e.g. town, shire, region, interstate
- communication strategy for the festival
- strategies to reach new audiences, e.g. communication, programming strategies
- if you are applying for marketing costs, you must attach a fully costed marketing plan for the festival as part of the support material.

5. The Management

- who will manage the project and their experience in organising festivals, professional arts programming
- festival planning and timelines
- outline of the festival's business and marketing plans
- revenue-generating strategies and broad revenue sources
- evaluation plans for the festival
- risk assessment strategies (i.e. people, plans and resources).

<www.arts.vic.gov.au>

Sporting events

In contrast to arts festivals, sporting events generally have a different focus and different funding arrangements. Many sporting events are run by volunteers and are not for profit. To attract funding they might need to show how the event will:

- meet the needs of participating players, volunteers and officials
- meet the needs of the event audience/spectators
- enhance the profile of the sport in question
- generate visitors to the city/town
- attract a key market segment (for example, retirees)
- provide an ongoing competition
- attract media exposure
- provide direct and indirect dollar returns to the community
- sit within the current calendar, compatible with other events
- show potential for long-term self-sufficiency
- utilise existing facilities
- create minimum environmental impact
- reinforce community health messages relating to sport and fitness.

Where a submission is made for an event involving children, the organisation would need to demonstrate an awareness of potential child abuse issues in sport, relevant legislation and guidelines for ethics policies. This is an example of a specific area in which these two types of bid might differ. The Play by the Rules website at the end of the chapter provides a user-friendly guide to relevant sport legislation. A guide for planning community sporting events is also provided by Bunbury, Western Australia, and is likewise listed under 'Links'. Similar guides are available from most councils.

TYPES OF BIDS

Bids are generally done at three levels: national, state and local. A bid to host an international meeting or event would usually be put together by a consortium of government authorities, the state convention bureau and the event management organisation. Tourism Events Australia has been developed at **federal** level to support Australia's branding as an events destination and to co-ordinate international bids. For many large conferences and events the bidding process is fiercely competitive. Issues surrounding the staging of the Rugby World Cup in 2003 created ill feeling between organisers in Australia and New Zealand when the event took place exclusively on Australian soil after earlier plans had games scheduled for both countries.

Many **state** organisations compete against each other for national events, all competing for high profiles in sport, business and arts/entertainment. Motor races, major conferences and performing art festivals are just a few areas in which the states are competitive.

Finally, event organisations compete with one another on a **local** level for the same event. Most government initiated events are listed as government tenders for which the process is highly regulated. Event bureaus in each state and territory also bring planned events to the attention of their members.

Woodford Folk Festival wins $650 000 boost

The Queensland Government says a funding boost for the Woodford Folk Festival will help secure the event as a major tourist attraction. The festival is held at Woodford north of Brisbane each year between Christmas and New Year. Premier Peter Beattie, who is on the Sunshine Coast for a community Cabinet meeting, has announced $650 000 for the festival over two years. He says the internationally recognised event attracts about 80 000 people each year. 'The good thing about that, almost a third of them ... were from interstate and just under 4 per cent were from overseas — that's good news for Queensland', Mr Beattie said. 'It has an estimated economic impact of just under $11 million to the state and so what we want to do is work with the organisers and the Sunshine Coast community to build on that.'

BID DETAIL

Below is an outline of the type of information that is included in a bid document or proposal:

- covering letter
- cover sheet
- executive summary
- event concept or theme
- event dates and program
- event city, tourism infrastrucure, event infrastructure, attractions, accessibility, etc.
- marketing and promotional activities
- event audience
- venue/s and floor plans, capacity
- event organisation/management
- budget
- ticketing, fees
- tours, travel and accommodation
- social activities
- event staffing
- staging and logistics
- special features
- event services
- technical requirements
- risk management plan
- impacts and evaluation methods.

Clearly not all would be relevant to every event. Bid documents for conferences, incentive tours, sporting events, arts festivals and community parades would all be quite different. For more detail, readers can refer to Appendix A, which provides a checklist for an event proposal.

As appendices the following would be included:

- letters of support (particularly from high-profile politicians or heads of government bodies)
- testimonials from previous satisfied clients
- previous event evaluation reports
- financial records/audits
- specified documents such as business registration and insurances.

PRESENTATION OF THE BID DOCUMENT

It is absolutely essential that the bid document is prepared in a timely manner so that there is sufficient time for professional desktop publishing and printing input. A complete project plan with timelines is needed for the bid process to ensure that the bid is delivered on time. When the document is prepared in a hurry, simple mistakes or failure to address all assessment criteria can ruin any chance of success with the assessment panel. For example, if the tendering specifications require a copy of the business registration or the public liability insurance policy and this is not included, the document will not reach the committee/panel for assessment.

In some cases the event bid is presented to a panel or client in person. Once again, this presentation needs to be highly professional and supported by a multimedia presentation of the event concept. Artist impressions, maps, diagrams, models and other visual aids can be impressive if the event is creative and concept based.

CASE STUDY

Hidden Valley (your local) Council would like to expand their event calendar while at the same time achieving a wide range of other objectives, including:

- promoting a sense of pride and community identity
- increasing access to community events to everyone in the community
- promoting cultural and disability awareness in the community
- contributing to the profile of the council
- creating an environment for innovation and creativity within the community
- leaving a lasting legacy to the community.

The council will provide funding to the value of $60 000 and this must be earmarked for specific components of the planned event. You will need other sources of funding to launch the whole concept.

Investigate the calendar of events in your local area and develop an event concept and bid which will meet the aims listed for Hidden Valley. Use the criteria and points allocated in Table 11.2 earlier in the chapter when preparing your submission. Ideally, you should work with other students, some playing the role of the council and assessing each of the bids presented, and then rotating roles. Detailed feedback should be provided on each bid document and presentation. This mirrors the real life experience of bid presentation.

ACTIVITIES

- *Visit the website for the Department of Sport and Recreation in your state or territory and find out whether there are grants for sporting events. Find out the basis on which these grants are approved.*
- *Visit the websites of five events listed in Appendix D and find out whether each event has been supported by government or similar grants.*
- *The Special Events website <www.specialevents.com.au> has an archive of magazine articles and media links. Read some of the articles and analyse two events in recent times that have struggled financially or recovered from a slump to become more financially successful.*

LINKS

Arts Victoria
www.arts.vic.gov.au

Australian Sports Commission (harassment free sport)
www.activeaustralia.org/hfs/child_prot.htm

Bunbury, WA Community and Sporting Events Guide
www.bunbury.wa.gov.au/Downloads/Parks%20Information%20Kit/Information%20Kit%202003.PDF

EventCorp
www.westernaustralia.com/en/Industry/Events+Opportunities/Events+Bidding.htm

International Olympic Committee (IOC) choice of host city
www.olympic.org/uk/organisation/missions/cities_uk.asp

Landmark Special Event (Peter Jones)
www.specialevents.com.au/archiveprev/centenary2001/cofmel.html

Play by the Rules
www.playbytherules.net.au/legislation.html

SUMMARY

Bids for events must show that the event is going to be successful. In most cases, the event organising committee establishes the criteria for success and the bid document must address those criteria. The same applies for grant applications. Understanding the potential impacts (economic, tourism, social and environmental) is helpful since the final evaluation of the event must demonstrate that the aims and objectives have been successfully achieved. Indeed, a bid document must include a range of past successes as evidence that this event will follow suit. Bidding for events is fiercely competitive, particularly on the international stage. At the local level, many community events rely on grants for their continued success as such events impact positively on the local community.

PART TWO

OPERATIONAL PLANNING

I n this section the detailed operational planning required for successful events will be covered, including the logistics of setting up an event and breaking it down afterwards. An event manager needs to plan the implementation of events at micro level, with attention to every detail. Forgetting the safety pins for attaching runners' bibs would be an example of a minor mistake that could have serious repercussions, including delayed telecast of a marathon. Extension cords, power boards, gaffa tape, pen knife, torch and brandy flask are essential components of the event manager's toolkit! This section will deal with production and staging, staffing, safety and security, spectator management, protocol, catering and waste management. These are some of the many operational details that need to be finalised before an event. In addition, it will look at event promotion and evaluation, as well as careers in a changing environment. The outline of the event proposal in Appendix A will prove useful for those interested in a career in this exciting industry.

COMPETENCIES

Chapter 12	Event Project Management	THHGGA09B (Element 02)	Manage projects
		THTFME02B	Provide on-site event management services (in part only)
Chapter 13	Event Promotion	BSBMKG503A	Develop a marketing communications plan
Chapter 14	Staging Management	THTFME06A CUEEVT03A	Manage event contractors Integrate knowledge of creative and technical production into management processes
Chapter 15	Staffing and Volunteer Management	SRXHRM001A	Manage volunteers

Chapter 16	People Performance Management	THHGLE08B	Lead and manage people
Chapter 17	On-site Management	THTFME02B	Provide on-site event management services
		THTFME07A	Organise and monitor infrastructure for outdoor events
Chapter 18	Safety and Security	THHGLE02B	Implement workplace health, safety and security procedures
		SRXOHS003A	Establish, maintain and evaluate occupational health and safety system
Chapter 19	Spectator Management	SRXEVT007A	Manage spectators at an event or program
Chapter 20	Event Protocol	THTFME09A	Develop and update knowledge of protocol
Chapter 21	Event Catering	THHSCAT02B	Plan the catering for an event or function
Chapter 22	Waste and Environmental Management	BSBCMN413A	Implement and monitor environmental policies
Chapter 23	Event Impact and Evaluation	THHFGGA09B Element 03	Manage projects
Chapter 24	Careers in a Changing Environment		
Appendix A	Integrated Assessment — Event Proposal	SRXEVT005A	Manage special events

CHAPTER TWELVE

EVENT

PROJECT MANAGEMENT

ON COMPLETION OF THIS CHAPTER YOU WILL BE ABLE TO:

- identify the purpose, aims and objectives of an event
- develop an event proposal or outline
- identify the team and the stakeholders involved in staging an event
- plan the location and layout of an event using maps/illustrations
- use charts and run sheets to develop timelines
- develop management control systems, such as checklists.

Successful event management involves many people undertaking separate tasks in a co-ordinated manner. In Mosman this involves staff from every section of Council, staff in several other state agencies, staff of companies and clubs, as well as volunteers. Events must be managed in accordance with not only Council's own policies, but also various state laws and regulations.

Only a small portion of this effort is visible to the general public. Even if the event runs smoothly there will be some negative feedback as some degree of inconvenience is inevitable. If the event is poorly managed, however, the impact can be profound with damage to property and to the natural environment, with public safety threatened, and with widespread dissatisfaction by visitors and local residents alike.

MOSMAN MUNICIPAL COUNCIL
SPECIAL EVENT MANAGEMENT OPERATIONS MANUAL

As this statement from a special event operations manual so clearly illustrates, planning and organisation are the key elements that determine the success of an event. For most event organisers, the first stop is the local council. The local council will provide guidelines on the possible impact of your event, such as the impact of noise. This may be a factor even if your event is not being held at a public venue. Another useful contact is the local tourism office. This office, with links to corporate offices in each state and territory, plays an important part in the strategic management of events and, in many cases, provides support in a number of other ways, such as listing events on their website.

However, before making these contacts, you need to develop the event concept. As we learnt in Chapter 2, this involves defining the event's purpose and aims, as well as the specific objectives on which the success of the event will be measured. Funding for your event may come from grants or from sponsors, but all stakeholders have to be provided with a good understanding of the event concept before you proceed further. If your client is the one funding the event, the provision of a clearly developed concept, plan and evaluation strategy will generally avoid problems down the line, including legal ones.

Effective planning ensures the provision of all necessary services and amenities at an event.

DEVELOP A MISSION/PURPOSE STATEMENT

The first step is to develop a simple statement that summarises the purpose or mission of the event. Too often, the purpose of the event becomes less and less clear as the event approaches. Different stakeholders have different interests and this can sometimes lead to a change of focus of which most stakeholders are unaware. The purpose of an event could be, for example, 'to commemorate the history of our town in an historically authentic parade that involves the community and is supported by the community'. In contrast, a sporting event may have as its mission statement 'to attract both loyal team supporters and first-time spectators (potential regulars) in an effort to improve ticket sales and thus the viability of the competition and venue'.

The mission statement should ensure that planning and implementation do not go off the rails and that the initial intent is realised.

The Adelaide Arts Festival is a very successful event, in some ways similar to the Edinburgh Festival mentioned in Chapter 7. The city also hosts the Adelaide Festival of Ideas which has a unique purpose: it is described as an 'intellectual celebration' that 'challenges current thought and practice'. The festival takes place over four days, gathering some of the world's most eminent and provocative speakers:

Ideas are the currency of our information age — they challenge the present and build our future.

Since the inaugural festival in 1999 the Adelaide Festival of Ideas has been committed to the presentation of new ideas and the exploration of issues and themes in a greater depth than global 'sound bite' mainstream media is capable of doing. Past topics have included explorations of population, reconciliation, water, inter-planetary exploration, and democracy, survival and co-operation.

The Adelaide Festival Centre

ESTABLISH THE AIMS OF THE EVENT

The purpose can be broken down further into general aims and specific measurable objectives. An event could have any one, or more, of the following aims:

- improving community attitudes to health and fitness through participation in sporting activities
- increasing civic pride
- injecting funds into the local economy
- raising funds for a charitable cause
- increasing tourist numbers to a specific destination
- extending the tourist season
- launching a new product
- raising revenue through ticket sales
- providing entertainment
- building team loyalty
- raising the profile of the town or city
- celebrating an historical event
- enhancing the reputation of a convention organiser/venue
- conducting an inspirational ceremony
- providing a unique experience
- increasing product sales
- acknowledging award winners (for example, tourism awards or staff awards)
- producing media coverage
- highlighting the main point of a conference.

Aims vary widely from one event to another, and this is one of the challenges for the event manager. One event might have social impact aims while another might be profit oriented. It cannot be stressed enough that everything to do with the event must reinforce the purpose and the aims. Choice of colours, entertainment, presentations, and so on must all work together in order to fulfil the purpose and aims of the event. A client may arrive at a meeting with an event organiser and say, 'I want a banquet for 200 people with a celebrity entertainer', and it may only emerge through questioning that the aim of the event is to recognise key staff, to present awards and to reinforce success. This is something that must be established early in the negotiation process and focused on during all the planning stages. The purpose is easily lost during the implementation phases.

The Edinburgh Festival was described in Chapter 7 as an artistic and marketing success. The aims of this event are:

- to promote and encourage arts of the highest possible standard
- to reflect international culture in presentation to Scottish audiences and to reflect Scottish culture in presentation to international audiences
- to bring together a program of events in an innovative way that cannot easily be achieved by other organisations
- to offer equal opportunity for all sections of the public to experience and enjoy the arts, and thus encourage participation through other organisations throughout the year
- to promote the educational, cultural and economic well-being of the City and people of Edinburgh and Scotland.

Edinburgh International Festival <www.eif.co.uk>

Like many of the arts festivals mentioned, Canberra's annual Floriade aims to enhance the perception of that city as a tourist destination and to achieve targets for attendance by domestic and international tourists as part of its more specific objectives. In 1999 this event attracted 162 000 visitors, over half of whom came from interstate or overseas.

The aims of an event provide the foundation for many aspects of the planning process. An event organiser who becomes distracted from the stated aims is likely to clash with the organising committee and other stakeholders. When working with clients, it is therefore essential to identify the aims early and to use them to inform the planning process. Too often, enthusiasm for the theme or the entertainment overrides the aims and planning goes awry. If, for example, the aim were to increase consumer recognition of the main sponsor, it would be necessary to develop specific objectives and to take steps to ensure that they were achieved. At the end of the event, there should be one or more measures in place to indicate the outcomes of the event, in this case the results of a survey indicating percentage levels of sponsor recognition by the event audience. As an event manager, you need to show, in a measurable way, how the aims have been achieved. Developing objectives helps you to do this.

ESTABLISH THE OBJECTIVES

The aims are used to develop detailed and specific objectives. Ideally, objectives should be realistic and measurable. Targets, percentages and sales are generally the factors used to measure objectives. As an example, an objective could be 'to increase the participation level in the local community's fun walk to 3500, including a cross-section of age groups, ranging from 15 to 60 plus, this target to be reached by the 2005 event'. The number of participants and the ages of participants would be measures of this objective, while a survey on training undertaken in preparation for the walk would indicate less tangible outcomes such as changes in community exercise patterns and attitudes towards fitness and health. As a second example, one objective of an event organiser might be to increase awareness of a sponsor's products, whereas the main objective might be to translate this awareness into sales totalling $3 million, which would be an even more successful outcome. Surveys of spectators and television viewers are used to demonstrate changes in awareness of a sponsor's products.

In summary, an objective is a specific and **measurable** target for achieving outcomes. Evaluation of event outcomes will be covered in more detail in Chapter 23. However, evaluation is not possible if the aims and objectives are not clear in the first place.

Objectives are generally evaluated by measures such as:

- size of audience
- demographics (age, country, place of origin, etc.) of audience
- average expenditure of audience
- sponsor recognition levels
- sales of sponsor products
- economic impact of event
- profit.

SMART objectives are specific, measurable, achievable, realistic and time related:
SPECIFIC — so that we know what is going to be achieved
MEASURABLE — so that we know how success will be judged
ACHIEVABLE — so that it is challenging but not impossible
RESULTS ORIENTED — so that we know what the result will be
TIME ORIENTED — so that we have target date/s.

Examples of specific objectives are to:

- increase the size of the event audience from 12 000 in 2004 to 14 500 in 2007
- attract 1500 international visitors to the 2005 festival, bringing the percentage to 11.5 per cent of the total audience
- increase tourist visitor nights from 6.5 to 7.7 nights
- attract a new major sponsor with naming rights for a five-year contract to 2009.

PREPARE AN EVENT PROPOSAL

A complete outline for an event proposal is included in Appendix A. At this stage of event planning, however, the proposal should include the purpose and the aims and objectives of the event, as well as details on organisation, physical layout and the social, environmental and economic impact, if applicable. Maps and models are extremely useful in illustrating the event concept and more detailed plans will ensure that the client's expectations are realistic.

MAKE USE OF PLANNING TOOLS

Organisation charts, maps and models, Gantt charts, run sheets and checklists are useful tools for presenting material and information to your clients, members of your staff and stakeholders. These are described and illustrated in the following sections.

Maps and models

Maps are a useful way to represent an event, particularly to contractors who may be required to set up the site. It may be necessary to develop more than one map or plan, using CAD (Computer Assisted Drawing) software, since different parties involved in the event will require this material for different purposes. The various people might include:

- builders and designers
- telecommunications and electrical contractors
- emergency response teams
- spectator services hosts
- artists, entertainers and exhibitors
- event audience.

Models are also extremely useful, as most clients find it difficult to visualise three-dimensional concepts. A model can also assist in many aspects of event management, such as crowd control. In this instance, bottlenecks and other potential problems are likely to emerge from viewing a three-dimensional illustration. Most CAD software can also present the information in this way, allowing the event management team to anticipate all design and implementation issues. Examples of maps and models are illustrated in Figs 12.1 and 12.2.

Gantt charts

A Gantt chart is generally used in the early planning days and in the lead-up to an event. In this type of planning sheet, dates are listed across the top of the chart and rules (or blocks) are used to

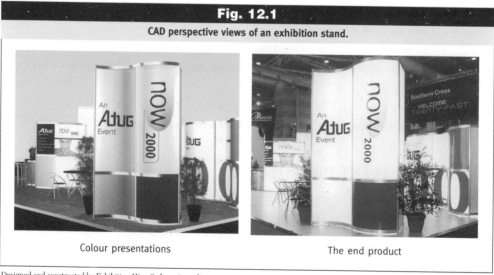

Fig. 12.1
CAD perspective views of an exhibition stand.

Colour presentations   The end product

Designed and constructed by Exhibition Hire, Sydney, Australia

Fig. 12.2

Map of National Folk Festival.

National Folk Festival 2004

Exhibition Park in Canberra

<http://www.folkfestival.asn.au/index.html>

illustrate how long each task (listed at the side of the chart) will take. The benefit of this type of chart is that the interdependence of the tasks can be clearly seen. For example, once you have plotted the process of recruiting, inducting, training and rostering staff for an event, you may realise that the recruitment process needs to start earlier than expected to enable staff to be completely ready for the big day.

Another aspect of planning is identifying the critical path: those elements of the plan that are essential to the successful outcome of the event and therefore high priority. Critical path analysis is beyond the scope of this text; however, the general principle of identifying planning elements on which all else is dependent can be done with a Gantt chart.

In the case of arrangements with sponsors, for example, these need to be finalised before any work can be done on print or promotional material as sponsors need to approve the use of their logos. If one sponsor pulls out of the arrangement, this will have an impact on print production which will, in turn, affect promotional activities and ticket sales.

Project planning software, including specialised event planning software, is available, while for smaller events a spreadsheet is probably sufficient. The trick is to identify the tasks that can be clustered together and to choose the ideal level of detail required in planning the event. At the extreme, the chart can be expanded to a point where even the smallest task is shown (but at this stage it will fill an entire wall and become unmanageable). As with maps, the Gantt chart must be a user-friendly planning tool in order to be effective.

Another point to take into account is that change is an integral part of event planning and it may be necessary to make significant changes that immediately make all your charts redundant. An experienced event manager is able to ascertain the level of planning required to ensure that everyone is clear about their roles and responsibilities, while remaining reasonably open to change.

A high-level planning chart for an event is illustrated in Fig. 12.3. It provides a broad overview of the main event tasks and a general timeline.

Each of these major tasks could also be used as the basis for a more detailed plan. This has been done in Fig. 12.4, which shows the planning process for recruiting and training staff for the above event. This Gantt chart is clearly an example of a fairly detailed level of planning although, even here, the training aspect is not covered fully as there would be many steps involved, including writing training materials and seeking approval of the content from the various functional area managers.

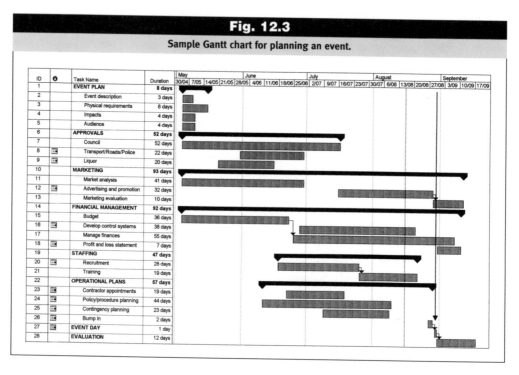

Fig. 12.3

Sample Gantt chart for planning an event.

ID		Task Name	Duration
1		EVENT PLAN	8 days
2		Event description	3 days
3		Physical requirements	8 days
4		Impacts	4 days
5		Audience	4 days
6		APPROVALS	52 days
7		Council	52 days
8		Transport/Roads/Police	22 days
9		Liquor	20 days
10		MARKETING	93 days
11		Market analysis	41 days
12		Advertising and promotion	32 days
13		Marketing evaluation	10 days
14		FINANCIAL MANAGEMENT	92 days
15		Budget	36 days
16		Develop control systems	38 days
17		Manage finances	55 days
18		Profit and loss statement	7 days
19		STAFFING	47 days
20		Recruitment	28 days
21		Training	19 days
22		OPERATIONAL PLANS	57 days
23		Contractor appointments	19 days
24		Policy/procedure planning	44 days
25		Contingency planning	23 days
26		Bump in	2 days
27		EVENT DAY	1 day
28		EVALUATION	12 days

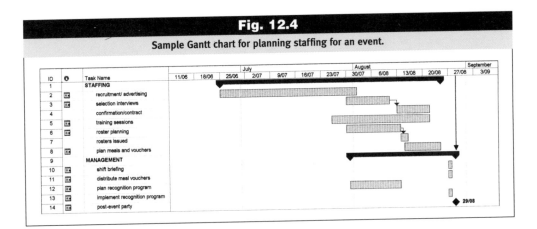

Fig. 12.4

Sample Gantt chart for planning staffing for an event.

ID	❶	Task Name
1		STAFFING
2		recruitment/ advertising
3		selection interviews
4		confirmation/contract
5		training sessions
6		roster planning
7		rosters issued
8		plan meals and vouchers
9		MANAGEMENT
10		shift briefing
11		distribute meal vouchers
12		plan recognition program
13		implement recognition program
14		post-event party

Run sheets

The run sheet is an indispensable tool for most event managers. It is the program, or schedule, of events. In the preliminary stages of planning, the run sheet is quite simple, with times allocated only to specific elements of the event (see the run sheet for a gala dinner in Fig. 12.5 on page 180). This overview of proceedings forms part of the event concept briefing.

As planning progresses, however, the run sheet becomes even more detailed with, for example, timings for dancers, technicians and other staff. This is illustrated in Fig. 12.6 on pages 180 and 181 where bump-in and bump-out are also shown.

Finally, an even more detailed run sheet can be developed (at this stage called the script) to identify each person's role and cues. This is illustrated in Fig. 12.7 on page 182 and the timing of meal service and the cues for recommencement of the 'championships' after the main course are outlined in detail.

Run sheets are an important tool for all stakeholders and participants, from the venue management team through to the subcontractors.

Organisation charts

An organisation chart is another important tool used in planning. Once all tasks have been identified and grouped logically, the staffing requirements for an event become much clearer and can be represented on an organisation chart. This will be described and illustrated more fully in Chapter 15. However, we have illustrated an event committee structure, as an example of an organisation chart, in Fig. 12.8 on page 182.

Checklists

At the most detailed level of planning, a checklist is indispensable. It is a control tool which ensures that the individual performing the tasks has not forgotten a single detail. For example, when checking fire-fighting equipment and emergency exits, it is imperative that a specific checklist be followed, and that it be signed and dated on completion. This is part of the record-keeping process, aimed not only at preventing potential problems, but also at reducing the risk of litigation if anything should go wrong. Detailed and correctly implemented plans reassure the client, allow the event team to work effectively and build confidence in achieving the objectives of the event. A safety checklist is illustrated in Fig. 12.9 on page 183.

Fig. 12.5

Preliminary run sheet for gala dinner — concept stage.

1900	Guests arrive. Pre-dinner drinks in foyer.
1930	Doors to Royal open. Guests move to tables.
1935	MC welcome.
1940	Entrée served.
2000	First 'Championship' (demonstration dance routine).
2010	Main course served. Band starts playing.
2050	Band stops. Second 'Championship' (demo dance routine). Guests drawn onto dance floor at the end.
2115	Dessert served. Band plays.
2140	Band stops. ABTA Awards Presentation (1 award, with 2 finalists).
2225	Ms & Mr Sparkly awarded. Dancing for guests starts properly.
2355	MC announces final winners (all!) and last dance.
2400	Guests depart.

Reproduced with permission of Events Unlimited

Fig. 12.6

Complete run sheet for gala dinner.

0800	Lay dance floor and stage, and lower vertical drapes. Scissor lift ready. Audio subcontractor commences bump-in. Rear projection screen set.
0900	Dance floor and stage set. Stage designer bumps in for stage decoration.
1000	Production meeting.
1100	On-stage set-up commences (audio and video).
1230 (approx)	Band set up.
1430	Technical set-up complete. Table set-up can commence.

Fig. 12.6 CONTINUED

Complete run sheet for gala dinner.

1500	Technical run-through.
1730	All decorations complete.
1745	Rehearsal with MC and SM (probably walk through with music). Band sound check.
1830	All ready.
1845	External sign ON.
1900–1930	Guests arrive. Pre-dinner drinks in foyer.
1900	Dancers arrive. Walk-through and music check.
1915	Pre-set lighting ON.
1925	Walk-in music ON.
1930	Doors open. Guests move to tables. All dancers ready.
1935	MC welcome.
1940	Entrée served.
2000	First 'Championship' (Demonstration dance routine).
2010	Main course served. Band starts playing.
2050	Band stops. Second 'Championship' (Demo dance routine). Guests drawn onto dance floor at the end.
2115	Dessert enters and is served. Band plays.
2140	Band stops. Awards presentation (1 award, with 2 finalists).
2225	Ms & Mr Sparkly awarded. Dancing for guests starts properly.
2355	MC announces final winners (all!) and last dance.
2400	Guests depart. Bump-out commences.
Tue 0230	All clear.

Reproduced with permission of Events Unlimited

Fig. 12.7

Script for part of gala dinner.

2010	Main course served.	
As main nearly cleared		MC and dancers stand by. Dance 2 music ready.
When clear 2050	Band stops and exits.	MC mic ON. Band OFF. MC spot ON. House down.
	MC: Welcome to our next championship, The Self-Booking Samba. Amazingly the finalists are our previous winners. Please welcome them back.	Vision — Self-Booking Samba. Dance floor ON.
	Dancers run on. (2nd dance routine 10 min). Dancers pause at end. MC: And once again it's a tie, isn't that fantastic! Now I know that there are some aspiring champions out there who are probably thinking 'I could never do that!' Well our champions have graciously agreed to teach you some of their steps, so come on up and join in ... MC somehow coaxes people up. When enough on dance floor he cues music with: OK. Let's dance! (About 10 minutes dance coaching)	MC spot OFF. Music 2 ON. MC mic OFF. When music 2 finished cue music 3. MC spot ON. MC mic ON. House UP ½.
		Music 3 ON. MC mic OFF. Kitchen advised 10 min to dessert.
At end		Dance music 3 OFF. Cue march in — SB track 14.

Reproduced with permission of Events Unlimited

Fig. 12.8

Event committee structure.

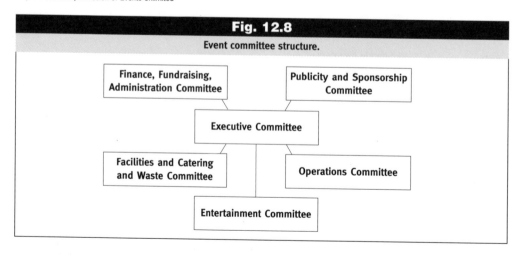

Fig. 12.9

Daily safety checklist.

DAILY SAFETY CHECKLIST

Name _____   Today's date and time _____

Task	Check ✓ ✗	Comment	Follow up required ✓
First Aid kit fully equipped			
Flammable goods signage correct, storage away from combustible materials			
Extinguisher visible, free of obstruction			
Cleaning products labelled and stored correctly			
All electrical appliances tested and tagged within last six months			
Extension cords tested and tagged within last three months			
Extension cords not presenting a hazard over walkways			
Boxes, rubbish, etc. not obstructing exits or fire-fighting equipment			
Gas cut-off valve visible and not obstructed			

FACILITATE COMMUNICATION

Effective communication is an essential feature of project management. Everyone involved needs to be aware of the goals and milestones and these have to be carefully monitored. In the stressful environment of event planning, trust and respect within the project team are essential. Ongoing consultation, in the form of meetings, telephone calls and emails, is one way to assess progress against project goals. Occasionally, additional resources will be required or the project timeline will need to be reviewed, but not the ultimate deadline, the event date, as that never changes! Actions must be agreed, with timelines and responsibility allocated. Everyone needs to be involved in ongoing communication — team members, colleagues and clients.

The nature of the event business is that most of the time is spent in planning and very little is spent in the execution phase. In fact, it often comes as a shock when the event is over so quickly. Things can go bad in an instant in the event environment but good planning can prevent this happening. In the best cases, the plans have been so thoughtfully developed that the event manager's role is simply to ensure that procedures are correctly implemented, resulting in minimal incidents and satisfied clients.

As the organiser of a product launch for a prestige motor car company, you need to reassure your client of your capacity to plan a successful event. The purpose of this event is to attract media attention to encourage widespread publicity for the new model. This will coincide with a national advertising campaign. Develop an overview of the event (event concept), a brief run sheet and a series of illustrations showing the event and staging layout. Finally, prepare a timeline or Gantt chart to show the planning process in the lead-up to the event.

ACTIVITIES

- *The concept, 'chain of events', is very relevant to event planning. Review three different types of event (such as a product launch, fete and sporting competition) and identify potential weak links in the planning process that could jeopardise each event if they were not thoroughly considered. For example, the lack of a back-up system for electrical supplies at an outdoor venue could jeopardise the event.*
- *Visit <www.travelsmart.gov.au/events/four.html> and compare two case studies of transport planning in terms of their travel solutions.*
- *Using the checklist at the above website, visit a public event and analyse transport arrangements, making observations and recommendations for the future.*

LINKS

Australia Day Council
www.adc.nsw.gov.au

Exhibition Hire Service, Sydney
www.exhibitionhire.com.au

Travel Smart Guidelines for Event Planning
www.travelsmart.gov.au/events/four.html

United Nations
www.un.org

SUMMARY

In this chapter we have explained the differences between the purpose, the aims and the objectives of an event, and have stressed the importance of these being clearly stated and adhered to. Using maps, diagrams, charts and checklists, the event manager can show how they can be achieved within the allocated time period. Unlike most other projects, deadlines in event management cannot be postponed since the date must be advertised and the event venue booked. The planning tools described and illustrated in this chapter will help to meet those deadlines, particularly as each aspect of an event is generally contingent on another. Nevertheless, planning needs to remain flexible since this is a very dynamic industry in which change is inevitable.

CHAPTER THIRTEEN

EVENT

PROMOTION

ON COMPLETION OF THIS CHAPTER YOU WILL BE ABLE TO:

- develop marketing communication objectives
- develop a brand or image for an event based on the theme
- determine the marketing communications mix
- set a promotional budget
- manage publicity and public relations.

Welcome to this year's Royal Easter Show

There's something for everyone at this year's Royal Easter Show, from 7 to 12 April at the Auckland Showgrounds.

Exciting new attractions for 2004 combine with traditional favourites, to provide entertainment for all ages and interests.

The Tweenies show, which sees the smash hit BBC children's series come to life in a live stage show, will be a sure hit with preschoolers. While the Butt Ugly Martians, appealing to primary school aged children, also feature in a live stage show with singing, popular music, funky dance moves and costumes.

The Weber Brothers Circus' 'Great Cadbury Easter Egg Hunt' is a new show exclusive to the Royal Easter Show that will appeal to all ages. So too will Club Physical's 2004 Mr Puniverse competition, which will see contestants brave the stage to compare their 'lack of muscle'.

All the show's traditional favourites are back including the carnival rides, street entertainers, Farmworld with its stables and petting pens and the A&P competitions which include shearing, dressage, show jumping, highland dancing, dog trials, equestrian and the Cat Show.

Add to that the Royal Easter Show Art Awards with hundreds of artworks on show and for sale, displays of award winning wines from the New Zealand Wine Society Royal Easter Wine Show and Cadbury's Great Bunny Show, and you have a winning holiday attraction for young and old alike.

Entry is only $30 for a family five, $15 an adult, $5 a child and free for under-two years, which represents good value family entertainment. All shows and attractions, excluding the carnival rides, are included in the entry price.

And with all attractions under cover except for the carnival, it's a great day out even if the weather is bad.

ROYAL EASTER SHOW

NEW ZEALAND

The New Zealand Royal Easter Show is an example of an annual event that is held in most countries and major cities. Agricultural shows continue to appeal to a wide audience ranging from rural farmers to city dwellers. For young children, the baby animal area is always popular, while side shows and stalls are perennial favourites. For rural exhibitors, these events provide the opportunity to have their livestock judged, thus increasing exposure and prices for breeding. The New Zealand event is particularly interesting, with new and exciting ideas capturing current interest in information technology, wine and cuisine. Their promotional information is available on the website listed at the end of this chapter.

Promotion and public relations are a crucial part of the marketing of any event, as we have mentioned in previous chapters, and they will be discussed below in some detail.

As part of the marketing strategy, event promotion involves communicating the image and content of the event program to the potential audience. Broadly, the aim of a promotional strategy is to ensure that the consumer makes a decision to purchase and follows up with the action of actually making the purchase. It is essential to turn intention into action and this is often the biggest obstacle of a promotional campaign.

IMAGE/BRANDING

The first step for most events is the development of a name, logo and image for the event. This includes the colour scheme and graphics that will appear on all event material ranging from registration forms to tickets to merchandise. Image and logo are closely linked and need to be agreed on well in advance. Together they are referred to as 'branding'. Where sponsors are involved, it is essential to obtain their approval of the branding, otherwise there could be conflict over the use of colour or the positioning and size of logos. The design must meet the needs of all stakeholders, as well as appealing to the event audience, particularly if the design forms the basis for merchandise such as T-shirts and caps. A slogan is sometimes developed as part of the image for an event and incorporated wherever possible. The result should be a consistent theme and colour scheme for all promotional materials. In most cases, the colour scheme is also carried through to the décor, including signs, fencing, flags, table settings, banners and posters.

PROMOTIONAL ACTIVITIES

Promotional activities include far more than advertising. Indeed, most community events rely on free editorial publicity in the local media. Other forms of promotional activity include direct marketing, sales promotion and personal selling. These approaches will be discussed in detail in this chapter. Event promotion has a direct link to the marketing plan and marketing objectives, and

One form of advertising.

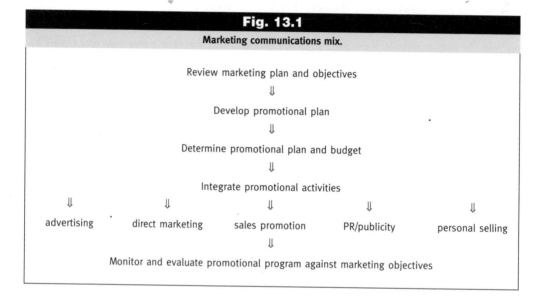

Fig. 13.1

Marketing communications mix.

Review marketing plan and objectives
⇩
Develop promotional plan
⇩
Determine promotional plan and budget
⇩
Integrate promotional activities

⇩ ⇩ ⇩ ⇩ ⇩

advertising · direct marketing · sales promotion · PR/publicity · personal selling

⇩

Monitor and evaluate promotional program against marketing objectives

a carefully crafted, integrated approach to communication with the client or customer is needed to ensure that the marketing objectives are achieved (see Fig. 13.1).

Having undertaken market research, the marketing department is in a better position to decide how to promote a particular product or how to launch a new product. There are a number of activities that are necessary for successful marketing and promotion of event products and services. Not all will be applicable to every situation, but awareness of them is essential. The most relevant of these are outlined below.

Advertising

Advertising is paid communication, using one or more types of media to reach potential buyers. It can be extremely expensive, particularly radio and television advertising, and for this reason it is essential to accurately identify the market and target the advertising as cost effectively as possible.

Advertising is one of the most effective ways of raising awareness of an event or event business. However, from a marketing point of view, the aim is to achieve more than awareness. Awareness and interest need to be converted into sales and loyalty.

The four steps to becoming a loyal customer are illustrated in Fig. 13.2.

Fig. 13.2
Stages in buyer behaviour.

awareness (positive appeal)

⇓

interest and knowledge of product

⇓

testing and evaluating of product

⇓

becoming a satisfied, repeat or recommending customer

Whereas advertising might attract a potential customer to a convention centre as the possible venue for a wedding reception, a tour of the establishment and a display of photographs from previous receptions would create interest and allow the client to evaluate the product. An invitation to sample various menus, in consultation with the chef, would more than likely clinch the deal — provided the food was of an appropriate standard. The buyer has expressed interest, developed knowledge of the product and tested some elements of the product. For such an important decision, these steps are critical. Signing the contract is almost guaranteed and so, too, are the couple's expectation of the event's success and the possibility of recommendation to others.

In the event industry, expectation and anticipation are part of the product. Anything that can be done to enhance this is adding to the product benefit. A well-designed website, such as that of Big Day Out (see link at the end of this chapter), can help to develop loyalty, while a website for an agricultural show is an essential source of information for visitors wanting to see specific exhibitions. Full colour brochures for this type of event are being reduced in size as more and more potential visitors access the required information online.

There are various types of advertising described in detail as follows.

Internet advertising

Site design and adequate listings with search engines are critical factors in the success of Internet marketing. Security for online transactions and privacy of information given by customers are other very important considerations. The potential of this method of advertising is well recognised, with exponential growth expected in the coming years, many events being leaders in the field.

Advertising can assist with decision-making on all types of bookings by providing detailed knowledge of the facilities, such as accessibility for displaying large items such as cars and boats. Some convention centres have interactive planning available, so that when the customer chooses a type of function (banquet, conference) and identifies the number of guests, various room configurations are shown on-screen using CAD software. Most websites also offer email links to facilitate questions and answers.

Internet advertising has the potential to be more than advertising — it can translate interest into purchase with bookings made, paid and confirmed online.

Print advertising

Newspapers and magazines are the media most commonly used for advertising, although a *Yellow Pages* listing is essential for most small event operations. Cost is related to the medium chosen and to the size and positioning of the advertisement. The front and back covers and inside front and back covers are usually the most expensive spaces to purchase, followed by the top part of right-hand pages. Choosing the appropriate newspaper or magazine is essential, as wide coverage or untargeted advertising tends to produce a very limited response. The circulation statistics for the publication need to be analysed, including the demographic profile of readers, and matched to event target markets.

As part of the marketing plan, it is necessary to identify the market to be reached and then to establish where these people live and which of the print media would be most likely to reach them. When selecting the most appropriate media, cost is generally the biggest issue. Then you need to decide when to advertise — a month before, a week before or the day before? Faced with budget limits and potentially expensive advertising, these are all crucial decisions.

When preparing an advertising budget, you should be aware that different time slots on radio and television cost vastly different amounts, as do different positions on the pages of print media, as mentioned above. Local newspapers and local radio stations are always more cost effective than national ones and are generally a most effective way to reach a local audience. Larger events may aim to attract international audiences and, if this is the case, you will need to clearly identify the potential overseas audience and perhaps develop a tourist package to include accommodation and other attractions. Partnership arrangements can often be reached with travel companies and the assistance of state and national tourism bodies obtained to support and promote the event.

The content of advertisements must be informative but, most importantly, it must inspire decision-making and action to attend or purchase. Let's look at the following advertisement by an event company for their wedding hire products and services:

We provide six-arm gold candelabra in the Victorian style, silk flowers, tea lights, fairy lights, table overlays (in organza, Jacquard and cotton), chair covers with sashes and ceiling drapes. We set up for you.

In this advertisement there is a lot of information but absolutely no inspiration. A number of descriptive adjectives would certainly have enhanced the text, as well as the possibility of customers buying their services!

In contrast, the advertisement for the unusual event opposite is much more creative.

It would be very difficult to attract an event audience if only the facts of a blood donation were presented, and the promotional team has realised this by making this event into something not to be missed.

The advertising message needs to meet the motivational needs of the audience, at the same time assisting the decision-making process by supplying the necessary facts.

Radio advertising

Radio advertising is effective if the message is clear. However, it is not possible to show images or provide very specific information and is thus used infrequently by all but the biggest event operators.

YOUR BLOOD!

Greendale Clinic Big Bleed Week

May 10–15 with the grand finale (don't miss this) on May 15

Greendale Clinic's last Big Bleed was a huge success. This year our target is 3000 units of blood. Sponsors have donated 10 major prizes as well as minor prizes for all other donors. The biggest prize, a trip to Cannes, will be presented at the grand finale. We will have free health advice, coffee shop and food stalls, a craft fair, children's entertainment, celebrities, races, a jazz band in the late afternoon and fireworks at the close each evening. Attendance is free and all donors receive a sponsor prize, plus go into the draw for the major prizes. Parking is available in Macleay Street. We start at 10 and finish at 9 pm.

Television advertising

While the impact of television advertising is greater than for most other media, it is extremely expensive. Specific marketing objectives would need to be developed and an advertising agency fully briefed on the proposed campaign. The timing of the advertising campaign should be linked to consumer decision-making, which is generally possible only when market research has been conducted on similar previous events. Celebrity endorsement does not come free unless the event supports a chartity. It costs around $2000 to $3000 for a minor celebrity and between $100 000 and $250 000 for a high profile celebrity.

Direct mail advertising

A substantial client list is a valuable resource for direct mail advertising and selling. A client list can be developed rapidly if an organisation is promoted at trade exhibitions where the list of attendees is made available to exhibitors. If the market can be clearly identified, then direct mail is a most effective form of advertising, and one that is cost-effective too. Where customers are transient, the expense of direct mail is unwarranted. Of course an invitation is a form of direct mail advertising.

Displays and signage

Signs are one of the most effective ways by which small event businesses advertise, even though most councils place limitations on the size of signs. Lighting, too, is an important element of outdoor signage, and one that is often neglected. Sky writing is expensive: one display of up to 12 characters costs $2600. For a second display on the same day the cost comes down to about $1800.

Brochures and fliers

Brochures and fliers are essential advertising items for many types of small events, and they need to be descriptive, informative and colourful. The quality of any photographs or artwork used in them is most important too.

Advertising collateral

This interesting term covers a range of advertising mediums, from tent cards to billboards. Posters and billboards are often displayed in public places and tourist information centres.

Personal selling

Personal selling involves face-to-face contact between seller and buyer. This enables the salesperson to talk directly to the buyer, and to persuade the buyer through negotiation to purchase the product. This type of promotion is most common for booking conferences, weddings, parties and incentive travel events. This is because the event details need to be planned and a quote provided.

For all personal selling, it is essential to prepare in advance by finding out as much as possible about the potential customer. Following are the steps and stages involved in meeting a potential client or making a sales call:

1 Welcome

Give a friendly greeting.

Open first.

Observe body language.

2 Explore

Ask about the planned event, including the purpose.

Explore and listen to what the client needs or wants.

Find out about the person's role in planning the event.

3 Offer information

Clarify the client's needs — what they really mean.

Focus on the buyer, not the product your company provides.

Outline the product (for example, function facility and catering) after clarifying the client's needs.

4 Close

Agree the next step or action to be taken.

Work out the follow-up required to finalise the event details.

Complete a sales report form.

5 Follow up

Follow up in a timely manner.

Provide a quote to the client.

Review status periodically.

Completion of sales call reports is essential since face-to-face meetings are costly and business development managers need to show a return on the time invested. An example of a sales call report is illustrated in Fig. 13.3.

Sales promotions

A sales promotion is intended to persuade a buyer to purchase immediately, so they often include incentives or discounts. Sales promotions may follow the introduction of a new product or may be implemented during a slow period. Examples of sales promotions include discounted event tickets, discounted off-season function facilities, incentive meeting packages, and newspaper or magazine competitions to win prizes such as tickets to a premiere. Giveaways would also fit into this category.

The Australian Promotion Marketing Association (see web address at the end of this chapter) provides a code of conduct for promotional activities, as well as advice to member organisations.

Fig. 13.3

Example of a sales call report form for meeting room/function bookings.

SALES CALL REPORT

Event venue details

Name of representative _____

Date and time of sales call/client meeting _____

Client details

Name of client, department and address _____

_____

Contact person's name and position/role _____

Person responsible for bookings and their department (if not as above) _____

Sales and promotions information

Purpose and type of event _____

_____

Types of rooms/facilities required _____

Other services _____

Number of guests/attendees _____

Specific entitlements or limitations (e.g. budget) _____

Other facilities currently used (competitors) _____

Opportunities for preferred supplier status (tendering) _____

Other needs (e.g. sales meetings, training sessions, conferences) _____

Outcomes of meeting _____

Action required _____

For example, if a discount is available to only a limited number of customers, this should be clearly stated on all promotional material. In both Australia and New Zealand, Gaming and Trade Practices Acts outline specific rules for promotions offering prizes.

Promotional events and trade shows

Hotel groups, casinos, resorts and convention centres frequently exhibit at promotional events where they distribute information to potential buyers, particularly in the area of incentive travel. So too do suppliers to the event business, such as staging and rental companies, event software companies and event planners.

Issues to be considered when assessing whether to participate in promotional events or trade shows may include:

- consistency of the activity with the overall marketing direction of the organisation
- level of exposure to be achieved by attendance at an event, or sponsorship of an event
- matching of attendees to an organisation's target markets
- available financial resources

- human resource requirements
- timing of the activity or event.

PUBLIC RELATIONS AND PUBLICITY

Public relations is stimulation of demand for a product or service by providing commercially significant news about the product or service in a published medium, or obtaining favourable editorial presentation in a medium, such as a newspaper, free of charge. The most commonly used form for public relations is the press release. Most major events have a press release page on their websites, although such releases would be sent primarily to specific contacts in the media. Editorial publicity in the form of an article or a story is highly sought after and valued. Of course this is not completely free as there is significant time cost involved in preparing and issuing press releases, following up journalists and producers by telephone, planning launches and so on. Thus while there is no cost associated with the space allocated to the story, a public relations budget must be factored into the marketing budget.

Publicity for an event can be secured by running a careful publicity campaign with the media. Sometimes photo opportunities and interviews with a spokesperson or celebrity will also be necessary to develop the feature.

There are different types of media release:
- backgrounder — providing general information about the event, history, previous success, etc.
- press release — story, newsworthy information
- media alert — invitation style alert to the fact that the event is imminent.

There are several points of contact. In the print media, these include the editor, the feature writers, and the editors responsible for individual sections of the newspaper or magazine. In the broadcast media, the people to contact include the station manager, producer or news director who in turn provide the story to the news announcers and radio personalities. In each case, the first question asked will be 'What makes this event newsworthy?' and the answer to this must be clear.

The aim of a press release is to stimulate media interest in the event and thus achieve positive and cost-effective publicity. Many large event organisers post their press releases on their web pages (see as an example the press release in this chapter for the International Genetics Conference). For mega and hallmark events, a launch is usually held prior to the event to which the media and the stars of the show are invited. These occasions are used to distribute the press release. It is essential that a launch be well attended and that the media report the event in a positive way, otherwise it will be counterproductive. The launch must be staged for photo opportunities and interviews. In the case of smaller events, sending a press release to a local paper is generally the best option. Since the staff working on these smaller publications are extremely busy, it is advisable to provide them with a ready-to-go article, including quotes as well as photos and logos where possible.

The following is an example of the sort of press release/article that would draw the attention of a local newspaper:

Media Release

WE HOST THE COUNTRY'S LARGEST CYCLE RACE
Thousands Pedal the Peninsula

This year's 54 km race will see 15 000 riders tackle the most scenic mountain and beachside race in the country. The race is the largest sporting event in the state and the largest bicycle race in the country. This indicates a trend towards competitive physical competition for all age groups and cycling is a popular choice. Contestants will be visiting from overseas countries including Japan, Korea, India and Holland. Some riders are fiercely competitive, while others ride as family groups. All age groups are represented, and last year's race was completed by an 84-year-old and his 7-year-old grandson. The race will raise funds for a community parkland project and will be run by 5 local clubs. An additional $3 million is the target for other deserving causes. To register for the event, contact Richard on 9879 6543 or register on-line at www.pedal.com.au.

The following guidelines for preparing a press release will help to ensure that the reader sits up and takes notice:

- There must be something newsworthy to appeal to the reader in the first two sentences: he or she must be motivated to read the whole press release.
- All the facts must be covered: what, when, why and how. This is particularly the case for negative incidents. The reader wants to know what happened, when it happened, why it happened and how things will be resolved. When something goes wrong, the facts are important because unsubstantiated opinion is dangerous. If the press release is promoting an event, all information such as the venue, date, time and so on should be included.
- The press release should be short and to the point.
- Layout is extremely important.
- Contact details should be provided.
- Photographs should be captioned.
- Quotes from senior staff and stakeholders (including sponsors) must be included.
- If the press release is promoting an event, it should describe all potential benefits for the audience.
- An action ending for booking or registering should include all necessary information.
- The style of writing should be appropriate for the targeted publication.
- There should be no errors in grammar or spelling.

Apart from media attention, it is also possible to obtain exposure through a number of official tourism organisations, many of which are listed at the end of this book. They provide tourist information to visitors through tourist information offices or their websites at state or national level. Brochures distributed to such offices or listings on their event calendars can provide valuable information to the potential (and sometimes very hard to reach) event audience. Every effort should be made to ensure that the event is listed as widely as possible.

The role of public relations is to manage the organisation's and the event's image in the mind of the audience and the public. This is mainly done through press releases as described above. These up-to-date information sources, together with photographs, provide the media with the background information they need to develop stories about the event. Media briefings can also be conducted before and during the event, particularly if high profile people such as celebrities, entertainers and athletes can enhance the publicity.

One of the most critical public relations roles is to inform the media if there is a negative incident of any description. For this reason, an incident reporting system needs to be in place so that senior members of the event management team are fully informed, including the Public Relations Manager, if this is a separate role. It may be necessary to write a press release or appear in an interview if such an incident occurs. In some situations it is essential to obtain legal advice regarding the wording used in the press release. The public relations role can be a highly sensitive one, and in some situations words need to be chosen carefully. A simple expression of regret, for example, would be more tactful than suggesting the cause of an accident before a thorough investigation or inquiry.

Another more positive public relations role is the entertainment of guests and VIPs attending the event, in some cases from other countries. In this public relations role you need to be:

- attentive to the needs and expectations of your guests
- mindful of their cultural expectations
- flexible in your response to their behaviour
- informative and helpful as a host
- proactive in designing hosting situations to meet the required protocol
- able to make easy conversation.

Particularly with overseas guests or guests of event sponsors, you need to know in advance who they are (official titles, correct names and correct pronunciation) and where they come from. Most importantly, you need to know the reason why your company is acting as host to these guests as often business objectives, such as sponsor product awareness or negotiations, are involved. Research is therefore essential to determine how to meet the needs of the guests and the expectations of, for example, the sponsors.

According to Roger Axtell (1990) the effective multicultural host is able to:

- be respectful
- tolerate ambiguity
- relate well to people
- be non-judgemental
- personalise their observations (not make global assertions about people or places)
- show empathy
- be patient and persistent.

As you can see from the above, there are a number of roles for the Public Relations Manager, or indeed for any member of the event team. The opportunity to sell an event occurs every time the telephone is answered or an enquiry is made by a potential customer. Customer relations becomes the role of everyone involved in an event and for this reason training in this area is recommended. This training should focus in particular on the event information likely to be requested by the customer, which is more difficult than it sounds since plans are often not finalised until very close to the event. Training ties in closely with the planning process, and the distribution of information to all concerned right up until the last minute is very important.

There are a number of situations in which an event manager might become involved in public relations, including:

- making travel arrangements by telephone or email
- meeting and greeting at the airport
- providing transport
- running meetings
- entertaining at meals
- entertaining at events
- providing tours and commentary.

If you had to lead a small group around a venue or an event, there are a number of additional recommendations:

- Plan the tour so that enough time is allocated to see everything.
- Advise your guests of your plan, however informal the group.
- Make sure that there is time for a break and refreshments.
- Provide maps so that people can get their bearings.
- Pause frequently so that the guests can ask questions.
- Be gracious — questions are never trivial or stupid.
- Make sure that everyone can see and hear.
- Treat everyone equally.
- Speak slowly and at an appropriate volume.

- Be patient and speak positively.
- Be flexible and change plans if necessary.
- Be attentive to fatigue or boredom and accelerate the tour if necessary.

In promoting an event, it is essential to analyse and understand the needs of the target market or markets. If, for example, one of the target markets were children aged eight to twelve, it would be necessary to understand the motivations of this group and to match the product to these motivational needs. It would also be necessary to keep in mind that the person purchasing the product might not be the consumer — in this case, it could be the parent and promotional efforts would need to assist with decision-making processes within the family. Likewise, a sponsor might be making a substantial investment in the event, and might have general, as well as specific, expectations of the event, which might or might not be consistent with those of the event audience.

To summarise, the task of promoting an event to the optimal audience at the most beneficial time is the first challenge. The second is to meet the needs of all stakeholders and to maximise public relations benefits to the satisfaction of customers at all levels.

PROMOTIONAL ACTION PLANS

Once the marketing and promotions strategy has been agreed, the following issues need to be considered when creating detailed plans for the various promotional activities outlined above:
- objectives and nature of the activity
- budget availability
- public relations implications
- staffing requirements and briefings
- availability of brochures and other promotional materials
- equipment requirements
- contracting of other services (e.g. display)
- travel arrangements
- strategies to ensure maximum benefits
- possible co-operative approaches (proactive or reactive)
- need for external assistance
- fulfilment of administrative and procedural requirements
- available technology
- potential e-commerce opportunities.

The promotional budget allocates funds to the various components of the promotional mix. This is illustrated for an event company in Fig. 13.4 on page 199.

The promotional effort is often closely linked to ticket sales. Box office software enables the capture of information on peak booking periods, profile of audience, ticket yield, ticket sales in the various price ranges and group bookings, as well as providing addresses for direct marketing, allowing further promotions to be directed towards the areas of lowest sales.

For mega events, the postcodes of ticket holders are used to anticipate demand for public transport. Ticket sales can form the basis for domestic and international travel packages,

Fig. 13.4

Budget allocation to event company promotions.

Type of promotion	Timing	Cost (including production, media and human resources) $
Advertising		
Yellow Pages	Annually	500.00
Magazine	Quarterly	1 200.00
Direct marketing		
Mailing list	Quarterly	450.00
Publicity/PR	Linked to key events (est. 4)	8 000.00
Sales promotion	August	810.00
Trade exhibition	June	950.00
Personal selling	Ongoing	21 000.00
Contingency		550.00
TOTAL		**33 460.00**

including hotel accommodation and transportation. In some cases, large numbers of tickets are reserved for organising bodies and returned for sale if not utilised. The primary benefit associated with ticketing programs is the opportunity to manage cash flow. For events where tickets are sold only at the gate, it is impossible to monitor promotional efforts and extremely difficult to anticipate audience numbers, particularly if the event can be affected by inclement weather.

For an annual event, ticketing data — part of customer relationship management (CRM) — is a valuable source of information for planning subsequent years' events. Popularity of ticket grades, profiles of customers and timing of decision-making are a few of the trends that can be monitored through ticket sale data.

*S*outh African culture and diversity will be the toast of London when the Celebrate South Africa campaign begins later this month, the High Commissioner to Britain, Cheryl Carolus, said yesterday. She said Londoners would have 'their socks knocked off' with South African arts, crafts, music, dance, theatre, film, cuisine and song from April 18 to May 31.

The focus of the six-week program will be to showcase South Africa as a nation in formation since achieving democracy in 1994. A huge concert will be held in Trafalgar Square to mark Freedom Day.

THE STAR, JOHANNESBURG, 6 APRIL 2001

Using the above newspaper article, and any materials you can find on the history and culture of South Africa, prepare the following promotional materials:

- a travel brochure promoting the campaign as part of a holiday in London
- a design for a web page (front page only) promoting the six-week program
- a backgrounder to explain the historical background of Freedom Day
- a press release designed for a feature story.

Links to tourism and other websites provided below and in Appendix D will assist with your research.

ACTIVITY

Select five advertisements for events and analyse the differences, deciding which has the most audience appeal in terms of:

- *attraction*
- *development of interest*
- *assistance in decision-making*
- *ability to lead to action/attendance.*

LINKS

Australia Promotion Marketing Association
www.apma.com

Big Day Out
www.bigdayout.com

Royal Easter Show New Zealand
www.royaleastershow.co.nz

SUMMARY

In this chapter we have dealt with event promotion in more detail, and have seen that branding or image is linked to the event purpose and theme, and that all of these aspects must be consistent and compatible in order to create the greatest impact on the consumer or event audience. There are many media options for advertising and these are often determined by the promotional budget available. Advertising and publicity need to be carefully planned to ensure the highest possible level of attendance at an event. We have also discussed the public relations role, communication with the media and other stakeholders being important during the planning phases and equally important when there are problems or incidents that threaten the success or reputation of an event. A more positive public relations role is the entertainment of guests and VIPs for which certain attributes are essential, including tolerance, patience, persistence, respectfulness and an ability to relate well to people of all cultures.

CHAPTER FOURTEEN

STAGING
MANAGEMENT

ON COMPLETION OF THIS CHAPTER YOU WILL BE ABLE TO:

- evaluate an event site to assess its suitability
- select a theme and plan the décor
- plan all staging elements, including lighting and sound
- plan all event services, such as catering
- understand the roles of staging contractors
- source, manage, monitor and evaluate the progress of contractors.

The biennial New Zealand Festival is presented by a charitable trust — The New Zealand International Festival of the Arts. Up to three hundred specialist arts administrators, communicators, production and technical staff are employed to help produce and present the Festival, but most are on short-term contracts, of between six weeks to eighteen months' duration. In the 'off' period between Festivals, a skeletal administration staff of only four is maintained.

The Festival operates on a financial knife-edge, with a mandate to break even at the end of each event, and the requirement to start from zero each time. It has 'core funding' by Wellington City Council, but relies heavily on public and private sector support for its existence; 62 per cent of income comes from ticket sales, and 31 per cent from sponsorship and grants. The Government, through its arts funding agency, Creative New Zealand, assists the development of new, New Zealand work for presentation at the Festival.

Approximately 75 per cent of the Festival's operating budget is spent on buying, producing and presenting the events which make up the Festival, with the remainder split between administration and marketing costs.

www.nzfestival.telecom.co.nz/home/page.aspx?page_id=22

The New Zealand Festival, with over 100 ticketed events, provides an introduction to the issues associated with staging. The staging of an event incorporates all aspects of the event that enable the performance to go ahead. Broadly speaking, by performance we mean

Jackie Clarke in the stage adaptation of 'The Underwatermelon Man' by Fane Flaws — New Zealand Festival.

Reproduced with permission of New Zealand Festival

entertainment: the sport, the parade, the ceremony. The topics covered in this chapter, such as theme, venue, sound and lighting, as well as all the essential services, are relevant to every one of the free and ticketed events of the New Zealand Festival. For every event in that festival, the organisers would have had to look at issues such as capacity, seating arrangements, emergency access, stage requirements and staffing.

Staging is an ancient concept: the Roman gladiatorial events were staged in spectacular, albeit gruesome, fashion, but these events certainly had the enthusiastic atmosphere every modern event organiser aspires to, although the modern audience would be unlikely to enjoy the same level of bloodshed.

CHOOSING THE EVENT SITE

Selection of an event venue must take the needs of all stakeholders into account. Stakeholders include emergency services, catering staff, entertainers, participants and clients.

Frequently, the client has an unusual idea for a venue, but however imaginative this may be, selection of the site must be tempered with rational decision-making. While a parking lot could be transformed into an interesting place to have a party, it would have no essential services, such as electricity, and would present enormously expensive logistical problems. An existing event venue, such as a conference centre, could more easily lend itself to transformation using decoration and props. Table 14.1 and Fig. 14.1 on page 204 illustrate useful information, such as hall size and capacity and layout of facilities, which is available from venues and convention centres on the Internet.

Choosing a venue that is consistent with the event purpose and theme is essential. It can also lead to cost savings as there is far less expense in transforming it into what the client wants.

The major considerations for selecting an event venue include:
- size of the event (including the size of the audience)
- layout of the site and its suitability for the event
- stage, field of play or performance area
- transport and parking
- proximity to accommodation and attractions
- supply issues for goods and services providers, such as caterers
- technical support
- venue management.

Table 14.1

Example of information, such as hall size and capacity, provided by venue providers on the internet.

CAPACITIES	AREA Sq m	AREA Sg f	THEATRE	BANQUET	CLASSROOM
Hall A	430	4628	540	300	210
Hall B	430	4628	540	300	210
Hall C	430	4628	500	300	210
Hall D	430	4628	500	300	210
Halls A&B	860	9256	1080	650	420
Halls C&D	860	9256	940	650	400
Halls B&C&D	1290	13884	1540	720	N/A
Great Hall A&B&C&D	1720	18512	2330	1300	730
Hall 2 (Auditorium)	1470	15817	5000	N/A	N/A
Hall 2 (Flat floor)	1470	15817	N/A	1080	630

Fig. 14.1

Layout of halls and facilities of a convention centre available on the Internet.

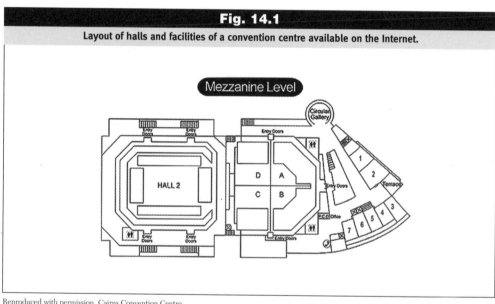

Reproduced with permission. Cairns Convention Centre

Cairns Convention Centre Hall 2 used for trade exhibition.
Reproduced with permission. Cairns Convention Centre

An inspection of the site should reveal any limitations, the aspects to consider including:

- compatibility with the event theme
- audience comfort
- visibility for the audience (line of sight)
- storage areas
- entrances and exits
- stage area (where relevant)
- equipment
- cover in case of poor weather
- safety and security
- access for emergency vehicles
- evacuation routes.

In viewing a potential event site, there are three major stakeholders who need to be considered and whose perspectives could be quite different: the **performers**, the **audience** and the **organisers**. By performers we mean those in the limelight, whether this involves providing an educational talk, dancing in a parade, presenting an award or scoring on a try line. Performers have specific needs that are fundamental to their success, such as the level of intimacy with the audience (often the result of the distance from the audience) or the volume of the sound. Secondly, the audience has needs, the primary one being to see what is going on! The level of lighting and sound, as well as access to and comfort of the seating, also contribute to audience satisfaction. Catering and facilities are generally secondary. Finally, from a management perspective, the venue must help to minimise risks, such as adverse weather, power failure, accidents and emergencies.

Staging elements

In order to choose an appropriate venue for an event involving a stage and set, it is necessary to know the types of props that will be required and the equipment needed to instal them. Staging can involve one or more of the following elements:

- framed scenery (e.g. flats, profiles, doors, windows)
- weight bearing scenery (e.g. rostra, ramps, steps)
- non-weight bearing scenery (e.g. columns, trees)
- soft scenery (e.g. canvas legs, borders, cloths, gauzes, cycloramas)
- furniture and other set props
- revolves
- trucks.

Equipment to be used could include the following (which must be used according to **Regulation** limits and licensing **Regulations**):

- tallescope
- maxi-lift or genie-type lifter
- cherry picker
- mobile scaffolding

- ladders and A-frames
- scissor lift.

If working outdoors, staging requirements could include stages, tents, scaffolding, fences, ground coverings and seating.

DEVELOPING THE THEME

As we have mentioned several times, the theme of an event must be supported in every aspect, including the décor, lighting, sound and special effects. The theme may be quite subtle: for example, in the case of a high-tech theme for a conference, the audience would only be subliminally aware of aspects of the theme, such as the colour scheme. In more dramatic cases, guests might be asked to support the theme by dressing appropriately or participating in entertainment that is consistent with the theme. Themes may be tried and tested, or quite unique.

A theme can be reinforced through such creative elements as:
- colour
- landscape and/or location
- film/theatre/art/dance
- humour
- fantasy.

Following are important aspects of the theme that need to be carefully considered by the event organiser. As you will see, there are many decisions to make!

Entertainment

There is a wide range of acts that can be used to enhance the theme of an event, and corporate events, in particular, often employ interesting performers such as snake charmers, hypnotists and belly dancers. Entertainment companies have a wealth of ideas and these can be investigated on the websites listed at the end of this chapter. Such companies need to be briefed in the early planning stages so that they become familiar with the event purpose and the event audience. They can then look at the event theme and come up with a range of concepts to suit the theme. If a band is recommended, the specific technical requirements should be discussed at this stage. (One event organiser illustrated the importance of briefing the entertainment provider with her own experience in organising an event for a young audience. When the teenager's parents heard that one of the band members had stripped, they were furious with her!)

Décor

Lena Malouf is one of Australia's foremost event designers and her work has recently earned her two awards, the first for Best Event Produced for a Corporation or Association (overall budget US$200 000 to US$500 000) and the second for Best Theme Décor (décor budget over US$50 000). Her guests were submerged in a magical 'underwater' world reminiscent of the fantastical journey in the children's classic, *Bedknobs and Broomsticks*. Malouf's events are characterised by extravagant displays, including imaginative moving art pieces that tie in perfectly with the chosen theme, her main aim being to surprise and transport the audience. She is now the President of the International Special Event Society (ISES). Her book, *Behind the Scenes at Special Events* (1998), is recommended for those interested in specialising in event design.

Décor encompasses many things, from the colour scheme to the drapes, props and floral arrangements. The challenge is to bring them all together into a cohesive theme. Staging rental companies can be extremely helpful with this task.

Layout

The layout of the event venue is clearly integral to the success of the event. Anyone who has worked on conferences and formal dinners knows that table layout is something that needs to be negotiated with the client well in advance. With large dinner events in large venues, all too often the audience at the back of the room has very limited vision of the stage. If this is compounded by poor sound and too much alcohol, it does not take long before the presenter is drowned out by the clink of glasses and the hum of conversation. This can be very embarrassing.

When planning an event at which guests are seated around a table, it is essential to plan the layout according to scale. If the dimensions of the tables and chairs are not considered, as well as the space taken by seated guests, there may prove to be no room for waiters or guests to move around. A number of common table and seating layouts are illustrated in Fig. 14.2. For each of these, a scale drawing would be used to calculate the capacity of the room and the appropriate use of furnishings.

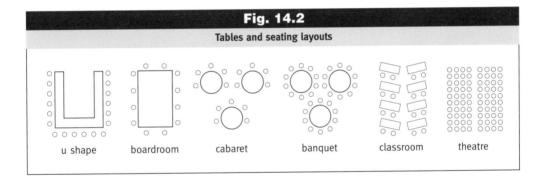

Fig. 14.2
Tables and seating layouts

u shape   boardroom   cabaret   banquet   classroom   theatre

Lighting and special effects

Lighting can be used to spectacular effect, and for this reason, events held at night provide the opportunity for more dramatic results than those held during the day. Lighting can be used both to create the general ambience and to highlight particular features. It is often synchronised with sound for special effect at dances and fireworks displays, and can also be used to highlight sponsor advertising. As with sound, lighting is used to create a particular mood, although it is important to remember that this must be consistent with the event theme. Subtlety is required, for there has been a tendency recently to use some of the latest patterning techniques too often. Professional advice from a lighting designer is recommended as lighting is more often than not one of the main contributors to staging a successful event.

Sound

Music is a powerful creator of mood. It can excite or calm an audience, while particular pieces can be highly emotive. The volume needs to be pitched at just the right level, and all members of the audience need to be able to hear clearly, particularly if the event is being staged in a large stadium. Professional sound engineers can be relied upon to give advice on equipment and the acoustic qualities of a venue. For example, a concrete venue with little or no carpeting or curtaining has a negative effect on sound, but this can be remedied by the incorporation of drapes in the design.

Vision

Vision incorporates all projected images, such as replays of sporting highlights on large screens or scoreboards. Video projectors, slide projectors and data projectors can project images onto screens for dramatic effect, and this can be extended to live broadcasts with satellite links. A wall of monitors can be used to project one large image across the whole monitor wall, achieving the effect of a large screen. The splitting of the image between monitors is done by computer programming.

Back-up projectors and duplicate copies of videos, slides and so on are essential. Most business and academic presentations use computer software packages to improve the visual quality of the images.

Stage

The stage is used for many reasons, including performances, prize-givings and presentations. Equipment rental companies can provide advice on the size and shape of the stage, as well as on screens and other devices on which to project images from the rear of the stage.

However, the needs of the audience are the most important consideration, particularly the line of sight, which must be considered when deciding on the size and shape of the stage and the placing of lecterns or screens.

Stage set-up and rehearsal before the performance.

Set

The set includes all objects on the stage: props, flats, lecterns, stairs, curtains, and so on. Sometimes these are hired; at other times they must be built.

The **cyclorama** is the drape at the back of the stage used to create a sense of distance, special lighting of the cyclorama providing different coloured backgrounds. **Borders** are used to mask parts of the rigging system and to trim the sightlines so that only the set may be seen by the audience. A **traveller** is a type of curtain that moves along a track. Often it is used as the main stage curtain, being configured so that one operating line moves curtains from both sides of the stage simultaneously.

The stage specifications from the Adelaide Festival Centre below would be most useful in planning operations by the event organiser. Most larger centres provide this level of detail, as well as plans and drawings.

Stage specifications
Adelaide Festival Centre

STAGE FACILITIES

Stage

Timber, covered with 6 mm masonite.

Painted: Matt black.

Traps

The Space has an understage trap in a T formation across the centre of the floor area. The trap is covered by a series of steel framed and timber covered lids, each measuring approx. 1.2 m x 1.8 m. Please refer to the 'Space Plans and Drawings' for further details.

The space also has a shallow audience seating trap with two levels. Please refer to the 'Space Plans and Drawings' for further details.

Power Supply

In addition to the Stage Lighting Power (distributed from the Drama Centre Rack Room) the Space has one 32 amp 3 phase outlet located in the grid.

Control Rooms

The Space Sound Control Room is at balcony level with a fully opening window. The Space Lighting Control Room is also at balcony level with a fixed, double glazed window. Some stage managers choose to call the show from the Lighting Control Room, although there is limited space.

Music Stands and Sconces

Music stands, sconce lights and orchestral chairs can be supplied out of the Festival Theatre stock subject to availability.

Pianos

Concert and rehearsal pianos are available by arrangement with the Production Co-ordinator. Moving and tuning charges apply.

Masking

The Space Theatre is stocked with the following masking items:

HARD MASKING

4 Flats	4500 mm high x 1600 mm wide	Wool covered ply
4 Flats	3000 mm high x 2000 mm wide	Wool covered ply
2 Flats	2300 mm high x 900 mm wide	Wool covered ply
2 Flats	3100 mm high x 600 mm wide	Wool covered ply
1 Flat	2700 mm high x 1500 mm wide	Wool covered ply
2 Flats	3400 mm high x 1400 mm wide	Wool covered ply (fit above balcony)
2 Flats	2800 mm high x 900 mm wide	Wool covered ply (fit below balcony)
1 Flat	2800 mm high x 1500 mm wide	Wool covered ply (fit below balcony)

SOFT MASKING

8 Curtains	5400 mm high x 3400 mm wide	Pleated velour (for hanging from bobbins on perimeter track)
6 Curtains	5400 mm high x 3100 mm wide	Flat velour (fair condition only)
7 Curtains	5400 mm high x 4000 mm wide	Flat velour (fair condition only)

Cyclorama

Cyclorama — approximately 36.57 m x 5.48 m drop (approx. 120 ft x 18 ft).

*Please note that one end of the cyc has visible water marks.

The Adelaide Festival Centre

Field of play

Each sporting event has specific requirements. These may include gymnastic equipment, which must be properly set up to very clear specifications, or simply a good quality pitch and wicket. In fact, there is nothing simple at all about a good quality wicket, as cricket fans would know only too well! The quality of the grassed field is important for most sports. The 2000 Olympic Games soccer semi-final held in Canberra was threatened with cancellation due to the poor quality of the newly laid turf. Fortunately the problem was solved in time for ticket-holders to enjoy the eagerly awaited match. Problems of this nature are not uncommon. For this reason, sporting fields are often covered when they are used for other events. However, while the cover protects the surface, it also blocks out the light so that damage can still be caused to the field. These days, professional grass specialists can replace the entire field within hours, but this is a very costly exercise.

Line of sight is clearly important for sporting enthusiasts, and one cannot afford to sell seats from which visibility is impaired. The placement of media equipment is often the cause of this type of problem, and discussions must be held before tickets go on sale to establish the proposed position of cameras and sound equipment. The same holds true for processions and street parades where an elevated position is preferable for camera crews. This may require authorisation by the local authority, and accreditation may be necessary for those eligible to enter the media area.

Finally, the use of giant screens with rear screen projectors, such as those used at the Mahler 8 concert at the Sydney Superdome, need to be considered for large venues where there is a risk that members of the audience will not be able to readily see the stage or field of play.

THE TECHNICAL TEAM

The production, or staging, of an event involves many specialists. As an example, members of the technical team supporting a performance would include:

- Artistic Director
- Production Manager
- Technical Director
- Stage Manager
- Choreographer
- Scriptwriter
- Lighting Designer
- Lighting Operator
- Sound Designer
- Sound Operator
- Vision Designer
- Vision Operator
- Front of House Manager
- Floor Manager.

The following staff would support the performance indirectly:

- Venue Manager
- Operations Manager
- Logistics Manager
- Catering Manager
- Cleaning and Waste Manager.

CONDUCTING REHEARSALS

The importance of rehearsal cannot be underestimated. This is the opportunity for all involved to integrate their efforts — everyone from the stage manager (who calls the shots for the presentation) to the technical support staff (who follow the appropriate cues for lighting and sound). A technical run-through allows the staff involved to test the set-up and to make sure that all elements work satisfactorily. Technical glitches at an event are unprofessional, to say the least, so a back-up plan for all aspects of the presentation is absolutely essential. This includes two copies of each video or sound clip, slide presentations in more than one format and multiple microphones. Every potential problem should have a ready solution. The final aspect, over which the event manager has little control, is the quality of the presentation given by the speaker, particularly at business and academic conferences. Giving some basic advice and encouragement beforehand can assist a presenter enormously. If rehearsals have been conducted and everything is under control, speakers are far less nervous and far less likely to feel uncomfortable under the spotlight. A 'ready room' where the speaker can set up and test the presentation before going on stage is recommended.

PROVIDING SERVICES

The supply of water, power and gas, a communications network, and transport and traffic management are essential to the staging of most events.

Reahearsal leads to perfection.

STAGING TERMS

Performance

Management and agent	Take care of performers' interests
Talent	Person who is not the main performer (demeaning term)
Green room	Area where performers wait and watch monitors
Dressing room	Area where performers dress and are made up
Wings	Area used for assembling performers and props
Stage-in-the-round	Circular stage allowing 360 degree views for the audience
Proscenium arch	Traditional theatre style, curtains at side and above

Thrust	Stage projecting into the audience, such as at fashion parades
Tracks	Fixed tracks used to move props
Lectern	Stand for speaker

Lighting

Mixing desk	Where the lighting engineer controls lighting effects, adjusting colours, brightness and special effects; also where the sound engineer controls sound, including volume and switchover between music and microphone
Rigging	Overhead truss
T-stand/tree	Upright stand for lights
Floodlight	Wide light
Spotlight	Narrow light
Fresnel	Circular soft-edged beam (can go from spot to medium flood)
Cyclorama	Curved white screen at the back of the stage for light projections
Parcan	Fixed beam with soft edge, cheaper than floodlight, usually above the front of the stage and usually used in groups of four
Lighting gels	Slip-over colours used to change the colour of spotlights and parcans
Wash light	General area cover
Key light	Used for highlighting an object
Back light	Rear lighting effect (should use for speakers)
House light	Lighting provided by venue

Sound

Sound spec sheet	Specifies the sound requirements for a particular group or performance
Sound amplifier	Used to project the sound (microphones are plugged into amplifiers which power up the sound and send it to the speakers)
Out-front speakers	Speakers which face the audience
Fold-back speakers	Positioned on stage, facing the performers, to help performers hear themselves
Microphones	Include battery, stage (dynamic voice), headset and lectern

Exhibitions

Floor plan	Two-dimensional layout of the venue
CAD drawing	Computer-generated, three-dimensional drawing of the design for a stand
Booth	Usually 3 m x 3 m stand at an exhibition
Corinthian	Walling covered with fabric to which Velcro will adhere
Pit	Service duct located in the floor, providing power and telephone cables (for some indoor and outdoor events, water and compressed air and gas can also be provided in this way)
Tracker/reader	Device for scanning visitor cards to capture their data

General

Pyrotechnics	Fireworks
Three-phase	Power for commercial use comes in three-phase (lighting, sound and vision equipment requires three-phase) and single-phase for domestic use

Essential services

Essential services include power, water and gas. While the provision of these may sound simple, various different electrical sources are often required, including three-phase power for some equipment and power back-up in case of emergency. Providing the venue kitchen with gas can also be a challenge. The choice of a complex site can add to the difficulties of providing these essential services to the event venue.

Communications

Many events have particular requirements for communications, which may even include the installation of a complete telephone and communications network. Where there is a high level of demand on the communications network, the issue of band width must be resolved, particularly if there is a significant amount of data being transmitted. A stadium often requires its own mobile phone base station owing to the number of people using mobile telephones, particularly at the end of an event.

Transport and traffic management

Transport to the event, including air, rail, bus, train and taxi, all need to be considered. So, too, does the issue of parking and its impact on local traffic. In some cases, streets have to be closed, traffic diverted, and special permission sought for this purpose, the event plan being an important part of the submission to the relevant authorities. Thought must also be given to access for people with disabilities, marshalling of crowds and notifying of businesses affected by any disruptions. A link to a traffic management planning guide for events is provided at the end of this chapter.

WORKING WITH CONTRACTORS

The legal aspects of contracting were discussed in Chapter 5. When working with contractors, work breakdown and specifications are vitally important. The organiser's aim is to:

- identify and source appropriate contractors to provide services for the event
- provide accurate briefings or specifications on precise staging requirements to contractors
- obtain complete and timely quotations for the provision of services
- analyse quotations and select contractors in consultation with key stakeholders
- confirm agreements with contractors in writing, including details and costs of all services.

When monitoring contract implementation the organiser needs to:

- monitor progress, including safety issues, at regular intervals through ongoing liaison with contractors and other stakeholders
- identify the need for adjustments and organise appropriate changes with confirmation in writing
- negotiate adjustments to maintain the integrity and quality of the event
- evaluate work completed against event requirements and time schedules, and take appropriate action to address delays.

The dynamic nature of the event environment generally brings about mulitiple additional requests or changes. For this reason, contract variations need to be negotiated and documented in writing.

Safety is a major consideration in the staging area, and this work is generally done by licensed professionals. Staging contractors are able to interpret stage plans, and they have a detailed knowledge of:

- types of control desks which operate stage machinery
- techniques for working out load capacity of stage machinery
- safe and efficient methods and procedures used in manoeuvring loads
- techniques for handling scenic elements (e.g. toggling flats and pin hinging)
- relevant legislative and/or organisational health and safety requirements, including safe manual handling techniques, working at heights, moving loads safely
- safety issues associated with using ladders
- signals to be employed when using stage machinery
- safety procedures to be followed in the event of lifting, revolving or trucking emergencies.

ARRANGING CATERING

A catering contractor usually does the catering for an event, taking care of food orders, food production and service staff. These contractors (or the venue catering staff) should provide menus and costings relevant to the style of service required. Photographs of previous catering and food presentation styles can be helpful in making a decision.

There are many approaches to event catering, the most common being:

- set menu, with table service
- buffet
- finger food
- fast food.

The style of cooking and the type of service have the main impact on cost. Food that is prepared off site and heated or deep fried on site can be very cost effective. If fully qualified chefs are to provide quality fresh food with superb presentation, and the guests are to be served by silver-service-trained waiting staff, then clearly the costs will escalate enormously.

When discussing catering contracts, the event organiser needs to be very explicit about food quantities, speed of service and type of food required. Despite expression of interest in healthier food at sporting events, findings show that the old favourites, such as pies and chips, are still popular and that fruit salad and sandwiches do not sell well.

A food safety plan is another essential item when planning an event. Food safety involves protecting the customer from food poisoning by implementing a plan to prevent cross-contamination and other factors that cause bacterial growth. For example, food needs to be kept at the correct temperature all the way from the factory/market to the store, into the kitchen and onto the buffet. Food safety plans look at every aspect of food handling and, if well implemented, ensure the measurement of temperatures at key points in the process in accordance with the guidelines of the plan. The best kitchens have refrigerated delivery areas and separate storage for vegetables, meat, seafood and other products at the correct temperatures. Planned food production processes, including plating food in a refrigerated area, can further reduce the risk of bacterial growth. Finally, it is essential for the food safety specialist to consider the length of time taken for the food to reach the customer (perhaps at the other side of the stadium) and the length of time before it is consumed. Health authorities in the various states and territories monitor food safety.

Catering for an event is extremely demanding for those in the kitchen. Producing several hundred hot meals is not for the faint-hearted. The chef should be aware of the planned time for service of all courses and this should be confirmed at an early stage of the planning. Most floor managers will ask the chef how much notice is needed for service of the main course and they will monitor proceedings and advise the chef accordingly.

Beverage supplied at functions and banquets usually comes in the form of beverage packages ('packs') which are available in a range of prices, depending mainly on the quality of the wine. A pack includes a specific range of wines, beers and soft drinks, and does not generally include spirits. The client may choose a selection of beverages, but this will clearly be more expensive, and may also specify a time limit for an open bar.

ORGANISING ACCOMMODATION

For many conferences, exhibitions, shows and sporting events, accommodation is an essential part of the package. The packaging of air travel and accommodation demands that planning for such events occurs well in advance in order to acquire discounted air fares and attractive room rates. If such rate reductions are essential to favourable pricing of the event, it is preferable to hold the event in an off-peak season. However, as soon as an event such as the Formula 1 Grand Prix in Melbourne reaches a significant size, discounted rates are out of the question as accommodation in the destination city will be fully booked.

The following extract illustrates the response of many accommodation providers as soon as they get wind of an event, although this approach to pricing is generally counterproductive. The negative image created by overpricing can have an impact on tourism in the long term.

The normally sleepy town of Mongu (in Zambia) is about to come alive this weekend for the Kuomboka ceremony. The ceremony stretches back several centuries and is about moving Lozi people from the flooded Zambezi Plains to the plateau. Hotel owners in Mongu say they immediately hiked room rates as soon as the announcement of the event was made, by between 600 and even 1000 per cent in some cases. They are also quoting their room rates in United States dollars as they expect more than 5000 tourists to witness Zambia's foremost traditional event.

The holding of the ceremony is dictated by the amount of rain that falls in a particular season. So much rain has fallen this year that staging the ceremony was never in doubt.

SUNDAY INDEPENDENT, SOUTH AFRICA, 25 MARCH 2001

This is a most unusual event — most event organisers dread the prospect of rain, while those organising this event require rain to ensure its success!

MANAGING THE ENVIRONMENT

One of the legacies of the Sydney 2000 Olympic Games is an increased awareness of environmental issues in Australia. For example, because of the enormous amount of takeaway food it was estimated would be consumed at the Stadium, the Sydney 2000 organisers knew that they had to come up with a plan for its disposal. Their solution was the development of plates and cutlery from cornstarch and other biodegradable products so that all food waste would be able to go into one bin for composting. In contrast, the foil pie plates and polystyrene containers used at other events generally end up as landfill.

Waste management is an important consideration for all event organisers and will be covered in detail in Chapter 22.

Pollution

Methods for reducing the environmental impact of noise, air and water pollution should be part of the planning process and advice on these can be obtained from the Environmental Protection Agency which has offices in each state. Professional contractors can advise you on the correct disposal of cooking oils and other toxic waste that could affect our water supply. As we all know, clearly marked bins should be provided to facilitate recycling of waste products. With regard to air pollution, releasing helium balloons into the atmosphere has been shown to be environmentally unfriendly and this practice is slowly dying out around the world.

Toilet facilities

Toilet facilities include those at the venue and any temporary facilities required. The number and type of toilets to be provided at an event, including the number allocated to men, women and people with disabilities, is another part of the decision-making process. The composition of the event audience — the number of men and women attending — and the average time taken by each also need to be considered! Theatre management has been working on this for years. Every woman has faced the problem of long queues during intermission and, believe it or not, there is a formula for working out how many toilets are required! Too many events provide substandard toilet facilities that cannot meet the demand.

It is essential to discuss the requirements for any event you are planning with a toilet facilities hire company as they are the experts.

Cleaning

There are a number of cleaning contractors which specialise in events, including Cleanevent, the company most widely used for events in Australia. In most cases, cleaning is done before and after the event. Maintaining cleanliness during peak times is challenging, particularly if there is only a short changeover time between event sessions. This means that you have to get one audience out, the cleaning and replenishment of stocks done, and the next audience in on time. The timing of this is part of logistics planning, which we will cover in detail in Chapter 17. Cleaning staff should be treated as part of the event staff and receive appropriate training so that they can answer questions from the people attending the event.

As you can see from the above, staging an event involves a myriad of tasks for the event organiser. With some events, the staging process may even include managing the fans who queue for days before the event for places at the event. At the Academy Awards, for example, the area designated for fans is occupied for up to two weeks before the big night, as one of the fans receives a free grandstand seat overlooking the red carpet. According to the *London Daily Telegraph*, 20 April 2001, 'The commitment of Oscar followers makes Wimbledon campers look like amateurs. A thriving industry has developed around their needs, from food stands to camping equipment.'

CASE STUDY

As an introduction to an academic awards ceremony in the Town Hall, you have been asked to organise a performance by contemporary or indigenous dancers. Unfortunately, the Town Hall is a large space, with limitations in terms of lighting effects. There will also be a significant difference between the requirements of the performance and the requirements of the awards presentation, which is a formal, traditional daytime event.

Investigate the options for props and drapes and/or create a model of the stage set-up for the dance production. Remember that the set will have to be easily removed or somehow integrated with the awards presentation.

ACTIVITIES

- *Develop a checklist for a venue inspection and then visit two or three venues and compare their various merits and limitations. In order to do this, you will need to have a specific event in mind, for example, a sporting event, a party, a conference or a wedding.*
- *Watch a video of* Gladiator *and review the staging and the audience response to the events portrayed.*

LINKS

Australasian Lighting Association
www.lighting-association.com/links/index.html

Cairns Convention Centre
www.cairnsconvention.com.au

Glossary of theatre terms
www.theatrecrafts.com/glossary/glossary.html

International Special Events Society
www.ises.com

Online special events magazine
www.specialevents.com.au

Rental equipment
www.onsiterentals.com.au

Traffic management planning guide
www.rta.nsw.gov.au

SUMMARY

In this chapter we have looked in detail at the staging of an event, including layout, décor, sound, lighting and vision. The staff and subcontractors have also been identified, and the services required at an event, including catering, cleaning, waste management and communications, have been discussed. Staging an event is probably the most creative aspect of event management and there is enormous scope for making an event memorable by using the best combination of staging elements. The selection of the right site for an event is essential as this can have a large impact on the cost of staging the event and the level of creativity that can be employed in developing the theme.

CHAPTER FIFTEEN

STAFFING

AND VOLUNTEER MANAGEMENT

ON COMPLETION OF THIS CHAPTER YOU WILL BE ABLE TO:

- develop an event organisation chart
- write job descriptions and specifications
- conduct recruitment and selection
- plan induction and training
- manage volunteers
- plan recognition strategies
- prepare staffing policies
- manage industrial relations and occupational health and safety.

There were two training sessions for volunteers. The first was very general and did not answer any of my questions. In fact, I was so confused I almost didn't return for the second session. All I really wanted was a realistic idea of where I would be and what I would do. Instead we were told about reporting relationships, incident reporting and emergency evacuation. When they started to talk about the VERP and the chain of command I was totally lost. The final straw came when the manager talked about the contractors 'attempting to claw back service in response to price gouging'. I had absolutely no idea what he was saying. All I really wanted was a map and my job description.

EVENT USHER

This comment, made by a newly employed usher, illustrates the importance of effective communication and understanding the listener's needs and expectations. In this chapter we will look at two important staff planning processes: developing organisation charts so that people understand their reporting relationships and developing job descriptions so that people understand their specific roles, thus avoiding situations such as the one outlined above. The human resource functions of recruitment, selection, training and performance management will then all fit into place.

DEVELOPING ORGANISATION CHARTS

Organisation planning for events can be complex as generally several organisation charts are required, one for each different stage or task.

Pre-event charts

Prior to the event, the focus is on planning and, as we know, this lead time can be quite long. The charts required during this period show:

- All those responsible for the primary functions during the planning stage, such as finance, marketing, entertainment, catering and human resource management. For example, the core event team for the Melbourne Comedy Festival includes the Festival Director, General Manager, Marketing Manager, Development Manager, Marketing Executive, Marketing Co-ordinator, Ticketing Manager, Office Manager, Production and Technical Manager, Artist Co-ordinator, Senior Producer and Producer's Assistant.
- Small cross-functional teams which manage specific issues such as safety and customer service.
- The stakeholders committee (including external contractors, suppliers and public bodies).

Charts during the event

When staffing levels for an event expand to the requirements of a full-scale operation, the size of the organisation generally increases enormously. In some cases, there may be more than one venue involved, so each of the functional areas, such as the catering manager for each event venue, needs to be indicated on the chart. Charts should show:

- Full staff complement, together with reporting relationships for the overall event operations.
- Emergency reporting relationships (simplified and streamlined for immediate response).

Post-event chart

After the event, the team frequently disperses, leaving only a few individuals and a chart showing key personnel involved with evaluation, financial reporting and outstanding issues.

An organisation chart can also include a brief list of tasks performed by individuals or the people performing each role. This clarifies roles and improves communication. An organisation chart for a team involved in a product launch is illustrated in Fig. 15.1 on page 222.

In Fig. 15.2 on page 223 is the organisation chart for Clean Up Australia. More than 300 000 volunteers turned up for the first Clean Up Australia Day and this number continues to rise each year.

PREPARING JOB DESCRIPTIONS

A job description, outlining the tasks that need to be performed, is required for each role. This document should show the position title, the reporting relationships and the duties. A position summary is optional. In addition to the sections shown in the job description for a Catering Services Manager in Fig. 15.3 on page 224, there should be a section showing the terms and conditions of employment. This job description would indicate the salary applicable, while those for many other positions would show the award and the pay rate under the award. As this position is likely to be a temporary one, the job description should also show the start and finish dates.

Fig. 15.1

Organisation chart for a product launch.

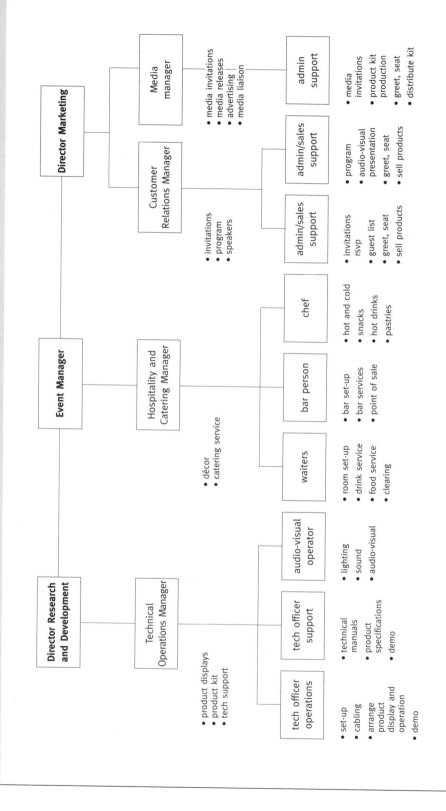

Fig. 15.2

Organisation chart for Clean Up Australia.

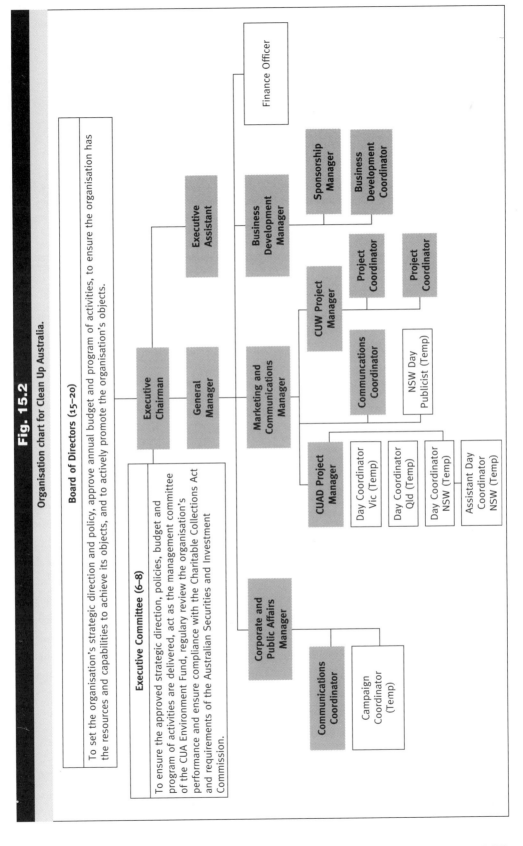

Board of Directors (15–20)

To set the organisation's strategic direction and policy, approve annual budget and program of activities, to ensure the organisation has the resources and capabilities to achieve its objects, and to actively promote the organisation's objects.

Executive Committee (6–8)

To ensure the approved strategic direction, policies, budget and program of activities are delivered, act as the management committee of the CUA Environment Fund, regulary review the organisation's performance and ensure compliance with the Charitable Collections Act and requirements of the Australian Securities and Investment Commission.

Executive Chairman

Executive Assistant

General Manager

Marketing and Communications Manager

Business Development Manager

Finance Officer

Sponsorship Manager

Business Development Coordinator

CUW Project Manager

Project Coordinator

Project Coordinator

Communications Coordinator

NSW Day Publicist (Temp)

CUAD Project Manager

Day Coordinator Vic (Temp)

Day Coordinator Qld (Temp)

Day Coordinator NSW (Temp)

Assistant Day Coordinator NSW (Temp)

Corporate and Public Affairs Manager

Communications Coordinator

Campaign Coordinator (Temp)

Fig. 15.3

Sample Job Description.

Job Description

Position title: Catering Services Manager

Reports to: Venue Services Manager

Responsible for: Sub-contracts with caterers/concessionaires

Position summary:

To meet the food and beverage needs of all customer groups through the selection and management of appropriate subcontractors and concessionaires. To ensure compliance with the negotiated agreements regarding menus, pricing, quality and service.

Duties:

• Develop tender documents for provision of food and beverage, including bars, fast food, coffee stalls, snack bars, VIP and staff catering.

• Select subcontractors and confirm agreements regarding menus, pricing, staffing and service levels.

• Develop operational procedures with special attention to integration of services, food hygiene plans, supply and storage of food and beverage, staffing and waste management.

• Work with venue operations on the installation of the required facilities and essential services (including power, water and gas) for food and beverage outlets.

• Monitor performance of contractors.

• Deal with daily operational and customer complaint issues.

As you can see from the job description, this person will not have a direct role in catering. Instead, he or she will be managing catering subcontractors. This means that experience in selecting organisations to tender for the catering contracts and managing supply of the products promised in the contracts would be essential.

Once the job description is complete, it is necessary to develop a person specification, as shown in Fig. 15.4 on page 225. This identifies the skills, knowledge and experience required for the role, and is used to inform the selection process. In this case, experience in a similar role, particularly in relation to tendering and contract management, would be required. In addition, knowledge of menu planning and costing would be essential, as would knowledge of food hygiene planning.

As you can see from the requirements for the position, experience in an event environment is desirable. However, experience in managing multiple contracts, such as in a resort, hotel or catering organisation, may be relevant in the absence of event experience.

The actual position description for a volunteer for the Australian Blues Music Festival in Fig. 15.5 on pages 226–228 is an excellent example.

RECRUITMENT AND SELECTION

Once the job description and person specification have been completed, they can be used to develop advertisements and interview questions.

Fig. 15.4

Sample Person Specification.

Person Specification

Position title: Catering Services Manager

Reports to: Venue Services Manager

Responsible for: Sub-contracts with caterers/concessionaires

Position summary:

To meet the food and beverage needs of all customer groups through the selection and management of appropriate subcontractors and concessionaires. To ensure compliance with the negotiated agreements regarding menus, pricing, quality and service.

Knowledge:

- Legal contracts (with professional advice where necessary)
- HACCP (food hygiene plans)
- RSA (responsible service of alcohol)
- Catering for large numbers
- Installation and management of bar and kitchen facilities

Skills:

- High level negotiation skills
- Verbal and non-verbal communication skills
- Preparing budgets and planning
- Development of operational procedures
- Problem solving

Experience:

- Managing large-scale catering subcontracts, multiple subcontractors, concessionaires
- Menu planning and catering control systems for large-scale catering
- Operational planning for new installations

Desirable:

- Experience in an event environment

The most common approach to recruitment is to advertise the position in local newspapers or major newspapers, on the Internet home page for the event or event-related sites, or on notice boards. Examples of advertisements for positions in the event industry are included in the final chapter. Employment agencies can also provide event staff — for a placement fee. This is an attractive method of recruitment as it cuts down your work by providing you with a short list of suitable applicants, as well as managing the administrative side of employment, such as taxes and insurance.

The best places to look for volunteers are volunteer organisations, schools, colleges and universities.

When selecting paid or volunteer staff, questions should be asked to check the candidates' suitability for the position. In the case of the position outlined in Figs 15.3 and 15.4, the recruitment officer could focus on, for example, food hygiene legislation and liquor licensing as both are relevant to the position of Catering Services Manager.

Fig. 15.5

Excellent example of a position description.

AUSTRALIAN BLUES MUSIC FESTIVAL
VOLUNTEER POSITION DESCRIPTION

DETAILS OF THE ACTIVITY

Date of Establishment:	October 2000
Date Last Reviewed:	September 2004
What is your official role?	Australian Blues Music Festival Volunteer
Activities?	Assist with the operations of the Australian Blues Music Festival
Who is your Supervisor?	Australian Blues Music Festival Volunteer Manager – Sarah Dawson
Availability?	Volunteers for this position will be required to be available for a minimum of 12 hours during the 2005 Australian Blues Music Festival.

Availability? — Volunteers for this position will be required to be available for a minimum of 12 hours during the 2005 Australian Blues Music Festival.
This activity is subject to varying hours. Volunteers will be required to be available for morning, afternoon and evening placements.
Availability will be required for 4 hours per placement and will take place between 9 am and 1 am.

Activity Requirements?

This role is in a voluntary capacity and volunteers do not receive a wage. They will, however, receive the following:
- Official Australian Blues Music Festival Volunteer Shirt
- Volunteers will be presented with Official Australian Blues Music Festival Certificates of Appreciation at an Official Ceremony Function
- Volunteering requires access to all ticketed venues and performances to undertake familiarisations, research and other volunteer duties

REQUIREMENTS
What do I need to do this activity?

- A desire to be part of the best Blues Music Festival in the country
- Passion for Australian music
- An ear for true blue Aussie talent
- Good communication skills
- Good time management skills
- Evidence of self motivation
- Flexibility
- Patience
- Ability to work as a member of close loyal team
- Ability to deal with a range of personalities and behaviours
- Ability to work under pressure

Fig. 15.5 CONTINUED

Excellent example of a position description.

	• Must be 18 years of age or over to work in venues with age requirements (ie licensed venues).
PHYSICAL ACTIVITY	Volunteering for the Australian Blues Music Festival may require, but is not limited to bending, lifting of boxes and merchandise, standing for lengthy periods where seating is not available and other activities that can at times be physically demanding. Where the physical demands of any activity are beyond your capabilities, you are requested to discuss the matter with your Supervisor.
TRAINING	One or two compulsory Volunteer training sessions will be conducted for all volunteers working for the 2005 Australian Blues Music Festival. Successful completion of this training will guarantee volunteer work placement with the festival. Where training has not been completed, your services cannot be utilised.
KEY TASKS/PERFORMANCE MEASURES	Many tasks are available to Volunteers of the 2005 Australian Blues Music Festival. Volunteers will be selected to fill various roles throughout the three days of the Festival. Depending on the role the volunteer is considered for, the key tasks and performance measures will be as follows:
Key Tasks – Customer Information Provision	• Volunteers need to have accurate knowledge of the Festival programme, venues, merchandise items and relevant prices, ticket structure and the festival band line-up. • Provide existing and prospective ticket holders with up to date information on the 2005 Australian Blues Music Festival
Performance Measures – Information Provision	• Minimal complaints received from festival patrons • Volunteers must attend one of the compulsory training sessions (date TBA) prior to the Australian Blues Music Festival
Key Tasks – Sales	• Sale of Australian Blues Music Festival tickets
Performance Measures – Sales	• Sale of tickets at the Belmore Park ticketing van and various festival venues, as specified by Festival organisers • All details are recorded accurately, and sales are to be receipted through the Point Of Sale machines and checklists immediately • Tills and stock levels must balance at the close of business every day

Fig. 15.5 CONTINUED

Excellent example of a position description.

Key Tasks – Wristband Checking	• To undertake door control at Official Australian Blues Music Festival venues to ensure only Festival patrons with correct wristbands or stamps gain entry to the ticketed areas
Performance Measures – Wristband Checking	• All patrons in the areas are wearing the required festival wristbands or stamps • All wristbands are the appropriate colour/s for the relevant days of the festival • Minimal complaints from Festival patrons and venues

ACTIVITIES

Tasks with each role will vary, but may include the following:

1. Supplying of accurate information on:
   - Ticket Structure & Costs
   - Festival Band Line-up
   - Key Personnel
   - Busking the Blues Competition
   - Blues Hall of Fame
   - Festival Venues
   - Local Knowledge
   - Festival Sponsors
   - Business Houses
   - Chain Awards
   - Shuttle Bus.
2. Attend face-to-face enquiries about the Australian Blues Music Festival.
3. Provide information to visitors and the local community.
4. Sale of Australian Blues Music Festival Official Merchandise through the cashiering system.
5. Handling of cash, and assisting with balancing the cashiering system at the end of the day.
6. Undertake shift stock take, and provide a report to the Australian Blues Music Festival Volunteer Manager.
7. Courteous and efficient ticket and merchandise sales.
8. Assist with the presentation of the Australian Blues Music Festival Headquarters (Goulburn Visitor Information Centre), and ticket/merchandise outlets.
9. Attend one compulsory volunteer training session (date TBA), as well as a pre-shift briefing and debriefing.
10. Work as part of a team.
11. Perform other duties as required that are consistent with the Principle Objectives of this position.

Permission kindly granted by the Australian Blues Musical Festival

DRAWING UP ROSTERS

Staff planning includes the development of work rosters. This can be quite difficult, particularly if multiple sessions and multiple days are involved and interrelated tasks have to be considered, as sufficient time needs to be factored in for each task. For example, if the site crew has not completed the installation of essential equipment for a particular session, work cannot begin on related tasks. Staff scheduled to be on duty will stand idle and become frustrated, knowing that deadlines are slipping. Having got out of bed at 3 am to arrive as scheduled at 4.30 am to set up for the day will contribute further to their frustration. In the event environment there is often limited time for transition from one session or show to the next and there are usually many interrelated jobs to be done, requiring extremely detailed planning and scheduling. A staffing crisis in the hours preceding an event can also contribute to the risk of accidents and poor service, again emphasising the importance of effective planning.

TRAINING

Event staff must be trained in three basic areas: the objectives of the event, the venue and their specific duties.

TAFE NSW volunteer training session for the 2000 Olympic Games.
Reproduced with permission TAFE NSW.

General outline

Staff need to be presented with a general outline of the event, as well as its objectives and organisational structure. They need to be motivated to provide outstanding service and reliable information to every member of the event audience.

Venue information

A tour of the venue enables staff to become familiar with the location of all facilities, functional areas and departments, and the spectator services provided. This is the ideal time to cover all emergency procedures.

Specific job information

Event staff need to know their duties and how to perform them. Maps and checklists can be extremely useful for this purpose, while rehearsals and role plays help to familiarise staff with their roles before the onslaught of the event audience.

Most trainees would rather move from the specific, which is more personally relevant, to the general. However, in some cases, access to the venue is only permitted at the very last minute and training has to focus on the more general aspects first.

Training days provide an ideal opportunity for team building. Team building activities, such as quizzes, games and competitions, should be included in all training so that comfortable relationships will develop. Such activities should be relevant to particular tasks. Event leaders need to accelerate all processes as much as possible in order to hold the attention of the trainee group and develop team spirit.

Reinforcement is essential and, at the end of training, the event manager should be confident that all staff have achieved the training objectives for knowledge, attitudes and skills. Too often these sessions are a one-way process, trainees becoming bogged down with an overload of information. Training materials need to be prepared in a user-friendly, jargon-free format for participants to take home. An illustration of how to use a stopwatch is provided in Fig. 15.6 to show how effectively simple training aids can support learning. A hotline staffed by volunteers who answer staff questions about rosters, roles and transport information is also a good idea.

Fig. 15.6

A simple training aid to assist learning.

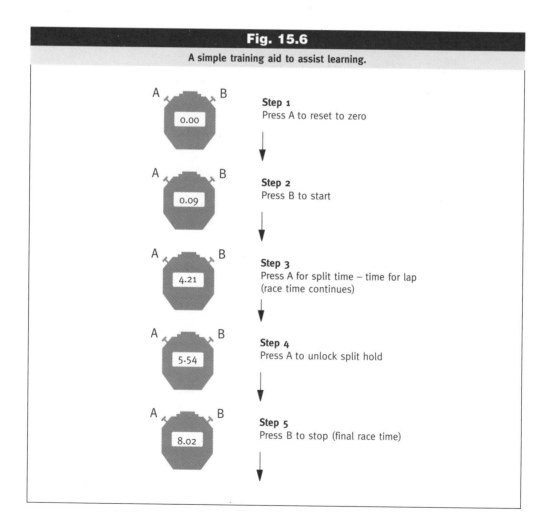

Step 1
Press A to reset to zero

Step 2
Press B to start

Step 3
Press A for split time – time for lap
(race time continues)

Step 4
Press A to unlock split hold

Step 5
Press B to stop (final race time)

The following checklist covers the type of information that might be included in training manuals and training sessions:

Shift routine and specific tasks

- location of check-in area and check-in procedure
- reporting for shift and briefing
- uniforms and equipment
- incident reporting system
- supervision
- specific roles
- breaks and meals
- debriefing and check-out

Moving stock quickly and safely from one area to another is an important task for event staff.

Venue operations

- venue organisation and support operations
- staffing policies/rules
- emergency procedures
- radio procedures
- other relevant procedures

General event information

- event outline and objectives
- event audience expectations
- transport
- related local services information
- contingency planning

Customer service training is a key component of all event training. As the general principles of quality service are well known, the focus should be on specific information required by staff in order to properly assist customers rather than on general skills. Most event staff rate training on specific event information for the event audience as being the most relevant to their training needs. Staff, however well intentioned, find themselves helpless and frustrated when asked questions that they cannot answer. Fig. 15.7 on page 232 shows the attributes of staff that event customers value.

Briefing staff

Briefing staff prior to every shift is essential. It is an extension of the training sessions and allows the venue or event manager to impart important, relevant information to staff before they commence work. Some information may be new, such as changes to spectator transport arrangements, while other elements may be a reinforcement of key information, such as incident reporting or emergency procedures.

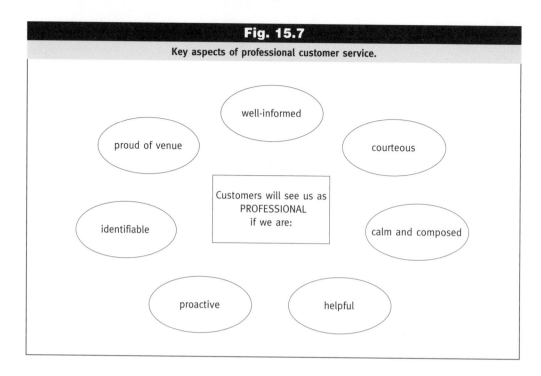

Fig. 15.7

Key aspects of professional customer service.

well-informed

proud of venue

courteous

Customers will see us as
PROFESSIONAL
if we are:

identifiable

calm and composed

proactive

helpful

Briefing volunteers.

MANAGING LEGAL REQUIREMENTS

Managers in charge of staffing need to be aware of the legal requirements of employing staff. The two main areas of concern are industrial relations and occupational health and safety.

Industrial relations

All paid staff should be remunerated in accordance with the relevant industrial award or agreement. Employers have a range of legal obligations, such as deduction of PAYG tax, that can be explored on the websites at the end of this chapter. Frequently a number of awards apply. This is due to the variety of occupations involved in staging an event, ranging from catering to electrical installation. For this reason, the use of agencies and subcontractors is common in the event industry as it reduces the administrative work of the event organiser. It is also possible to put in place a specific workplace agreement, as was done by the Sydney Organising Committee for the Olympic Games (SOCOG) for the 2000 Olympic Games, though this is not generally feasible for smaller events.

Occupational health and safety

The topic of occupational health and safety is covered in detail in Chapter 18. The most important element of this legislation is the responsibility it places on the event organiser for training and supervision of staff.

Employers have a duty of care for the health and safety of employees. Any issue which places employees in the workplace at risk should be considered a duty of care issue, including matters not typically seen as OH&S issues, such as aggression from customers, working alone at night or working long hours with limited rest periods. An employer's responsibilities include the provision of a safe place of work and training in safe systems of work.

A five-step approach is recommended in implementing an OH&S system. The five steps are:

1 Develop OH&S policies.
2 Set up consultation meetings with employees.
3 Establish training programs and communication plans (including posters).
4 Establish a hazard identification process.
5 Develop, implement and continuously improve risk control strategies.

PREPARING STAFFING POLICIES

Staffing policies should be developed as part of any human resource planning strategy and should cover such aspects as health and safety, misconduct, poor performance, sexual harassment and contravention of safety procedures. These policies are then simplified and summarised as rules for all paid and volunteer staff:

1 Work in a safe manner.
2 Do not endanger the health and safety of others.
3 Report all accidents and incidents.
4 Protect the confidentiality of the event organisation and sponsors.
5 Do not say anything derogatory about any aspect of, or person involved in, the event.
6 Refer media questions to the correct person.
7 Look after equipment, uniforms and other assets.
8 Act in a polite and courteous way to spectators and team members.
9 Use and abuse of alcohol or drugs while on duty is prohibited.
10 Act in a financially responsible manner.
11 Follow reasonable instructions of supervisors and senior event staff.

DEVELOPING RECOGNITION STRATEGIES

Recognition of the work of both paid and volunteer staff can have a huge impact on motivation. One of the most effective strategies is the development of realistic goals for staff as this allows individuals to see that their work has contributed to the success of the event.

Intangible rewards include:
- goal achievement through individual and team targets and competitions
- job rotation
- job enrichment
- meeting athletes, stars, musicians and artists
- working with people from overseas
- providing service and information and performing other meaningful tasks
- praise and verbal recognition
- training and skill development
- opportunities for building relationships and friendships
- media recognition.

Tangible rewards include:
- merchandise
- tickets
- post-event parties
- recognition certificates
- statement of duties performed
- meals and uniforms of a high standard
- badges, memorabilia.

Linking performance to individual or team goals should be considered carefully by those in charge of motivating staff. When recognition is given to individuals, it needs to be done with caution, otherwise it can lead to accusations of inequity. Team targets are more likely to improve team performance and to develop camaraderie.

MANAGING VOLUNTEERS

Volunteer management is particularly relevant to the event business since many events are staffed by volunteers. The Australian Council of Volunteers provides training in volunteer management and the following guidelines summarise the main principles of their training:
- Volunteers have the right to be treated as co-workers.
- They should be allocated a suitable assignment, task or job.
- They should know the purpose and ground rules of the organisation.
- Volunteers should receive continuing education on the job, as well as sound guidance and direction.
- They should be allocated a place to work and suitable tools and materials.
- They should be offered promotion and a variety of experience.
- Volunteers should be heard and allowed to make suggestions.
- They must be adequately insured.
- They should be given a reference at the end of the event.

In return, the event organisation can expect:
- as much effort and service from a volunteer as a paid worker, even on a short-term basis
- conscientious work performance, punctuality and reliability

- enthusiasm and belief in the work of the organisation
- loyalty to the organisation and constructive criticism only
- clear and open communication from the volunteer.

The organisation has the right to decide on the best placement of a volunteer, to express opinions about poor volunteer performance in a diplomatic way and to release an inappropriate volunteer.

The roles most commonly performed by volunteers include:
- usher
- marshal
- time-keeper
- results co-ordinator
- referee
- administrator
- media co-ordinator
- protocol/public relations assistant
- logistics co-ordinator
- transport officer
- information officer
- customer relations officer
- first aid officer
- physiotherapist/sports medicine
- access monitor/security officer
- shift co-ordinator
- uniform/accreditation officer
- safety officer.

From a survey done by the Australian Bureau of Statistics (cat. no. 4441.0) it was shown that 2 639 500 persons, or roughly 20 per cent of the Australian population, performed some form of voluntary work. It was also shown that two fields of voluntary work claimed almost half of all volunteer hours: sport/recreation/hobby (24 per cent) and welfare/community (24 per cent).

The personal benefits, as perceived by volunteers, were:
- personal satisfaction
- social contact
- helping others in the community
- doing something worthwhile
- personal or family involvement
- learning new skills
- using skills and experience
- being active.

From another ABS survey (cat. no. 4172.0) into cultural trends, it was shown that 200 000 people Australia-wide were involved each year in organising cultural festivals. (Note that this does not include events from other categories as discussed in Chapter 1.) The following data revealed by

CLEAN UP AUSTRALIA DAY

The first Clean Up Sydney Harbour Day in 1989 achieved an enormous public response with over 40 000 Sydneysiders donating their time and energy in an attempt to clean up their harbour. The next year **Clean Up Australia Day** was born, after Ian Kiernan, AO and his committee thought that if a city could be mobilised into action, then so could the whole nation. Over 300 000 **volunteers** turned out on the first Clean Up Australia Day and the numbers have risen ever since.

The subsequent step was to take the concept of **Clean Up Australia** to the rest of the world. After gaining the support of the United Nations Environment Programme (UNEP), Clean Up the World was launched in 1993. The success of **Clean Up the World** (40 million people from 120 countries took part in the event in 1998) has shown that the environmental effort in Australia has been noticed and the environment is a concern to all people globally.

Every official clean up site needs to have at least one supervisor on **Clean Up Australia Day**.

Site supervisors must be over 18, and should be responsible people who are happy to commit their services for the entirety of the clean up activity. Site supervisors are volunteers who report to the state coordinator in their state or territory.

Site supervisors are responsible for:
- ensuring they have read the Clean Up Australia Day Site Guide
- selecting and surveying a site
- registering the site with Clean up Australia
- correct registering of volunteers
- volunteer briefing and ensuring volunteers are aware of safety requirements
- distributing Clean Up Bags and gloves
- reporting back to the state coordinator.

It is easy to organise a **Clean Up Australia Day** site in your local area. Once you register your interest in joining the national campaign, **Clean Up Australia** will provide you with a step-by-step guide explaining exactly what you need to do to get involved! Simply contact **Clean Up Australia** by telephoning us on 1800 CUADAY 1800 282 329 or e-mailing **cleanup@cleanup.com.au**.

the survey is also interesting: 28.5 per cent of festival involvement was for a duration of one to two weeks and 24.9 per cent involved three to four weeks work. Most people were not paid for their involvement — only 14.2 per cent received any payment for their work.

These findings are useful in understanding the contribution and motivation of volunteers and the importance of developing recognition strategies to meet their needs. In the job description for volunteers for the Australian Blues Music Festival earlier in this chapter, a number of benefits are listed that would meet the stated needs of volunteers for social contact and being active. These volunteers also received rewards in the form of merchandise and meeting musicians. After the Sydney Olympics, IOC President Juan Antonio Samaranch described Australia's volunteers as the 'most dedicated and wonderful volunteers ever'. This was a richly deserved accolade for a country in which volunteering is part of the social fabric. However, not only volunteers embraced the Olympic spirit. An experiment by one of the radio stations showed that a person posing as an American tourist with a map and a puzzled look was offered immediate assistance by those who witnessed his dilemma. The average response time to offer help was 66 seconds (Column 8,

Sydney Morning Herald, 18 September 2000). This illustrates the positive attitude of most Australian citizens towards tourism and the importance of the role of events in increasing tourist numbers. Intangible rewards, such as achievement of specific service targets, should therefore form part of the motivation strategy for both paid and volunteer staff.

CASE STUDY

You have been asked to run a tourism destination promotional forum. The aims are to raise the profile of your region as a tourist destination; provide a platform for the public and private sectors of the local tourism industry to gather, discuss and address regional tourism issues; and assist in the expansion of marketing networks and opportunities to promote local tourism destinations and events.

The Buyers and Sellers Business Session will enable delegates to network and conduct business with high-level government officials and representatives of the national, state and local tourism organisations, as well as entrepreneurs, hoteliers, travel agents, tour operators and the media. Break-out sessions at which all delegates will be invited to voice their opinions will aim to generate ideas and solutions. Also on the discussion table will be issues such as standards, product ranges, joint promotional efforts, and marketing opportunities and strategies.

You are to invite:

- tourism representatives and tourism information officers
- investors and financiers seeking new opportunities and business partners
- hoteliers, tour operators, ground transport providers and tourism facility operators
- transport operators serving the area
- buyers and tourism suppliers
- media representatives.

You have two major tasks:

- Develop an organisational chart similar to the one illustrated in Fig. 15.1 in this chapter.
- Develop your own job description as Tourism Forum Event Manager.

ACTIVITY

Investigate the occupational health and safety legislation in your state or territory by visiting the NOHSC website listed below. In the process of this investigation, identify the particular problems related to workplace health and safety facing employees and their employers in the event industry.

LINKS

Australian Blues Music Festival
www.australianbluesfestival.com.au

Department of Employment, Workplace Relations and Small Business
www.dewrsb.gov.au

National Occupational Health & Safety Commission
www.nohsc.gov.au

Wagenet (wages information)
www.wagenet.gov.au

SUMMARY

Staffing is a very important part of event management and crucial to the smooth running of an event. In order to cover this adequately, we have discussed many topics ranging from the preparation of organisation charts, which allow employees to understand their reporting relationships, to the importance of writing clear job descriptions. Recruitment and selection help to bring staff on line, while induction and training prepare them for their event roles. These topics, too, have been covered, and we have also looked at the management of volunteers and the development of recognition strategies for paid, volunteer and contract staff. Finally, the event manager needs to be able to manage industrial relations and occupational health and safety issues, as well as prepare human resource policies.

CHAPTER SIXTEEN

PEOPLE

PERFORMANCE MANAGEMENT

ON COMPLETION OF THIS CHAPTER YOU WILL BE ABLE TO:

- manage staff by planning, organising and controlling work processes
- manage staff by informing, leading and reinforcing outstanding performance
- accelerate group development processes
- manage diverse and temporary teams, including volunteers
- manage communication effectively
- plan and manage meetings.

The volunteer took one look at the uniform, refused to wear it and walked off the job. Of the twenty people I had in my team on the first day, only six remained by day five. Three of my best people were reassigned to another team on the second day. Some of those who remained beyond the second day found the work too hard; others found it too boring. People assume that when they work at a major event they will be directly involved in the action. We were long gone by the time the bike race began each morning, rushing ahead to set up the next night's camp. In reality most event employees work behind the scenes, handling difficult situations such as spectators trying to gain access to secure areas. In our case drunkenness, aggression and general horseplay by both riders and spectators were hard to handle. The work was physically hard too. Holding a team together is a real challenge, especially when there are many other opportunities for them, or nothing to hold them.

CYCLING EVENT MANAGER

This story is indicative of the problems that face many event managers. Staff are often hard to come by owing to the short-term or unpaid nature of the work. In the above scenario, the event manager was struggling to keep the event team together for the duration of a six-day, long-distance bike race. While her team may have been enthusiastic to support the charity involved in the race, as well as excited to be on the road with the cyclists, the harsh realities are often quite different from the team's expectations.

Although the event planning team may work together for months or even years, the bulk of the event team works together for an extremely short period, ranging from one day to about one month. Staff expectations are hard to manage under these conditions, and there is little time for building relationships and skills. Therefore, the focus of the event leader should be on giving clear guidelines, facilitating efficient work, energising people and celebrating successes. The event must be extremely well planned and the event leader must concentrate on developing tools for organising and controlling activities, as well as on innovative ways to inform, lead and motivate employees and volunteers who may need to reach job maturity within minutes or hours.

DEVELOPING LEADERSHIP SKILLS

The leadership model on which this chapter is based is shown in Fig. 16.1. The two main dimensions of this model are task management and people management, the basis for many other models used in organisational behaviour.

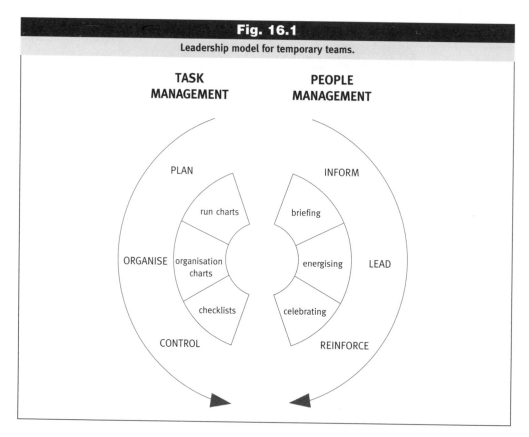

Fig. 16.1
Leadership model for temporary teams.

Task management

Task management involves the skills of planning, organising, co-ordinating and controlling work processes, using tools such as run charts, organisation charts and checklists.

Plan

Planning is probably the most important aspect of event management. It encompasses the development of policies and procedures to cover all situations, from disputes over ticketing/seating to summary dismissal of alcohol-affected employees. Planning is necessary for the development of staff rosters and the provision of meals for paid and volunteer staff, as well as for restocking, careful scheduling of stock being most important for multi-session events. When a venue is still under construction, architectural drawings are used in logistics planning to ensure, for example, that materials and equipment can be unloaded and set up easily.

There are a number of useful tools which can facilitate the planning process. A simplified version of a run chart (see Chapter 12) is helpful for all team members, and charts and maps should be displayed and discussed during training. Sometimes it is necessary to modify them so that they can be easily understood by all event staff. While the event management team needs to focus on the macro level of the event (the big picture), the micro level must not be ignored. It is essential that all members of the team be clear about the specific jobs that they are expected to do, otherwise they will become frustrated and their performance will deteriorate.

Organise

Organisation charts have been covered in Chapter 12 on 'Event Project Management' and in Chapter 15 on 'Staffing and Volunteer Management'. You will notice that including the main tasks of those involved has enhanced the chart illustrated in Fig. 15.1 on page 222. An organisation chart enhanced with task lists is a useful tool for providing everyone with a more accurate idea of roles and responsibilities at a glance. There should be no ambiguity as to who is responsible for what. In addition to the organisation chart, every person should have a job description listing their duties.

Job rotation is an important organisational task, particularly where paid or volunteer staff are required to man remote locations. Change from one role to another during a shift can alleviate boredom and reduce feelings of inequity.

Control

Checklists are useful control mechanisms. They can be used to check cleanliness, monitor the temperature of food, check for safety or security risks, and to ensure that procedures are followed for setting up and shutting down. A completed checklist is also intrinsically satisfying for the person carrying out tasks, especially if their job has no visible output. Most events are high risk, making control measures absolutely essential for risk and hazard minimisation. Tours of the venue (both front and back of house) to check that everything is safe are invaluable. Frayed carpets, loose wiring and chairs stacked in fire exits can all be dealt with using simple control tools, such as checklists.

People management

The three skills shown in the model in Fig. 16.1 that are required for good people management are informing, leading and reinforcing. Briefings, energising strategies and celebratory activities can achieve closure on short-term targets and are necessary for keeping staff interested and motivated.

People management is one of the most significant challenges for the event manager. Due to the short-term nature of events, the frontline staff do not have the commitment of employees embarking on careers with traditional organisations. A volunteer or casual employee who finds the work boring, the location unappealing, the weather unpleasant or the food unsatisfactory may simply not return the following day. Indeed, he or she may not return from a meal break! The ability to keep people informed, to inspire and motivate them through positive leadership, and to reinforce the attainment of specific results, is the key to successful people management in this fast-paced environment.

Inform

Briefings before and after shifts provide the opportunity to advise staff on the order of proceedings and to clarify issues of concern. If a single important piece of information is left out, and several hundred spectators ask the same question about it, it is frustrating for everyone involved and a mistake most event managers make only once in their career. If staff understand why they are performing what appear to be unnecessary tasks, such as checking accreditation or photocopying results, they are far more likely to understand how they fit into the big picture. Well-informed staff members (including all uniformed staff who are always the target for questions from customers, regardless of their role at an event) also respond well to positive feedback from guests and spectators.

Lead

Most event staff expect to have some fun at an event and most look forward to joining in the atmosphere. Positive actions on the part of management (including good verbal and non-verbal communication and the initiation of a range of activities to energise the team) can help to create positive staff morale. Event managers who are burnt out before an event begins are unlikely to provide inspired leadership or to solve problems with tact and diplomacy. Time and stress management are vital for everyone involved. As role models, event leaders demonstrate to their staff how to provide quality service to customers. Depending on the level of formality of the event, the service provided will vary in subtle ways. Staff look to management for these cues.

Finally, it is important that each staff member has accurate expectations of his or her role, especially the more mundane tasks. (Sometimes, jobs will be oversold and underdelivered, or undersold and overdelivered.) This provides the opportunity for the event manager to encourage the staff member to go beyond initial expectations by introducing motivational strategies such as job rotation, viewing the performance, meeting the stars and athletes, or assisting the public. Accurate expectations of the less exciting parts of the job, combined with a positive team spirit, are the outcomes of good leadership.

Reinforce

Positive reinforcement of key messages can enhance safety and service, two essential responsibilities of the whole event team. The range of ways in which core messages can be reinforced are outlined in Table 16.1. Event staff are well known for their capacity to celebrate success at every stage of a project, so recognition strategies for individuals and groups, including parties and prizes, are essential in this industry where people work under tremendous pressure to pull off an event.

In summary, event leadership is about:
- planning for short-term assignments
- organising and simplifying work processes
- developing checklists and other control processes.

Table 16.1

Communication strategies.

Verbal	Visual	Written	Behavioural
Briefings	Photographs	Training material	Videos
Meetings	Displays	Memos	Working practices
Radio conversations	Models	Letters	Role modelling
One-to-one discussion	Demonstrations	Email	Non-verbal communication
Instruction	Printed slogans	Handbooks	
Telephone	Posters	Staff newsletters	
conversations	Videos	Reports	
Training	Internet	Information bulletins	
Word-of-mouth		Checklists	
messages			

One-on-one computer demonstrations are very useful for reinforcing core messages.

It is also about:

- briefing and communicating with the team
- motivating and energising on an hourly or daily basis
- reinforcing key messages and targets
- celebrating success.

The work of the event leader may extend to some or all of the following challenging contexts quite unlike those of the traditional business environment:

- one shift for one day
- single or multiple venues
- single or multiple session times
- a team separated by physical distance
- routine and dull jobs away from the action
- busy, pressured and high-stress roles in the midst of the action.

And the team itself may include all or any of the following:

- contractors
- volunteers

- temporary workers
- students
- committee members
- police and other stakeholders.

MANAGING TEMPORARY AND DIVERSE TEAMS

The characteristics of temporary groups differ dramatically from those of long-term groups. Long-term groups are able to focus on quality improvement initiatives, with quality teams contributing to ongoing improvements over a period of time. This is seldom the case for temporary teams. The differences are summarised in Table 16.2.

Table 16.2	
Differences between long-term and short-term teams.	
Long-term teams	**Temporary teams**
Commitment to organisation's mission	Commitment to task
Decisions by consensus	Leader solves problems and makes decisions
Group cohesion over time	Limited relationship building
Career development within organisation	No career/organisation orientation
Intrinsic satisfaction	Tangible rewards
Empowerment	Limited responsibility
Lifelong learning	Limited learning
Positive performance management	Positive reference

In the event environment safety instructions need to be clear and concise.

Not only is the event team temporary, it is also, as a rule, extremely diverse. The general approach to managing a diverse workforce is to assimilate everyone into a strong organisational culture. When individuals share common codes of behaviour and communication, and solve problems in routine ways, the positive benefit is consistency and this can be achieved in the normal organisational life cycle. However, this is hard to achieve in the dynamic event environment where there tends to be more on-the-spot decision-making and a wider acceptance of diverse standards of behaviour. With limited time, an event leader simply does not have the opportunity to assimilate the team into a strong organisational, or group, culture. Working with a diverse range of people with wide-ranging needs and interests is inevitable.

MOTIVATION THEORIES

In common business operations, such as real estate offices and banks, most employees are permanent and motivation considerations are quite different from those in the dynamic and project focused event environment. Here the workforce is made up of contract, casual, temporary and volunteer labour and a small team of event staff who generally work much more flexible (and longer) hours than the norm.

Event employees are motivated by a wide range of factors, from hours compatible with study in unrelated fields to the potential for promotion and career development in the event industry. The first type of employee is probably looking for a position in which the tasks are simple, the work is routine and well paid, and the problems are few. The second is looking for a challenge: variable and complex work and new learning experiences. This diversity is matched by diversity in cultural expectations. Some employees are comfortable in a society in which individual effort is acknowledged, while others are more accustomed to a group-oriented environment in which social harmony is more important than competition.

With these challenges in mind, the modern event manager needs to evaluate contemporary theories of motivation to understand how best they can motivate their own work teams. A number of these theories are summarised below.

Three needs theory

David McClelland (1961, 1975) suggests that there are three motivating needs: the need for achievement; the need for power; and the need for affiliation. Those motivated by achievement are goal oriented and focus on career development. Those who are motivated by a need for power prefer to influence others, either through formal or informal leadership. Where such influence occurs informally, it is essential that leadership skills are harnessed for the good of the organisation. If the informal leader is a troublemaker, then their goals will not be compatible with those of the organisation. Finally, those who are motivated by affiliation look for a friendly, group-oriented workplace where there is positive social interaction.

Equity theory

In the workplace, people make comparisons between the effort they make and the rewards they receive and the effort and rewards of others. If there is a perception that other employees or volunteers are better rewarded or make less effort, this will result in a lack of motivation. To redress the issue, the person who feels that their treatment is inequitable is likely to become less productive or to leave. Inequity can be perceived by teams as well, with employees at one venue comparing their rewards and effort with those of employees at another venue. 'Not fair' is the usual comment made in this situation and is applicable to any number of rewards, including meal breaks, shift allocation, uniform design, and allocation of new equipment or incentives. The perceived imbalance between effort and reward is illustrated in Fig. 16.2 on page 246.

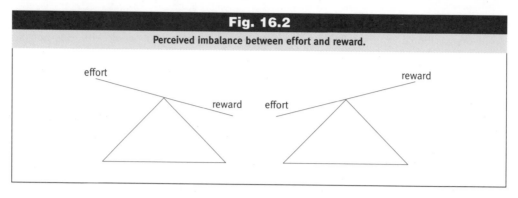

Fig. 16.2

Perceived imbalance between effort and reward.

effort

reward

reward

effort

reward

When evaluating the benefits and equity of rewards another consideration is whether it is best to reward individuals or teams.

Opportunities for individual recognition, development and reward may include:

- internal training/professional development
- external training/professional development
- change in job responsibilities
- opportunity for greater autonomy or responsibility
- formal promotion
- contests and prizes
- rewards for loyalty
- incentives.

Goal-setting

Edwin Locke et al. (1984) suggests that achievable goals are highly motivating. However, as well as being achievable, goals must be specific and relevant. Goal achievement is an **intrinsic** (internal) motivator, while prizes and other tangible rewards are **extrinsic** (external) motivators. Many events with social impacts attract volunteers who are intrinsically motivated, because their efforts are directed towards fundraising for charities and other social causes. If this is the case, these goals need to be well articulated, and communication of the milestones towards achieving these goals needs to be timely and encouraging.

Reinforcement theory

The origin of the theory of reinforcement is the work of B. F. Skinner (1953). Reinforcement theory is based on the premise that people's behaviour is determined by feedback. In the simplest sense, positive feedback is likely to enhance behaviour. So it follows that productivity will improve if the correct behaviours are identified, monitored, recognised and rewarded, often by praise, which is most effective when linked to specific behaviours and goals.

It is important to remember that unacceptable behaviour, too, can be reinforced by positive feedback or actions. For example, a lazy employee who arrives late to find that everyone else has set up the function room is being rewarded for laziness, and an employee taking credit for the work of others is being rewarded if management gives him or her a bonus. Managers need to be aware that they may be positively reinforcing the wrong behaviour. 'Let me do it' can encourage future demonstrations of incompetence!

Another outcome that can follow certain behaviours is punishment. In the event industry, this often involves criticism, and sometimes yelling. The effect is demotivating, even though the behaviour that provoked the outburst may be eliminated.

The use of rewards, including encouragement, can have wide-ranging benefits. A positive working environment can have a dramatic impact on motivation and, in turn, on customer satisfaction. Thus, there is a **customer benefit** associated with a positive environment. When an individual is rewarded for learning new skills or for working efficiently, this can have a direct, constructive effect on the reinforced behaviour. It can also have a spin-off benefit, by **influencing other positive behaviours**. Indeed, psychologists have shown that rewards do not have to be given every time the behaviour is exhibited. A variable ratio of reinforcement, given at random, can be even more effective. This principle is evident in the behaviour of gamblers. While gamblers may only win, say, once out of five times, that win is sufficient to encourage them to gamble again and again. This means that a manager can have a powerful influence over an employee's behaviour if the rewards follow the desired outcomes, even if these only occur from time to time. In addition, **positively reinforced behaviours are stable**, even in the absence of the reinforcer.

In contrast, when a manager has a punishing, critical style, employees may comply when he or she is present, but will take the opportunity to misbehave in his or her absence — 'While the cat's away the mice will play'. For many managers in busy event workplaces, the temptation is to notice errors and omissions. 'Your attitude towards customers is bad' is a negative, punishing reaction that will do little to improve performance. It takes a shift in thinking to provide constructive feedback and encouragement of good performance.

The challenge for the manager is to explain to the employee what a 'good attitude' looks like. 'Stop what you are doing, smile and acknowledge the customer, greet the customer and take time to listen' are some of the signs of a positive attitude towards the customer. Once these behaviours have been established, practised and understood, the employee can be encouraged for exhibiting a positive service ethic. The customer may also reward this orientation with an enthusiastic response. As mentioned, rewards can take many forms. However, in everyday life, simply noticing effort and complimenting it is often all that is needed to create an upbeat event environment which everyone on site can enjoy.

Role modelling

Role modelling is often used in training in the service industries. At events where the ambience is created by senior staff, the tone is set for subsequent relationships with clients and colleagues. For this reason, behaviour by senior personnel should demonstrate best practice, and employees who model this type of behaviour and uphold the service vision of the organisation should be appropriately rewarded. This may sound very simple, but in practice far too many managers in event workplaces exhibit autocratic, egocentric styles of behaviour that are not conducive to a positive service ethic.

Expectancy theory

This theory, developed by Victor Vroom (1973), looks at the motivators of performance and the outcomes of performance. It also considers the important issue of perception and how the balance between effort and reward is perceived by the individual, thus combining elements of some of the preceding theories. If the expectation is high, but the performance target is achievable, the individual or team will achieve the outcome, providing that the outcome has sufficient appeal.

Expectancy theory is one of the most comprehensive explanations of motivation, and identifies three variables:

- expectancy (effort linked to performance)
- instrumentality (performance linked to reward)
- valence (attractiveness of rewards).

Expectancy theory stresses the importance of the individual's perception: their perception of effort leading to performance; their perception of the likelihood of rewards being delivered as promised; and their perception of the rewards promised.

GROUP DEVELOPMENT

Studies by B. W. Tuckman as far back as 1965, and still applicable today, have shown that groups tend to go through five defined stages in their development:

1 **Forming** This is the period during which members grow used to one another and tentatively formulate goals and behaviours that are acceptable.
2 **Storming** In this stage there is generally some conflict over control and leadership, including informal leadership, known as sorting out 'the pecking order'.
3 **Norming** Once the hierarchy and the roles of all group members have been defined, the group tends to adopt a common set of behavioural expectations.
4 **Performing** During this productive stage, members focus on performance within the framework of the team.
5 **Adjourning** Faced with disbandment, successful teams share a sense of loss. In this stage, feelings of achievement are tempered by sadness that the group will be disbanding.

This analysis of group development is useful to those of us who are in the event business because the process of group formation does require special attention in this environment. Sometimes, the early stages of group development can be accelerated so that the performing, or productive, stage is reached quite quickly. This can be done effectively by using ice-breakers in team training sessions.

Where group members exhibit a wide range of individual differences, particularly in language or culture, the following strategies can help to develop effective communication between them:

1 Identify specific information needs of group members.
2 Use plain English.
3 Allocate buddies or develop sub-teams.
4 Use graphics to impart information.
5 Rotate roles.
6 Provide all members with opportunities to participate in the group.
7 Develop group rituals and a group identity.

Geert Hofstede (1980), well known for his work in cross-cultural communication, has identified the following value dimensions in communication.

The first value dimension he termed **power distance**. This indicates the extent to which a society accepts differences in power and authority. In some cultures, employees show a great deal of respect for authority, so Hofstede suggests that these employees have a high power distance. They would find it difficult to bring problems out into the open and discuss them with senior staff. The low power distance prevalent in other cultures encourages closer relationships at all levels, and questions and criticism from employees are more readily accepted. As you can imagine, if employees in an event team were to come from both high power and low power distance backgrounds, the first would be aghast at the audacity of the second when they brazenly pointed out problems and the low power distance employees would find it difficult to understand why the others did not speak up.

The second value dimension identified by Hofstede was **individualism/collectivism**. Some societies have a strong sense of family, and behavioural practices are based on loyalty to others. Such societies display higher conformity to group norms, and it follows that employees of these cultural backgrounds would feel comfortable in a group. In contrast, employees from highly individualistic societies would defend their own interests and show individual (as opposed to group) initiative.

These are just two cultural dimensions. There are many other variations in people's responses to situations, for example, their different attitudes towards punctuality.

Hofstede suggests that the main cross-cultural skills involve the capacity to:

1 communicate respect

2 be non-judgemental

3 accept the relativity of one's own knowledge and perceptions

4 display empathy

5 be flexible

6 take turns (allow everyone to take turns in a discussion)

7 tolerate ambiguity (accept different interpretations of what has been said).

IMPROVING COMMUNICATION

While the topic of event briefings has been covered briefly above, here are some additional guidelines for improved communication in the event team.

Establish the level of priority

It is important to establish the level of priority straightaway. Emergency situations are of course the highest risk for any event and communication about an incident or potential incident should be given top priority.

Identify the receiver

By identifying the receiver, you will be able to match your message to the receiver's needs, thus demonstrating empathy. Your message will also reach the correct target.

Know your objective

Clarity in communication is often linked to the development of an action objective. If you know what you want to achieve, you will be able to express yourself more easily and clearly. Stating a problem and its ramifications is often only the first stage. By indicating what needs to be done, you can more easily achieve your objective and reach an agreed outcome.

Review the message in your head

In preparing to send a message, you should structure your communication effectively. It is also useful to review the receiver's likely response.

Communicate in the language of the other person

If you use examples and illustrations that the receiver will understand, your message will be more easily comprehended.

Clarify the message

If the receiver appears from their non-verbal behaviour not to understand your message, clarification is essential.

Do not react defensively to a critical response

Asking questions can help you to understand why your receiver has responded defensively and can diffuse the situation. By seeking feedback you can ensure that you have reached a common understanding.

In most event situations you are running on adrenalin from the start. There is never enough time. You have to deliberately stop yourself, focus on the person, look them in the eye and use their name. It is so easy to forget to do this when you have a hundred unsolved problems and the urge is to be short with them. Something as simple as using the person's name makes the difference between a good event leader and a mediocre one. The worst event leaders are so stressed they can't remember their own names!

EVENT STAFFING MANAGER

TIME MANAGEMENT

To work effectively with event teams, which may be together for a very short period of time, an event manager needs to:

- plan effectively
- identify critical issues and tasks
- analyse and allocate tasks
- manage work priorities
- make quick but informed decisions
- build relationships quickly
- provide timely information
- remove barriers
- simplify processes
- solve problems immediately

- manage stress for self and others
- develop creative and flexible solutions
- constantly monitor performance
- reward the achievement of outcomes.

From this list, it is clear that outstanding time management skills (on a personal and a group level) are required in order to gain maximum benefit from the planning phases. An ability to develop instant rapport with new people is also essential when time is limited.

PLANNING AND MANAGING MEETINGS

Meetings are an important feature of the management of events, starting in the early planning phases and building to pre-event briefings and post-event evaluations. Meetings can be highly productive, or they can waste an incredible amount of time. In fact, a poorly focused, poorly managed meeting will simply confuse and frustrate everyone. One event management company introduced the idea of a standing meeting to curtail the length of their meetings.

Timelines should be set and an agenda for discussion distributed beforehand with all relevant material so that everyone is prepared. During meetings a chairperson should manage the pace and outcomes of the meeting and someone should be designated to keep notes for the record. The most important aspect of note-taking is the recording of actions and deadlines for those attending. Documentation from the meeting should be distributed and actions identified, prioritised and included in the planning process.

In addition to focusing on tasks at event meetings, focusing on people should be a priority. Meetings can be an excellent venue for relieving stress, building team spirit and motivating all involved.

CASE STUDY

I knew what I had to do. I had to stand at an access gate all day on my own and check staff passes. I was prepared for the boredom but I didn't bring my thermos or a portaloo. Can you believe it? I wasn't given a break for six hours! By then I was really looking forward to some relief. You would think that these managers would learn something about people's basic needs. In this situation I needed to keep warm and dry. A folding chair would have made all the difference. A drink and an opportunity to go to the toilet would have been welcome! In terms of the hierarchy of needs, I wasn't expecting self-actualisation but I was hoping to have my physical needs met by being given scheduled breaks and possibly having my job rotated. In fact by the time my shift was over for the day, my supervisor had long left the scene. It's good for some.

EVENT VOLUNTEER

- How could this person's needs be better catered for?
- Are there any strategies for helping to motivate this volunteer?
- What leadership approach would you take to managing your event team?
- Is a different approach needed for managing paid staff and volunteer staff? Explain.
- Explain one way in which you would energise your staff or celebrate success.

ACTIVITY

Select an event and develop a list of pros and cons of working in three different roles at the event. Describe the leadership challenges and your solutions for the management team of this event.

LINKS

Australian Human Resources Institute
www.ahri.com.au

Australian Workplace
www.workplace.gov.au

Volunteering Australia
www.volunteeringaustralia.org

SUMMARY

In this chapter we have discussed the time constraints in staging an event and the temporary nature of the event workforce, both of which have a major impact on event leadership. The event staff manager must be able to plan, organise and control tasks in such a way that all concerned are able to see their contribution to the aims and objectives of the event. In managing these temporary, and often diverse, teams, the event staff manager also needs to accelerate group development processes, communicate effectively, lead constructively and develop recognition and reward programs.

CHAPTER SEVENTEEN

ON-SITE

MANAGEMENT

ON COMPLETION OF THIS CHAPTER YOU WILL BE ABLE TO:

- plan the logistics of an event
- develop policies and procedures for on-site management
- develop performance standards to measure success against objectives
- organise and monitor infrastructure for outdoor events
- oversee event set-up
- monitor event operation
- oversee event breakdown.

Melbourne is recognised as Australia's event capital and in recent years has consolidated this position with respect to golfing events. In 1998, Melbourne hosted the President's Cup, followed by the Accenture World Match Play in 2001. Melbourne held its first Heineken Classic in 2002. This event has been secured for a four-year period. These international events attract leading international and Australian golfers, along with global media, including television broadcasters. They are supported by significant State Government funding and enable Melbourne and Victoria to build on its reputation as an events capital and ultimately will contribute to an increased level of awareness of the world-class golfing facilities available in Victoria.

www.tourismvictoria.com.au

The Heineken Golf Classic, previously held in Perth, Western Australia, is now held at the Royal Melbourne Golf Course. This golf tournament has many operational demands. Firstly, a logistical plan would need to be developed to ensure that all competing golfers (and their entourage of managers, caddies, etc.) arrive as scheduled, that they are settled into the correct accommodation and that all their golfing equipment is accounted for and secure. Secondly, there would be the whole process of preparing the course, which the greenkeeper would start many months before the competition. This would also involve setting up spectator stands, scoreboards and crowd barriers closer to the actual time of the event (this could not be done overnight and adequate time would need to be allowed for this process). The setting-up process is often called bump-in. Finally, at the end of the competition, everything would need to be dismantled and stored, as most items would be valuable assets, and the course restored to its original state for normal operation. This is referred to as bump-out. In between bump-in and bump-out, there is the event to run. (Naturally, with all events, the costing for the facility needs to include the period required for bump-in and bump-out.)

The focus of this chapter is managing the operation of an event, which is the culmination of many months, at least, of careful planning.

Setting up crowd barriers is just one of the operational procedures for a major golf tournament.
Reproduced with permission EventsCorp, Perth.

PLANNING LOGISTICS

Simply put, logistics is about getting things organised, getting things (and people) in the right place at the right time and pulling everything down. Rock concerts and entertainment events featuring international artists present many logistical problems, particularly if the group is on a tour of several cities. Sometimes a complex array of musical equipment, some of which might have been airlifted into the country only days, or even hours, before the event, has to be set up. However, in most cases, the team supporting the artists would have identified specific requirements, at times down to the last detail, to be met locally. (These might even include requests for exotic foods and special dietary items.) Arranging accommodation has been known to be complicated by the inclusion of a weird range of pets, not commonly cared for in five star hotels, in the entourage.

The most amusing example of a logistical dilemma was that reported by the organisers of an equestrian cross-country event. A decision had to be made as to how to manage 'comfort breaks' for volunteers deployed over an enormous open venue. Should a buggie pick up the staff member and take them to the facilities? No, it was decided that a roving portaloo on the back of a small truck was the answer. Take the toilet to the staff member, not the staff member to the toilet! This avoided redeployment of replacement staff.

In most cases, however, logistics planning focuses on setting up and changing sets. Athletics events are particularly challenging as there are often several concurrent and consecutive events requiring different equipment. An event that involves catering also presents enormous demands when the product has to be served hot, often to hundreds of people in a very short time. One event co-ordinator describes an event where there was only one set of plates for each guest so that the plates had to be washed between the entrée and the main course. This involved a trip up and down lots of stairs and a very tiny washing-up area with a single cold tap, placing pressure on the kitchen

Operations staff busy at an athletics event.

to plate the main course and serve it at the correct time. Cutlery (teaspoons in particular) is one of the biggest bugbears of the banquet department as a search for matching cutlery can delay a room set-up by an hour or more. Some chair covers take so long to stretch and position correctly that significant time can be lost carrying out this task (and significant labour costs incurred). The logistics manager needs to be one of the most efficient and organised people on the event team. With event operations, workflow planning becomes a fine art.

Figure 17.1 outlines the steps necessary in preparing for the effective management of on-site operations.

Fig. 17.1

Preparation for on-site management.

Develop plans for on-site management in accordance with agreed procedures

⇓

Check final arrangements for all aspects of the event

⇓

Create and collate materials to facilitate effective on-site management

⇓

Brief operational staff and contractors prior to the event

Infrastructure

The level of difficulty associated with running an outdoor event at a temporary facility cannot be underestimated. Each element of the proposed infrastructure must be discussed with key stakeholders and suppliers. Licensing requirements also require special attention. A licence may be required for:

- building work
- electrical work
- plumbing work
- gas fitting
- handling hazardous materials
- forklift operations
- special effects (e.g. rigging)
- pyrotechnics.

Outdoor infrastructure may include all or any of the following:

- power supply
- water supply
- heating or air-conditioning
- public toilets
- erection of temporary structures
- scaffolding
- emergency services
- car and coach parking
- transport systems
- camping sites or other temporary accommodation
- signage
- media services
- disabled access
- waste management facilities.

Naturally safety, security and risk management principles need to be considered throughout the operations process. Accurate plans and briefings to suppliers of infrastructure and related services will ensure a more efficient procurement process. Careful co-ordination and monitoring needs to be done, particularly during the bump-in phase when several contractors are working simultaneously on site.

Bump-in

Once final arrangements have been checked and staff and contractors have been briefed, the process of setting up all structures and facilities required for the event begins. For some tasks, such as installing sound and lighting equipment, the services of specialist engineers are needed. Setting up can be a time-consuming process and a run-through must be built into planning. This is absolutely essential as it is imperative that all facilities and equipment work. Perimeter fencing is required for most outdoor events. Computer network and other cables are laid along the fence line, and these must be covered for safety reasons and tested to ensure that the network is up and running.

Figure 17.2 illustrates the level of checking that needs to be done to ensure that an event will run smoothly.

Bump-out

At the end of the event, all temporary structures and equipment need to be dismantled. If this needs to happen immediately after the audience has left, sufficient staff will be required because at this stage everyone is generally exhausted, which itself presents a safety risk. If bump-out does not occur immediately, security staff will be needed to monitor the site until all materials and equipment have been removed. Some items are particularly expensive, and if they are lost, stolen or damaged, this can have a dramatic effect on the bottom line of an otherwise successful event.

Figure 17.3 indicates what is involved in efficiently managing the breadown of an event.

Fig. 17.2

Overseeing event set-up.

Establish contact with the nominated contractor personnel at the appropriate time and
reconfirm and agree all requirements

⇓

Agree to and make any necessary adjustments with the contractor

⇓

Check all aspects of the event set-up against the pre-arranged agreements
(materials and equipment, room set-up, staging, technical equipment, display and signage,
food and beverage facilities, registration areas)

⇓

Check all areas of the venue, and equipment, are accessible and safe

⇓

Identify any deficiencies and discrepancies and take prompt action to rectify the situation

⇓

Brief any additional on-site staff on the full details of event operation (including communication and
control mechanisms)

Fig. 17.3

Overseeing event breakdown.

Oversee the breakdown of the event to ensure it is completed in accordance with agreements

⇓

Co-ordinate the packing and removal of all materials and equipment

⇓

Check the venue to ensure items and belongings are not left behind

⇓

Debrief with contractors to discuss any difficulties or suggestions for future improvements

⇓

Check and sign accounts in accordance with contractor agreements

⇓

Note any outstanding items requiring post-event action

In most other industries, logistics involve managing the processes of manufacture, supply
and distribution (including storage and transport) of the product to the ultimate consumer. The
same general principles apply in event management, requiring an organised and structured alignment of key logistics functions. Procurement, transportation, storage, inventory management,
customer service and database management are all examples of logistical aspects of, for example,
event merchandise sales. In the same way, the supply of food and beverage to the event audience
starts right back with the producer of the food and beverage products. For most events, food

supply is unproblematic. However, in the case of a very large event, such as the Commonwealth Games, provision of sufficient stock of potatoes for fries may require importation of frozen fries, while ensuring an adequate supply of lettuce may mean the sourcing of an out-of-season vegetable. For events that run over multiple days, food storage is also an issue, as is the logistics of fresh supplies needing to be delivered overnight, which has ramifications for staffing rosters and security.

DEVELOPING OPERATIONAL POLICIES AND PROCEDURES

Every event requires policies. These describe the general principles, or 'what is to be done'. For example, policies may be drawn up to prevent fraud, to limit misrepresentation, to manage the performance of staff and to promote the right image for the event. Having prepared the policies, the procedures for implementing the policies are then developed. For example, there may be a policy on customer complaints and a procedure to follow in the event of a complaint. There may be a policy on the recruitment and training of time-keepers and a procedure for reporting and recording performance times for athletes. The policy equates to 'what is to be done' and the procedure equates to 'how it is to be done'.

A uniform policy would say that event staff are to wear specific shirt colours, that they are supplied and laundered by the event company, and that staff who lose their uniforms have to pay for replacements. The policy might also list the personal items that staff are not allowed to wear and might recommend a certain type of footware. Uniform procedures would cover the steps involved in issuing uniforms to staff at the first training session, the steps involved in handing in and retrieving uniforms from the laundry using a ticket system, and the steps to take if a uniform were lost.

A procedure can take the form of a list of tasks or a checklist. Once procedures have been developed and integrated across the event functions, all the pieces begin to fit together. Sometimes, the timing of a procedure needs to be modified to meet the needs of another functional area. For example, if the grass surrounding the greens of a golf course were scheduled to be mowed the day before a golfing competition, it would not be possible to erect the crowd control fencing until this had been done.

A procedure for entertaining sponsors for a full day is illustrated in Fig. 17.4 in the form of a run sheet.

A procedure for checking the safety of a kitchen could be outlined in a checklist, as shown in Fig. 17.5 on page 260. This procedure could also be shown as a flow chart or it could be based on a logical tour of the kitchen, with items re-ordered to match the kitchen set-up.

ESTABLISHING PERFORMANCE STANDARDS

By establishing performance standards and inspection schedules, the operational success of an event can be more confidently assured. For example, in the case of a contract with a cleaning company, with clear expectations on both sides the result should be excellent customer service. In the case of the cleaning contractor, specific details about the level of service required would be outlined for the following:
• pre-event cleaning
• pre-event day cleaning

Fig. 17.4

Daily run sheet — sponsor hospitality.

Start	Finish	Tasks
7.00 am		Security hand-over to Assistant Operations Manager.
7.00 am	7.30 am	Venue opened and checklists completed for safety, cleaning, layout and par stocks.
8.00 am	8.30 am	Staff check-in and briefing.
8.30 am		Staff commence first shift. Hospitality area opened for light meals/coffee/breakfast.
10.00 am	7.00 pm	Staff break area open.
11.00 am		Entertainment staff arrive. Acts as per daily schedule held by Operations Manager.
11.00 am	3.00 pm	Lunch service.
2.00 pm		Hand-over from Assistant to Operations Manager. Meal numbers for following day confirmed.
3.00 pm		Second shift commences, staff briefing. Catering staff meeting — Operations and Kitchen production.
3.30 pm		Deadline for lunch cash reconciliation.
4.00 pm	10.00 pm	Dinner service.
10.30 pm		Deadline for dinner cash reconciliation
11.00 pm	12.00 mid	Set-up for following day service.
12.00 mid	1.00 am	Cleaning all areas, kitchen, dining area and facilities.
2.00 am		Security lock-up.

- during session cleaning
- turnover cleaning (between sessions)
- post-event cleaning
- removal of waste materials.

The criteria for performance standards may include efficiency (e.g. speed of set-up), accuracy (e.g. checklist 100 per cent), revenue (dollar sales per outlet) or courtesy (customer feedback).

FUNCTIONAL AREAS

While the division of responsibilities into different functional areas has already been discussed in previous chapters, it is useful to review the roles of these areas, known in most other businesses as 'departments'. Each of these functional areas develops their own policies, procedures and performance standards.

Procurement and Stores

This area is responsible for purchasing, storage and distribution of all products required for the event. Such items may include radios, computers, sound equipment and drapes, and are often hired from specialist suppliers.

Fig. 17.5

Checklist for kitchen safety procedure.

Kitchen Safety Checklist

1	Food contact surfaces are clean and clear.	☐
2	Chopping boards for meat, chicken, vegetables are colour coded.	☐
3	Non-food surfaces clean and clear.	☐
4	Floors are clean and not slippery.	☐
5	Equipment is correctly cleaned and stored.	☐
6	Wiping cloths and cleaning equipment for different purposes correctly colour coded.	☐
7	Plumbing is functional.	☐
8	Refrigerator and freezer temperatures meet standards.	☐
9	Hand-washing facilities meet standards.	☐
10	Garbage disposal containers are labelled and covered.	☐
11	Storage areas are clean and clear.	☐
12	No evidence of insects or rodents.	☐
13	Lighting and ventilation is adequate.	☐
14	Gas supply is checked.	☐
15	All cooking equipment is functional.	☐
16	First aid box is fully equipped.	☐

If catering, for example, were contracted out to a subcontractor, the subcontractor would be responsible for food purchasing and storage, and the same would apply to other subcontractors. They, too, would be responsible for their product or equipment procurement and storage.

One of the main roles for this functional area during an event is the supply of event merchandise to the sales outlets.

Marketing

In the lead-up to an event, this functional area is responsible for the overall strategy for product, pricing and promotion. As the event draws near, image, sponsor liaison and sales promotion become priorities.

Ticketing

The ticketing area looks after ticketing in the lead-up to an event and during the event. In some cases this function is managed by the local Tourism Information Office; in other cases, tickets are sold by charitable organisations. For most profit-making events, the ticketing function is managed wholly by a major ticketing organisation.

Registration

Most sporting events, particularly those with large numbers of participants, need a functional area to manage the registration of participants in the race or the event. This involves completion of relevant forms by participants as well as the signatures of participants to acknowledge that participation is at their own risk.

Merchandising

The merchandising area is responsible for the sale of merchandise, ranging from caps and posters to CDs and videos. The range is frequently extensive and is sometimes advertised on the Internet.

Finance

As the event draws near, the main concern of this functional area is to maintain control processes, minimise expenditure and manage cash during the event.

Legal

In most cases, legal advice is sought before the event and it is only with very large events that a specific functional area is established to cover this role.

Technology

Networks linking different reporting systems can be developed to include those for sales of tickets and merchandise, registration of athletes and recording of results, as well as managing rosters and payroll.

Media

This functional area deals directly with the media, and during an event it needs to be constantly informed of progress. If a negative incident should occur, it is the media unit that writes the press releases and briefs the press. It also manages media interviews with the stars or athletes.

Community Relations

Generally speaking, this functional area is only represented when there is a significant community role, for example, at non-profit events.

Staffing

As the event approaches, the staffing area looks after training, uniforms, rosters and other schedules, and staff meal vouchers.

Services and Information

The provision of services and information to the event audience is obviously at its peak during the event, requiring staff to be extremely knowledgeable and resourceful.

Cleaning and Waste Management

Very often this function rests with venue staff who undertake cleaning as a routine operation before, during and after an event. For larger events, such as street festivals, the local council may ask current contractors to expand their role for the period of the festival. For major sporting events, contract cleaners are often called in to manage this functional area.

All staff need to be able to provide event information.

Catering

In most cases, venue catering is outsourced to a catering company and there is generally a long-standing contract in place with that company. Sometimes, however, a decision needs to be made as to whether to employ one caterer to take on this role or several caterers, each offering different types of cuisine. Most event organisers leave this area to catering professionals.

Catering for both takeaway and fine dining at event venues is mostly outsourced, so that this functional area is generally managed by contractors.

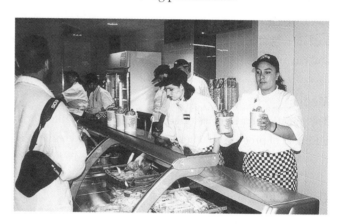

Venue Operations

The management of the venue, in particular the operation of facilities and equipment, maintenance and the like, is the responsibility of the venue team. Health, safety and emergencies are the key areas of concern of this functional area.

Sports Operations

All aspects of a sporting competition, including results management and award ceremonies, are managed by sports operations.

Medical

The medical functional area provides first aid to both spectators and athletes. In some cases, this area is responsible for drug testing.

Security

Access to the event site by accredited personnel is managed by security, which also plays an important role in crowd management.

MANAGING STAFF, VOLUNTEERS AND CONTRACTORS

In addition to organising the tasks that need to be performed, an event organiser needs to focus on managing staff, volunteers and contractors during the operational phase of the event. Since there are few long-term job prospects for most of the frontline staff working at an event, there is a higher than average chance that they might not return the next day, or that they might disappear during a break, or simply walk off the job. Some of the reasons they might give include:

- My skills are being wasted.
- I am not suited to this job.
- I feel as if I am being used and abused.
- My help is not appreciated.
- There is a lack of support.
- I don't understand how I fit in.
- I don't have all the information I need.
- I don't have the equipment I need to do the job.
- The procedures are not clear.
- I feel unwelcome and ignored.
- I didn't expect to be doing this.
- Getting here was too difficult.

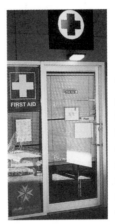

This is one of the most important functional areas. If there is more than one event venue, medical facilities need to be available at all of them.

Unhappy staff say things such as:

'My supervisor arrived two hours late and I was kept waiting after getting up at 5 am.'

'Why can't we be given more information so that we can answer questions?'

So you can see why good leadership and an ability to motivate staff are crucial to the smooth running of an event. This is what experienced event managers say about staff management during the pressured moments of an event:

'One of the most difficult things is assigning jobs. All staff want to be able to see the show.'

'Nothing can prepare you for it. Being faced with huge numbers of people descending on you, filling a venue within minutes, is incredible. Nothing can prepare you for the time-consuming nature of it. There are so many conflicting demands. You have to keep focused.'

'There is no quicker way to destroy team morale than for the manager to complain about the situation.'

'Take the time to use the person's name and give clear and concise directions.'

'Once they are committed and settled, they will do anything. If you manage well, your team will walk over hot coals for you.'

'Information is provided to team leaders to pass on. They need to recognise the value of getting the information to the staff at the briefing, otherwise their radio will run hot all day answering the same question.'

'Remember to be fair with recognition — you don't want to create a nasty competitive spirit in your team, especially in relation to give-aways.'

'Most of the organising committee were burnt out before the event began. Look after your physical health. It is like running a marathon. Prepare for it. Your tolerance for stress needs to be high.'

'Crack a few jokes when the going gets tough; initiate a dynamic and energetic team spirit.'

'Think about appreciation strategies beforehand — you have to plan celebrations for reaching milestones. This takes time and you won't have the time during the event.'

'People working at events expect to enjoy themselves; if they don't, the customers won't.'

CASE STUDY

You are organising a race for 20 000 runners. The biggest logistical problem you will face will be at the end of the race. At this time, runners crossing the finish line are exhausted and don't want to run or walk another step. Media wanting to take photographs and interview front runners compounds this problem. Enthusiastic supporters wishing to congratulate those who finish only adds to it. All runners need to get across the line without hold-ups, otherwise their times will be affected.

You need to make plans to ensure that all runners cross the line, that they are advised of their times, and that they receive free sponsor products, retrieve their belongings and attend the prize-giving ceremony. Some participants and spectators will not wait for the final ceremony and will wish to take the transport provided back to the race starting point and go home.

Develop detailed operational plans for the end of the race, using estimates of finish times and crowd flow patterns for participants and spectators.

ACTIVITIES

- *Draw up an operational timetable for a wedding. This should include hire of outfits, table linen, candlesticks and chair covers. It should also include organisation of the cake, hire cars, floral arrangements and entertainment. The focus of this activity is the logistics of getting everything and everyone into place at the right time for the reception party.*
- *Develop a mid-event appreciation strategy and a plan for a post-event party in order to celebrate the success of the event with your staff.*

LINKS

Department of Local government (guide to events)
www.dlg.nsw.gov.au

Events NSW
www.events.nsw.gov.au

Our community
www.ourcommunity.com.au

Traffic management
www.rta.nsw.gov.au

TravelSmart events planning
www.travelsmart.gov.au/events/two.html

SUMMARY

This chapter has looked in more detail at logistics, including the often problematic bump-in and bump-out phases of an event. The task of identifying resources and equipment needed, bringing them on site and setting up in the required time takes careful planning. The emphasis in this chapter has therefore been on organisation and co-ordination to ensure that all functional areas work together smoothly and co-operatively through all phases of the event. The development of policies and procedures can assist in the fulfilment of this goal by outlining the interrelationship between functional areas and will also help to ensure that the event performance standards and objectives are successfully achieved.

CHAPTER EIGHTEEN

SAFETY

AND SECURITY

ON COMPLETION OF THIS CHAPTER YOU WILL BE ABLE TO:

- identify situations in which police or security staff are required
- comply with laws, regulations and standards relating to occupational health and safety
- implement and monitor procedures for controlling hazards and risks
- implement and monitor health, safety and security training
- establish a system of communication for reporting incidents and emergencies.

The woman from Sydney's northern beaches was found clinically dead shortly after Limp Bizkit was forced to stop during its first song because of a crowd crush.

A witness said they carried the woman into a St John Ambulance area by the stage.

The witness said, 'It was like a war scene in the tent. There were 25 kids on their back. Drips were being connected to them. It looked like a mass resuscitation was going on. It was absolute pandemonium.

SUN HERALD, 28 JANUARY 2001

During this event, 12 people were taken to hospital and up to 600 treated, mainly for heat exhaustion. Prior to the event, the band had requested a T-style barricade through the centre of the audience to provide security access to the mosh pit, but the organisers had refused, saying that this measure was untested.

In the management of this type of event, careful analysis of crowd behaviour and the methods proposed for controlling crowds is required. Crowd management encompasses the steps taken to organise and manage crowds, while crowd control is the term used for dealing with crowds that are out of control. Security staff and security organisations play a major role in crowd control, particularly in events of this nature. First aid is also a necessity.

On the same day as the event described above, 220 000 people celebrated Australia Day with only a few minor incidents, none relating to crowd management. The behaviour of event visitors thus has an important role to play in the level of potential risk at a particular event and should form

A well-behaved crowd at the Federation Day parade in January 2001.

part of the analysis that begins with the risk management policy discussed in Chapter 10 and follows through to the contingency plans for safety and security discussed in detail in Chapter 19.

Safety of the event audience, staff and subcontractors should be of paramount concern for every event manager, since all events carry safety risks which may result in anything from accidents to the evacuation of a venue. In this and the following chapter, we will look more closely at risks associated with the safety of the audience and staff and the security procedures used to manage such risks. In addition, we will look at the potential for injury being caused by fixed or temporary structures, which may in turn be subjected to damage.

Another issue for consideration for most events is that of queuing. Queuing can be managed very well or very badly. The delays getting into events such as Grand Final matches are sometimes so long that the event manager has to direct staff to stop taking tickets and simply open the gates. Clearly this can lead to problems inside the venue if non-ticketed people manage to find their way in. On the other hand, if the Grand Final has commenced, and perhaps a goal scored while the spectators remain outside, there would be little else that could be done. However, if there were a number of people without tickets outside the venue, this would not be a viable option.

Orderly management of spectators leaving the venue is just as important, with clear directions and signage necessary to guide them to public transport. Sometimes revellers enjoy themselves so much at an event that they have to be marched out by security staff.

In this chapter we will deal with general security issues, occupational health and safety, first aid and effective communication of incidents. The topics of crowd control and emergency evacuation will be covered in more detail in the next chapter.

SECURITY

Security is generally required for premises, equipment, cash and other valuables, but the predominant role of most event security staff is to ensure that the correct people have access to specific areas and to act responsibly in case of accident or emergency. Accreditation badges (generally a tag hanging around the neck, showing the areas to which staff, media and spectators have access) allow security staff to monitor access. Ejection of people who are behaving inappropriately, sometimes in co-operation with police personnel, is occasionally necessary.

There are several considerations in the organisation of security for an event. Firstly, it is necessary to calculate the number of trained staff required for the security role. If the venue covers a large area, vehicles and equipment may also be required. (Four-wheeled buggies are usually used to deploy staff to outlying areas.) And secondly, the level of threat will determine whether firearms are needed.

In all cases, security staff should be appropriately licensed and the security company should carry the appropriate insurance.

Security is generally provided by the Police Service and/or security companies.

Police Service

The Police Service often provides some of the required security services, generally at no cost to community events. However, with the growth of the event industry and the increased demands on police for spectator control, charges are now being levied by some Police Services for every officer attending a profit-making event. For major sporting events, about four police officers are provided free and the remainder are hired by the event organiser. The number of police required is negotiated by the police and the event manager, the number depending on any history of incidents and the availability of alcohol.

Mounted police often attend large street festivals and processions.

Security companies

Laws exist in relation to security companies and security personnel. The industry is well regulated and an event company must ensure that the appropriate licences are secured. A master licence is held by the security company, and there are various classes of licence for officers, depending on training and experience. All security officers are required to undergo a criminal record check.

The roles of security officers include:
- acting as a bodyguard, bouncer or crowd controller
- patrolling or protecting premises
- installing and maintaining security equipment

- providing advice on security equipment and procedures
- training staff in security procedures.

Security companies must hold appropriate general liability insurance cover. General liability insurance cover is, in fact, a requirement of almost all contracts between event organisers and subcontractors. Subcontractors, including security companies, also need to cover their staff for work-related health and safety incidents.

OCCUPATIONAL HEALTH AND SAFETY

Occupational health and safety legislation aims to prevent accidents and injury in the work environment and is of particular relevance to the event organiser. The duties of employers, people in control of workplaces and suppliers of equipment and services are all described in the relevant state or territory legislation. The following extract from *Making the workplace safe: A guide to the laws covering safety and health in Western Australian workplaces* (2002) gives a broad overview of these responsibilities:

Duties of Employers
The Act lists a number of specific duties for employers, all of which depend on what is practicable for the workplace.

For example, employers must:
- *provide and maintain workplaces, plant and systems of work that do not expose employees to hazards (This refers to the whole working environment, premises, machinery, methods of work, lighting, ventilation, dust, heat, noise, fumes, and other factors such as stress, fatigue and violence in the workplace.)*
- *provide information, instruction, training and supervision so that employees can perform their work safely*
- *consult and co-operate with safety and health representatives, if any, and other employees at the workplace, on occupational safety and health matters*
- *provide employees with adequate protective clothing and equipment free of charge where hazards cannot be avoided*
- *ensure safe use, cleaning, maintenance, transportation and disposal of substances and plant in the workplace.*
- *notify the WorkSafe Commissioner of employee deaths in the workplace. Certain injuries and diseases listed in the Regulations myst also be reported.*

An employer also owes these duties to any contractors or subconstractors he or she engages, in relation to matters over which the employer has control.

Duties of Persons who have Control of Workplaces
Persons in control of a workplace where people who are not their employees are likely to be in the course of their work, must ensure that the workplace is safe. Similarly, persons in control of the means of entering or leaving a workplace must ensure that anyone can safely enter or leave it.

Owners, lessors, lessees and others who control any part of a workplace are bound by this duty. This includes persons with a contract or lease which gives them responsibility for maintenance or repair of a workplace, including the means of entering or leaving the workplace. This duty is limited to matters under the person's control.

Duties of Manufacturers, Importers, Suppliers and Designers

Persons who design, manufacture, import or supply plant for use in workplaces have a duty to ensure, as far as is practicable, that the article is designed and constructed so that persons installing, maintaining or using it properly are not exposed to hazards.

Plant must be tested and information supplied about its safe use and its hazards.

Manufacturers, importers or suppliers of workplace substances, such as chemicals, must provide toxicological and other information about safe handling, transport, storage and disposal. This information should be given in a material safety data sheet (MSDS), and on the container label. MSDSs should be provided when the substance is supplied and whenever requested by a purchaser or intending purchaser.

Persons who design or construct buildings or structures for use as a workplace have a duty to ensure that persons constructing or using them are not exposed to hazards.

Reproduced courtesy of WorkSafe, Department of Consumer and Employment Protection, Western Australia <www.safetyline.wa.gov.au>

All employers must take out workers compensation insurance. This covers all staff for work-related accident or injury, including their medical expenses, payment for time off work and rehabilitation. Volunteers are not covered by this insurance because they are not, by definition, 'paid workers', but they are covered under general liability insurance. Workers compensation insurance generally covers the employee in transit to and from their workplace, provided that they travel directly to and from their place of work. The most important element of this legislation is the **responsibility placed on supervisors and managers** for ensuring that employees have a **safe place of work** and **safe systems of work**.

Policies and procedures in relation to safety are essential, and these procedures need to be part of all employee training. In the sections below we will discuss the safe handling of items and the safe performance of certain activities that otherwise may be a threat to the safety of workers in the event environment.

Safe lifting techniques

Lifting techniques are generally part of training for anyone involved in lifting, carrying or moving heavy objects, such as sporting equipment or display stands. Two useful training aids for this purpose are illustrated in Fig. 18.1 and Table 18.1.

The correct way to lift a heavy object is to squat close to the load, keeping your back straight. Do not stoop over the load to get a grip and pick it up. Test the weight of the object before attempting to lift it. Lift using your knees and legs (not your back) as leverage. Keep your back straight, not bent forwards or backwards. Do not twist or turn your body while carrying the object or putting it down.

The WorkSafe Western Australia Commission's 2000 Manual Handling Code of Practice (Appendix G) provides the following guidance for the handling of heavy objects.

In conclusion, they suggest that a definitive, absolute safe lifting weight is not possible to determine and that a commonsense approach is required for assessing manual handling tasks. Weight

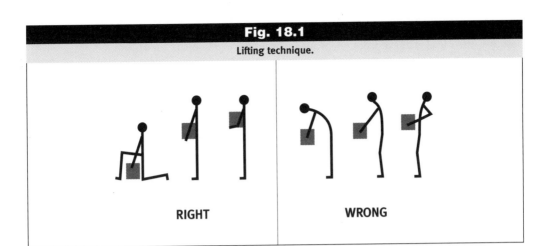

Fig. 18.1

Lifting technique.

RIGHT   **WRONG**

Table 18.1

How to prevent injuries caused by lifting and moving heavy objects.

Avoid	Common Causes of Injury	Common Solutions
Lifting and moving	Lifting boxes from the floor	Do not store items on the floor.
	Carrying boxes or equipment	Use proper lifting techniques. Get help or use a lifting aid. Use a cart. Avoid over-reaching, twisting or lifting over head.
	Pushing carts	Maintain casters in clean, operating condition. Match the casters to the floor type.

2.1 Heavy

The risk of injury increases as the weight of the load increases.

Evaluating the risk of weight of the object needs to take into account:

- how long the load is handled
- how often the load is handled.

As a guide, the risk of back injury increases when loads over 4.5 kg are handled from a seated position or when loads over 16 kg are handled from positions other than seated. As weight increases, the percentage of healthy adults who can safely lift, lower or carry decreases.

Generally, no single person should be required to lift, lower or carry loads over 55 kg. **This limit would only apply, however, when the load is within the person's capabilities and no other risk factors are present** (e.g. no bending or twisting is required to pick up the load; the load is compact and easy to grasp; it is held close to the trunk and not carried frequently or for long distances).

On occasions, objects over 55 kg may be moved but not lifted, e.g. rolling a 200 litre drum.

Reproduced courtesy of WorkSafe Department of Consumer and Employment Protection, Western Australia <www.safetyline.wa.gov.au>

should be considered, along with all other factors in the context of the task, including actions or postures, other load characteristics, the work environment and human characteristics.

Safety steps for electrical equipment

Electrical equipment is a significant hazard in the event environment, particularly in wet weather. All safety steps must be taken to prevent accidents involving electrical equipment, including routine tagging, lockout and inspection of equipment. Many venues are extremely rigorous in their demands for documentation demonstrating correct licensing and inspection.

The following extract from Electricity: Residual Current Devices (RCDs) (Worksafe Western Australia Commission, 1998) outlines the duties of employers and employees:

Duties of an Employer

Section 19 of the Occupational Safety and Health Act requires an employer to provide, so far as is practicable, a workplace where employees are not exposed to hazards and to provide a safe system of work. In the case of using portable electrical equipment the employer should establish whether the fixed socket outlets to be used by his or her employees are protected by RCDs and whether they are identified as being protected.

The employer must inform the employees if and where protection is provided. If the employer is not satisfied that non-portable RCDs have been installed, the employer should provide a portable RCD and consult with the employee on when and where the portable RCD is to be used. If there is any doubt regarding the installation of RCDs at the workplace, portable RCDs must be provided and used.

The use of a portable RCD in a circuit already protected by a non-portable (or portable) RCD has no detrimental effect on the operation of either RCD.

Duties of Employees

Under section 20 of the Occupational Safety and Health Act, employees have a duty to take reasonable care of their own safety and avoid harming the safety or health of other people. Before connecting portable electrical equipment to an electrical power source, an employee should seek the advice of the employer as to whether the outlets are protected by non-portable RCDs. Where neither the employer nor an employee is satisfied that non-portable RCDs have been installed, the employer must provide a portable RCD. The employer and the employee should consult on when and where the portable RCD is to be used.

Reproduced courtesy of WorkSafe, Department of Consumer and Employment Protection, Western Australia <www.safetyline.wa.gov.au>

Safe use of machinery

Regulations for safeguarding machinery in the workplace are provided in the Australian Standard, AS 4024.1-1996 Safeguarding of Machinery — General Principles.

This Standard identifies the hazards and risks arising from the use of industrial machinery and describes methods for the elimination or minimisation of them, as well as for the safeguarding of machinery and the use of safe work practices. It also describes and illustrates a number of safety principles and provides guidelines by which it is possible to assess which measure or method it is practicable to adopt in particular circumstances.

This Standard is intended for those who design, manufacture, supply, instal, use, maintain or modify machinery, machinery guarding or safety devices, and identifies the existence of Standards for a number of particular classes of machine. It is also designed to be used by those concerned with information, instruction and training in safe work practices.

Safe handling of hazardous substances

Because different chemicals have different safe use requirements, it is important for staff to know as much about hazardous substances used in the workplace as possible. Material Safety Data Sheets should be used to provide the following advice on these substances to staff members:

These cylinders contain a hazardous substance, requiring clear instructions for safe handling and storage.

- ingredients of a product
- health effects and first-aid instructions
- precautions for use
- safe handling and storage information
- emergency procedures.

Safety signs

Safety signs are particularly important in the event workplace since staff are generally only at the venue for a very short period. This does not allow much time for reinforcement of safety issues, however these can be stressed during briefing sessions. Posters and safety signs, such as those reproduced below, can be used to reinforce key messages, helping to prevent many accidents.

First aid

In most cases, first aid is provided by organisations such as St John Ambulance, although venue and event staff should also be trained in first aid procedures. Some of these procedures will be specific to the event in question. For example, at road races, common first aid emergencies that occur include exhaustion, collapse, dehydration, road burns, and bone and muscle injuries, and procedures should be in place for dealing with them. In addition, participants in races such as these sometimes do not wish to accept help and staff would need to be trained in the correct procedure for dealing with such an occurrence.

RISK MANAGEMENT

This chapter extends the approach to risk management outlined in Chapter 10 to look at risk management principles in relation to safety and security. Access control, theft prevention and emergency are examples of areas for which detailed risk analysis must be undertaken. Risk management is an ongoing process, involving constant evaluation of the impact of change and the risk factors associated with that change. Analysis and consultation are necessary when change in the workplace occurs. For example, storage of excess flammable recycling material could result in a small area loading dock becoming extremely hazardous. A supervisor would need to evaluate this risk and put in place control measures. Most major events will not allow anyone to commence work before undertaking safety and evacuation training.

The Australian and New Zealand standard for risk management (AS/NZS 4360:1999 Risk Management) simplifies the process of systems development and is a useful resource for supervisors and managers in the event industry. Risk management plans for event safety can also be required from contract organisations working on site. This process is indentical to that illustrated in Chapter 10 but is applied here at operational level. It bears repetition as the ability to plan all work using a risk management approach is one of the key attributes of professional employees in the event field.

PROCESS OF RISK MANAGEMENT

Risk management involves a three-step process:
1 Identify risks and hazards.
2 Assess risks and hazards.
3 Manage risks and hazards.

This process allows the manager or supervisor to establish and prioritise the risks, to take steps to prevent problems occurring and to make contingency plans if problems do occur.

Identifying risks and hazards

Identifying the risk or hazard involves ascertaining when and how a problem might occur. Hazards representing potential risk include:
- fire
- plant and equipment
- hazardous substances
- electrical equipment
- spills
- stacking of unbalanced heavy items
- moving vehicles
- hold-ups

- threats to visitor/spectator safety
- threats to staff safety.

Brainstorming by the event management team helps to identify potential risks.

Temporary structures and ladders present a safety risk.

Assessing risks and hazards

Once potential risks and hazards have been identified, their likelihood of occurring needs to be evaluated. This allows the management team to prioritise the issues for attention. It is a good idea to set up a committee to manage risk, safety and security issues, and to establish operational guidelines for such aspects as operating equipment and testing schedules. The following questions need to be asked:

- What is the likelihood of this happening?
- Who will be exposed to the risk?
- What impact has this risk had in similar circumstances?
- How will people react to this risk/hazard?

With hazards that might pose a risk to health and safety, the following three classifications are recommended:

Class A hazard This has the potential to cause death, serious injury, permanent disability or illness.
Class B hazard This has the potential to cause illness or time off work.
Class C hazard The resulting injury or illness will require first aid.

While this example refers mainly to injury, the principle of looking at potential consequences is well illustrated. The potential consequences of fire, bomb threats, hold-ups and electrical failure can be evaluated in the same way.

Managing risks and hazards

Once the risks and hazards have been prioritised, the final step is to look at the most effective ways of managing them. Control measures include:

- elimination plans to eliminate the risk altogether (for example, removal of dangerous children's equipment)
- substitution plans (for example, replacing slippery floor tiles in a wash-up area)

- isolation plans (for example, isolating dangerous or noisy equipment)
- engineering controls (for example, using fences to prevent access to waterways or busy roads)
- administrative controls (warning signs, trained staff and well-developed procedures, for example, all help to minimise risk)
- contingency plans (where risk cannot be completely avoided, contingency plans for, say, evacuation, need to be developed).

An example of a simple risk management plan is shown in Fig. 18.2. This plan shows the analysis of risk associated with an armed hold-up, the potential impact, and the management strategies and contingency plans put in place to control them. For a much more detailed analysis, the Australian Institute of Criminology website listed at the end of the chapter is a valuable source of detailed information

Fig. 18.2
Risk management plan — armed hold-up.

Nature of risk	Likelihood of event A (almost certain) – E (rare)	Consequences of event 1 (insignificant) – 5 (catastrophic)	Preventative measures NO SHORTCUTS, AVOID COMPLACENCY	Contingency measures MONEY AND PROPERTY NOT WORTH A LIFE, NO HEROICS
Hold-up	D (unlikely)	4 (major)	• Develop procedures relating to cash handling • Assign responsibilities • Conduct training • Distribute standard hold-up form • Develop posters — 'stay alert' • Report suspicious circumstances • Check doors and locks when opening • Lock rear entrances; monitor by CCTV • Monitor identification • Watch for bogus tradesmen • Remove excess cash and hold in strongroom • Check alarm systems weekly	• Staff to stay calm • Staff to do as told by offender • Staff to stay out of danger • Observe bandits and vehicles • Avoid panic • Raise the alarm when safely possible • Phone police when safely possible • Provide name and address of premises to police • Provide offender's description to police • Provide vehicle description to police • Give travel directions to police • Close premises to public • Retain witnesses • Do not interfere with crime scene

Fig. 18.2 CONTINUED
Risk management plan — armed hold-up.

Nature of risk	Likelihood of event A (almost certain) – E (rare)	Consequences of event 1 (insignificant) – 5 (catastrophic)	Preventative measures NO SHORTCUTS, AVOID COMPLACENCY	Contingency measures MONEY AND PROPERTY NOT WORTH A LIFE, NO HEROICS
			• Check CCTV monitors daily • Provide escorts for cash • Change routines and carriers • Alert employees to confidentiality requirements • Employ security when large amounts being handled	• Complete offender description form (all witnesses) • Avoid statements to media • Refer media to manager **Post hold-up** • Issue press release • Provide counselling for staff • Review procedures • Improve security for cash handling

HEALTH AND SAFETY TRAINING AND MEETINGS

All induction and training programs should include a component on health, safety and security, with a particular emphasis on duty of care. The topics that should be covered in training sessions include:

- review of the risks to health and safety
- magnitude of actual and potential problems
- review of issues that could arise, such as public liability actions
- specific job and individual risk factors
- control strategies
- reasons for procedures, rules and regulations
- outline of the most prevalent areas of risk (for example, slips and falls, and manual handling)
- responsibilities of the parties.

Every staff meeting should have health and safety on the agenda so that employees are able to identify risks and consult on procedures and systems. Both awareness and action are necessary, and when serious risks are identified, they should be referred to the organisation's occupational health and safety committee. The role of this committee is to:

- help to resolve any health and safety issues
- carry out regular safety inspections
- develop a system to record accidents and incidents
- make recommendations to management about improving health and safety
- access any information about risks to health and safety from any equipment or substance or occupational disease.

All accidents and incidents need to be reported, even in cases where medical attention is not required.

INCIDENT REPORTING

For any event there are standard reporting relationships on all operational issues. On the whole, these reporting relationships concur with the organisation chart. However, there are many instances where communication is less formal and less structured, no less in the case of the event working environment where 'mayhem' or 'controlled chaos' may best describe it.

Despite some tolerance of rather haphazard communication before and during the event, **any communication relating to an incident or emergency needs to be very clear**. (An example of an incident report card is illustrated in Fig. 18.3.) It must also **follow a short and specific chain of command**. The chain of command, or organisation chart, for an emergency is seldom the same as the organisation chart for the event as a whole. Emergency reporting tends to go through very few levels, and all staff must be trained in emergency reporting. Many stakeholders may be involved — general staff, security staff, first aid personnel, police, emergency services — but absolute clarity is needed as to who makes key decisions and how they are to be contacted. These lines of reporting and responsibility will be reviewed in the next chapter.

Communication methods

Most event teams use radios as they are the most effective tool for maintaining communication. Different channels are used for different purposes, and it is essential that the correct radio procedures be followed. In Fig. 18.4 on page 280 radio links to the Event Operations Centre are illustrated, with 'Control' serving as the link to the decision-makers. For example, in response to a request to remove a hazard, Control would ensure that the Site team responded to the call. If a spill were reported, Control would report to Cleaning, requesting that the spill be cleaned up. The Operations Centre also has links to emergency services that can be called if required.

At some events, mobile telephones are used, but the drawback of this method of communication is that the information transmitted can be overheard. Networks can also become overloaded if spectators are using their mobile phones, particularly during intermission and at the end of a match or concert.

A railway security officer in radio contact with Operations.

Meetings between event staff, including security staff and emergency services, are necessary to plan and monitor security and safety, as difficulties can occur if the communications technology of the various services is not compatible. It is crucial that this issue be anticipated and that contingency plans be put in place to deal effectively with any communication problems.

Fig. 18.3

Sample incident report card.

INCIDENT REPORT CARD

Time ....

Date ....   FUNCTIONAL AREA/DEPARTMENT

                          YOUR POSITION

YOUR NAME

....

NAMES OF PERSON/S INVOLVED IN THE INCIDENT

....

CONTACT DETAILS OF PERSON/S INVOLVED IN THE INCIDENT

....

NAME AND CONTACT DETAILS OF WITNESS/ES IF ANY

....

INCIDENT DETAILS

_____

_____

_____

_____

TIME OF INCIDENT

LOCATION OF INCIDENT

CAUSE OF INCIDENT

CONSEQUENCES OF INCIDENT

CAN ANY ACTION BE TAKEN TO PREVENT REOCCURRENCE?

....

DATE AND TIME RECEIVED AND LOGGED

OUTSTANDING ACTIONS

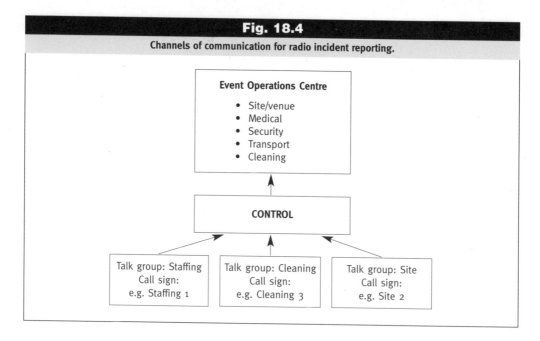

Fig. 18.4

Channels of communication for radio incident reporting.

Event Operations Centre
- Site/venue
- Medical
- Security
- Transport
- Cleaning

CONTROL

Talk group: Staffing
Call sign:
e.g. Staffing 1

Talk group: Cleaning
Call sign:
e.g. Cleaning 3

Talk group: Site
Call sign:
e.g. Site 2

SAFETY AT OUTDOOR EVENTS

The code of practice for safety at outdoor events reproduced below was developed in the United Kingdom. It can be modified for any event, large or small. When staging an event, organisers need to consider all of the points outlined in order to demonstrate their duty of care to employees, contractors and spectators.

Code of practice for outdoor events

- A Hazard and Risk Assessment should be carried out.
- All Statutory Requirements should be met.
- Identification, registration, marking of safe working loads and capacities in accordance with construction and lifting operation regulations should be initiated.
- Materials and components used on site should comply with current Building Standards, where they exist.
- The number of people likely to attend the event, along with plans for their arrival, departure and emergency evacuation should be in place.
- Adequate provision of services to the site should be available, e.g. water, electricity, gas, toilet facilities, waste disposal, hygiene facilities for catering areas.
- Plans for provision of Fire Fighting Equipment and on-site access for Emergency Service Vehicles should be drawn up.
- Sufficient First Aid cover and treatment facilities should be arranged.
- Food hygiene controls should comply with the code of practice issued by the Mobile Outside Caterers Association.
- No temporary structures should be used unless it is of a 'type' having a certificate of approval from the relevant government department.

- All electrical wiring, fittings and appliances should be installed in compliance with Electricity at Work Regulations 1991.
- Stages and platforms, lighting towers and temporary grandstands should be inspected by an independent structural engineer and a certificate of stability obtained.
- Lasers, strobes or other high intensity lighting to be used must be authorised by the licensing authority.
- Marquees, tents and tented structures should be erected in accordance with manufacturers' recommendations in a safe position; all marquees and drapes should comply with BS for fire retardation.
- The provision of the noise at work regulations must be met with regards to sound systems and the environmental issue with regard to the travel distance of sound must be considered.
- Records should be kept of all inspections carried out and of all visitors to the site during build-up and breakdown. All certificates issued for structures and documentation referring to build-up, or breakdown, should be retained and be available for inspection.
- Any accident occurring (no mater how small) should be recorded and investigated by a competent person immediately.
- An Event Control Point should be established and manned throughout the duration of the build-up, event and breakdown.
- A final checklist should be compiled and a pre-event inspection carried out of all areas before the public are permitted onto the site.
- A specialist firm should be appointed to arrange and establish security.
- Adequate provisions for insurance must be arranged.
- The statutory Emergency Services should be contacted at the early planning stage of an event and their guidance should be sought and complied with.
- Organisers should bear in mind that the Health and Safety of an event is of paramount importance and should be carried out in a professional manner.

<www.medinet.co.uk/event.htm>

CASE STUDY 1

The Gold Mining Company is a nightclub venue that is popular during the months of May, June and July for its Friday night dance events. The staff working at this venue are all casuals and turnover is high. During a conversation, two of the staff, Jason and Malik, find out that they have both been mugged on their way home from work in the early hours of the morning, but on different Friday nights. In both cases, the perpetrators waited in a nearby alley and threatened them with knives. Jason lost his wallet and $400 and Malik broke his ankle when trying to run away. Candice, another employee, has been harassed by patrons and was once burned deliberately with a cigarette by a particularly drunk and obnoxious customer. Management gave her some cash to get medical attention.

Discuss the occupational health and safety issues of the staff concerned. What are the responsibilities of the management in each of these cases?

The 2003 exhibition of Designer Jewellery — Artists of the South Pacific is being held in the foyer of a large city hotel. The State Premier will open the exhibition and several dignitaries from visiting countries will be in attendance. Some of these countries are currently experiencing political turmoil so there will be security risks associated with the guests, as well as with the items on display. Threats and protests could also disrupt the opening.

Discuss the following issues:

- Who will be responsible for security (probably more than one body)?
- What are some of the potential security problems?
- What are the occupational health and safety issues?
- What steps can be taken to prevent a security incident?
- What plans should be in place should an incident occur?

ACTIVITY

Identify some of the security issues at the following events and prepare plans to prevent or deal with these issues:

- *dance party with mosh pit*
- *street festival*
- *private party for a celebrity*
- *product launch*
- *road race.*

LINKS

Australian Institute of Criminology, Preventing Armed Robbery
www.aic.gov.au/publications/

Cash logistics; security personnel
www.chubb.com.au

International site for occupational health and safety
http://oshweb.me.tut.fi/index.html

Internet safety resources
www.christie.ab.ca/safelist/

OH&S sites
www.worksafe.gov.au

Standards Australia
www.standardsaustralia.gov.au

Workplace Health and Safety Act Queensland
www.detir.qld.gov.au

WorkCover
www.workcover.gov.au

WorkSafe Western Australia
www.safetyline.wa.gov.au

SUMMARY

The health, safety and security of staff and the event audience are very important concerns of the event management team. In this chapter we have discussed many measures for ensuring that this is achieved, including the safe handling of heavy objects and hazardous substances and the safe use of electrical equipment and machinery. Safety and security are risks that need to be dealt with by assessing the risk, managing the risk and developing contingency plans for dealing with the risk. Not only must people be protected but also assets, and security personnel and the police are there to assist the event manager in managing these risks. Most importantly, an effective system of communication for reporting incidents will prevent the escalation of a situation and help staff to deal promptly with any emergency.

CHAPTER NINETEEN

SPECTATOR

MANAGEMENT

ON COMPLETION OF THIS CHAPTER YOU WILL BE ABLE TO:

- develop and implement a plan to minimise the risks associated with crowds of spectators
- develop and implement spectator management and spectator control systems and procedures
- identify the types of events and situations that might involve emergency management of spectators
- identify the types of occurrences that may require evacuation
- develop procedures for managing spectators in an emergency, including evacuation.

Paramedics from all across the city rushed to the scene, then battled to get through the crowds to attend to the injured. In some cases, police had to baton-charge a path through hordes of hysterical people in order for doctors and rescue workers to get into the stadium. An already appalling situation appears to have been worsened by security guards who fired tear gas at a stampeding crowd outside the stadium. People ran everywhere, dozens falling down and being crushed to death and many more severely injured.

THE CITIZEN, JOHANNESBURG, 12 APRIL 2001

As this article illustrates, contingency plans need to be in place in case of emergencies at an event and, clearly, easy access for emergency services is one of the first aspects that needs to be considered. Evacuation and spectator management are others. In this chapter we will deal with all three.

The initial task of the event manager is to develop a spectator management plan.

SPECTATOR MANAGEMENT PLAN

Following are the key things to consider when developing a spectator management plan:
- the number of people at the venue (the event audience, staff and contractors)
- the likely behaviour of spectators (especially for events with a history of crowd behaviour problems)
- the timing of the event, including session times and peak periods

- the layout of the venue and/or other facilities
- the security services to be provided or contracted
- the legal requirements and general guidelines.

The last of these requires adherence to occupational health and safety legislation and the laws relating to fire egress (exits), as well as to a number of guidelines provided by Standards Australia, if applicable to the event, such as:

- **AS 2187.4 Pyrotechnics — Outdoors**, which specifies the precautions to be carried out in storage, handling and use of pyrotechnics for outdoor displays.
- **AS 2560.2.3 Lighting for Outdoor Football**, dealing with the level of lighting required for training, competition and spectator viewing for all football codes.
- **AS 1680 Interior Lighting — Safe Movement**, which sets out the minimum requirements for electric lighting systems within publicly accessible areas of buildings in order to provide visual conditions that facilitate the safe movement of people in the normal use of the buildings.
- **AS/NZS 2293.3 Emergency Evacuation Lighting for Buildings**, providing building, maintenance and inspection guidelines for emergency evacuation lighting.

All the above Standards, and many more that are relevant to building permanent and temporary structures, are available on the websites listed at the end of this chapter.

There are also many considerations in relation to transport to the event site, parking and access to the venue. An outstanding website, TravelSmart, mentioned overleaf and at the end of this chapter, provides extensive guidelines in this regard and also lists the relevant legislative guidelines and policies for the states and territories. Special events involving street closures require careful planning and negotiation with the authorities (such as the Roads and Traffic Authority, local council and the police) many months before the event takes place. Events are classified as follows:

Class 1 Event
Impacts major traffic and transport systems, disrupts the non-event community over a wide area

Class 2 Event
Impacts local traffic and transport systems, disrupts the community in the area around the event

Class 3 Event
Does not impact local or major traffic systems, disrupts immediate area only

Class 4 Event
Small street event requires police consent only

Consideration of event transport and access should cover:
- pedestrian facilities
- cyclist facilities
- public transport facilities
- access for people with mobility or visual impairments
- car parking.

In relation to pedestrian facilities, for example, the TravelSmart site suggests asking the following questions:

1   *Have you marked pedestrian routes on your access map?*
2   *Have you used walk times, rather than distances? Times are more effective in journey planning.*
3   *Are pedestrian routes good quality?*
4   *Are there any 'missing links', such as missing pedestrian crossings at busy roads?*
5   *Have you organised queuing facilities at stations, or other places where pedestrians may have to wait?*
6   *Could you arrange for staff to entertain and inform waiting pedestrians?*
7   *Could you provide televisions at queue points to inform and keep people relaxed? You may be able to subsidise these through advertising or sponsorship.*
8   *Do you have staff on hand to answer questions about public transport services and timetables? You could give staff an information sheet to help them answer questions.*
9   *Are queuing areas covered from the sun and rain?*
10 *Have you told people attending the event about the safest pedestrian routes?*
11 *Do you need to contact police about organising temporary crossing facilities?*
12 *Could you contact the state road authority to discuss temporarily making pedestrian crossing times longer at key intersections?*
13 *Do you need to provide mats or floor covers for outside areas?*
14 *Are pedestrian routes well lit if people will be walking to or from your event in the dark?*

<www.travelsmart.gov.au/events/four.html>

The spectator management plan covers readily available information, such as the dimensions of the venue or site, but it also goes further to encompass the probable number of spectators at particular times of the event and their flow through the site. Clearly the peaks are the most problematic from a crowd management perspective and the plan needs to address this and other challenges by covering the following:

• Estimate the level of attendance for specific days and times.
• Estimate the number of people using public corridors, specific entrances, specific aisles and seating at particular times.
• Estimate the number of ushers and service and security personnel needed for spectator management.
• Establish the requirements for crowd control measures, such as barriers.
• Identify the areas that need to remain restricted.
• Develop accreditation plans for restricted access by specific staff.
• Identify particular hazards (for example, scaffolding, temporary structures).
• Identify routes by which emergency services personnel will enter and leave the site.
• Establish the means of communication for all staff working on the site.
• Establish a chain of command for incident reporting.
• Check safety equipment (for example, the number of fire extinguishers and also that inspections have been carried out according to legal requirements).

- Identify the safety needs of specific groups of people, such as people with disabilities, children and players/performers.
- Identify first aid requirements and provision.
- Develop an emergency response plan (ERP).
- Develop an evacuation plan and initiate training and drills for the staff concerned.

As we know, there are many different types of event venue, each having specific features and some being safer than others. They range from outdoor environments, such as streets and parks, to aquatic centres, indoor facilities and purpose-built venues. The last of these is generally the safest since spectator management and evacuation would generally have been considered at the time these structures were built, and rehearsed again and again by the venue team. However, a spectator management and evacuation plan would still need to be developed for each event held at the venue, as factors such as spectator numbers and movement would generally be different.

RISK MANAGEMENT PLAN

In addition to the spectator management plan, a risk management plan specifically for managing spectators is required. This follows the format covered in Chapter 10.

Identifying the risk

The major incidents that need to be considered in relation to spectator management and evacuation include:
- fire, smoke
- bomb threat, terrorism, threats to VIPs
- flood, earthquake or other natural disasters
- heat, failure of air-conditioning or lighting
- gas leaks or biological hazards
- crowd crush, overcrowding, congestion
- riots, protests
- vehicle accidents
- collapsing fences or other structures.

For each of the above, the response of the public to the emergency should be evaluated so that the emergency team has procedures in place for preventing panic. Reassuring messages on the public address system is one way of reducing panic and ensuring orderly evacuation.

Analysing and managing the risk

Once the risks have been identified (such as congestion, overcrowding and crowd crush), the circumstances that may lead to negative or destructive behaviour in these contexts need to be analysed. The risks then need to be prioritised and plans put in place to avoid them (known as preventative measures) or to deal with them should they occur (known as contingency measures). An example of a preventative measure for reducing congestion at turnstiles would be to employ staff to assist spectators and to monitor the area. However, impatient crowds might simply jump over the turnstile or knock it down, so there would need to be a contingency plan in place for

The density of this event audience illustrates the importance of appropriate crowd control measures.

dealing with this situation. Property damage by spectators would also need to be covered and procedures put in place for ejecting the offending spectators. At worst, the police may charge them. (Streakers who disrupt play during sports matches spring to mind in this instance.) The more serious risk, however, are non-ticketed spectators who gain illegal entry.

---

21 die in Chicago nightclub stampede
Tuesday, February 18, 2003, Associated Press

Hundreds of screaming guests rushed the exits of a crowded nightclub Monday after someone used pepper spray or mace, and at least 21 people were crushed to death or smothered in the panic, officials said. There were more than 1,500 people in the two-storey nightclub when the pepper spray was released sometime after 2 a.m., officials initially estimated. They could not immediately say what the legal capacity of the building was. "It appears a disturbance from within led to a mass chaos where people headed for the door. Most of the fatalities appear to have been crushed or had injuries due to suffocation," said police officer Ozzie Rodriguez.

The melee marks one of the nation's deadliest stampedes. In December 1991, nine young people were crushed to death in a gymnasium stairwell while awaiting a celebrity basketball game in New York. In December 1979, 11 people were killed in Cincinnati in a crush to get into a concert by The Who.

The following strategies (adapted from the Crowdsafe website at the end of this chapter) may help to prevent deaths and injuries suffered by fans at rock concerts and other large events:
- Review the behaviour of crowds attending similar past events.
- Review crowd responses to specific bands and performers at past rock concerts.
- Conduct an evaluation of all structures available for mosh pit management.
- Obtain engineering and specialist advice.

- Isolate the mosh pit from the general audience.
- Limit mosh pit capacity and density.
- Provide easy exits from the mosh pit area.
- Ban alcohol and cigarettes from the mosh pit.
- Station special first-aid assistance near the mosh pit.
- Ban stage diving, body surfing/swimming.
- Provide specially trained private security and 'peer security'.
- Provide special ventilation and drinking fountains for moshers.
- Pad the floor and all hard surfaces, including barriers and railings.
- Ban certain types of clothes and accessories worn by moshers in the pit.
- Introduce mosh pit safety announcements in advance of the show and during shows.
- Seek assistance from the performers in managing or preventing moshing.

In particular, consideration should be given to entrance management, barrier controls and exit management. Throughput capacities need to be calculated and crowd flows planned.

EMERGENCY PLANNING

Emergency Management Australia (see website at the end of this chapter) has very useful guidelines for planning safe and healthy mass gatherings. This extensive document covers the psychology of crowds and is essential for anyone planning an event of this magnitude.

Emergency planning is Standards based. The following is a summary of the guidelines that are provided in **DR00180 Emergency Control Organization and Procedures for Buildings (Standards Australia)**.

A committee called the Emergency Planning Committee (EPC) should be convened to:
- establish the emergency response plan (ERP)
- ensure that appropriate people are assigned to specific roles, such as Chief Warden, and that their responsibilities in the Emergency Control Organisation (ECO) are clarified
- arrange training for all members of the ECO team
- arrange for evacuation drills
- review procedures
- ensure that ECO staff are indemnified against civil liability in situations where they act in good faith in the course of their emergency control duties.

When developing the emergency response plan, specialist advice is recommended. Most security organisations offer this type of consultancy support. When developing the emergency procedures, the following should be taken into account:
- peak numbers of people in the venue
- assembly and evacuation routes, and signage
- people with disabilities
- lifts and escalators (assume that these are not used, except by fire authorities)
- people check (making sure everyone has left)
- marshalling points (especially for very large venues)
- safeguarding of cash and valuables

- communication systems (emergency warning and emergency intercom system — AS2220.1 and AS2220.2) as well as public address systems
- emergency equipment
- control and co-ordination point/s (location/s) for emergency response by the Chief Warden and liaison with emergency services
- co-ordination with other agencies such as council and emergency services.

The Emergency Control Organisation is the team responsible for responding to the emergency. This team includes the following personnel:
- Chief Warden
- Deputy Chief Warden
- Communications Officer
- Floor/Area Wardens
- Wardens.

During an emergency, instructions given by ECO wardens should override those given by any other person in the organisation structure.

The structure of the ECO, together with identifying features, is illustrated in Fig. 19.1.

Selection and training of emergency personnel should follow the comprehensive guidelines provided in the relevant Standards document. It is essential that you read the full text of the Standards as this chapter provides only an overview of the Standards, roles and procedures.

In general terms, the people selected for roles in the ECO should be in attendance during the hours of operation, should show leadership qualities and sound judgement under pressure, and

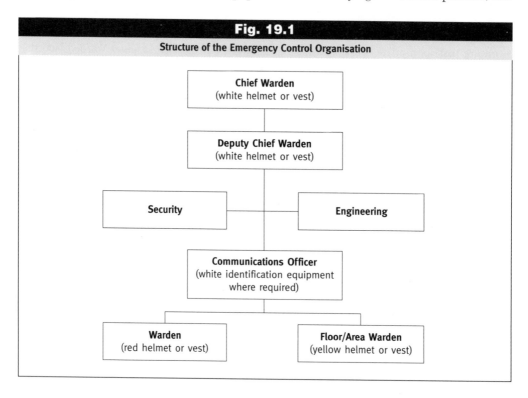

Fig. 19.1

Structure of the Emergency Control Organisation

should be able to communicate clearly. The first of these attributes is the most problematic in the event business. For leased premises, the venue team is generally limited in number and few work for the full duration of an event. The question of availability during an event, especially one with multiple sessions, is a key consideration for the committee. There is no point in having a well-trained ECO that is not in attendance!

Below are the chief roles of each person in the ECO team.

Chief Warden

The duties of the Chief Warden include ascertaining the nature and location of the emergency and determining the appropriate action; ensuring that emergency services and floor wardens are advised; initiating evacuation; and briefing emergency personnel on their arrival.

Deputy Chief Warden

The Deputy will take on the roles of the Chief Warden if unavailable or assist as required.

Communications Officer

The duties of the Communications Officer include ascertaining the nature and location of the emergency; confirming that the emergency service/s have been notified; and notifying, transmitting and recording instructions and progress.

Floor/Area Wardens

Implementing the emergency procedures for their area, checking the floor/area, and co-ordinating and communicating with the Chief Warden are all roles of Floor/Area Wardens.

Wardens

Checking, searching, giving instructions during an evacuation and reporting to the Floor/Area Warden are the tasks undertaken by the Wardens.

For all officers in the ECO, ensuring that emergency services have been notified is part of the job.

Full details of the roles and tasks of these officers are available on the Standards websites at the end of this chapter, as well as a number of videos on this type of planning and training. Specialist assistance in this area is recommended, as well as the use of Emergency Warning and Intercommunication Systems (EWIS).

IMPLEMENTING EMERGENCY PROCEDURES

In order to effectively implement emergency procedures, the following steps should be taken:

- Review implementation issues and integrate them with all other event operational plans.
- Ensure broad awareness of the procedures through wide dissemination of information and consultation with all concerned.
- Use signage and well-designed communication materials in a simple format to provide information.
- Train all staff.
- Test the procedures by conducting evacuation exercises.
- Review procedures to check effectiveness.

Fire procedures

There are four major steps that ideally should be initiated concurrently:

1 Ensure the safety of everyone within the vicinity of the fire.
2 Call the fire brigade in any circumstance in which there is suspicion of fire.
3 Conduct evacuation.
4 Fight the fire with appropriate equipment or retreat and close all doors.

Note that there is no need for anyone to give permission for a call to the fire brigade. This call can be initiated by anyone.

Evacuation procedures

The evacuation procedure for most venues follows the same process: the Chief Warden uses the tone BEEP … BEEP … BEEP for alert and WHOOP … WHOOP … WHOOP for evacuation on the public address system.

The warden intercommunication phone (WIP) is used to advise the Chief Warden of danger in specific areas. All staff should be trained in their specific roles in this situation.

In the event of an evacuation it is important for staff to:

• remain calm
• be observant
• listen to and follow instructions
• provide information and instructions to staff and spectators when advised to do so
• maintain radio protocol (do not block channels)
• follow all safety precautions (such as not using lifts in case of fire).

The emergency response plan is reliant on the warden system and the chain of command. Early warning means fast intervention.

Bomb threat procedures

As with fire and evacuation procedures, there is a recommended procedure for dealing with bomb threats. Details are available from the Australian Bomb Data Centre which publishes a handbook, giving standard guidelines, that can be kept near all telephones. These include:

• evaluation (deciding whether or not to take action, and whether to search, with or without evacuation)
• notification (police should be advised)
• search (the aim is identification of the suspicious object, which should not be touched or moved).

In Fig. 19.2 is a checklist, which should also be kept near the telephone, outlining the questions to ask and information to secure about the caller.

Fig. 19.2
Bomb threat checklist.

PHONE THREAT CHECKLIST©

REMEMBER TO KEEP CALM

WHO RECEIVED THE CALL

Name (print): _____
Telephone number: _____
Date call received: /   /   Time received: _____
Signature:

GENERAL QUESTIONS TO ASK

1. What is it ?

2. When is the bomb going to explode ?
   OR
   When will the substance be released ?

3. Where did you put it ?

4. What does it look like ?

5. When did you put it there ?

6. How will the bomb explode ?
   OR
   How will the substance be released ?

7. Did you put it there ?

8. Why did you put it there ?

BOMB THREAT QUESTIONS

1. What type of bomb is it ?

2. What is in the bomb ?

3. What will make the bomb explode ?

CHEMICAL / BIOLOGICAL THREAT QUESTIONS

1. What kind of substance is in it ?

2. How much of the substance is there ?

3. How will the substance be released ?

4. Is the substance a liquid, powder or gas ?

OTHER QUESTIONS TO ASK

1. What is your name ?

2. Where are you ?

3. What is your address ?

- DO NOT HANG UP -

PHONE THREAT CHECKLIST

REMEMBER TO KEEP CALM

EXACT WORDING OF THREAT

_____
_____
_____
_____
_____
_____

CALLER'S VOICE

Accent (specify): _____
Any impediment (specify): _____
Voice (loud, soft, etc): _____
Speech (fast, slow, etc): _____
Diction (clear, muffled): _____
Manner (calm, emotional, etc): _____
Did you recognise the caller ?
If so who do you think it was ?_____
Was the caller familiar with the area ?

THREAT LANGUAGE

Well spoken: _____
Incoherent: _____
Irrational: _____
Taped: _____
Message read by caller: _____
Abusive: _____
Other: _____

BACKGROUND NOISES

Street noises: _____
House noises: _____
Aircraft: _____
Voices: _____
Music: _____
Machinery: _____
Other: _____
Local Call: _____
STD:

OTHER

Sex of caller: _____   Estimated age: _____

CALL TAKEN

Duration of call: _____

Number called: _____

ACTION (OBTAIN DETAILS FROM SUPERVISOR)

Report call immediately to: _____

Phone number: _____

- DO NOT HANG UP -

The ABDC Phone Threat checklist may be obtained from the ABDC at a minimal cost. Visit the AFP website <www.afp.gov.au> or contact ABDC at <abdc@afp.gov.au> for further information.

Y̶ou are going to hire a venue for a fashion parade. The venue you have in mind is an old theatre that lends itself well to the event, with excellent sight lines for the audience. However, the décor and lighting planned by your Artistic Director for your fashion parade may compromise safety. Drapes over the ceiling area will obscure the normal lighting and prevent the fire sensors and sprinklers from working correctly. And there are a number of props that may hinder access into and out of the venue. On the other hand, the audience expected is quite small.

Answer the following questions:

- What are some of the safety risks associated with this event?
- Who is responsible for the safety of the venue and the audience?
- With whom should you discuss the risks associated with your event concept?
- How could the risks be reduced?
- What sorts of contingency plans could be developed?
- What should the evacuation plan include?

ACTIVITIES

1 Visit <www.crowdsafe.com> and list five major crowd control problems that have led to significant numbers of casualties at rock concerts.
2 Visit an event venue and evaluate the emergency plan in terms of:
- the venue's physical features and likely emergency risks
- the venue map, emergency equipment and access for emergency services
- entrances and exits for the event audience
- the clarity of roles for staff involved
- reporting relationships
- communication technologies
- record keeping
- other legal compliance or adherence to Standards.

LINKS

Australian Bomb Data Centre (Australian Federal Police)
www.afp.gov.au

Emergency Management Australia
www.ema.gov.au

Standards Australia
www.standards.org.au

Standards New Zealand
www.standards.co.nz

Strategies for ensuring crowd safety
www.crowdsafe.com

TravelSmart
www.travelsmart.gov.au

SUMMARY

In this chapter we have dealt with one of the most problematic issues for event managers: spectator control. Unfortunately, there are many examples of events at which people have lost their lives through fire or riot, and there are many examples of near misses. For this reason, it is necessary to prepare both a spectator management plan and a risk management plan for every event, as well as emergency response plans for crowd control and evacuation in case of fire or other major risk. These plans must comply with the relevant legislation and Standards and be properly implemented. All possible preventative measures and contingency plans need to be put in place prior to events, and appropriate staff training is essential.

CHAPTER TWENTY

EVENT

PROTOCOL

ON COMPLETION OF THIS CHAPTER YOU WILL BE ABLE TO:

- explain the concept of protocol
- identify protocol associated with a range of events
- identify sources of information regarding event protocol
- avoid breaches of protocol
- use national symbols correctly.

The ceremony is a major state function, with the Royals granting an audience at the event, hence certain restrictions regarding the observation of the ceremony are unavoidably necessary. They apply to all persons who are not actual participants in the ceremony. The Royal Household requests the kind co-operation of all visitors to this ceremonial event to observe the following:

- *Dress code for international media. Members of the Press are requested to dress in formal business attire with 'Press/Media' accreditation. For men: shirt, jacket and necktie. For ladies: blouse and skirt or dress. (Please refrain from wearing trousers or pants.)*
- *Photographers must have their cameras and accreditation passes checked by Security at approximately 9.00 am at tent number 19.*
- *Photographers who are authorised to take photos at the event must be dressed in a business suit with the appropriate press accreditation status. Other unauthorised photographers will be excluded.*
- *After 11.30 guests and tourists must remain within the tents assigned.*
- *Photographers are not permitted to walk into or with the procession. Photographing is permitted only from both sides of the procession. Three specific locations with elevated seating have been prepared for photographers at the eastern side of the procession.*
- *Following the arrival of the Royals at the gala luncheon, guests and individuals without Media accreditation are not permitted to take photos. Photographers are allowed to take photos from the designated vantage points.*

The above example illustrates the protocol for a Royal ceremonial procession. If VIPs and dignitaries are present at an event, protocol is an important aspect of planning. Functions where protocols need to be used include:

- civic receptions
- formal parades
- freedom of city ceremonies
- national day receptions
- citizenship ceremonies
- private functions.

Sources of information on protocol include:
- libraries
- Internet
- federal, state and local government protocol departments
- Aboriginal Land Councils
- Australia Day Councils
- Office of the United Nations.

For example, if you visit the website for the Queensland Government listed at the end of this chapter, you will find all relevant information about the state, its government, its emblems and its icons. This type of information is available from government departments at state and federal level, as well as at local government level. Accessing this information can assist the event planning team with issuing invitations, preparing running sheets, preparing briefing papers, liaising with dignitaries and officials, and providing services during an event.

The formalities outlined below are among those you might be called upon to put in place when managing events.

ORDER OF PRECEDENCE

Outlined in Fig. 20.1 on page 298 is an abbreviated version of the order of precedence for Australian Commonwealth, state and territory dignitaries. Besides these basic requirements, there are additional rules for more complex situations, such as establishing order of precedence based on the date of taking or leaving office. Those dignitaries included range from the Governor-General to ex-ministers of state to those who retain the prefix 'Honourable'.

An event planner would consult the order of precedence in order to make seating and other arrangements, and would also need to contact state or federal government protocol officers for any specific information on protocol. The late Sir Asher Joel's book, *Australian Protocol and Procedures* (1998), is a very useful reference on this subject.

TITLES

Style guides, available in most public libraries, provide guidelines on the correct titles for people such as Prime Ministers ('Right Honourable') and Commonweath Ministers ('Honourable').

Rolling out the red carpet is usually associated with formal or ceremonial events.

Fig. 20.1

Abbreviated order of appearance for Commonwealth, state and territory dignitaries.

The Governor-General

The Governor of the State
The Governor of the other States according to their date of appointment
The Administrators of the Northern Territory and Norfolk Island

The Prime Minister

The Premier within his/her own State
The Chief Minister of the Northern Territory and Norfolk Island

The President of the Senate and the Speaker of the House of Representatives according to seniority of appointment

The Chief Justice of Australia

Ambassadors and High Commissioners
Chargés d'affaires en pied or en titre
Chargés d'affaires and acting High Commissioners

Members of the Federal Executive Council under summons

The Administrators of the Northern Territory and Norfolk Island

The Leader of the Opposition

Former Governors-General
Former Prime Ministers
Former Chief Justices of Australia

The Premiers of the States according to the population of their States
Chief Minister of the Northern Territory and Norfolk Island

The Lord Mayor within his/her city

If high-ranking overseas visitors were attending an event, an event organiser would contact the relevant embassy to obtain information on the table of precedence and the titles to be used.

STYLES OF ADDRESS

Styles of address for foreign dignitaries are summarised in Table 20.1. Again, style guides can assist you with this form of protocol, as well as with the correct form of address for the clergy.

Table 20.1			
Styles of address for foreign dignitaries.			
Dignitary	**Salutation**	**Final Salutation**	**In Conversation**
A King/An Emperor	Your Majesty/Sire:	I have the honour to remain, Your Majesty's obedient servant,	'Your Majesty' first, then 'Sire'
A Queen	Your Majesty/Madame:	I have the honour to remain, Your Majesty's obedient servant,	'Your Majesty' first, then 'Ma'am'
A Prince/Princess With title 'Royal Highness'	Your Royal Highness:	I remain, Your Royal Highness, Yours very truly,	'Your Royal Highness' first, then 'Sir/Ma'am'
With title 'Serene Highness'	Your Serene Highness:	I remain, Your Serene Highness, Yours very truly,	'Your Serene Highness' first, then 'Sir/Ma'am'
Without title 'Highness'	Prince: Madame:	Yours very truly, Yours very truly,	'Prince' first, then 'Sir' 'Princess' first, then 'Madam'
A President of a Republic	Excellency:	Yours sincerely,	'Excellency' first, then 'President' or 'Sir/Madam'
The President of the United States	Dear Mr. President:	Yours sincerely,	'Mr. President' or 'Excellency' first, then 'Sir'
A Prime Minister His/Her Excellency (full name) Prime Minister of (name) Address	Dear Prime Minister:	Yours sincerely,	'Prime Minister' or 'Excellency' first, then 'Sir/Madam' or 'Mr./Mrs./Ms./Miss (name)'
Ambassadors/High Commissioners of foreign countries	Dear Ambassador/ High Commissioner:	Yours sincerely,	'Your Excellency' or 'Excellency'

Based on Styles of Address from the Canadian Heritage website <www.pch.gc.ca>

DRESS FOR FORMAL OCCASIONS

The appropriate dress for formal occasions should be included on the invitation. This might include morning dress for formal day functions or black tie (or sometimes white) for formal evening events. Protocol also needs to be observed as to the correct insignia to be worn at ceremonial events.

PROTOCOL FOR SPEAKERS

Speakers need to be briefed in advance and provided with a list of the guests to be welcomed, in order of precedence. The timing and length of speeches need to be discussed with the speakers before the event and must also be canvassed with the chef so that food production coincides with the event plan and speakers are not disturbed by food service or clearing of plates.

SEATING PLANS FOR FORMAL OCCASIONS

Correct seating arrangements for occasions such as awards ceremonies and formal dinners must be observed by the event organiser. The guest of honour always sits at the right of the host unless the Governor-General or Governor is present, in which case the guest of honour sits at the left of the host. If other government dignitaries are present, the order of precedence outline in Fig. 20.1 on page 298 is then followed.

The seating plan illustrated in Fig. 20.2 is designed for an event at which all dignitaries are male and accompanied by their spouses. If some of the dignitaries are female, or some are unaccompanied, this adds to the level of difficulty in planning the seating. In general terms, those with higher rank sit closer to the official party, and the guest of honour sits at the right of the host. As mentioned above, protocol officers based at federal and state government level are an invaluable source of information, as are their counterparts in other countries.

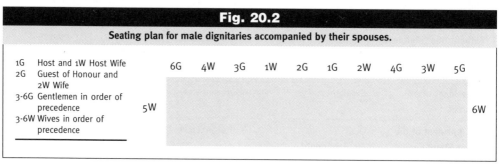

Fig. 20.2

Seating plan for male dignitaries accompanied by their spouses.

1G   Host and 1W Host Wife
2G   Guest of Honour and 2W Wife
3-6G Gentlemen in order of precedence
3-6W Wives in order of precedence

Adapted from Joel (1998)

WELCOME TO COUNTRY

Many Australian events commence with a 'Welcome to Country' opening ceremony. This ceremony recognises Australian Indigenous culture and custodianship of country. The following guidelines from the Musicological Society of Australia illustrate their policy:

The policy
It is the policy of MSA to recognise the Indigenous custodianship of country where MSA public events are held, and acknowledge the continuing significance of Indigenous culture in Australia.

This policy embraces the spirit of reconciliation between Indigenous and other Australians and reflects the national process of reconciliation as guided by the national Council for Aboriginal Reconciliation.

What is Welcome to Country?

Recognition is made through a formal process called Welcome to Country. It always occurs in the opening ceremony of the event, preferably as the first item. Welcome to Country is conducted by a representative (or representatives) of local Indigenous custodians who welcome the delegates to their country. Indigenous protocols in relation to Welcome to Country are wide and diverse and will vary according to region and locality. The form of the welcome is negotiated between the Indigenous people and the event organisers. For example, Welcome to Country may consist of a single speech, or it may include some kind of performance (a song, dance, didjeridu solo, etc), or it may be a combination of these. It is important to remember that the Indigenous representative/s must feel comfortable with the arrangements. Rather than a gesture of tokenism and political correctness, MSA acknowledges that Welcome to Country is a right of the local Indigenous custodians and not a privilege.

Who performs Welcome to Country?

Who performs Welcome to Country is agreed between appropriate representatives (individual or organisation) of local Indigenous custodians and the event organisers.

<www.msa.org.au/welcome.html>

RELIGIOUS AND CULTURAL PROTOCOL

Formalities attach to most religious and cultural ceremonies, although these may or may not be observed by the client. The event organiser may therefore be required to assist with the protocol for such an event or to provide advice if the client wants a more relaxed arrangement.

Following are examples of traditions associated with a number of wedding ceremonies from around the world.

Scottish wedding

The stag night is a tradition of Scottish — and Australian — weddings, male friends taking the groom out to celebrate with lots of drinking and practical jokes at the expense of the groom. Another old Scottish custom requires the groom to carry a basket of stones on his back until the bride can be persuaded to kiss him. The groom and his groomsmen often wear kilts to the wedding (traditionally with no undergarments), and the groom may present the bride with an engraved silver teaspoon on their wedding day as a pledge that they will never go hungry. A traditional sword dance is sometimes performed at the wedding reception.

Greek Orthodox wedding

There are two parts to this service: the betrothal ceremony and the marriage ceremony. During the marriage ceremony, the priest crowns both bride and groom three times and all three parade around the altar table three times. The entrance of the families of the bride and the groom to the reception area, as well as the arrival of the bride and groom at the reception, are greeted with a fanfare.

Japanese wedding

The bride's wedding gown is often a traditional wedding kimono. The first sip of sake drunk by the bride and groom at the wedding ceremony symbolises the official union of marriage. The ceremony is generally quite small and is held at a Shinto shrine or in a chapel. Guests invited to the wedding reception make gifts of money to the couple and they, in turn, are given a gift to take home.

Macedonian wedding

Prior to the wedding ceremony, an unmarried relative or friend of the family makes a loaf of bread and decorates it with sweets. Once the bread is cooked, the family members dance and sing, and then give the loaf to the best man who carries it to the reception. Towards the end of the reception the bread is taken apart by all the single males. The story goes that if they eat some and keep some under their pillow they will see their future wife.

The formalities for weddings of different nationalities can often be found on the Internet (see one such website at the end of this chapter) or from the many books on wedding etiquette available in bookstores.

For the modern bride and groom there are many variations on the old traditions and these must be discussed with them before the ceremony. For the organiser of the wedding, the most crucial elements are the timing of the music, the speeches and the meal at the reception. From a planning perspective, there are many details which need to be agreed upon, including:

The day a Sydney woman married a Zulu warrior

When talk turned to ritual sacrifice, the Cogley family from Sydney wondered what kind of wedding they were in for. They had flown to South Africa to see their daughter, Sofi, 31, marry Robert Ntshalintshali, also 31, a Zulu from a small village in the foothills of the spectacular Drakensberg mountain range.

The night before the April 18 ceremony they were summoned to the spirit hut to witness the village chief call upon his ancestors. Three boys held down a bleating goat while a man slaughtered it, collecting the blood. With a piece of dried sage burning and the skinned goat strung from the ceiling, the chief called the names of his ancestors, one by one, telling them about Sofi, about the wedding and asking them to accept the couple into the family.

He sprinkled bile on Ms Cogley's forehead, arms and legs, then rolled a thin piece of goat skin around her wrist, a symbol that she was now a member of the family.

Custom dictated that Mr Ntshalintshali should give Ms Cogley's family 11 cows for her hand in marriage. Not surprisingly, both families were relieved to quietly drop the whole subject — not just because of the unwanted excess baggage for the Cogley family but because the cost is prohibitive for the average Zulu.

The Cogleys tried to get some idea of the number of guests who would attend the festivities, only to be met with a shrug. 'Maybe 100, maybe 300, maybe 1000 — it depends who hears about it', their daughter said. 'There are no invitations here. The word spreads and people start coming.'

Danielle Teutsch, *Sydney Morning Herald*, 13 May 2001

- décor
- seating plans for the bridal party (see Fig. 20.3) and other guests
- timing and duration of the reception
- menu and special food requirements
- beverages and payment for beverages
- timing of food service, speeches, dancing, etc.
- music, sound system and microphones for those giving speeches
- rooms where the bride and groom can change.

Fig. 20.3

Seating plan for bridal table.

| Chief Bridesmaid | Groom's Father | Bride's Mother | Groom | Bride | Bride's father | Groom's Mother | Best Man |

A run sheet (see Chapter 12 for other examples) for a wedding reception would need to include the following steps and the timing of these steps:

- music on arrival
- arrival of guests
- drink service commences (generally champagne, wine, beer and soft drinks)
- arrival of bride's and groom's families
- guests seated
- entry and introduction of the bridal party approximately half an hour later
- entrée served, starting with the bridal table
- main course served, starting with the bridal table.

Approximately two hours after commencement:
- all guests are served champagne in anticipation of the speeches and toasts
- speeches by father of the bride, the groom and the best man (this may vary)
- cutting of the cake
- bridal waltz
- dessert and coffee served
- dancing
- throwing of garter and bouquet
- farewell of bride and groom through an arch formed by guests
- close bar and music stops
- guests leave.

Note that an open bar (which does not generally include spirits) may extend only for a number of hours, after which guests pay for their drinks.

PROTOCOL FOR SPORTING CEREMONIES

There are a number of formalities for sporting events, including the awarding of trophies, cheques or medals at the ceremony held soon after the event has finished. Traditionally, in team sports, the press interviews the team captain of the runner-up before the winner is announced. However, different sports have different conventions. For example, at motor racing events, champagne is sprayed over spectators by the winner and this ritual is followed by a press conference at which the drivers remain seated. Press interviews for a number of other sports take place in the locker rooms. Generally, there is a major presentation at the end of the season. An outline of the procedure at a sporting awards ceremony is illustrated in Fig. 20.4 The briefing provided for the MC lists the order of precedence of those attending so that the MC can make the appropriate introductions (see Fig. 20.5).

Fig. 20.4

Order of ceremony for a sporting awards evening.

6 pm	Arrival of guests
	Pre-dinner drinks
6.25 pm	Guests seated
6.30 pm	MC welcomes everyone
	President's welcoming speech
	Junior sportsman award presented by Vice-President
	Junior sportswoman award presented by Vice-President
7 pm	Entrée
7.20 pm	Official of the year presented by Sport & Recreation representative
	Administrator of the year presented by Sport & Recreation representative
	Coach of the year presented by Life Member
	Team of the year presented by Life Member
7.40 pm	Main course
8.10 pm	Introduction of new Life Member by the President
	Presentation to state players selected in national squads by former Australian representative
8.40 pm	Dessert
9 pm	CEO thanks all sponsors and presents a small token of appreciation to major sponsor
	Speech by major sponsor
	Sportsman of the year presented by major sponsor
	Sportswoman of the year presented by major sponsor
9.30 pm	MC thanks all presenters, congratulates all winners and wishes everyone the best for the next year
9.35 pm	DJ plays music

© Jennifer Anson. Reproduced with permission

Fig. 20.5

Briefing notes for presenters at a sporting awards evening.

- MC will announce title of next award and will welcome the presenter to the stage.
- Walk to the stage, proceed up centre stairs and then to the lectern.
- MC will shake right hands and pass the envelope to you with the left hand.
- At the lectern announce the nominations for the ... award are ...
- The award goes to ...
- As the winner proceeds to the stage the awards assistant will hand you the award.
- Meet the winner in the centre of the stage.
- Shake right hands and present the award with the left hand.
- Face the front for official photographs.
- The awards assistant will direct the winner to return to their seat.
- You will either return to lectern for second presentation or return to your own seat.

Briefing notes for awards assistant

- All awards are set up on the presentation table in the order of proceedings to the side of the lectern.
- All envelopes are placed under the appropriate award.
- Hand envelope to MC as the presenter moves to the stage.
- Hand award to presenter as the winner moves to the stage.
- As the official photographer and family/friends finish taking photographs, indicate to the winner to return to their seat.
- Indicate to the presenter to return to their seat or, if they have a second presentation to make, hand them the next envelope.

Briefing notes for MC

Guests in order of importance:

- Major sponsor
- State Sport & Recreation representative
- Former Australian representative
- Life Member
- President
- Vice-President
- Board Members
- Athletes (members of Association)
- Staff of Association
- Family and friends

© Jennifer Anson. Reproduced with permission

RULES OF FLAG FLYING

There are many conventions involved in flying the national flag and the flags of other nations. Take, as an example, an international sporting event staged in Australia. The Australian flag, as Australia's national emblem, should take precedence over all flags of other nations and should always be presented properly (it should not be used as a tablecloth or seat cover!). When flying with flags from other countries, the Australian flag should be in the position of honour, for example, immediately opposite the entrance to the stadium; when carried in procession, the Australian flag should lead. The Australian flag may be used for advertising purposes, although it must be displayed clearly and be unobscured by other logos or images (Joel, 1998).

ACTIVITY

You have been asked to run an event with an Australian theme for a senior American executive who is about to return to the United States after working in Adelaide for three years. This event will be held outdoors and up to 400 staff members will attend. The Australian theme should be evident in all aspects of the event, including the décor, music, food and beverage. (A link to a recipe for 'Dogs in Blankets' is provided at the end of the chapter.) Since this is a large multinational company and the media will no doubt attend the event, you must observe the correct protocol for use of Australian symbols. You also need to ensure that you do not breach copyright in your use of images, music, etc. and seek permission for usage or pay licensing fees as necessary.

- *Expand on the approach to the theme of this event.*
- *Explain how you will use Australian images and music.*
- *Illustrate your use of the Australian flag.*

LINKS

Australian Department of Foreign Affairs and Trade
www.dfat.gov.au/protocol/index.html

Australian Honours System
www.itsanhonour.gov.au

Australian symbols
www.pm.gov.au/aust_focus/nat_symbols/flag.htm

Canadian protocol and events
www.pch.gc.ca

'Dogs in Blankets' recipe
http://members.tripod.com/virtaus/volume3/cuisine

Flags of the world
http://fotw.digibel.be/flags/

Queensland Government
www.premiers.qld.gov.au/Government/

Wedding traditions
www.chicagomarriage.com/wedding_traditions.htm

SUMMARY

This chapter has dealt with the topic of event protocol. Protocol encompasses the traditions associated with government functions, official ceremonies, sporting events, weddings and the like. Such rules and guidelines assist event planners in working out seating arrangements, making introductions, and protecting the privacy and security of VIPs, such as overseas dignitaries. Our national symbols often form part of event décor and an event manager needs to be aware of the rules pertaining to their use. Awareness of the importance of protocol and the ability to locate the relevant information prior to the event will ensure that the event runs smoothly.

CHAPTER TWENTY-ONE

EVENT

CATERING

ON COMPLETION OF THIS CHAPTER YOU WILL BE ABLE TO:

- determine the scope of event catering requirements
- develop a catering concept for an event
- prepare and implement an operational catering plan
- monitor food safety for event catering
- manage catering contracts and client relationships.

An outbreak of food poisoning at the Darling Harbour Convention Centre that saw five ambulances, including a medical mini-bus, called to treat diners, is believed to have been caused by a rare mushroom toxin. Both NSW Health and the convention centre management are conducting investigations into the incident last Friday night.

Ambulance officers treated 17 diners, but no-one was admitted to hospital. The sudden onset of the illness saw some of the 700 guests at the NSW Master Builders' Association awards throw up at the table. A spokeswoman for the convention centre said a commercial laboratory report released yesterday afternoon showed there were 'no hygiene or food pathogen factors at fault'.

KIRSTY NEEDHAM, *SYDNEY MORNING HERALD*, 6 SEPTEMBER 2003

Food safety is a major concern for event participants. In this chapter, food safety planning will be linked to the development of plans for catering at functions and outdoor events. In the above case, there were no food safety issues or, indeed, any fault found with food safety planning and implementation. This was instead a rare outbreak of mushroom poisoning similar to that experienced during a banquet for 482 people in Vancouver, British Columbia, which was reported in June 1991. Concerns of the public are no doubt reinforced by incidents such as that of a young man at an event stand blowing into hot dog bags to inflate them prior to packing them with hot dogs, and then leaving these in a heating unit for his germs to multiply in the packaging!

Knowledge of basic food safety requirements is absolutely necessary for all event catering staff. Most events involve bulk catering, and the risks associated with food safety are particularly significant

Outdoor catering presents special challenges

for those staged at outdoor venues. In comparison with convention centre facilities, which use cook chill methods and state-of-the-art refrigeration, outdoor venues seldom provide an ideal environment for food safety. Surveys conducted by Boo, Ghiselli and Almanza (2000) show that foods served at outdoor fairs and festivals and fast food restaurants are considered the least safe compared with food served at other locations, such as in the home or at a restaurant. Food poisoning/spoilage was the major safety concern, while fat or cholesterol was the major health concern at all locations. Insect and dirt or dust contamination was a major concern for customers eating at outdoor fairs and festivals.

Before looking in detail at food safety planning, we will deal with the skills and knowledge required to plan the catering for an event or function. This is a specialised area for Catering and Functions/Banquet Managers but an overview of the field is valuable for every event manager.

CATERING RESPONSIBILITIES

The functions and responsibilities associated with event catering generally follow similar lines. However, the level of specialisation differs between a large organisation, such as a hotel chain or convention centre, and smaller events where the catering team is likely to be quite small, with most roles undertaken by a few individuals. For most large outdoor events, catering is contracted out.

Sales

A Director of Catering is generally responsible for the catering sales team, which includes salespeople and administration staff. The sales staff have titles such as Convention Sales Manager, Banquet Sales Manager, Function Sales Manager, Convention Sales Manager, and Event Co-ordinator. The sales function involves negotiation with clients about their catering needs, preparation of quotes and finalisation of contracts.

Service

Once all details of the proposed contract have been finalised, the details are handed over to the service staff for execution. The title, Functions Manager, is used to cover management of service for meetings, weddings, conventions and exhibitions, and is largely synonymous with the more old-fashioned title of Banquet Manager. The Functions Manager reports to the Director of Food and Beverage. Functions/Banquet staff members are responsible for room set-up and food and beverage service. These employees have direct contact with the client, customers and guests at the event. In all cases where alcohol is served at least one barperson is also allocated to the event. The kitchen crew which prepares the food is likely to include the Executive Chef, a Banquet Chef, apprentice chefs, stewards and other kitchen workers. The senior kitchen staff are responsible for food safety and are supported by a purchasing department for food and beverage supplies.

Figure 21.1 shows the functions and responsibilities of the Sales and Food and Beverage staff and their reporting relationships.

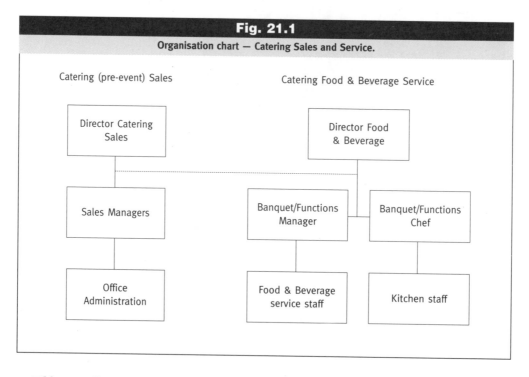

Fig. 21.1
Organisation chart — Catering Sales and Service.

Catering (pre-event) Sales

Catering Food & Beverage Service

- Director Catering Sales
- Director Food & Beverage
- Sales Managers
- Banquet/Functions Manager
- Banquet/Functions Chef
- Office Administration
- Food & Beverage service staff
- Kitchen staff

Table 21.1 illustrates how performance standards can be developed for each of the tasks associated with catering provision.

Table 21.1
Procedures and performance measures for Functions Manager.

Standard procedure	Performance measure
Confirm bookings	• Acknowledge and confirm booking confirmation and reconfirmation within 24 hours by responding to catering sales manager • Liaise with chef regarding function catering in week prior to function
Plan function set-up	• Plan function layout two weeks prior to event • Check stock levels, for example, tablecloths, cutlery • Develop function specifications such as table layouts
Schedule and manage staffing	• Plan staffing requirements • Roster staff • Contact staff one week prior to function • Confirm rosters 24 hours prior to function • Brief staff immediately prior to function set-up

Table 21.1 CONTINUED	
Procedures and performance measures for Functions Manager.	
Supervise function set-up	• Monitor function set-up in progress • Check all physical specifications met two hours prior to function (tables and stage set-up, etc.) • Schedule service of food and beverage and confirm with chef three hours prior to function (for example, timing of main course and dessert)
Manage customer requests on the day or refer to catering sales manager	• Respond to customer needs by meeting requests, or refer to catering sales manager immediately
Clear and clean up after the function	• Supervise staff clearing and cleaning up • Monitor occupational health and safety • Evaluate function and record outstanding or emerging problems • Where necessary, supervise function set-up for following day

As mentioned previously, catering is generally outsourced for most outdoor or large events. This may involve one master caterer or several smaller caterers. In a large sports stadium, for example, there is likely to be one large catering organisation serving the needs of the corporate boxes and several smaller caterers servicing concession stands selling hot and cold food. The types of catering provided for most large events include:

• VIP catering
• sponsor catering
• performer/athlete catering
• staff catering
• fixed concessions (fast food, beverages)
• mobile concessions (coffee carts, ice-cream units, hot dog units).

Speedy service is needed at half-time

During the 2003 Rugby World Cup organisers planned for over 23 000 servings of hot chips, 15 000 pies, 15 000 hot dogs, 3500 pizzas, 3500 hamburgers, 600 boxes of stir-fried noodles, 500 salads and 3000 sandwiches. These quantities are mind-boggling. For mega events, the purchasing process is commenced several years beforehand since supplies of potatoes, lettuce, etc. need to be planned in collaboration with farmers. These contracts have to be signed in good time for planning, planting and production of raw foods. Flowers are another good example of a purchasing dilemma, particularly if large quantities of national floral emblems are required. Many products, such as eggs, have to be imported since it is not worthwhile for producers to increase their number of laying hens for a short selling period.

In addition to planning and providing support to contract caterers, in some cases the Catering Manager is also responsible for managing environmental issues associated with catering, such as waste disposal. This job description is illustrated in Fig. 21.2.

Fig. 21.2

Sample Job Description — Catering and Waste Services Manager.

Catering and Waste Services Manager

Job Summary

The Catering and Waste Services Manager is responsible for working with the venue Master Catering Organisation and relevant subcontracting caterers and concessionaires to finalise food and beverage specifications and control procedures in accordance with their contracts. Responsible also for working with the Cleaning contractor and Waste Management contractor for the best possible outcome for an environmentally friendly event.

Duties

- Establish operational specifications and procedures for catering, cleaning and waste management.
- Monitor day-to-day performance of contractors in accordance with contract specifications such as opening hours, service levels, quality, etc.
- Liaise with customers, including external customers such as sponsors and internal customers such as staff, to monitor satisfaction levels.
- Manage meal service for staff, contractors and performers.
- Liaise with Health Department and catering contractors in relation to food safety Regulations, planning and control systems.
- Attend daily meetings with contractors, including Catering, Cleaning and Waste.
- Solve immediate problems or refer to venue or other managers as required.

Reports to: Venue Manager

As this job description illustrates, the Catering and Waste Services Manager in this position has no direct involvement in catering. The primary role is planning, negotiating and overseeing contracts with the catering contractors. The process of negotiation would, for example, involve developing specifications for menus, prices and service levels. Following planning, the manager would then oversee all event catering, putting control measures in place to evaluate whether contractors were meeting contract stipulations. Problem-solving is another feature of this job, with unusual requests and issues emerging as an event unfolds.

FOOD PREPARATION AND SERVICE

Food is an integral part of any event. Any experienced event manager knows that complaints about food are serious indeed and extremely difficult to remedy during or after an event. On the other hand, where client expectations are surpassed, food quality can contribute to high satisfaction ratings. Since, generally speaking, the cost of food in relation to all other costs is relatively low, food should always be served in reasonable portion sizes and reasonable quantities. Careful planning is essential, and advice must be given to the client about menu selection to ensure that it meets the needs of the audience or spectators at the event.

Styles of service

There are several styles of service, ranging from plated meals to snacks, from which a client may choose.

Buffet

A buffet style set-up, which offers a wide variety of foods, is one way to ensure that all customers will be satisfied. Generally the only mistake made with buffet style food is the unexpected demand for vegetarian dishes — these appeal to non-vegetarians and it is common to find that dishes have run out before the vegetarians get to the front of the queue. Buffet queues are another matter of concern, but with careful planning and layout, queues can be avoided. If a queue forms, it can take some time for the last person to help themselves, by which time some dishes, such as seafood, will have run out.

Plated meals

For many functions and conventions, food is already plated and everyone gets the same meal unless a special dietary request has been made. In other cases, there is a 50:50 drop with different meals served to alternate guests. Customers at the table are then free to swap meals if they please. Again, demand for vegetarian meals is often higher than expected, even when guests have been asked about special meal requests at the time of booking. One of the many menus offered by Suntec Singapore International Convention and Exhibition Centre is illustrated in Fig. 21.3 on page 314. This convention centre can organise events ranging from small cocktail parties for 10 people to weddings, corporate dinners, banquets, functions and other special events for 10 000 people. The centre's world-class chefs provide a gourmet selection of Asian, Western and Halal menus. In the competitive field of convention bidding, catering plays a big part in the decision-making processes of organisers.

Grazing stations

A contemporary approach to function food is a grazing station, a small table with light snacks such as cheese and fruit. Healthier items are becoming increasingly popular, with fruit often being

Fig. 21.3

Example of gourmet menu offered by convention centres.

GOLDEN PEONY MENU

Sashimi on Ice

taro, deoduck clam, salmon and lobster

Buddha Jumps over the Wall

top broth with abalone, sea cucumber,

shark's fin, scallops and fish maw

Stuffed Spiny Sea Cucumber

served with crab roe

Braised Abalone

served with Hong Kong kai lan

Pepper Beef Tenderloin

served with Oriental apple sauce

Imperial Pearl Rice

with crabmeat, dried scallops and prawns

Double-boiled Bird's Nest

with hasma, ginseng, red dates in young coconut shell

Suntec Singapore International Convention and Exhibition Centre

‹www.suntecsingapore.com/contactus.asp›

served for morning and afternoon tea. A large basket of red apples is a welcome change from a platter of processed biscuits.

Food stalls

Food stalls are commonplace at many events and here it is essential that food quality and food safety are carefully monitored. The caterers should be evaluated before the event, menu and food specifications agreed and food safety plans reviewed.

Types of meals

All meals can form the basis for event catering, including breakfast, lunch and dinner. Refreshment breaks and cocktail parties also require catering. Whatever the event, the professional skills of a qualified chef are needed for planning purposes. Food can range in quality from frozen processed meals to sophisticated, unique gourmet offerings. In all cases, attention must be paid to nutrition, product quality, quantity, presentation, special dietary needs and food safety. Surpassing expectations by, for example, providing an espresso cart at an exhibition or serving hot snacks during a meeting break can contribute to the success of the event concept. Trends and themes are another consideration for menu planners.

Athletes provide a particular challenge for event caterers, and advice can be obtained from their managers or sports institutes. Food poisoning and food contamination are serious concerns for high profile athletes — one memorable team blamed their host country for gastroenteritis and poor performance on the field!

A major consideration, linked to the bottom line, is the quantity of food necessary to meet demand. For many festivals and events, the audience is hard to predict and the number of meals purchased on the day can vary depending on the weather and other factors. On a cold day, hot foods and beverages are in high demand, while on hot days these stalls could have little business. Nearby storage facilities, such as refrigerated units, can be most useful for storing food until just before it is required.

Logistics of food supply

Moving large quantities of food can be highly problematic, particularly if there is a full-scale accreditation system that limits access to the site. This means that only certain individuals and vehicles can deliver food. Traffic delays are also likely to occur. Most large events have to develop a delivery schedule for the early hours of the morning, with limited times available for each operator. Supply chain analysis is useful in estimating the time needed for delivery and off-loading of supplies and equipment, which allows the venue hire period to be extended if necessary to ensure adequate delivery time. This also has implications for security of the site.

Storage is another logistical consideration, the importance of which is illustrated in the following example. It is not rare for an Executive Chef working at a stadium to have to supervise the preparation of 28 000 meals to be served in one day. Production of this number of meals would need to commence five days in advance, using cooking and storage methods to achieve a 7 to 21 day shelf life.

Profitability

For hotels, events such as meetings and weddings are more profitable than other food and beverage operations. However, food purchasing needs to be very accurate (little or no waste), the food component of the price quoted to the client should be low, and production and service should be tightly scheduled. Planning should occur well in advance, with menu engineering identifying the best items to include on menus for the highest profit margin.

BEVERAGE SERVICE

There are many considerations for beverage service at events, not the least of which is the legislative requirement for responsible service of alcohol. The banning of 'beer wenches' has occurred in response to poor crowd behaviour at sports matches. Sponsorship arrangements generally have a major impact on beverages sold, with exclusive arrangements, for example, negotiated with sponsor beer and soft drink companies, including major promotional activities. This can involve changing the beer supply from one company to another at a sports stadium, a significant effort when the beer lines run for 3.5 kilometres around the stadium to the various outlets!

Legislative compliance and profitability are the main considerations for beverage service.

Legislative compliance

In addition to all liquor-related responsibilities, such as correct signage, all staff must have RSA (responsible service of alcohol) certificates. This should not become a last-minute staffing issue. Poaching trained and accredited staff is a well-known feature of major events when staffing shortages occur. All sorts of prizes and monetary inducements are used to attract casual staff when outlets become desperate.

Profitability of selected beverages

Choice of brand and profit margin need to be considered when deciding what to stock and serve at events. House brands are generally selected on the basis of a regular, large supply with resulting discount. The quality of house brands is important as it must be acceptable to the public. Some clients will require both regular and premium brands to be served and this must be negotiated before the event. Drink sizes should be monitored, and the correct glass used for each beverage. The temperature of beer and wine is also a consideration as is an adequate supply of ice for spirit-based drinks. This can be particularly problematic for outdoor events.

Prices for alcohol for functions such as weddings should be negotiated beforehand. This can be done on the basis of an open bar where the host pays for all individual drinks or a cash bar where guests pay for all their own alcohol. A compromise is an agreement by the host to pay for all beer, wine and soft drink but no spirits. In other cases, the host might set a limit on the budget, and once this is reached guests must pay for their own drinks. Or a full package deal might be negotiated where the establishment charges a flat rate based on average drinking at a similar type of function. This of course includes a margin for profit. In rare cases, the client may wish to provide wines, in which case corkage rates need to be discussed before the event.

NEGOTIATING CATERING CONTRACTS

When outsourcing catering, or booking catering for an in-house event, the following questions form part of the planning process, leading to quotes and contracts with caterers:

1 What is the nature of the event?
2 Does the event have a theme?
3 Is it a one-off event?
4 How many people will attend (is this an estimate or guarantee)?
5 When will the final head count be done?
6 What is the budget?
7 Where will the event be held?
8 Is there a properly equipped kitchen with hot and cold running water, cooking equipment, cool room and freezer? When can this be inspected?
9 Does the site have storage?
10 How easily can the site be accessed (accreditation and road closure)?
11 Can food be prepared off site and transported in?
12 How soon will the menu be finalised (impacts on costing)?
13 Are there preferred foods, items which must be avoided or special dietary or nutritional requirements?
14 Will alcohol be served? Who will pay for the alcohol?

15 What is the schedule for access to the venue and setting up?

16 When does the event run sheet (running order) allow for food service (e.g. after speeches)?

Prior to the event the caterer's references should be checked, cooking and service facilities should be inspected, and staffing levels and qualifications should be discussed along with menu planning. Food safety plans and registration are the most important control measures, requiring attention before the contracts are finalised.

IMPLEMENTING THE CATERING PLAN

A detailed operational plan for catering should be provided to all stakeholders identifying steps, activities, sequence and responsibilities. All event details should be confirmed prior to the event, with any adjustments fully documented in the plan. In the following section on food safety planning, many elements of the catering plan are covered in detail. There are many operational constraints, such as limited space at the venue, small work areas, limited food storage and refrigeration space, and different climatic conditions. A risk management plan for catering is highly recommended and should follow the guidelines given in Chapter 10. This would identify the things that could go wrong (such as interrupted power supply to refrigeration units). Contingency plans should then be developed to meet the most likely and the most serious possibilities.

Mobile cool rooms are essential for food safety.

FOOD SAFETY PLANNING

Food safety planning involves identifying critical control points in food production and service. The process of purchasing through to food service is illustrated in Fig. 21.4 on page 318, along with the parallel processes of cleaning, garbage removal and pest control. At any one of these stages, raw materials or cooked food could become contaminated. For example, during the receiving process, there may be long delays at the loading dock resulting in all seafood being defrosted. Each control point must be identified as part of the HACCP (Hazard Analysis Critical Control Point) plan and it is essential that such a plan forms part of the tender and contract with the caterer/s. For catering operations at a large stadium, for example, there would be a scientific approach to commodities delivery and storage and food production, and procedures would be well documented for regular monitoring of food temperatures. In the more informal environment of a small event, such concerns require careful attention.

The following guidelines are adapted from information provided by the Victorian Government Food Safety Authority and can be found in the form of templates on their website at <www.foodsafety.vic.gov.au/downloads/events_template.pdf>.

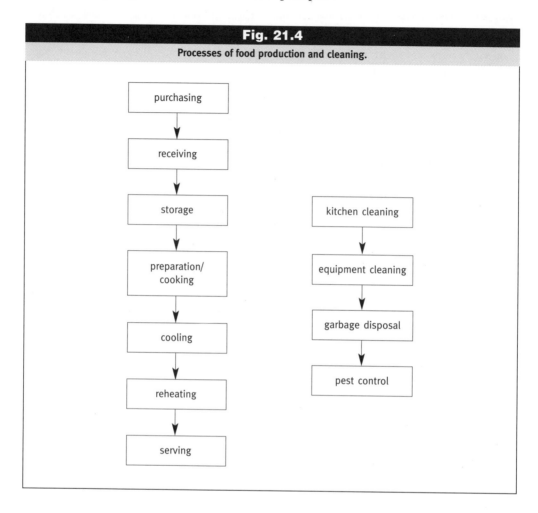

Fig. 21.4

Processes of food production and cleaning.

Temporary premises

The event co-ordinator should ensure that a permit is obtained from the local council or relevant authority for setting up temporary food premises and that the following items are available:
- benches or tables with smooth, easy to clean surfaces or plastic tablecloths
- hand-washing facilities near the temporary premises, with water, a basin, soap and paper towels
- a place to wash up cooking equipment, dishes and utensils
- a fridge to keep cold food cold (below 5°C) and a freezer to keep frozen food frozen (a calibrated thermometer is needed to check temperatures)
- facilities to keep hot food at 60°C or above
- a sufficient number of rubbish containers to collect and store waste away from food.

There must also be a way of dealing with waste water from cooking, cleaning and hand washing. If there are no sinks near the food stall, these will need to be created by providing a drum with taps filled with cold water and a hot water urn. Detergent, food grade sanitiser and disposable towels are also required. Dishes should be washed in hot soapy water and rinsed before and between uses.

Cross-contamination

Most food poisoning cases are linked to **high risk food** such as meat, seafood, poultry, dairy products, small goods and cooked rice, or any food that contains these foods such as pies.

Bacterial contamination can occur when germs contaminate food via physical food handling or via cutting boards and other utensils, or from one type of food touching another type (for example, where cardboard boxes soaked in chicken juices are placed on food preparation surfaces).

In the right conditions, bacteria multiply rapidly — the **Temperature Danger Zone** is between 5°C and 60°C (see Fig. 21.5). Thus hot foods left on a buffet for too long provide an ideal breeding ground for bacteria.

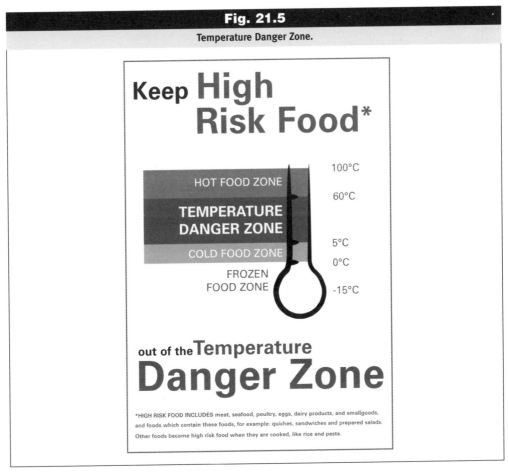

Fig. 21.5
Temperature Danger Zone.

Adapted from ‹http://www.foodsafety.vic.gov.au/downloads/events_template.pdf›

More detailed guidelines are provided on the Food Safety Authority's website for specific purposes, such as product labelling and packing of food sold at market stalls, display and service of food, and temperature checking, but in general terms, food safety can be improved by:

- safe and hygienic handling of food and beverages, including beer lines
- regular hand washing (between, say, handling poultry and peeling vegetables)
- use of gloves when appropriate
- correct food storage (not on the floor)
- checking manufacturers' labels for storage instructions (e.g. length of time permitted under refrigeration)
- use of suitable containers for storage
- correct labelling of items, including expiry dates
- correct stock rotation (first in, first out)
- appropriate and clean clothing (a damp apron is a perfect place for bacterial reproduction)
- avoidance of cross-contamination (e.g. avoiding using the same preparation areas for fish and salads)
- safe disposal of linen and laundry (especially when contaminated with bodily fluids)
- appropriate handling and disposal of garbage
- cleaning and sanitising surfaces (sanitising kills germs too)
- cleaning and sanitising floors, etc. (environmental hygiene)
- personal hygiene (including clean hair and wearing hair covering in the kitchen).

All the above guidelines, as well as more specific ones for specific purposes, are generally developed as part of the HACCP plan. For event managers who contract out catering provision, an awareness of these issues is essential so that the implementation of food safety plans can be monitored by regular inspections prior to and during an event. It is also essential that the event organiser has a complete record of food providers so that sources of contamination can be traced should any food poisoning cases occur.

WASTE MANAGEMENT

Bulk waste resulting from catering operations is significant. By prescribing the use of biodegradable plates and cutlery (made from starch, not plastic), all food waste can go into a single bin and the contents used for compost. Depending on the waste stream, dedicated bins are generally allocated in the proportions indicated in Fig. 21.6.

This topic is covered in more detail in the next chapter.

Fig. 21.6
Allocation of dedicated bins.

Waste stream	Estimated
Cans and bottles	20%
Paper and cardboard	10%
Food waste (for composting)	50%
Residual waste (non-recyclable)	20%

CASE STUDY

Y̶ou are planning an agricultural exhibition and the committee has asked you to weigh up the pros and cons of having one master caterer providing a range of food stalls with different types of food, or several small stall holders with their unique products. One of the purposes of this event is to showcase produce of the local area.

For this case study, you will need to answer the following questions:

- How can catering contribute to the event purpose?
- What are the benefits of employing a master caterer?
- What are the benefits of having several stall holders?
- When selecting caterers, list five key questions that you would ask them in the early selection process.

ACTIVITY

Visit the website of the Victorian Government Food Safety Authority below and investigate the guidelines for product labelling and packing for food sold at events for charity or community causes.

LINKS

Australian and New Zealand Food Safety Authority
www.anzfa.gov.au

Victorian Government Food Safety Authority
www.foodsafety.vic.gov.au

SUMMARY

This chapter has looked at the catering elements of an event. This function can vary widely from in-house catering teams at major convention centres to small stall holders at local markets. In all cases, the choice of foods served is the critical factor as this can enhance or diminish the event concept and customer satisfaction. Logistical issues of transport, storage, food production and service are particularly problematic at outdoor events, and such issues should be covered in catering plans. There is nothing more frustrating for the event audience than a queue for food that is so long that they cannot return to their seats before the end of intermission or half-time! Finally, guidelines for food safety, which are a legislative requirement, have been outlined and sources provided for the relevant authorities for obtaining more detailed and specific information. While responsibility for this is generally delegated to a contractor, the event manager needs a good understanding of the general principles of food safety to ensure that procedures are implemented correctly.

CHAPTER TWENTY-TWO

WASTE AND
ENVIRONMENTAL MANAGEMENT

ON COMPLETION OF THIS CHAPTER YOU WILL BE ABLE TO:

- develop an environmentally friendly waste management plan
- implement and monitor operational procedures for reducing, recycling and reusing waste
- implement and monitor operational procedures for storage and clearing of waste
- implement and monitor operational procedures for cleaning
- organise appropriate sanitary facilities in accordance with council guidelines
- train staff in waste management
- communicate waste management strategy to all stakeholders.

The aim is not just to ensure that holding the Games has no negative net impact on the environment, but also to try to improve this environment and leave behind a positive green legacy.

The environmental element has become one of the most important aspects of any bid to host the Olympic Games; the candidate cities for the Games in 2008 all presented detailed projects in this respect. The candidate cities' statements are checked by an Evaluation Commission which includes an expert on environmental issues named by the Sport and Environment Commission.

www.olympic.org/uk/organisation/commissions/environment/games_uk.asp

Environmental issues form the basis for both summer and winter Olympic Games' bids. These issues are also considered in competitive bids for major sporting events such as the Soccer World Cup and Rugby World Cup. Bid documents need to clearly spell out details of the intended plans for managing solid waste, sewage treatment and energy, and state how the organisers see this influencing the city and region in the future. Planning for even the smallest event must include consideration of environmental issues. Local councils are responsible for waste management and will look for a waste management plan. Councils demand assurances that the environmental impact will be minimal and that the area will be left in pristine condition. As mentioned in the previous chapter, environmentally friendly waste disposal is a major consideration of event organisers.

Scheduled clearing of waste avoids the problem of bins overflowing.

This chapter deals with cleaning and waste management. Such services are most likely to be outsourced to companies such as Cleanevent, well known around the world for event and venue presentation and waste management consultancy services. This company can even provide, through a subsidiary, executive washrooms that are stocked with toiletries, perfumes and flowers — and every washroom comes with its own attendant.

Professional waste consultants can provide assistance in:

• identifying the event venue's total potential waste stream
• tailoring the waste stream to maximise the use of recycled materials
• identifying biodegradable, cost-effective food and drink packaging
• providing recycling collection, storage and transportation equipment
• providing environmental audits post-event.

If waste management is not outsourced, it is the responsibility of the event organiser or local council to decide on the method of dealing with waste streams.

Standard colour codes and bin labels are recommended to simplify waste management for the event organiser and to educate the public. Other types of bins and recycling equipment, such as recycling cages, are also recommended where needed.

Medical and contaminated waste needs special care as these items must be collected, stored and disposed of in accordance with legal guidelines. This is particularly relevant where there is doping control at an event and blood tests are carried out. Oil used in catering also requires special treatment (in a restaurant a waste trap is used) and should not be disposed of in the sewage system.

PLANNING A 'WASTE WISE' EVENT

EcoRecycle, Victoria's Waste Wise Event Program, helps event organisers integrate simple and cost-effective waste, recycling and litter management systems into their events. This program has been successfully road-tested at large and small events, including Moomba and the Melbourne International Flower and Garden Show. The website is extremely informative with a detailed waste management plan included with associated templates. The site also provides artwork for bin stickers, such as the one illustrated, and sample pre-event and post-event press releases on the subject of waste management.

To get the best results, EcoRecycle suggests introducing the Waste Wise Event Program into your planning as early as possible:

1 Commit to becoming a Waste Wise Event. Create waste minimisation policies and ensure waste minimisation clauses are inserted into event applications, contracts and agreements.

2 Review packaging materials to see which materials can be eliminated, reduced, reused, recycled or composted. Work with suppliers, caterers, stall holders and retailers to select appropriate materials. For example, encourage the use of plastics that can be recycled or organise to return timber pallets used to deliver materials to the supplier for reuse.

3 Choose event equipment which allows materials to be separated into recyclable groups, is easy for the public to use and is simple to maintain. Purpose-built event recycling equipment and standard signage are available to organisers following the program.

4 Determine how waste will be managed during the event. For the most effective waste management, equipment must be positioned strategically and regularly maintained. Overflowing bins attract more litter and make more work for event organisers.

5 Create signage for equipment to prevent confusion about bin use. EcoRecycle has created Waste Wise Event artwork, which is clear, bright and sits comfortably in an event environment.

6 Communicate the program to suppliers, caterers, stall holders, retailers and the general public before, during and after the event.

7 Evaluate your success using sample do-it-yourself audit sheets provided in the kit.

<www.ecorecycle.vic.gov.au/www/default.asp?casid=2694>

Another Waste Wise Event site, developed by Resource NSW, is a one-stop shop offering the event organiser, stall holder, council representative or venue owner the resources to plan and implement an effective waste management and recycling program. This site also provides the template for a waste management plan and some excellent case studies, including a case study on a Korean Food Fair, which is reproduced on page 325–238.

LOGISTICS OF WASTE MANAGEMENT

Suppliers of waste bins and recyclable products are available through an Internet search or via links on the two websites already mentioned. Event organisers need to plan the location of bins and the best time to have them installed. Clearing bins and storing waste is another major consideration for event organisers. In many cases, clearing is done by the cleaning contractor and waste is removed by a recycling/waste contractor, and it is essential that these companies work in partnership. In other situations, councils may provide waste management solutions.

COMMUNICATING THE WASTE MANAGEMENT MESSAGE

The most important element of any waste management program is effective communication with stakeholders to enlist their support in the implementation of green initiatives. Stakeholders include staff, contractors, volunteers and, of course, the event audience.

Korean Food Fair 2001
Waste Management Report

1. Event Details

Name of Event:	Korean Food Fair
Dates:	Saturday June 23, 2001
Time:	10am – 4pm
Address of venue:	Anzac Mall & Beamish St, Campsie
Anticipated crowd size:	Up to 20,000

Event Activities:
Food stalls & eating areas, information stalls, speeches & entertainment at main stage, Korean dance troupes, music groups & martial arts demonstrations, amusement rides (see program), children's stage, Hyundai car auction.

Venue Description:
Beamish St is the main street of Campsie. The fair was held in the area north of the station and the Anzac Mall. Anzac Mall is a paved pedestrian mall, closed to traffic. There is a variety of Korean shops which line the mall & were open during the festival.

The event attracts families, with a majority of Korean visitors (over 80%) and the remainder a combination of Chinese and other ethnic mixes. There is public parking in nearby streets. The venue is also readily accessible from Campsie railway station.

Existing Facilities
The street litter bins (approx. 55 litre bin inside a metal frame) along Beamish Street & Anzac Mall were supplemented with 60 240 litre wheelie bins for the event.

Other Relevant Information:
Canterbury City Council has in the past offered free cleaning & waste disposal at the Korean Food fair as the event is a Council run event. The value of labour & tipping fees is approx. $3000.

For the past 2 years, the Southern Sydney Waste Board has sponsored the festival by supplying the envirotrays and biodegradable cutlery for use by all of the food vendors via the packaging supplier D&JC Trading. A standard size envirotray was used as a unit of measurement as all stalls were charging $5 for a selection of foods in the same tray. The food vendors are discouraged from bringing their own packaging and were not charged to use the envirotrays and corn starch sporks (combination of spoon & fork).

2. Catering

Food or drink type	Packaging or tableware	Material type
e.g. hot chips	*Cups and bags*	*Paper*
Sample Korean food	Envirotrays	Cardboard
	Spork	Corn starch
	Serviettes	Paper
Soft drink	Can/bottle	Aluminium/PET plastic
	Take away container	Non recyclable plastic
Fairy floss	Stick	Wood
Express kebabs	Bag	Foil/paper

3. Activity Wastes

Activity	Waste types
Stall holders	Cardboard boxes
Distribution of programs/flyers	Paper
Hyundai car auction	Paper

4. Catering Wastes

Stall type	Waste types
Food vendors	Paper, serviettes, aluminium foil, plastic packaging, wood sticks, plastic cups, used cooking oil

5. Waste Generation and Quantities

Approximately 5 tonnes (15 cubic metres) of waste was collected. The recycling measured approx. 1 cubic metre in volume and was not accepted by the recycling contractor due to high contamination (15%) of food waste and was also landfilled.

Stall holders were responsible for the collection and takeback of bulk food packaging, a large proportion of which were in plastic tubs & as such a very small volume of cardboard was put out for collection.

6. Waste Stations

Twenty recycling stations consisting of a bin cap over 3 x 240 litre wheelie bins were distributed throughout Beamish St and Anzac Mall. The configuration of the stations consisted of a garbage bin on either side of the recycling bin in the centre.

Korean language labels for garbage and recycling were prepared by the Board and added to the English and pictorial signage on both sides of the bin caps (shown on right).

Used cooking oil containers were supplied by contractor Auscol and were placed in the food vendor compound in the centre of Anzac Mall.

The servicing of the bins involved Canterbury Council staff lifting the caps and wheeling the garbage bins to the compactor truck for emptying via automatic lift at the end of Anzac Mall. The recycling bins were lined and the bags of recycling were collected and taken back to the Council depot for a visual audit where the decision was made whether to send the material to Collex, the domestic recycling contractor.

In addition to the bins in the recycling stations, an additional 20 x 240 litre garbage bins were scattered around the border of the Anzac Mall seated areas and in the food vendors' back-of-house compound areas.

7. Waste Station Locations

The recycling stations were placed strategically next to food stalls, at eating areas, inside the bar, around the main stage. They remained in the same position for the day. See map below:

8. Promotion of Waste System/Handling

Action	Who	Done (tick)
Arrange for signage, bins	Sonya/Gary	
Educate stall holders of waste system	Janelle/Joanna	
Script announcements for PA or Master of Ceremonies	Janelle/Joanna	

9. Activities Required before the Event

Action	Who	Done (tick)
Set up waste stations at predetermined location	Gary – staff	
Check on bin location & signage	Sonya	
Liaise with caterers re packaging	Janelle/Joanna	
Ordering of cooking oil recycling containers	Angelo	

10. Waste Management during the Event

Action	Who	Done (tick)
Master of Ceremonies reads announcements re waste & support of Waste Boards/Council	Janelle/Joanna	
Monitor waste & recycling bin content quantities	Monitoring crew	
Arrange recycling bin clearing schedule	Gary – crew	
Garbage collection	Gary – Crew	

11. Waste Management after the Event

Action	Who	Done (tick)
Cleaning – litter picking, emptying of garbage into designated truck, street cleaning	Gary – crew	
Provision of final report including data, contamination rates, future recommendations	Janelle/Gary/Sonya	

12. Contact List

Person/organisation	Contact numbers	Area of responsibility
Sonya Williams		Southern Sydney Waste Board
Janelle Mackintosh		Environmental Health Officer, Canterbury City Council
Angleo Tsirekas		Environmental Health Officer, Canterbury City Council
Gary Smith		Depot Manager, Canterbury City Council
Joanne Stubinski		Events Co-ordinator, Canterbury City Council

13. Recommendations
(results, conclusions, recommendations)

? ? Explore receival options for organic waste; food, cutlery, contai
? ? Limit the distribution of stand alone garbage bins in the eating areas & replace with recycling stations
? ? Increase frequency of public announcements

Department of Environment and Conservation <www.wastewiseevents.resource.nsw.gov.au>

One of the biggest problems with recycling is contamination of the waste stream. This occurs, for example, when a load destined for composting is contaminated by plastic, foil or other non-biodegradable items having been placed in the wrong bin, necessitating its disposal as landfill.

The concept of a composting stream is new to most people attending events. As mentioned previously, only food scraps and biodegradable foodware (plates, cutlery and cups made from cornstarch and sugarcane) should be placed in the maroon bin provided for this purpose. The important message is 'right rubbish, right bin'. When procedures work well the amount of landfill resulting from an event can be reduced dramatically.

The following principles form the basis of the waste management plan and need to be communicated to both internal and external customers

Reduction

Waste reduction can be achieved through purchasing strategies aimed at reducing the amount of material brought into a venue, for example, by ordering supplies in large boxed quantities rather than small plastic packages. However, there is sometimes a conflict between waste management and food hygiene, for example, where food safety authorities recommend provision of individual portions of sauces, butter and jam to customers. If individual portions are dispensed with in favour of jars, bottles or other larger containers in the interest of waste management, the caterer must be confident that the condiments can be dispensed in a hygienic way in accordance with food safety legislation. The pumps illustrated on the Heinz stand meet this requirement. Using this system

avoids small plastic sauce packages being included in the compost waste stream. The idea is that all food-related items are binned together in this one stream — a simple message for inattentive event fans.

Reuse

Waste reduction can also occur if items are reused. A good example is polystyrene boxes in which some vegetables are delivered. These should not be allowed to remain on the site and should be removed for reuse if this can be done hygienically.

Recycling

Most members of an event audience will be familiar with recycling messages in relation to glass bottles, plastic bottles, paper and cardboard.

PLANNING SANITARY FACILITIES

Planning the correct number of toilet facilities for an event is very scientific. In fact, council guidelines can sometimes be very specific in respect of the number of toilet facilities to be provided for events. This is illustrated in Tables 22.1, 22.2 and 22.3. As you can see from these tables, there are a number of considerations for the event organiser, including the duration of the event, the number of males and females attending the event and service of alcohol. Provision of toilets for people in wheelchairs and for baby change rooms also needs to be considered. Facilities provided can range from the most basic to the luxury complex described earlier in the chapter. There is no doubt which one the consumer would prefer.

No doubt this type of analysis will be refined even more, with more variables such as the number of intermission periods, type of seating etc. being taken into account.

What is clear is that careful consideration must be given to this issue, particularly for events held out of doors or at temporary venues. Anyone who has spent some time in a long toilet queue at an

Table 22.1

Toilet facilities for events where alcohol is not served.

Patrons	WCs	MALES			FEMALES	
		Urinals	Hand basins		WCs	Hand basins
‹500	1	2	2		6	2
‹1000	2	4	4		9	4
‹2000	4	8	6		12	6
‹3000	6	15	10		18	10
‹5000	8	25	17		30	17

Blue Mountains City Council Event Guidelines <www.bmcc.nsw.gov.au/index.cfm?L1=1&L2=65>

Table 22.2

Toilet facilities for events where alcohol is served.

Patrons	WCs	MALES			FEMALES	
		Urinals	Hand basins		WCs	Hand basins
‹500	3	8	2		13	2
‹1000	5	10	4		16	4
‹2000	9	15	7		18	7
‹3000	10	20	14		22	14
‹5000	12	30	20		40	20

Blue Mountains City Council Event Guidelines <www.bmcc.nsw.gov.au/index.cfm?L1=1&L2=65>

Table 22.3

Reductions for duration of event.

Duration of event	Quantity required
8 hours plus	100%
6–8 hours	80%
4–6 hours	75%
less than 4 hours	70%

Blue Mountains City Council Event Guidelines
<www.bmcc.nsw.gov.au/index.cfm?L1=1&L2=65>

event will agree that this important element of customer service is sometimes poorly planned. At one event, organisers forgot to turn on water supplies to the toilet facilities, causing dismay on the part of the event audience and incredulity on the part of the emergency plumber who was called in after most toilets had blocked up. The importance of using pre-event checklists is well illustrated by this story.

GENERAL CLEANING

The cleaning function for most events is handled by the venue staff or by a contract cleaning company. The staff involved must be trained in all areas of waste management and policies and procedures developed specifically for cleaning, including cleaning routines and inspections. Responsibility for specific areas needs to be clearly defined. For example, while public areas and toilet facilities are generally the responsibility of the cleaning contractor, the catering contractor may be responsible for cleaning in the kitchen, particularly during service. Staff involved in cleaning need to be very knowledgeable about the event itself as they are frequent targets for questions, the most common one being 'Where are the toilets?'

CASE STUDY

As the event co-ordinator for the Corumbah International Food and Music Festival, plan the type and number of bins needed as part of your waste management plan. Draw a site map showing the 20 food stalls and the location of public use bins and bins used by the stall holders. Show also the larger skip bins and illustrate how and when these will be installed and accessed by the waste management company during the three-day event. The event is expecting around 25 000 people over the three days. One of the case studies on the Waste Wise Events NSW website below may provide some relevant ideas.

ACTIVITY

Visit a waste management site in your state or territory to find bin labels. (Labels are also provided on the EcoRecycle and Waste Wise Events NSW websites listed below.) Using these labels, develop a communications strategy to train staff in the area of waste management.

LINKS

Beverage Industry Environment Council
www.biec.com.au

EcoRecycle Victoria
www.ecorecycle.vic.gov.au/www/default.asp?casid=2694

VISY Recycling
www.visyrecycling.com.au

Waste Wise Events NSW
www.wastewiseevents.wasteboards.nsw.gov.au/default.asp

SUMMARY

An environmentally friendly approach to waste management at every event is recommended and, in many cases, a waste management plan is a requirement of local councils. It is an important element of operational planning and one likely to cause dissatisfaction on the part of the customers if anything goes wrong. An increasing level of sophistication is evident at most large events in the provision of facilities, cleaning procedures and waste management, with customers having increasingly higher expectations. Effective communication with all stakeholders, including the audience, is imperative for the successful implementation of the waste management plan.

23

EVENT

IMPACT AND EVALUATION

ON COMPLETION OF THIS CHAPTER YOU WILL BE ABLE TO:

- develop and implement preventative and feedback control systems
- plan an evaluation strategy
- use research methods to identify the composition of an event audience
- use research methods to evaluate the success of an event from the customer, staff, management and sponsor viewpoints
- write an event evaluation report.

The 2004 event, despite forecasts of wet weather on event day, proved an outstanding success by attracting a large field of over 1450 entrants. There has been a 23.6% increase in the popularity of the event over the past four years in comparison to the previous four-year period that began in 1997, when the event won a national award from the Heart Foundation as 'Australia's Best Community Recreation Event'.

These results indicate that a local 'fun walk' is capable of attracting at least twice as many people as the average 'fun run'.

By 2004, the number of local entrants had increased to 82.6% of the total field, yet over 17% of entrants continue to travel from outside the Macarthur region. The popularity of the event with residents of the greater Sydney metropolitan area, the Southern Highlands, the Blue Mountains, the Illawarra region and the South Coast indicates that the event could have a positive impact on non-health fields such as local tourism and the local hospitality industry.

It is significant that over 85% of the field selected the 6 km distance and that entrant details showed considerable involvement by family and neighbourhood groups, as well as teams from schools, clubs and workplaces.

These results indicate success in targeting participation rather than competitiveness and reinforce the findings of the 2004 entrant survey, which revealed that, when asked their reasons for participating, 28% chose 'family outing' as their first priority and 15% chose 'a fun day with friends/ work colleagues'.

CAMPBELLTOWN CITY COUNCIL HEALTH PROMOTION UNIT

This is an outstanding example of event evaluation in that it demonstrates the council's achievement of its objectives, which were to raise awareness of walking as a viable form of exercise and to provide a motivational goal for commitment to regular exercise as an integral part of a healthy lifestyle. However, in addition to the findings that supported the health-related objectives, it was found that over 17 per cent of the participants were from outside Macarthur, resulting in a positive economic impact from tourism on the region. More than a quarter of the participants saw the walk as a family outing, demonstrating a positive social impact as well.

In this chapter we will look at two aspects of event management: control and evaluation. Control systems are essential in ensuring that procedures are followed (for cash handling and recording entrants, for example) and that performance measures are achieved. Evaluation is the process of measuring the success of an event against its objectives. The data from performance measures is used in this analysis. Taking the example of the fun walk above, control systems would ensure that all participants were registered, while evaluation would involve an analysis of the questions on the registration form and feedback after the event. If a significant number of local residents joined the walk without registering, this would indicate a lack of control measures, and would naturally have an impact on the evaluation findings.

MONITORING AND CONTROL SYSTEMS

The challenge for the event manager is to delegate and monitor effectively and not to micromanage (become too involved with detail). While attention to detail is positive, this should be left to the event manager's team. A successful event manager needs to be aware that during the peak time of an event non-standard situations and incidents will require his or her time, which means that all routine procedures and control systems need to be in place before the event. Such control systems ensure that information filtering to the top of the event organisation will prompt management to make decisions to intervene only if things are not going according to plan.

Take, for example, the simple situation of T-shirts and caps being sold through an outlet at an event. How would an event manager know if the cash passed over the counter were reaching the till? Or if all the merchandise were reaching the outlet? A simple procedure for recording the number of boxes of stock issued and an hourly check of stock and cash levels would immediately show any shortfall.

Preventative controls and feedback controls

There are two types of controls: preventative and feedback. A preventative control is established early in the planning process. For example, checking the quality of incoming food for a banquet is a preventative control measure, as is monitoring food temperatures to avoid food poisoning. Signed requisition forms are another preventative measure designed to curtail unauthorised spending and budget blow-outs. A checklist for setting up sporting equipment before an international gymnastics event is another example of a preventative control measure. This would need to be designed to ensure that set-up would meet international specifications: if measurements were inaccurate, injury could be caused to an athlete or an athlete disqualified. In Fig. 23.1 on page 334 we have included an example of a site inspection checklist.

Fig. 23.1

Site inspection checklist.

Venue Checklist

Plans to scale (all venue dimensions)	✓
Disability access	✓
Capacity for seating and standing	✓
Sight lines for event audience (no pillars, obstructions)	✓
Capacity for storage	✓
Appropriate number of toilets, suitable locations	✓
Suitability of food and beverage preparation and service areas	✓
Accessibility for delivery and installation of equipment, food, etc.	✓
Correct number of tables, chairs, plates, glasses, etc.	✓
Emergency evacuation plan	✓
Safety of venue (fire equipment, access and egress)	✓
Preferred contractors (e.g. security, catering)	✓
Fixed and hire equipment requirements	✓
Electrical supply	✓
Water supply (especially for temporary kitchens)	✓
Venue limitations	

Outstanding issues/actions

Feedback controls are put in place to assist with decisions during an event. For example, feedback would be required to decide on the point at which event merchandise should be discounted to avoid having stock left over. If you discount too early, you lose revenue. If you discount too late, you find yourself with stock that has no sale value after the event. Incident reporting is another form of feedback control: if a series of similar incidents have occurred, preventative measures will need be implemented. As an example, the reporting of a number of slips and falls in the kitchen over a period of days would require the implementation of a preventative measure, which might be thorough overnight cleaning, sandpapering the floor and painting it with a non-stick surface, or providing mats to cover the slippery areas.

In most industries, information from point-of-sale and stock control systems are the feedback used for measuring and managing sales and profit levels over a particular period. However, in the event industry, decisions about price and other product features are made before the event, with sales occurring over a very short time period, allowing little opportunity to respond to financial information during an event. This is why it is so important to collect and store information on aspects of an event, such as merchandise sales, for use as a precedent for the next event of a similar nature.

OPERATIONAL MONITORING AND CONTROL

There are a number of issues in relation to operational procedures that need to be addressed before an event begins. These include the necessity for delegation of responsibility, as well as flexibility in carrying out procedures, the effect of control systems on customers and the importance of financial controls.

Implementation of priority or high risk procedures

If the procedure is one that involves high risk, it must be fixed, detailed and well documented. There can be no deviation from this type of procedure. It must be part of training and readily available to those who need to use it. The procedure for emergency evacuation is a good example. Posters and signs must be erected to assist staff to remember their training on evacuation, and controls must be put in place for checking on emergency systems, such as exits, fire fighting equipment, announcement and crowd management equipment (for example, loud hailers), and access for emergency vehicles.

Delegation of decision-making

A flat organisational structure is essential for the successful operation of an event, so some parts of the event manager's role must be delegated. At most events, the pace is so fast that it is crucial that staff be in a position to make decisions on the spot. This is particularly important for volunteers (many of whom are well qualified in other roles) who generally need to know that they have a part to play in the problem-solving process. Only decisions on such important matters as evacuation need to be referred to the more senior staff on duty. Event staff need to be trained to make decisions when minor incidents occur, and each of these incidents needs to be recorded in a logbook for analysis at the end of the shift or at the end of the day. Checks and monitors will ensure that delegation is managed well, that quality service is provided and that costs are contained.

Flexibility in operational procedures

Flexibility is required in many aspects of event management, most particularly in the operational phase, so it is important that the desired outcomes are fully understood by all staff. Staff, too, need to be able to think on their feet and make quick decisions about changing non-critical procedures where circumstances demand it. This is in fact one of the most desirable attributes of event operations staff.

Assuring customer satisfaction

In some cases, control systems can serve to frustrate customers and, at times, customers will endeavour to circumvent the system by trying, for example, to:

- enter areas without accreditation
- purchase alcohol for underage drinkers
- change their seating to a better area
- break the rules for rides (about height, attire or use of safety equipment, for example)
- cut across crowd control barriers
- stand or sit in the aisles.

In each of these cases, a decision needs to be made by event staff as to what to do. If a customer is refusing to wear safety equipment for a ride, for example, customer safety considerations should come before customer satisfaction. On the other hand, if you were confronted by customers frustrated by having to walk an extra distance as a result of crowd control barriers, when there are clearly no crowds, you may decide to move the barrier to allow them through.

Controlling finance

Financial control can be assured by:

- using a requisition system for purchases/expenditure that limits those authorised to spend over a certain dollar limit
- ensuring that all expenditure is accounted for and documented
- checking goods against requisition and order forms
- checking stock levels
- using financial systems that maintain up-to-date information on income and expenditure
- using financial systems to forecast cash flow
- ensuring that everyone understands the budget and current financial position.

Control of point-of-sale systems, or registers, can be achieved by:

- checking and securing cash floats
- checking that cash received is accurately recorded and/or processed through the point-of-sale system/register
- checking that point-of-sale terminal/register print-outs have been balanced against cash takings (after removing cash float)
- checking that cash and documents have been securely transported and stored
- checking that banking documentation has been retained and balanced against statements issued by the bank.

The following suggestions for monitoring and controlling event operations have been provided by experienced event organisers:

- CHECK everything, over and over.
- Write everything down, including promises made by your contractors and requests made by your client.
- Develop checklists for everything possible.
- Check the venue before you move in and note any existing damage.
- Never leave the venue until the last staff member has finished.
- Check the venue before leaving — some things may be left on (gas) or left behind (including people).
- Pay attention to detail at every stage.
- Schedule carefully as the audience has little patience with, for example, long-winded speeches.
- Maintain a contingency fund for unexpected expenses.
- Involve the sponsor at every stage.
- Get approvals for use of logos before printing.

- Don't take safety knowledge for granted; repeat often.
- Train staff to be observant.
- CHECK everything, over and over.

EVENT EVALUATION

Evaluation is an area which is frequently neglected following an event. This is unfortunate as there are many benefits to be gained from a critique of an event. From a quality viewpoint, it allows those involved to learn from their experience and to improve operations. For those not involved, it provides a body of information for future planning of events. If you can't learn from your own experience, at least you can learn from someone else's.

Evaluation needs to be planned before the event, the event objectives generally guiding the evaluation process. In Chapter 12 on 'Event Project Management', the concept of developing event aims and objectives was introduced, and in Chapter 7 on 'Event Marketing', the importance of understanding the target audience was discussed, together with the consumer's decision-making process. As an example, the history and objectives of the Melbourne Comedy Festival are described in the section that follows. The detailed analysis of audience characteristics (including technology use) illustrated in Chapter 6 shows how this festival carefully evaluates its audience. This research is conducted on an annual basis. The most up-to-date audience analysis is provided on their website, which is listed at the end of this chapter.

Melbourne Comedy Festival

Background

The Melbourne International Comedy Festival began in 1987. It was very much a grass roots organisation, springing from the abundance of comic talent in Australia (particularly Melbourne), the public demand for access to Australian and international comedy at its finest, and the local comedy community's desire to shine a spotlight on what we have here and celebrate it. The pubs, clubs, cabarets and back bars of this city are an extraordinarily fertile breeding ground for funny people. Even the Melbourne Town Hall, once the no-mess fortress of the ruling class City Fathers, has embraced the role of Melbourne Comedy Festival and becomes an overflowing Comedy Central every April. Melburnians love comedy and comedians from all over the world love Melbourne, because our city generously nurtures and appreciates their

work. The Melbourne International Comedy Festival is a celebration of this dynamic.

What are the Comedy Festival's Objectives?

The Art of Comedy

To promote and encourage the knowledge, understanding, appreciation and enjoyment of the musical, visual, performing, literary and comedic arts through an annual Comedy Festival.

Culture

To promote the importance of comedy as an artistic element in the cultural fabric of Melbourne, Victoria and Australia, and to ensure the legitimate place of members of the Comedy industry in the artistic community.

Melbourne Comedy Festival *continued*

Profile

To maintain and further develop the Melbourne International Comedy Festival's national and international profile.

Community Participation

To organise a Comedy Festival that is accessible and encourages the general public to participate as audience members, performers or employees.

Tourism

To generate tourism to Melbourne by building on the competitive strength of Melbourne as the arts capital of Australia.

Advocacy

To be a public voice for, and to serve the interests of, the Comedy Community by operating year round as a representative and advocate of the Australian Comedy Industry.

Education

To contribute to the development of new talent in the field of comedy writing and performance, and to conduct educational activities in the musical, visual, performing and literary comedic arts.

Melbourne International Comedy Festival Report 2003, Quantum Market Research

Evaluation methods

When planning evaluation, it is very important to work out what information you require. For example, participants entering a cycling race may be asked for their age and address, which would allow an analysis in terms of their general demographics. What a pity if they were not asked if they had participated before, how they had heard about the event and when they had made the decision to take part. This information would greatly assist the organisers of the next event.

The type of information described above can be obtained from surveys conducted before, during and after an event by completion of forms or through personal interviews. Alternatively, a small focus group of participants can provide valuable information through group discussion.

The following are examples of questions that may be included in a customer survey for an informal post-evaluation report. However, to obtain a more reliable report, the survey would need to be designed and analysed by a market research company.

- How did you find out about this event?
- Why did you decide to come to the event?
- When did you decide to come to the event?
- Did you come to the event with other people?
- Who was the main decision-maker?
- How did this event meet your expectations?
- Was the transport/parking adequate?
- Did you get value for money?
- Was the food and beverage adequate?
- Were the seating, sound and vision adequate?
- Would you attend this event again?

- Why would you recommend/not recommend the event to others?
- How could the event be improved?

In the case of an exhibition, the questions would be something like:
- Why did you come to this exhibition?
- Do you have the authority to purchase at this exhibition?
- Did you place any orders at this exhibition?
- Do you plan to place any orders as a direct result of the exhibition?
- Did you come to this exhibition last year?
- When did you decide to come to the exhibition?
- Have you travelled interstate to visit the exhibition?
- What were the best features of the exhibition?
- How could the exhibition be improved?

Staff debriefings

Meetings of event staff and stakeholders can generate valuable information for the evaluation report. Some of the questions addressed in this type of meeting include:
- What went well and why?
- What went badly and why?
- How could operations be improved?
- Were there any significant risk factors that we did not anticipate?
- Was there a pattern to any of the incidents reported?
- Are there any outstanding legal issues, such as injuries or accidents?
- Are there any implications for staff recruitment and training?
- How would you describe the organisation and management of the event — in the planning and the operational phases?
- What can we learn from this event?

Financial records

Audited financial records, together with a number of planning and other documents, are an essential component of post-event analysis and reporting. These include:
- audited financial statements
- budgets
- revenue, banking and account details
- point-of-sale reconciliation
- payroll records
- the risk management plan
- incident reports
- minutes of meetings
- insurance policies
- contracts with other agencies and organisations, such as hire companies and cleaning companies
- asset register
- promotional materials

- operational plans
- policies and procedures
- training materials
- database of attendees/participants if possible
- record of results of competitions
- event evaluation and statistics (including attendance)
- event or sponsor report.

It is one thing to know that you have managed a successful event but quite another to prove it. The event manager needs more than informal feedback from the after-event party. A summary report evaluating the event against specific aims and objectives is an absolute necessity.

SPONSORSHIP EVALUATION

Evaluation of sponsorship outcomes is required in order to provide accountability to sponsors in relation to their investment. This post-event report needs to include the aims and objectives and the measures used to evaluate them. Sponsors such as brewers, communications companies and banks will have a presence at the event, some selling their products and others advertising their organisation and its products. Sponsors want more than intangible benefits; they want evidence that the sponsorship dollar has achieved a return on investment. There are a number of measures that can be used:

- **Demographics** of both event attendees and television viewers (to tie in with the sponsor's strategic marketing plans).
- **Signage** Range of exposure, such as website, posters, T-shirts, screen displays, directional signs, tickets and all places where the sponsor's logo appears.
- **Audience response** The number of products sampled or purchased at the event as a percentage of the total audience attending.
- **Surveys** Audience opinions regarding the sponsor's product — how the product was evaluated on site, whether the product was recognised, whether future purchase was intended.
- **Publicity** Number of times the sponsor was named in publicity. This involves collection, taping etc. of all media exposure, estimating the time of television coverage and its dollar value and analysing print media exposure and its dollar value. Samples should be included in an appendix to the report.
- **Image** Surveys can be undertaken with the non-attending public to demonstrate their response to the sponsor's image.
- **Sales** An analysis of pre- and post-event sales can be done to estimate the impact on sales. This is an estimate only as a number of other variables might influence sales in the short term. For example, sales of beer might drop soon after the event due to unseasonally cold weather, but this would have nothing to do with the promotional effort.
- **Employee benefits** Identify employee benefits accrued to the sponsor organisation.
- **Corporate hospitality** Identify business networks and the value of new alliances.

BROADER IMPACT OF EVENTS

Events can have an economic, political, physical and social impact on the community (Hall, 1992; McDonnell et al., 1999). The economic impact of an event can be both direct (spending by international visitors) or indirect (the flow-on effect that occurs when related businesses benefit from the expenditure of event visitors). For example, farmers, wholesale suppliers of flowers and food production companies would benefit from increased sales and this in turn would prompt further expenditure on their part as demand for their products increased. Economists and tourism analysts have shown that events such as the Goodwill Games and the Sydney Gay and Lesbian Mardi Gras have an impact on the Australian economy. Tourism makes an important contribution to Australia's export earnings. In 2001–02, international visitors consumed $17.1 billion worth of goods and services produced by the Australian economy. This represented 11 per cent of the total exports of goods and services. Exports of tourism goods and services compare favourably with other Australian 'traditional' export products. For example, exports of tourism products are greater than coal, or iron, steel and non-ferrous metals, but less than food and live animals (ABS cat. no. 5249.0).

Events such as festivals, meetings, conventions and exhibitions that increase the level of international tourist visitation have a positive economic benefit by increasing export earnings.

Political benefits clearly accrue when events raise the profile of a town, city or country. When a region enjoys a surge in tourism, increased economic benefits and the associated reduction in unemployment lead to support for politicians at both local and state levels. Of course the reverse occurs when an event has a negative impact on the community.

Events often increase community spirit, bringing social benefits as well. For example, the many multicultural events held in Australia expand our cultural perspective, while on the other hand rave parties where drug abuse is prevalent can have a negative impact.

The physical impact of events is evident in the construction of new infrastructure, such as roads, railways and sporting venues. However, events can have a negative environmental impact by causing damage or creating offensive noise. The best example of an event with an extremely positive environmental impact on the community is Clean Up Australia Day, which now operates in countries throughout the world.

Measuring economic impact

Arts Victoria has worked with CRC Tourism to develop a kit for evaluating the impact of regional festivals. This kit is specific to Victoria (since the multiplier effect is different for different regions). The approach is standardised and can be adopted throughout the state. This type of comparative research is extremely valuable in a field in which there is little research information to aid decision-making. The aim is to assess the economic impact of a festival by determining the amount of new expenditure attracted to the region by the festival. This new money is made up of expenditure by festival visitors from outside the region and festival income funded from outside the region and spent within the region.

The report on the Australian Open opposite is an excellent example of the economic impact of a large sporting event.

Major Events Brief

The 2002 Australian Open

The 2002 Australian Open was held at Melbourne Park in January. The event is one of four Grand Slam tennis tournaments and attracts most of the world's top tennis players. The 2002 event was another huge success for organisers with 518,248 people passing through Melbourne Park's gates over the 14 day and 10 night sessions.

The staging of the Australian Open in Melbourne creates direct and indirect economic benefits to the Victorian and Australian economies. The benefits include expenditures by interstate and overseas patrons, media representatives, players and entourage, officials, umpires, and the follow on effects as these work there way through the economy.

Event Details 2002

Date of event 14 to 27 January 2002

Total attendance 518,248

Origin of Visitors

Melbourne	127,429	55.9%
Other Victoria	42,507	18.6%
Interstate	44,344	19.4%
Overseas	14,023	6.1%

Please note that the **Total attendance** *figures do not equate to total visitors, as the same person may attend on a number of days.*

Additional Visitors to Victoria Generated by The Australian Open

	Total Visitors	Length of Stay (Victoria)
Interstate	28,824	5.6
Overseas	4,908	12.1

The estimate of additional visitors to Victoria **only** *includes persons who come to Victoria specifically for the event.*

Extended Visitors to Victoria as a result of The Australian Open

	Total Visitors	Length of Stay (Victoria)
Interstate	3,104	7.5
Overseas	1,823	16.1

The estimate of extended visitors includes visitors to Victoria who extended their stay because of the event but did not come to Victoria primarily for the event.

Major Events Brief

Average Duration of Stay in Melbourne, Victoria and Australia (nights – all visitors)

Interstate Visitors	
Melbourne	4.9
Victoria	6.1
Overseas Visitors	
Melbourne	12.8
Victoria	14.0
Australia	30.1

Economic Impacts

Total visitor expenditure in Victoria ($million)

	Interstate	Overseas
Patrons	38.4	12.3
Media representatives	0.6	2.9
Players and entourage	1.2	4.8
Officials/umpires/other	0.2	0.5

This expenditure estimate includes expenditure by persons who traveled to Victoria specifically for the event or extended their stay in Victoria as a result of the event.

Contribution to Victorian Economy $189.0 million

This estimate includes the impact on Victoria's economy by visitor expenditure, business investment, international and interstate trade and Victorian State Government Tax receipts. Multipliers were further applied to obtain flow on effects resulting in this figure. The full effect will occur over 4 years, with 81% of the economic gain occurring in 2002.

Employment

The economic contribution of the 2002 Australian Open is the equivalent to employing 3,530 people full time for one year in Victoria

---

Source: Economic impact evaluation of the 2002 Australian Open, National Institute of Economic and Industry Research, trading as National Economics, March 2002

Prepared by: Research Unit, Tourism Victoria, June 2002

Tourism Victoria

You'll love every piece of Victoria

Economic Impact Report, Australian Open, Tourism Victoria, <www.tourismvictoria.com.au>

The Australian University Games brought together tertiary students from all over Australia to compete in 16 team and individual sports at venues across Perth.

Many of Australia's finest international competitors in track and field, swimming, Rugby Union and soccer are past participants of the Australian University Games.

The Games were conducted over five days in an atmosphere of friendly competition, with a strong focus on social activity and interaction.

Universities compete in regional lead-up competitions to qualify for the Australian University Games — 53 universities were represented by more than 3500 participants. The Australian University Games generated $10.3 million in revenue for Western Australia.

More information can be obtained from <www.eventscorp.com.au/history/index.html>.

Develop a range of objectives for this event and a corresponding strategy for evaluating the success of the event.

ACTIVITY

Investigate a control system to be put in place at an event and evaluate its effectiveness (or lack of it). This system may relate to:
- *registration of participants*
- *cash handling*
- *safety*
- *food hygiene*
- *purchasing and control*
- *staff accreditation.*

LINKS

Arts Victoria DIY Event Impact Kit
www.arts.vic.gov.au/index.htm

Australian Open Impact Study
www.tourism.vic.gov.au/index.php?option=displaypage&Itemid=114&op=page&SubMenu=

Australian University Games
www.eventscorp.com.au/history/index.html

Melbourne Comedy Festival
www.comedyfestival.com.au

SUMMARY

This chapter has looked at two neglected aspects of event management: control and evaluation. Control systems are necessary to ensure that plans are carried out, yet often the event deadlines draw near too soon for these systems to be developed. Preventative controls are established during the early planning phase of an event, while feedback controls help with decisions during the event. If control systems meet best practice standards, they will reduce risk and ensure that there will be ample evidence if a court action should occur. Evaluation is required to ensure that an event meets the aims and objectives identified in the planning strategy. The capacity to show that these objectives (for example, financial, safety, customer satisfaction) have been met is one way of guaranteeing that the event management team is selected for future events and that sponsors will continue to give their financial or in-kind support. The impact of events from a wider point of view — economic, political, social and physical — has also been considered.

CHAPTER TWENTY-FOUR

CAREERS

IN A CHANGING ENVIRONMENT

ON COMPLETION OF THIS CHAPTER YOU WILL BE ABLE TO:

- discuss economic, social and other changes that will have an impact on employment in the field of event management
- discuss the attributes of a successful event manager
- evaluate a range of career choices in the area of event management.

Cultural tourism is based on the culture of a destination — the lifestyle, heritage, arts, industries and leisure pursuits of the local population. Australia is increasingly being recognised as a distinctive, diverse, vibrant and sophisticated tourist destination which has much to interest visitors beyond its world-renowned natural attractions.

Many tourists are keen to learn about and experience the culture of the places they visit — from planned attendance at cultural events to meeting local people. More and more domestic and international visitors are looking for cultural experiences as a major component of their holidays. Cultural tourism encourages us to showcase those qualities and experiences that make us distinctly Australian and to demonstrate to the world our excellence in internationally recognised art forms. The cultural and tourism industries, and the wider Australian economy, can benefit from the development and pursuit of the dual themes of cultural identity and excellence.

www.isr.gov.au/scripts/search/sthome_search.idq

Cultural festivals include arts festivals, popular and classical music festivals, film festivals, and dance and craft festivals. In addition to cultural events, Australia hosts numerous sporting events, some with international profiles, such as the Australian Masters Golf Tournament. The meetings, incentives, conference and exhibition industry (MICE) also contributes to the total number of events held in Australia, as do all product launches and large-scale private parties.

The Tourism Forecasting Council estimates that the number of international visitors to Australia will grow from nearly 5.2 million in 2004 to 8.7 million in 2013. With this projected growth rate, the level of interest in Australian festivals and events will undoubtedly grow. In addition to the level of international interest, there is the long-standing support for festivals and events by local residents and domestic tourists. This continues to be the mainstay for event organisers: Australia Day celebrations and Anzac Day parades are being attended by increasing numbers of people, while the level of interest in the Corroboree Walks in support of Aboriginal reconcilation also illustrate this trend.

This chapter is about employment prospects and specialisations for those planning a career in the event industry which, as you can see from the above, is a growth area. It also covers the current issues of concern for event organisers since up-to-date knowledge of the industry is essential for everyone involved in it.

Spectator management and crowd control are the most problematic areas. Attending or participating in an event is a risky leisure pursuit and event organisers have ethical obligations to ensure that the latest knowledge and the latest technology are applied to ensuring the safety of staff, the audience and the participants. Knowledge of audience psychology, as we have seen, can help to more accurately predict crowd behaviour and some of the problems that might occur.

An event manager thus needs to be an expert in psychology, crowd behaviour, consumer decision-making, financial management, human resource management, marketing, safety and logistics. Legal knowledge is also helpful, as is a solid understanding of risk issues.

Nonetheless, the event business provides an adrenalin rush for all those involved. As happy and excited faces stream out of the venue, the memories of all those planning problems — and your tiredness — soon fade. While the event manager's role is hardly that of party host and more about long hours and hard work, it is still fun.

JOB OPPORTUNITIES

Apart from the position of Event Manager for which you would require education, training and experience in other roles, there are many other jobs available in the industry. As someone wishing to enter the event industry, you could consider positions in one of the functional areas described in Chapter 17, such as venue operations, catering, technology or registration. These positions include:

- Operations and Logistics Manager
- Entertainment Manager
- Sports Competition Manager
- Risk Manager
- Tourism Event Co-ordinator
- Security Co-ordinator
- Venue Manager
- Catering and Waste Manager
- Pyrotechnics Consultant
- Administration Co-ordinator
- Sponsorship Manager
- Lighting/Sound Engineer
- Technology Support Officer — Meetings
- Technology Support Officer — Exhibitions
- Event Designer
- Registration Manager
- Equipment Rental Sales Manager.

There are many jobs for catering staff in the events industry.

The following job descriptions (lists of tasks) provide some insight into just a few of the above-mentioned positions.

Event Manager

As the overall organiser of an event, the manager performs a large number of roles. Below are some of the duties you may find in a job description for Event Manager.

Tasks
1   Develop an event concept, purpose and objectives.
2   Establish a committee and/or event planning team if not already in place.
3   Review the feasibility of the event to maximise strengths and opportunities.
4   Conduct a risk management analysis to miminise weaknesses and risks.
5   Develop a marketing plan for the event.
6   Develop budget, break-even and cash flow analyses.
7   Prepare detailed event plans and obtain the support of the stakeholders, as well as all required approvals.
8   Organise specific theme and staging effects.
9   Recruit and select staff, train and lead staff effectively.
10 Develop detailed plans for event safety and security, including emergencies.
11 Develop policies and procedures for event logistics and daily operation.
12 Develop monitoring and control systems, as well as evaluation procedures.
13 Write a post-event evaluation report to be presented to sponsors/stakeholders.

Venue Manager

The Venue Manager is generally a permanent employee who is familiar with all aspects of the venue and provides a service to anyone who books the venue. It is essential that the roles of the Venue Manager and the Event Manager are clear as these two individuals are often employed by different organisations. For example, a venue will have preferred security contractors and/or cleaning contractors and this can sometimes lead to conflict with the event organising committee if it, too, has preferred suppliers of these services.

Tasks

1 Develop a site diagram, site dimensions and specifications.
2 Negotiate contracts and deposits/fees.
3 Negotiate organisational structure and staffing with the event organiser (e.g. responsibility for cleaning and/or security).
4 Discuss site needs for performers.
5 Discuss site needs for the event audience/spectators.
6 Review the feasibility of plans for logistics and operations.
7 Provide support for bump-in (set-up), including signs and spectator management facilities.
8 Ensure development and implementation of safety and security plans.
9 Monitor the site for health, safety and cleanliness.
10 Work with the event team to ensure that the emergency evacuation plan is in place and that roles are clear.
11 Check entrances, exits and equipment (e.g. public address system, warden communication system).
12 Assist with bump-out at the end of the event.
13 Check all assets and monitor security during bump-out.
14 Manage payment of fees.

Exhibition Registration Manager

The registration of people visiting an exhibition is a key role, and in many cases exhibition organisers do their best to register participants beforehand for two reasons: it saves time on entry to the exhibition and it allows for the registration of participants who intend to visit but do not make it on the day. When completing the registration form, the person indicates their area of interest in the exhibition and this allows exhibitors to target this person for advertising. The database of visitors to an exhibition is a most valuable asset. Therefore, technical hitches must be avoided at all cost as they can cause delays and, at worst, loss of data. (One exhibition manager reported that the loss of his data resulted from a 'spike' in electrical supplies.)

Tasks

1 Meet with the committee/organiser to establish registration requirements, in particular the system for registration and the data to be captured.
2 Develop a registration plan, including selection of software or specialist subcontractor, and a schedule for the complete process.
3 Develop an operational plan and diagram for the registration area and review feasibility with the venue concerned, with particular emphasis on network cabling and back-up electrical supply.
4 Recruit, select and train staff for registration duties.
5 Assist with planning of advance mail-out advertising, including information on pre-registration.
6 Organise name tags, magnetic cards or other materials for registration.
7 Set up registration area.
8 Allocate duties to staff and schedule tasks to suit level of demand.
9 Manage operational issues, questions, problems and complaints.
10 Monitor and manage queues.
11 Close registration and provide required reports to exhibition managers.

The positions available in the event business are many and varied. Quite often people find themselves working on events having come from other fields such as sports administration, entertainment, television production and even nursing. (This last example is indicative of how a medical background can be highly relevant to other roles such as first aid training and occupational health and safety training, leading ultimately to a role in risk management.)

Figure 24.1 shows the types of positions available within the various sectors of the event industry. These are not linear career pathways, but a range of the positions and career possibilities available in the event business. Most individuals in fact move laterally during the course of their working lives. Extracts from a number of recently advertised positions are also given on page 352.

While managing events is nothing new, the field is a newly emerging 'profession' with community acknowledgement of the contribution that events make to society and the economy.

KEEPING UP TO DATE

Anyone planning a career in events must stay up to date with trends. Fashions change rapidly and one cannot afford to come up with stale or outdated ideas. It is thus essential to stay up to the

Fig. 24.1

Positions available in various sectors of the event industry.

ENTERTAINMENT	SPORT	CHARITY/ COMMUNITY ORGANISATIONS	TOURISM	LEISURE	ATTRACTIONS	HOSPITALITY	MEETINGS INDUSTRY	VENUE MANAGEMENT	EVENT STAGING SERVICES
Festival Artistic Director	Executive Director	Agency Director	Director Tourism Development	Club Director	Director Special Events	Executive Director Convention Centre	Director Convention Bureau	Director Park Authority	Chief Executive Officer
Director	Operations Manager	Marketing Director	Manager Regional Tourism Development	Club Manager	Festival Promotion Manager	Special Projects Manager	Marketing Director	Stadium Manager	General Manager – Staging
Producer	Corporate Sponsor Account Manager	Sponsorship Co-ordinator	Group Sales Manager	Food and Beverage Manager	Retail and Sponsorship Manager	Catering Director	Account Manager	Venue Manager	Executive Assistant Manager
Stage Manager	Club Manager	Public Relations Assistant	Tourism Centre Manager	Events Co-ordinator	Park/Facility Manager	Executive Chef	Conference Organiser	Venue Safety Manager	Media Manager
Choreographer	Tournament Manager	Marketing Co-ordinator	Executive Assistant	Food and Beverage Assistant Manager	Exhibition Co-ordinator	Sous Chef	Conference Sales Co-ordinator	Booking Agent	Creative Consultant, Multimedia
Performer/actor	Event Co-ordinator	Fundraiser	Tourism Sales Co-ordinator	Catering Sales Co-ordinator	Exhibit Developer	Banquet Chef	Administrative Assistant	Chief Safety Officer	Electronics Engineer
Production Assistant	Sports Administrator	Volunteer	Tour Guide	Bar Manager	Animal Trainer	Chef	Data Entry Operator	Engineer	Production Technician
Crew	Team Manager		Tourism Information Officer	Bartender	Zookeeper	Apprentice		Technical Assistant	Audio Visual Technician
	Coach					Kitchenhand			
	Player/athlete								

EVENTS MANAGER

We are a city of over 38 000 people with surrounding towns and villages adding a further 20 000 people. The city provides a vibrant cultural atmosphere with visual, performing and literary arts joining the expanding food and wine industry. Council is seeking a highly motivated person with excellent customer service skills to manage our hospitality, entertainment, events and venues management area.

EVENT CO-ORDINATOR

The Council is about to start implementing an array of exciting events for the community, such as open-air cinema nights, bush symphony series, sport awards and food and wine festivals, to name but a few. To co-ordinate this program we are seeking a highly motivated and enthusiastic event specialist with a proven track record in overseeing major celebrations and community events.

ENTERTAINMENT DIRECTOR

Guest relations professional with flair, creativity and initiative is required to take on a new and exciting opportunity. The position will involve creating and managing entertainment, as well as social activities for

our guests, and assisting the sales team in liaising with journalists and photographers. If you have energy to burn and love to be on stage please apply.

CONFERENCE AND TRAINING PROGRAM MANAGER

The role involves the extensive research of topical issues and development of strategic and forward-thinking programs for senior business executives. This stimulating, creative and dynamic role has fast-track promotional prospects and overseas opportunities.

FUNCTIONS SALES MANAGER

This is a pivotal role responsible for dealing with enquiries regarding the planning, booking and execution of conferences and functions. Working within the sales team, the role will maximise the revenue of the conference/function facilities, ensuring excellence in customer service and therefore repeat and referral business.

BUYER

We are back for another exciting tour and you are invited to join our multi-talented crew. Reporting to the Technical and Site Operations Manager, the successful candidate will be responsible for

purchasing, co-ordinating, reception and despatch of goods on site, and scheduling of courier and runner in each city. Responsibilities will include updating the bank of suppliers in each city; set-up and tear-down of technical department; managing petty cash; and inventory of all tour assets. Must be available for full-time travel in the Asia Pacific region.

COMMUNICATION EXECUTIVE

We are looking for a special person with strong communication skills to manage the content, production and presentation of all event communication material, whether written, published or electronically presented. You will be required to manage a comprehensive media program.

CATERING AND CONVENTIONS EXECUTIVE

You will co-ordinate catering and convention activities, ensuring that our guests receive the very best in hospitality when attending their function. Experience in a similar role is essential.

SPONSORSHIP EXECUTIVE

In conjunction with our external consultants, you will be involved in the development of

proposals and identification of prospective sponsors. You will be responsible for developing and delivering all sponsorship benefits to a large sponsor base.

TRAINING MANAGER

Working with our Human Resources Manager and all functional area managers, the training professional will be involved in conducting a training needs analysis for volunteer staff, preparing training materials and arranging for print production before training commences.
You will be responsible for delivering core components of the training and will thus need a proven record as a trainer/facilitator. You must be able to demonstrate your success in developing and delivering customer service training. Tourism, hospitality or event experience would be a bonus.

EVENT SUPERVISORS

This role involves overseeing the service provided by ushers and event staff. This involves managing a team for a minimum of three shifts over four days. Previous experience with two-way radio, large crowds and volunteers would be useful. You must have excellent communication and team leadership skills. These are paid positions.

CATERING MANAGER

This position involves the selection and management of the event contract caterer. It is thus a co-ordinating as opposed to a hands-on role. You will work closely with the caterer on menu planning and costing, on service standards and food hygiene plans. Qualifications at certificate level and relevant experience in similar environments, such as hotels or sports venues, is essential.

PROMOTIONS CO-ORDINATOR

Our bar and nightclub requires an enthusiastic, creative and energetic person to create and promote theme nights, special events and all aspects of the bar, restaurant and nightclub with a capacity to cater for over 600 people. The position entails organising promotions from concept design to execution. A marketing or event management background would be ideal.

BANQUET SALES CO-ORDINATOR — CONFERENCES

Boasting one of the city's biggest conferencing facilities, the hotel currently has an opening for a Banquet Sales Co-ordinator. Sales and project management experience in a similar role would be an advantage.

RISK MANAGER

Responding to a senior executive, the appointee will be responsible for the ongoing assessment of risk exposures, controls and responses and overseeing compliance. A major focus will be the enhancement of risk management systems, policies and strategies and the analysis and reporting of risks.

SPONSORSHIP AND EVENTS MANAGER

We are a non-profit organisation. Your role would involve managing the delivery of all fund-raising activities, developing and maintaining relations with corporate sponsors, planning and budgeting, as well as management of operational committees. You must have the ability to communicate with the 'top-end of town' and need to demonstrate your experience in business development.

minute with trends in entertainment and the arts. The website for Bizbash provided at the end of this chapter is just one site that will stir your imagination. The website also lists a number of event fiascos from which some good lessons can be learned, such as remembering to turn off the sprinkler system before the guests assemble on the lawn! The activity suggested at the end of this chapter involving the development of a portfolio relevant to the event industry is also designed to stimulate your creativity.

However, in addition to creative ideas, it is also essential to stay up to date with economic trends. Regular visits to tourism websites, particularly to the corporate planning areas, will keep you informed of the latest in strategic planning for events. Collecting this information will ensure that you are both informed and creative — an ideal combination for the rapidly changing event environment.

CASE STUDY

Having read a number of job descriptions for event roles in this chapter, develop a letter of application and résumé for two of these jobs at any event discussed in this book. Note that each time you apply for a position you need to modify your résumé to stress your relevant knowledge and experience. For example, one résumé might stress your knowledge of marketing principles and the other might illuminate your understanding of operational issues. If your experience is limited, you can fabricate some relevant experience for the purpose of this exercise.

ACTIVITY

Develop a scrapbook of newspaper and magazine articles that are relevant to the event industry so that you can remain up to date with current trends and issues.

LINKS

Imaginative ideas for events
www.bizbash.com

mice.net (online magazine)
www.mice.net.au/home.html

Special Events magazine
www.specialevents.com.au

SUMMARY

This final chapter has looked at a range of social, economic and other changes that have had, and will continue to have, an impact on the field of event management in the future. Staying up to date with fashion, entertainment, tourism trends and the like is essential. A number of employment choices are available for those considering a career in the event industry, and a number of these positions have been described in this chapter. Most importantly, the management skills developed by event managers are relevant to many other occupations in which risk is high, deadlines are tight, people management skills are a priority and there is only one opportunity to get it right.

APPENDIX A

INTEGRATED

ASSESSMENT

EVENT PROPOSAL

Develop a detailed event proposal covering all aspects of your planned event from concept to risk analysis, marketing strategy, budget, human resources and evaluation strategy. This is an opportunity to fully develop a concept in an area of interest to you, whether in business (corporate), arts, entertainment, sport, community or outdoor public festivals.

The following guidelines for a detailed event proposal are not prescriptive. In some cases the individual elements will not apply to your project and can be ignored. For the purposes of assessing the knowledge gained in this text, the event needs to provide scope to illustrate your ability to plan in detail. For this reason, an event such as a meeting or a wedding held at a hotel venue is an example of one that offers little scope since the venue would provide staff, catering, security, etc. The level of difficulty will be a consideration when grading this assessment. Events that would be considered difficult include the following:

- outdoor event, no infrastructure
- event with multiple stakeholders
- multi-session event
- multi-venue event
- new concept event
- event with tourism impact
- event with higher than average risk (such as financial, safety)
- event with operational or logistical challenges.

You are expected to present your proposal using the outline below, which in many respects follows the text chapters. The proposal should be in report format with a matching folder containing relevant appendices. It is up to you to decide what should appear in the main report and what should be included as an appendix. For example, an overall risk management plan and budget are essential parts of the main report. More detailed plans, job descriptions, volunteer advertisements etc. should be included as appendices. Imagine that the report will be read by a major client, sponsor or government body. It should be more detailed than usual, and it should be readable and flawlessly presented.

Read through the following sections carefully, as you will need to select an event that will provide the scope to cover many of these elements.

Event concept

In this section you need to describe the event concept. The reader should have a clear picture of the event before moving on to the planning details. Note: It is surprising how many assumptions are made in this section, so make sure that you paint a good picture.

Some of the elements you might cover include:

- event name
- event type
- location, suburb and council
- date(s)
- duration/timing
- event overview and main purpose
- aims
- measurable objectives (e.g. audience size).

Event feasibility

This is a brief justification for the event (probably easier if summarised later when more detailed planning has been completed) covering the following as an overview for the reader:

- management responsibility for the event
- major stakeholders and agencies
- physical requirements (venue/route/layout)
- marketing strategy
- financial management strategy (including income generation)
- human resources strategy
- event impacts (social, environmental, economic)
- risk management plan (overview)
- operational planning (overview)
- evaluation strategy (overview)
- timelines (Gannt chart of macro level plans; more detailed timelines can be provided in later sections).

Approvals and consultation

This section should describe all relevant compliance issues and insurance requirements, as follows:

- state and federal government
- council
- Roads and Traffic Authority/Department of Transport
- liquor licensing
- police
- building

- health
- environmental
- entertainment
- music licensing
- security
- contracts for service
- insurances (including public liability).

Marketing

In the marketing section you look at marketing the event product (promotion comes later) and need to carry out:

- competitive analysis
- market analysis and planning
  — customer segmentation
  — meeting audience needs
  — consumer decision-making
  — price and ticket program
- event promotion (overview).

Sponsorship and other forms of income

If these are sources of income for your event, they need to be covered in detail:

- sponsorship (minor, major, cash or in kind)
- grants
- donations
- merchandising
- other.

Financial control

You should present more than one budget model, based on different assumptions (for example, different ticket pricing, choice of indoor/outdoor venue). You need to justify both income and expenditure and include the following:

- capital and funding requirements
- fees (police, council, transport, music, etc.)
- expenses (including insurance)
- control systems (e.g. cash handling)
- taxation
- cash flow analysis (you need to predict when suppliers will demand payment, usually prior to the event)
- profit and loss statement.

Risk management

In this section you will need to look at the strategic risks, such as the loss of a key sponsor (this section is not about detailed health and safety planning):

- identification of risks
- assessment of risks
- management of risks

When you have completed this section, you might like to look at Chapter 11, 'Event Proposals and Bids', to ensure that you have covered all strategic elements of planning before focusing on operational planning.

Operational planning

In this section you will look at the operational and logistical challenges of the event and start to provide more detail about the site and the services required:

- site/venue maps and plans
- logistics and schedules (bump-in, bump-out)
- services
  — electricity
  — water
- transport (including air travel, access to venue)
  — traffic management
  — street closure
  — impact on local traffic
  — notification of affected businesses, etc.
  — diversions
  — marshalling
  — support vehicles
  — parking
  — disability access
- catering
  — providers
  — facilities
  — food safety plans
- waste and environmental management
  — toilets
  — waste management (e.g. recycling)
  — noise
  — water pollution
- cleaning.

Event promotion

Your promotional plan might include developing a website, advertising in the press and a publicity campaign. The content, cost and timing of all these strategies need to be elaborated:

- advertising (messages, look, media)
- public relations (who, where)

- event program design and printing
- website design.

Event staging

Staging covers the peformance, entertainment or competition aspect of the event and most of the terms are theatrical terms. For example, the stage manager is responsible for the stage when the show is being performed and is the director's right-hand person in the lead-up to the performance. In this section you need to show how the event will be delivered to the audience, finishing (or starting if you wish) with the production schedule, which shows how the performance will come together. While earlier sections covered mainly public areas and audience issues, the focus for this is on the cast (also known as the talent) and crew and the physical area in which they will perform. Other events, such as conferences and sports competitions, also require similar considerations, including MC, stage manager and other production roles. For a sporting competition, substitute field of play for stage.

You should consider:
- theme
- décor
- layout/seating
- stage
- entertainment
- special effects, lighting
- sound
- production schedule.

Staffing

This section describes your human resources strategy and approach to management of a temporary or volunteer workforce. Job analysis is vitally important so that roles are clear. Organisation charts should show all stakeholders and contractors, as well as full-time, temporary and volunteer staff. This is what you would include in the staffing section of your event proposal:
- organisational charts (pre-event, event and post-event)
- work breakdown and job descriptions
- selection and recruitment
- rosters
- training (including OH&S)
- briefing
- recognition strategies
- workplace relations
- volunteer management.

Safety and security

In this section you address some of the issues in more detailed risk management plans:
- safety of the event audience
- safety and security of the performers, VIPs, etc.

- health and safety of the staff
- security for premises, equipment, cash, etc.
- communications
  - meetings
  - reporting relationships
  - emergency reporting relationships
  - communication methods (radio)
- emergency access and emergency management
- first aid.

SPECTATOR MANAGEMENT

This section has an emphasis on policy, procedure and contingency planning:
- signage, way-finding
- spectator flow planning
- admission control
- policies (e.g. complaints, lost children, violence)
- contingency plans
  - weather
  - electrical supply, lighting
  - fire
  - accident
  - crowd crush
  - delay or cancellation
  - bomb or other threat
  - security incident.

EVENT EVALUATION

As we have discussed throughout this book, evaluation is a very important part of every event, and informs future events of a similar nature. It is a process of measuring the outcomes against the objectives using a variety of methods (such as customer surveys, focus groups, etc.). The evaluation report prepared for the customer should include all information used in its preparation, including statistical summaries.

APPENDIX B

EVENT OBSERVATION
AND ANALYSIS QUESTIONNAIRE

This list of questions is provided as a guide for a structured observation and analysis of an event. By looking closely at the following event features and elements you can learn a great deal. For this exercise it is not necessary to contact the event organiser for information. The exercise should be limited to your own observations. Comparisons across a number of events can also be very productive, as this will demonstrate the many different dimensions and solutions offered by event planners.

OVERVIEW

1 What is the name of the event?
2 What type of event is it?
3 Who is the audience for this event? Can the audience be described in terms of market segments? Does the event have a tourism impact?
4 Who are the participants/players/performers in this event?
5 Can you identify the stakeholders in the event (local council, police, traffic authority, etc.)
6 Is there evidence of sponsorship of the event in naming rights, signage or product sales?
7 What type of pre-event promotion has been done?
8 Has there been a system of pre-event registration or ticket purchase?
9 What is included in the event program?
10 What do you see as the main purpose of the event?

OPERATIONAL ELEMENTS

Comment on the following operational arrangements:
11 Suitability of venue
12 Accessibility of venue (wheelchairs, prams, etc.)
13 Parking

14 Public transport

15 Access for emergency vehicles

16 Lighting

17 Directional signage

18 Maps, plans

19 Fences and perimeters

20 Admission control system

21 Location, size and type of entries and exits

22 Pass-out system

23 Spectator flow through the venue

24 Crowd management (e.g. mosh pits)

25 Provision of information

26 Décor and furnishings

27 Toilet facilities

28 Catering provision (what food is on offer to event audience)

29 Beverage provision, including alcohol and drinking water

30 Refrigeration and other cooking and food storage facilities

31 Cleaning services

32 Waste management, including recycling

33 General condition and maintenance of facility

34 Sound systems, sound spill/acoustics

35 Seating and line of sight for audience (obstructions such as pillars)

36 Visual or special effects

37 Cooling and heating systems, shade

38 Staffing (adequate number for tasks)

39 Uniforms

40 Service provision

41 Security system/staff

42 Staging requirements

43 Seating, aisles, tables, etc.

44 Safety (hazards)

45 Merchandise for sale

46 Lost and found

POST-EVENT ANALYSIS

47 Has there been any media comment on the event, positive or negative?

48 What are the primary reasons for the success or failure of this event?

49 What are five recommendations for improvement you would give to the event organisers?

HERITAGE FESTIVAL

EDMONTON 2003 ANNUAL REPORT

Heritage Festival
EDMONTON

2003 Annual Report

President's Report

The 39 cultural pavilions participating at the 2003 Edmonton Heritage Festival were rewarded with outstanding weather and crowds. The Kurdish Pavilion enthusiastically showcased their culture at the Festival for the first time this year.

Visitors were enriched by the tapestry of cultures displayed. The entertainment, food, educational material and crafts provided attendees with appreciation and understanding of the diversity of our heritage.

The Honourable Judge Bahtia welcomed 53 new citizens at Citizenship Court. Our long-term partner, the Edmonton Food Bank, received donations of 35000 kg of food. Edmonton Minor Soccer Association once again hosted their All-Star games at the Festival and also showcased a match with a Chilean team.

We welcomed our not for profit partners on site this year, Juvenile Diabetes Research and Canada World Youth.

The Amphitheatre saw crowds up to 2900 for performances by the Mill Creek Colliery Band, Tilo Paiz and Friends Sunday Night Salsa Party, Laura Vinson and Free Spirit, and 11 Multicultural dance groups.

Heritage Festival
EDMONTON

Children's Corner programming, including Through the Eyes of a Child, was expanded this year thanks to the efforts of Marnie Law and numerous volunteers.

The enthusiasm of the hundreds of volunteers was contagious. It was a privilege to work with the volunteers, sponsors, cultural associations and our committed staff. It was only through their combined efforts that the Festival was a success. To mention a few: Princess Candace Grant and Prince Nenad Dumanovic who proudly made numerous appearances, Arlene Giroux who devised the ticket sale and redemption system and supervised the bank trailer, Danette Ross who supervised the ticket sellers and Relan Crosby, our volunteer of the year, who recruited enough volunteers to cover three of six ticket shifts, and manned the administration trailer throughout the Festival.

Steve Nixon, our Site Operations Manager, did a great job. Through his efforts we now have a CAD drawing of our site and a manual for future Festivals. Steve, Frank, Ewald and his crew had the site set up early, which allowed early access by the pavilions. Kurt Stallknecht organized security to his normal high standards. He has provided the Festival with yeoman service over many years and has trained his replacement, Matt, to take on this job in the future. It has been a real pleasure for me to work with him over the past eight years.

Josh Nodelman and his assistant, Jenny, promoted the Festival and provided high quality and a high energy level to their work. This is the second year I've had the pleasure to work with them, this year with their roles reversed.

I was saddened by the untimely death of our auditor, Ed Jestin. I recognize his contribution to the Festival over the past decade.

Marnie has been our institutional memory this year and made an outstanding contribution not only to the volunteer program and administration, but the whole Festival. I would be remiss if I did not thank Executive Director Raj Nigam for his contribution this year. We wish him well at the Alberta Lung Association.

We have many loyal sponsors and partners to thank. Without their contributions, the Festival would not be possible. Please see the listing on page 17.

Through the introduction of the food ticket system, the association has a new sustainable funding source. Problems with inadequate change were corrected early Sunday and pavilions indicated they were very satisfied with the redemption process and the fact that fewer volunteers were required for their pavilions. This ticket system, modified by improvements recommended by pavilions and the Foot Ticket Committee, will be utilized in 2004. The ticket system was the first step in restoring the Association's financial health.

Heritage Festival
EDMONTON

I am extremely grateful for the support and cohesiveness of the Board not only last year but throughout my term as president. We dealt with challenging issues regarding the pavilions, the City, staff turnover and our fiscal position. We were able to keep the best interests of the Festival in mind and move forward, even when the decisions and changes were not popular. I believe we have learned from our poor communications with our stakeholders and have taken positive steps to improve them.

I have enjoyed the contribution of Ed Faford on the Board and on the Festival Committee. I know the Board will miss him and wish him and Clair well on their extended cross-Canada tour. We also will miss the contribution of Ron Symic who will no longer sit with the Board as past-president.

In December, the Board hired Jack Little as our Executive Director. I believe Jack's business, management, marketing and volunteer background will provide the Festival with sound management and fund raising expertise.

Jack has already taken steps to obtain another secure alternate funding source for the Festival. It is through his and the Board's efforts that a number of the pavilions that withdrew last year have submitted applications for 2004.

As my term draws to a close, I also thank our past presidents who have provided wise counsel. With the new Executive Director, a strong president and Board, I am confident the Association is in good hands.

Donna Kline, FCA
President

Heritage Festival
EDMONTON

Mission Statement

To promote public awareness, understanding, and appreciation for cultural diversity through an annual summer festival, as well as to provide educational events, programs, and/or projects on a year-round basis.

2003 – In Review

'Imagine All the People – Now meet Them'

The twenty-eighth annual Edmonton Heritage Festival was held in Hawrelak Park in Edmonton August 2–4, 2003. The theme selected for the 2003 edition of the Edmonton Heritage Festival was 'Imagine All the People – Now Meet Them'. Festival visitors had the opportunity to experience, first hand, the diverse traditions of the many people from other lands who have chosen to call Canada their home.

The 39 participating cultural pavilions showcased a variety of entertainment, cuisine and arts and crafts, with offerings that appeal to all ages and tastes. The Edmonton Heritage Festival was proud to welcome one new pavilion in 2003, the Kurdish Pavilion. The main attraction for visitors to the Edmonton Heritage Festival are the cultural pavilions, each operated by a non-profit ethno-cultural organization. Each pavilion is responsible for presenting the cuisine, entertainment, and arts and crafts traditional to their culture. This diversity of pavilions reflects the vibrant nature of Edmonton's multicultural communities. Activities and presentations at each cultural pavilion are done by volunteers, with over 6,000 individuals among these groups offering their time, energy, pride, talents, and expertise to present the traditions they are so very proud of and have brought to Canada for the enjoyment of all.

Festival History

In 1975, eleven ethno-cultural communities came together to present their food, entertainment, arts & crafts and cultural traditions to stage the first Edmonton Heritage Festival. From these humble beginnings the Edmonton Heritage Festival has grown from a one-day event, into the World's largest three-day celebration of cultural diversity with more than sixty cultures working in harmony to showcase the richness they have added to our Canadian culture with respect for each other's differences and accenting their similarities. The Festival is held each year in Edmonton's scenic Hawrelak Park, which provides a stunning backdrop to showcase this unique event.

Heritage Festival
EDMONTON

The Edmonton Heritage Festival strives to be a Festival for everyone by remaining admission and alcohol free. Almost perfect weather conditions greeted the over 300,000 visitors to the 2003 Festival.

Festival visitors were encouraged to donate non-perishable food items for the Edmonton Food Bank Patrons in lieu of paying an admission fee to attend the Festival. The result has made our event the Edmonton Food Bank's single largest annual food drive, with over 35,000 kilograms of food collected in 2003.

Heritage Amphitheatre

In addition to the Pavilion entertainment, performances are held at the Heritage Amphitheatre, situated in the heart of Hawrelak Park. The Amphitheatre is an outdoor venue, constructed by The Edmonton Heritage Festival Association in 1986. With fixed seating of approximately 1150, there is room for an additional 2000 spectators in the surrounding bowl via grass seating. The Amphitheatre plays host to a variety of performances and events over the course of the 3-day Festival.

The 2003 performances included:

- Mill Creek Colliery Band
- Tilo Paiz and Friends Sunday Night Salsa Party
- Laura Vinson & Free Spirit
- Eleven Multicultural Dance Groups (representing the Polynesian, Middle Eastern, Filipino, Spanish, East Indian, Irish, and African cultures)

On Monday afternoon, the Heritage Amphitheatre was the site for a Citizenship Ceremony. This year, 53 new Canadians took the oath of citizenship in an impressive ceremony that has been part of the Festival since 1987.

Prince and Princess

Each year a boy and a girl between the ages of eight and twelve, representing two different participating cultures at the Festival, are selected as Festival Prince and Princess. These children serve as goodwill ambassadors during the Festival, and symbolize the hope we have in our children that theirs will be the first generation to carry no prejudices towards people of other cultures. The Prince and Princess attend, and are present at many of our formal functions. This year:

- Princess Candace Grant was from the Caribbean Pavilion
- Prince Nenad Dumanovic was from the Serbian Pavilion

Heritage Festival
EDMONTON

Children's Corner

Another program offered is the Children's Corner and Through the Eyes of a Child. This is an area where younger children are educated about different cultures, through games and play. All the activities are provided free of charge, and included such standard activities as face painting, making ethnic related crafts and learning games and dances from other lands.

Community Partners

Other community partners in 2003 were:

- Edmonton Minor Soccer Association – For the second consecutive year, the Association organized an all-star tournament, featuring both girl's and boy's teams in all age categories.
- Juvenile Diabetes Research Foundation and Canada World Youth were on site to provide information on the programs and services they provide to the community.

Food Tickets

2003 saw the introduction of a new fund raising venture. Over the last few years, the Edmonton Heritage Festival Association had experienced declining revenues. Grants from the three levels of government had declined, while corporate sponsors reduced their sponsorship or marketing expenditures. At the same time, the Association experienced increases in the costs to operate the Festival. A number of new fund raising methods were considered, including charging admission to the public and raising the participation fee to the pavilions.

It was decided that the most effective means of raising additional funds was a food ticket program. Festival attendees purchased tickets from a number of ticket booths located around the park. The tickets were redeemed for food and beverages at the participating pavilions. The pavilions then redeemed the tickets.

Some initial problems were quickly resolved and by Sunday afternoon the food ticket system was working well. The public accepted it and the pavilions reported they required fewer volunteers to operate with food tickets as opposed to cash. A summary of the food ticket program is:

- Ticket Commission Revenue $89,428

Heritage Festival
EDMONTON

- Ticket Printing   ($11,607)
- Cash Supervision and Security   ($4,186)
- Legal and other Costs   ($6,491)

- Net Food Ticket Revenue $67,144

The food ticket system, with improvements from the 2003 Festival, will continue in 2004.

Financial Summary

Overall, net operating results were much better in 2003, with a net loss of $19,183 as compared to a loss of $163,705 in 2003.

Overall revenue increased to $337,682 this year, mainly helped by ticket commissions and a positive return on the investment portfolio:

- Food ticket commissions brought in net revenue of $67,144
- Tent charges and entrance fees were down 27%, from $89,050 to $65,055, with the decrease in the number of participating pavilions from 52 to 39
- Advertising and sponsorship revenues decreased again from $59,277 to $48,053, continuing a multi year trend of increasing difficulty in getting grants and sponsors to support the Festival

The following chart provides summary of the revenue received.

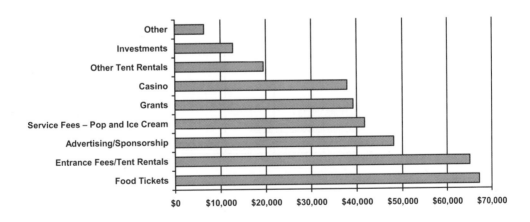

Heritage Festival
EDMONTON

Total expenses decreased to $356,685 from $375,129 the year before:

- Public relations and advertising costs declined from $60,398 to $49,892
- Insurance tripled from $6,173 to $19,977
- Two large expenses from 2002 were not repeated, the retiring allowance and a consulting contract
- Direct Festival expenses were up by 2.5%, to $149,197. Festival expenses included:

o	Site foreman and labour	$26,603
o	Main stage show	$14,242
o	Portable toilets/waste removal	$13,993
o	City of Edmonton	$12,296
o	Equipment rentals	$8,125
o	Non recoverable GST	$7,684
o	Golf carts	$7,427
o	Security	$6,778

The following chart provides a summary of the expenses incurred in the operation of the Association.

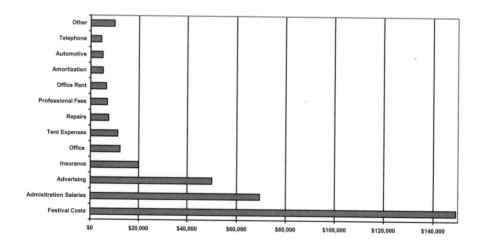

Heritage Festival
EDMONTON

Strategic Plan

The Edmonton Heritage Festival Association started a review of its Strategic Plan during 2003. Following a meeting with Past Presidents and current board members, it was decided to focus on four strategic areas:

1. Operational, including volunteers, on-site Festival improvements and year-round activities
2. Governance
3. Communications
4. Finance

To provide input to the Strategic Plan, the Association created a survey that was sent to all cultural groups who had participated in the Festival over the last five years. They included questions regarding:

- The optimal number of pavilions on-site during the Festival
- Operational improvements
- The placement of entertainment stages

While the Strategic Plan is not yet final, elements of it have already moved forward to respond to concerns from stakeholders. During the year, a number of current and former pavilion partners expressed concern over the lack of pavilion representation on the board of the Edmonton Heritage Festival Association. Following discussions with the Community Services Committee of Edmonton City Council, the City agreed to participate in a mediation process with the Association and some of the pavilion groups.

Governance Committee

To assist the Association in reviewing how the Association is governed, the Board established a Governance Committee, with representation from Past Presidents, current board members and pavilion organizations. The Committee's mandate is to look at the following aspects of governance:

- Membership criteria
- Election of directors
- Should pavilion representatives be on the EHFA Board of Directors?
- What are the logistics (e.g. legal and procedural) of making changes?
- Make recommendations on all the above including how it would work if change is proposed, and how the change would take place.

Heritage Festival
EDMONTON

The Committee is tasked to put forward a draft plan at the Spring 2004 pavilion meeting. By putting forward a draft proposal at that time, feedback can be sought throughout the summer of 2004, and the Committee can make changes, if necessary based on that feedback, for final approval before the Fall 2004 pavilion meeting.

Executive Director

After the 2003 Festival, our Executive Director, Raj Nigam, decided to accept another career opportunity. All the Board and staff would like to express our appreciation for his efforts and wish him well in his new endeavours.

2004 – A Look Forward

2004 marks Edmonton's 100th anniversary as a City. The Edmonton Heritage Festival looks forward to showcasing Edmonton's cultural history and diversity during our 29th Annual Festival to be held July 31 to August 2, 2004.

During the year, our updated Strategic Plan will be completed. This will provide a plan to ensure that the Festival is put on a stable financial footing and provide an operational framework for future Festivals. It will form the basis of planning for the 2005 Festival, which will coincide with the 100th anniversary of the Province of Alberta.

By year-end, the Governance Committee will have reported. Our goal is to provide stakeholders the opportunity to be involved, in some manner, in the planning and operation of the Festival.

Subsequent to the end of the 2003 fiscal year, the recruitment of a new Executive Director was completed. Jack Little took over the position in December 2003. Jack's marketing and management background, as well as extensive experience in the volunteer sector, will greatly benefit the Association.

Heritage Festival
EDMONTON

Financial Summary

Statement of Financial Position
October 31, 2003

	2003	2002
ASSETS		
CURRENT		
Cash	$ 20,912	$ 25,995
Accounts receivable and accrued	14,633	46,283
Prepaid expenses	13,931	14,507
	49,476	86,785
INVESTMENTS	295,952	283,477
CAPITAL ASSETS		
Tents	306,326	306,326
Equipment	126,997	121,939
Buildings	49,338	49,338
	482,661	477,603
Accumulated amortization	(482,661)	(477,603)
	$ 345,428	$ 370,262
LIABILITIES AND NET ASSETS		
CURRENT LIABILITIES		
Accounts payable and accrued	$ 31,171	$ 27,915
Retiring allowance payable	-	8,500
Deferred revenue	1,000	1,407
	$ 32,171	37,822
CONTINGENT LIABILITY		
NET ASSETS		
Restricted for tent replacement	464,632	464,632
Unrestricted	(151,375)	(132,192)
	313,257	332,440
	$ 345,428	$ 370,262

Edmonton Heritage Festival Association
2003 Annual Report

Page 11

Heritage Festival
EDMONTON

Statement of Changes in Net Assets
Year Ended October 31, 2003

	Restricted	Unrestricted	2003 Total	2002 Total
BALANCE, beginning of year	$464,632	$(132,192)	$332,440	$496,145
Net loss for the year	-	(19,183)	(19,183)	(163,705)
Tents purchased (net)	-	-	-	-
Internally imposed Restriction	-	-	-	-
BALANCE, end of year	$464,632	$(151,375)	$313,257	$332,440

Heritage Festival
EDMONTON

Statement of Operations
Year Ended October 31, 2003

	2003	2002
REVENUE		
Food ticket commissions	$ 67,144	$ -
Tent charges and entrance fees	65,055	89,050
Advertising, sponsorship & donations	48,053	59,277
Festival service fees	41,713	19,357
Grants	39,220	44,601
Casino proceeds, net	37,910	37,910
Tent rentals	19,460	17,065
Investment Income (loss)	12,732	(19,690)
Parking passes	6,050	8,366
Miscellaneous	345	4,570
	337,682	260,506
EXPENSES		
Festival	149,197	145,566
Salaries and benefits, administration	69,382	52,679
Publicity and advertising	49,892	60,398
Insurance	19,977	6,173
Office and miscellaneous	12,158	11,264
Expenditures in respect of tent rentals	11,160	6,893
Repairs and maintenance	7,449	5,192
Professional fees	6,926	6,839
Office rent	6,500	6,500
Amortization of capital assets	5,059	3,545
Automotive	4,998	2,154
Telephone	4,394	3,029
Meetings	3,380	2,639
Bad debts	2,973	1,445
Scholarships	2,500	1,900
Conventions, workshops and seminars	920	4,288
Administration consulting contract	-	32,000
Retiring Allowance	-	22,625
	356,865	375,129
LOSS FROM OPERATIONS	(19,183)	(114,623)
WRITE-DOWN OF INVESTMENTS TO MARKET VALUE	-	(49,082)
NET LOSS	$ (19,183)	$(163,705)

Heritage Festival
EDMONTON

Statement of Cash Flows
Year Ended October 31, 2003

	2003	2002
CASH PROVIDED BY (USED FOR)		
OPERATING ACTIVITIES		
Net loss for the year	$(19,183)	$(163,705)
Items not affecting cash:		
Amortization of capital assets	5,059	3,545
Write-down on investments	-	49,082
	(14,124)	(111,078)
Changes in non-cash current operating assets and liabilities:		
Accounts receivable and accrued	31,650	(20,566)
Prepaid expenses	576	(13,424)
Accounts payable and accrued	3,256	4,914
Deferred revenue	(407)	1,407
Retiring allowance payable	(8,500)	8,500
	26,575	(19,169)
	12,451	130,247
INVESTING ACTIVITIES		
Withdrawn from investment fund	-	120,000
Purchase of investments	(12,475)	(90,427)
Purchase of capital assets	(5,059)	(3,545)
	(17,534)	26,028
DECREASE IN CASH	(5,083)	(104,219)
CASH, beginning of year	25,995	130,214
CASH, end of year	$ 20,912	$ 25,995

Heritage Festival
EDMONTON

Our Partners

Cultural Associations

Aboriginal
Afghan
Arabic
Bangladeshi
Bosnia-Herzegovina
Caribbean
Chilean
Chinese
Croatian
Ecuadorian
Ethiopian
Fijian
Filipino

Greek-Hellas
Guatemalan
Hong Kong
Hungarian
Indian
Israeli
Italian
Japanese
Korean
Kurdish
Malaysian-Singaporean
Nicaraguan
Nigerian

Pakistani
Peruvian
Polynesian
Portuguese
Romanian
Scandinavian
Serbian
Sri Lankan
Taiwanese
Thai
Turkish
Ukrainian
Welsh

Sponsors

ATCO Gas
Alberta Carpet Cleaning
Alberta Co-op Taxi
Capital City Savings

The Coast Edmonton Plaza
The Driving Force
GE Capital Modular Space
Kiwanis Club – Edmonton
    Oil Capital

Mobilcom
Second Cup
Vision Design
Yellow Pencil

Heritage Festival
EDMONTON

Media Partners

The Edmonton Journal
Access – The Education
    Station

CKER Radio
A-Channel
Power 92

630 CHED
CISN Country
Cool 880

Government and Related Partners

The City of Edmonton
The Edmonton Arts Council
Alberta Community
  Development

Alberta Foundation
  for the Arts
Department of Canadian
  Heritage

The Wild Rose
  Foundation

Community Partners

Canada World Youth
Capital Health Authority
Child Find Edmonton
Citizenship and Immigration
  Canada
Edmonton Bicycle
  Commuters' Society

Edmonton Minor
  Soccer Association
Edmonton Police Service
Edmonton Transit System
Edmonton Food Bank
John Janzen Nature Centre

Juvenile Diabetes
  Research Association
Precision Giant Systems Inc.
Valley Zoo

APPENDIX D

SUPPLEMENTARY

INTERNET LINKS

Event planning

Ballarat Council Event Planning
Guide
www.ballarat.com/events/pdf/
COB%20Event%20Planning%
20Guide%201st%20Ed%20May
%202003.pdf

Blue Mountains City Council,
Guide for festival/event
organisers
www.bmcc.nsw.gov.au/index.
cfm?L1=1&L2=65

City of Sydney, Waste Minimisation
and Management Policy —
Events in Public Places
www.cityofsydney.nsw.gov.au/
catz_council_policies.asp

Community Builders NSW
www.communitybuilders.nsw.
gov.au/events_guide/alcohol.html

CRC for Waste Management
www.crcwmpc.com.au

Department of Local Government
1997, *Major and special events
planning: a guide for promoters
and councils* (1997) (search
'event')
www.dlg.nsw.gov.au

Emergency Management Australia
www.ema.gov.au

Entertainment
www.entertainoz.com.au/
article/event_management.
html

Event Project Management System
www.personal.usyd.edu.au/
~wotoole/epmspage1.html

Events NSW
www.events.nsw.gov.au

Guidelines for Event Organisers
(Southern Waste Strategy)
www.southernwaste.com.au/
community/organiserguide
lines.html

Nowaste ACT, Guidelines for
Recycling at Public Events
www.nowaste.act.gov.au

NSW Department of Environment
and Conservation
www.epa.nsw.gov.au/index.htm

Our community
www.ourcommunity.com.au

Party Oz
www.fancydresshire.com.au

Queensland Liqour Licensing
www.liquor.qld.gov.au/our
products/brochures/
planning_guide/page_1.
asp#obtain

Special Events online
www.specialevents.com.au

*Traffic management for special
events* 1999 (available through
the Roads and Traffic
Authority)
www.rta.nsw.gov.au

TravelSmart Australia
www.travelsmart.gov.au/events/
four.html

Victorian Government Food Safety
Guidelines for Events
www.foodsafety.vic.gov.au/
downloads/events_template.
pdf

Volunteering Australia
www.volunteeringaustralia.org/
sheets/rights.html

Tourism

Australian Tourist Commission
www.atc.net.au

Canberra Tourism
www.canberratourism.com.au

Northern Territory Tourism
Commission
www.nttc.com.au

South Australian Tourism
Commission
www.southaustralia.com

Tourism New South Wales
www.tourism.nsw.gov.au

Tourism New Zealand (market
research)
www.tourisminfo.govt.nz

Tourism New Zealand (travel)
www.purenz.com

Tourism Queensland
www.queenslandholidays.
com.au/pfm/index.htm

Tourism Tasmania
www.discovertasmania.com.au

Tourism Victoria
www.tourismvictoria.com.au

Western Australia Tourism
Commission
www.westernaustralia.net.au
World Tourism Organisation
www.world-tourism.org.au

Tourism training

NT Tourism Training Board
www.ntttb.org.au
Tourism Training ACT & Region
Email: ttact@interact.net.au
Tourism Training Australia
www.tourismtraining.com.au
Tourism Training NSW
www.ttnsw.com
Tourism Training QLD
www.ttq.org.au
Tourism Training SA
www.ttsa.com.au
Tourism Training TAS
Email: tourtraintas@bigpond.
com.au
Tourism Training VIC
www.ttvic.com.au
WA Hospitality & Tourism Training
Council
www.wahtitc.com.au

Statistics and forecasts

Australian Bureau of Statistics
www.abs.gov.au
Bureau of Tourism Research
www.btr.gov.au
Commonwealth Department of
Sport and Tourism
www.tourism.gov.au
Festivals Australia
www.dcita.gov.au
World Tourism Organisation
www.world-tourism.org
World Travel and Tourism Council
www.wttc.org

Government

Australian Commonwealth
Government Information and
Services
www.fed.gov.au
Austrade
www.austrade.gov.au
Australian Local Government
www.algin.net.au
City of Sydney
www.cityofsydney.nsw.gov.au

New South Wales Government
www.nsw.gov.au
Northern Territory Government
www.nt.gov.au
Queensland Government
www.qld.gov.au
South Australian Government
www.sa.gov.au
Tasmanian Government
www.dpac.tas.gov.au
Victorian Government
www.vic.gov.au
Western Australian Government
www.wa.gov.au

Meetings and events associations

Australian Amusement, Leisure and
Recreation Association
www.aalara.com.au
Australian Incentive Association
www.aia.com.au
Australian Tourism Export
Council
www.atec.net.au
Exhibitions & Events Association of
Australia
www.eeaa.org.au
International Congress and
Convention Association
www.icca.nl
International Festivals & Events
Association
www.ifea.com
International Special Events
Society
http://ises.com
International Association Exhibition
Management
www.iaem.org/default.asp
Media, Entertainment & Arts
Alliance
www.alliance.org.au
Meetings Industry Association of
Australia
www.aia.com.au
Meetings, Incentives, Conferences
and Exhibitions
www.mice.net.au
Pacific Asia Travel Association
www.pata.org
Venue Management Association
www.vma.org.au

Convention bureaus

Cairns and Region Visitors Bureau
www.tnq.org.au/crcb/
Canberra Convention Bureau
www.canberraconvention.
com.au
Conventions New Zealand
www.conventionsnz.co.nz/
conventions/index.asp
Melbourne Convention and Visitors
Bureau
www.mcmb.net.au
Perth Convention Bureau
www.pcb.com.au
Sydney Conventions and Visitors
Bureau
www.scvb.com.au/index_s.html

International events

Clean Up the World
www.cleanup.com.au
Dakar Rally
www.dakar.com
Edinburgh Festival
www.eif.co.uk
Fairs and Festivals of India
http://travel.indiamart.com/
fairs-festivals/
Fédération Internationale de
Football Association (FIFA)
www.fifa.com
International Events
www.frontrow.com/international.
shtml
Oscars
www.oscar.com
St Patrick's Day Events
www.emigrant.ie/patrick/events.
htm
Superbowl
www.superbowl.com
Tall Ships Races
www.cutty-sark.com/
tallshipraces/
Tourism Thailand
www.tourismthailand.org
Webnet World Conference
www.aace.org/conf/webnet/
Wimbledon
www.wimbledon.org

Australian events

Australia Day Council (National)
www.nadc.com.au

Australian Motorcycle Grand Prix
www.grandprix.com.au/bikes/
Australian Open
www.ausopen.org
Australian Science Festival
www.sciencefestival.com.au
Big Day Out
www.bigdayout.com
Camel Racing
www.camelraces.asn.au
Canberra Floriade
www.floriadeaustralia.com
City to Surf Sydney
www.coolrunning.com.au/races/
citysurf.shtml
Classic Car Rally
www.classicrally.com.au
Clean Up Australia
www.cleanup.com.au
Comedy Festival
www.comedyfestival.com.au
Gay & Lesbian Mardi Gras
www.mardigras.org.au
Goodwill Games
www.goodwillgames.com/2001/
2001_index.html
Grand Prix
www.grandprix.com.au/cars/
Henley-on-Todd Regatta
www.henleyontodd.com.au
Hobart Fringe Festival
http://hobartfringe.com
Hunter Valley events
www.atn.com.au/nsw/syd/
event-e.htm
International Horse Trials
www.adelaidehorsetrials.com.au
Juvenile Diabetes events
www.jdfa.org.au

Le Mans
www.lemansadelaide.com.au
Melbourne Comedy Festival
www.comedyfestival.com.au
Melbourne Cup
www.acn.net.au/articles/1998/
10/melbcup.htm
Melbourne Flower Show
www.melbflowershow.com.au
Melbourne Food and Wine Festival
www.melbfoodwinefest.com.au
Mercedes Fashion Week
www.afw.com.au/html/
Mt Isa Rodeo
www.isarodeo.com.au
National Days of Commemoration
www.awm.gov.au/atwar/
commemorative_days.htm
National Folk Festival
www.folkfestival.asn.au
Perth Festival
www.perthfestival.com.au
Reef Festival
www.reefestival.org.au
Royal Easter Show
www.royalshow.com.au
St Kilda Film Festival
www.stkildafilmfest.com.au
Scarecrow Festival
www.maleny.net.au/scarecrow
Summernats
www.summernats.com.au
Surf Lifesaving Championships
www.slsa.asn.au
Sydney Events Listing
www.sydney-events.com/
sydney/
Sydney Writers Festival
www.swf.org.au/about/

The Big Swim
www.thebigswim.org.au
Womadelaide
www.womadelaide.ozemail.
com.au
Woodford Folk Festival
http://woodfordfolkfestival.com
World Solar Challenge
www.wsc.org.au

New Zealand events
New Zealand Events
www.nz-events.co.nz
NZ Festival
www.nzfestival.telecom.co.nz
Rally NZ
www.rallynz.org.nz
Royal Easter Show
www.royaleastershow.co.nz
Volvo Ocean Race
www.volvooceanrace.org/
homepage.html
Winter Festival
www.winterfestival.co.nz

Other event sites
Eventclicks
www.eventclicks.com
Events Unlimited
http://eventsunlimited.com.au
Special events ideas
www.bizbash.com
Special Events Magazine online
www.specialevents.com.au
Visual Event Management
www.vem.com.au

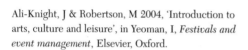

Ali-Knight, J & Robertson, M 2004, 'Introduction to arts, culture and leisure', in Yeoman, I, *Festivals and event management*, Elsevier, Oxford.

Allard, A, Fitzclarence, L, Nakata, M & Warhurst J 2001, *Evaluation of the 2000 Croc Eisteddfod Festival in Weipa* [Online], Available: <www.crocfestivals.org.au/evaluation_reports/index.htm> [Accessed 18 March 2004].

Allen, J 2003, *Event planning ethics and etiquette: a principled approach to the business of special event management*, Wiley, Etobicoke, Ontario.

Allen, J, Harris, R, Huyskens, M & Australian Centre for Event Management 2001, *Event management: an Australian bibliography*, Australian Centre for Event Management, Lindfield, NSW.

Allen, J, Harris, R & University of Technology Sydney, Australian Centre for Event Management 2002, *Regional event management handbook*, Australian Centre for Event Management, Lindfield, NSW.

Allen, J & McDonnell, I 2002, *Festival and special event management*, 2nd edn, John Wiley & Sons, Milton, Qld.

Allen, J & University of Technology Sydney, Australian Centre for Event Management 2000, *Events beyond 2000: setting the agenda: proceedings of conference on event evaluation, research and education, Sydney, July 2000*, Australian Centre for Event Management, Lindfield, NSW.

Allen, J & University of Technology Sydney, Australian Centre for Event Management 2002, *Events and place making conference: abstracts of papers at international event research conference, held in Sydney, July 2002*, Australian Centre for Event Management, Lindfield, NSW.

American Sport Education Program 1996, *Event management for sport directors*, Human Kinetics, Champaign, Illinois.

Appenzeller, H 1998, *Risk management in sport: issues and strategies*, Carolina Academic Press, Durham, NC, US.

Australian Bureau of Statistics 1997–98, *Australian national accounts: tourism satellite account*, cat. no. 5249.0, ABS, Canberra.

Australian Tourist Commission 2000, *Research and Statistics, MICE profile* [Online], Available: <www.atc.net.au/intell/market/mice/profile.htm> [Accessed 20 January 2003].

Australian Tourist Commission 2001, *Australia climbs world conventions ladder* [Online]. Available: http://atc.australia.com/enews.asp?art=159> [Accessed 22 January 2003].

Axtell, R 1990, *The do's and taboos of hosting international visitors*, Wiley, New York.

Baranoff, E 2003, *Risk management and insurance*, Wiley, New York.

Betteridge, D 1997, *Event management in leisure and tourism*, Hodder & Stoughton, London.

Boo, HC, Ghiselli, R & Almanza, BA 2000, 'Consumer perceptions and concerns about the healthfulness and safety of food served at fairs and festivals, *Event management*, 6 (2), 85–92.

Bureau of Tourism Research 1998, *International visitors survey 1997*, BTR, Canberra.

Catherwood, DW, Van Kirk, RL & Ernst & Young 1992, *The complete guide to special event management: business insights, financial advice, and successful strategies from Ernst & Young, advisors to the Olympics, the Emmy Awards, and the PGA Tour*, Wiley, New York.

Cook, S 1997, *Customer care*, Kogan Page, London.

Cordato, A 1999, *Australian travel and tourism law*, 3rd edn, Butterworths, Sydney.

Cutlip, S, Center, A & Broom, G 2000, *Effective public relations*, 8th edn, Prentice Hall, New Jersey.

Denvy, D 1990, *Organising special events and conferences*, Pineapple Press, Sarasota, Florida.

Getz, D 1997, *Event management & event tourism*, Cognizant Communication Corp., New York.

Goldblatt, JJ 1997, *Special events: best practices in modern event management*, 2nd edn, Van Nostrand Reinhold, Wiley, New York.

Goldblatt, JJ 2002, *Special events: twenty-first century global event management*, 3rd edn, The Wiley event management series, Wiley, New York.

Goldblatt, JJ, McKibben, CF & International Special Events Society 1996, *The dictionary of event management*, Van Nostrand Reinhold, New York.

Goldblatt, JJ, Nelson, KS & International Special Events Society 2001, *The international dictionary of event management*, 2nd edn, Wiley events, Wiley, New York.

Golik, B 2003, *Not over the hill, just enjoying the view: seniors market for tourism* [Online], Office of the Ageing, Available: <www.families.qld.gov.au/seniors/publications/> [Accessed 4 July 2003].

Graham, S, Goldblatt, JJ & Delpy, L 1995, *The ultimate guide to sport event management and marketing*, Irwin Professional Pub, Burr Ridge, Illinois.

Graham, S, Goldblatt, JJ & Neirotti, LD 2001, *The ultimate guide to sports marketing*, 2nd edn, McGraw-Hill, New York.

Hall, C 1992, *Hallmark tourist events: management and planning*, Belhaven Press, London.

Handy, C 1993, *Understanding organizations*, 4th edn, Penguin Books, London.

Hofstede, G 1980, *Culture's consequences: international differences in work related values*, Sage, Beverly Hills.

Hoyle, LH 2002, *Event marketing: how to successfully promote events, festivals, conventions, and expositions*, The Wiley event management series, Wiley, New York.

Joel, A 1998, *Australian protocol and procedures*, 2nd edn, Angus and Robertson, Sydney.

Johnston, J & Zawawi, C 2000, *Public relations, theory and practice*, Allen & Unwin, Sydney.

Karpin Task Force 1995, *Enterprising nation: report on the Industry Task Force on Leadership and Management Skills*, AGPS, Canberra.

Locke, E, Frederick, C & Bobko, P 1984, 'Effect of self-efficacy, goals and task strategies on task performance', *Journal of Applied Psychology*.

Making the workplace safe: a guide to the laws covering safety and health in Western Australian workplaces 2002 [Online], WorkSafe Western Australia Commission, Available: <www.safetyline.gov.au> [Accessed 17 August 2004].

Malouf, L 1998, *Behind the scenes at special events*, John Wiley & Sons, Milton, Qld.

McCaffree, M and Innis, P 1977, *Protocol: the complete handbook of diplomatic, official and social usage*, Prentice Hall, New York.

McClelland, D 1961, *The achieving society*, Van Nostrand Reinhold, New York.

McClelland, D 1975, *Power: the inner experience*, Irvington, New York.

McColl, R, Callaghan, B & Palmer, A 2000, *Services marketing*, McGraw Hill, Sydney.

McConnell, J 1996, *Managing client-server environments: tools and strategies for building solutions*, Prentice Hall, New Jersey.

McDonnell, I, Allen, J & O'Toole, W 1999, *Festival and special event management*, John Wiley & Sons, Milton, Qld.

McGill, M, Slocum, J and Lei, D 1992, 'Management practices in learning organizations', *Organizational Dynamics*, 42.

McMahon-Beattie, U & Yeoman, I 2004, 'The potential for revenue management in festivals and events', in I Yeoman et al. (eds), *Festival and events management*, Elsivier, Oxford.

Molloy, J 2002, 'Regional festivals: a look at community support, the isolation factor and funding sources', *The Journal of Tourism Studies*, December, 13 (2).

National Volunteers Orientation Kit 2000, Volunteering NSW, Sydney.

Office of Multicultural Affairs 1994, *Best practice in managing a culturally diverse workplace*, AGPS, Canberra.

Reader's Digest book of the road 1999, Reader's Digest (Australia), Sydney.

Richardson, J 1995, *Travel and tourism in Australia: the economic perspective*, Hospitality Press, Melbourne.

Risk Management [Online], Standards Australia Publications, Head Office, 286 Sussex Street, Sydney, Available: <www.standards.com.au> [Accessed 10 May 2004].

Robbins, S & Coulter, M 1996, *Management*, 5th edn, Prentice Hall, New Jersey.

Robbins, SP 1998, *Organizational behaviour*, 8th international edn, Prentice Hall, New Jersey, 1998.

Salter, B & Langford-Wood, N 1999, *Successful event management in a week*, Hodder & Stoughton, London.

Schaumann, P 2004, *The guide to successful destination management*, The Wiley event management series, Wiley, Hoboken, New Jersey.

Schmidt, A 2001, *The banquet business*, 3rd edn, Van Nostrand Reinhold, New York.

Shone, A & Parry, B 2001, *Successful event management: a practical handbook*, Continuum, New York, London.

Shone, A & Parry, B 2004, *Successful event management*, 2nd edn, Thomson Learning, London.

Silvers, J 2004, *Professional event coordination*, The Wiley event management series, Wiley, New Jersey.

Skinner, B & Rukavina, V 2003, *Event sponsorship*, The Wiley event management series, Wiley, New York.

Skinner, BF 1953, *Science and human behaviour*, Free Press, New York.

Smith, PB & Peterson, MF 1988, *Leadership, organizations and culture: an event management model*, Sage, London.

Sonder, M 2003, *Event entertainment and production*, The Wiley event management series, Wiley, Hoboken, New Jersey.

Tarlow, PE 2002, *Event risk management and safety*, The Wiley event management series, Wiley, New York.

Toffler, A 1980, *The Third Wave*, Pan Books, London.

Tuckman, BW 1965, 'Developmental sequence in small groups', *Psychological Bulletin*, 63, 384–99.

Vecchio, R, Hearn, G and Southey, G 1996, *Organizational behaviour*, Harcourt Brace, Sydney.

Vroom, V 1973, *Work and motivation*, Wiley, New York.

Watt, DC 1998, *Event management in leisure and tourism*, Addison Wesley Longman, Harlow.

Weaver, D & Opperman, M 2000, *Tourism management*, John Wiley & Sons, Milton, Qld.

WorkCover News, 16, WorkCover NSW, Sydney.

Zeithaml, VA & Bitner, MJ 1996, *Services marketing*, McGraw Hill, New York.

INDEX

Page numbers followed by fig indicate figures; those followed by tab indicate tables.

accessibility, of venues, 45–6, 49–53, 286
accommodation, 216–17
account codes, 130–1
action planning, 104
advertising, 188–91
advertising collateral, 191
alcohol provision, 65, 315–16
ambulance services, 71
ambush marketing, 96, 116
anti-discrimination legislation, 66
arts festivals, 9
associations, 13–14
audiences, 22–3, 36–8, 52
    identifying, 90–1, 103
    meeting needs of, 91
    surveys, 77, 80–1
Australian Open, 342–3

balance sheets, 132
beverage service, 216, 315–16
bidding and tendering, 158–67
    addressing the criteria, 161–5
    bids and bid documents, 165–7
    interpreting the brief, 160
    researching for, 160–1
bomb threats, 292–3
branding, 186
break-even points, 128
briefings
    for official bodies, 71
    for performers and speakers, 206, 300

for staff, 231, 242, 249–50
    for suppliers, 355–6
brochures, 191
budgets and budgeting, 123–32
    sample budgets, 125–7figs
bump-in, 356–7
bump-out, 356–8
burglary insurance, 70
business environment analysis, 97–103
business interruption insurance, 70
business negotiations, 82–4
business registration, 63–4

cancellation insurance, 71
career opportunities, 346–53
cash flow analysis, 129–30, 130fig
cash flow planning, 122–3
catering, 28–9, 215–16, 262, 308–20
    contracts, 316–17
    food and beverage service, 313–16
    food safety, 67, 216, 260, 308–9, 317–20
    food supply, 259–60, 315
    functions and responsibilities, 309–12
charitable fundraising legislation, 67
checklists, 179, 183fig, 241
Clean Up Australia, 236
cleaning, 258–9, 261, 330–1
clients
    analysing needs of, 76–8
    business negotiations with, 82–4
    evaluation reports for, 84
common law, 62–3
communication, 248–50
communications services, 214
community impact, 25

community relations, 261
community support, 34–5
competition, 24, 103
compliance, legal, 59–73, 123
concept development, 18–29
concerts, 34–40
consumers, 77, 91–2
contingency expenses, 124, 133
contractors, 24, 214–15, 263–4. *see also* suppliers
contracts, 71–2, 316–17
control systems, 333–7
conventions, 9–10
copyright, 67
crisis management, 150, 154
critical path analysis, 41
cross-cultural communication, 248–9
crowd control, 266–7, 287–8, 292
cultural festivals, 9
cultural protocol, 301–2
customers, 78–80, 90–2

decision-making, by consumers, 91–2
décor, 26, 206–7
delegation, 334
designing. *see* event designing
direct mail advertising, 190
displays and signage, 191
dress protocol, 300
duty of care, 62–3

economic impact, 341–3
Edmonton Heritage Festival, 363–78
electricity supply, 214
emergencies, 289–93, 335
Emergency Control Organisation (ECO), 290–1
emergency services, 71
entertainment, 28, 206
entertainment events, 9
environmental issues, 217–18
environmental protection legislation, 67
equity theory, of motivation, 245–6
essential services, 214
ethical issues, 14–15
evacuation procedures, 292
evaluation
  of events, 337–40
  of marketing, 92, 104–6
  reports for clients, 84
  of sponsorship, 116–18, 340
event cancellation insurance, 71
event concept development, 18–29
event designing, 26–9
event feasibility planning, 31–43
event industry. *see also* business environment analysis
  job opportunities, 346–53
  relations in, 13fig

updating knowledge in, 15, 350–3
event management associations, 13–14
event managers, 239–40, 348
  leadership skills, 240–4
  managing teams, 241–2, 248–50
  time management, 250–1
event marketing, 86–107. *see also* event promotion;
    market segmentation; marketing; ticket pricing
  developing a marketing plan, 97–106, 98fig
  evaluating, 92, 104–6
  identifying target markets, 78–80, 90–1, 103
  legal aspects, 103
  marketing mix, 93–5
  nature, 87–9
  sponsorship, 95–7
  steps in, 89–93
event promotion, 104, 186–99. *see also* event marketing
  action plans, 198–9
  advertising, 189–91
  branding, 187
  personal selling, 192
  publicity, 194–8
  sales promotion, 192–3
event proposals, 175
event teams, 12, 24, 241–5, 248–50
event technology, 12–13
events
  characteristics, 4–5
  classification, 5–12
  defined, 5
  impacts, 158–9, 340–1
  as products, 89–90, 94–5, 103–4
  purpose and objectives, 19–21, 32–3, 172–5
  themes, 19–21
  timing, 23–4
  types, 8–12
exhibition registration managers, 350
exhibitions, 9–10
expectancy theory, of motivation, 247–8

family events, 10
feasibility planning, 31–43
feedback controls, 334
festivals, 162–4, 341
fetes and fairs, 10–11
fidelity guarantee insurance, 70
financial management, 23, 25, 121–39, 261
  account codes, 130–1
  assessing financial viability, 38–9
  balance sheets, 132
  budgeting, 123–32
  cash flow analysis, 129–30
  contingency expenses, 133
  financial control systems, 123, 132–3, 336
  financial planning, 38–9, 41–3
  first steps, 122–3

food and beverage, 315–16
income strategy, 128–9
post-event reporting, 133–4
profit and loss statements, 131–2
fire insurance, 70
fire procedures, 292
fireworks, 285
first aid, 273–4
flags, protocol for, 305–6
fliers, 191
food. *see also* catering
logistical aspects, 315
safety, 67, 308–9, 317–20
styles of service, 313–14
Functions Manager, 309–12
fundraising events, 10–11

Gantt charts, 176–9
gas supply, *214*
general insurance, 70
general liability insurance, 269
goal achievement, 246
grant applications, 160, 161tab
group development, 248–9
guests, 196–8, 298

hallmark events, 6
Hazard Analysis Critical Control Point plans, 317–20
hazardous substances, 273
heritage festivals, 363–78
Hofstede, Geert, 248–9

ICMS Australia, 6–7
image creation, 186
incident report forms, 196, 278–80
income sources, 122, 128–9. *see also* bidding and
tendering; merchandising; sponsorship; ticket
pricing
Indigenous Australians, 300–1
industrial relations law, 64–5, 102–3, 232–3
insurance, 68–71, 269, 270
Internet advertising, 189

job descriptions, 221, 224, 224fig, 226–8fig

Korean Food Fair, 325–8

LAN nights, 33–40
laws and regulations
concerning events, 25, 63–8, 103, 233, 261, 316
information about, 60
sources of law, 60–3
layout, 26
Life Concert, 32–40
lifting techniques, 270–2
lighting, 207, 285

liquor licensing, 65
local events, 9, 162–4, 340–1
local government regulations, 63
Locke, Edwin, 246
logistics, 28, 315, 324, 354–62
loss of profits insurance, 70

machinery
breakdown insurance, 71
safe use of, 272–3
major events, 6–7
Maleny Scarecrow Carnival, 20
Man from Snowy River Arena Spectacular, 27
management fees, 122–3
maps (of venues), 56–7, 176
market research, 80–1, 104–6
market segmentation, 78–80, 90
marketing, 25, 186–7, 260. *see also* ambush marketing;
event marketing; event promotion; services
marketing
concept, 86–7, 103
versus selling, 103–4
marketing events, 9
Marketing Information System (MKS), 106
marketing mix, 93–5
McClelland, David, 245
media releases, 194–6, 261
media support, 38
medical services, 262, 273–4
meetings
for event management, 251
as events, 9–10
mega-events, 5–6
Melbourne Comedy Festival, 337–8
Mercedes Australian Fashion Week, 28
merchandising, 118, 261
minor events, 7
mission statements, 172–3
modelling, financial, 41–2
models (of venues), 176
money in transit insurance, 70–1
morale. *see* motivation: staff
motivation
customer, 91
staff, 233–4, 242–3, 245–8, 263–4
theories, 244–8

National Folk Festival, 132–9
needs theory, of motivation, 245
negotiations
with clients, 82–4
with sponsors, 113–16
non-appearance insurance, 71

occupational health and safety, 269–74, 277
legislation, 68, 233, 269–70

order of precedence, 297, 298fig
organic food markets, 32–40
organisation charts, 179, 182fig, 221, 222–3figs, 241
outdoor events, 278–81

panic payments, 133
pedestrian access, 286
performance standards, 258–9
personal selling, 192
planning. *see also* project management
    catering, 317–20
    for emergencies, 150
    event feasibility, 31–43, 42fig
    financial, 41–3, 123–30
    logistical, 354–8
    marketing the event, 97–106
    planning tools, 176–83
    spectator management, 284–7
    waste management, 323–9
police services, 71, 268
pollution, 217
position descriptions, 224, 226–8fig
power supplies, 214
press releases, 194–5
preventative controls, 333–4
pricing. *see* ticket pricing
primary research, 76, 80–2
print advertising, 190
privacy law, 66
product development, 103–4
product launching events, 9
profit and loss statements, 131–2
project management, 171–84
    establishing aims and objectives, 173–5
    event proposals, 175
    mission/purpose statements, 172–3
    planning tools, 41, 176–83
promotion. *see* event promotion
promotional events, 9, 192–3
protocol, 296–306
public liability insurance, 68–9
public relations, 194–5, 197
publicity, 194–8
pyrotechnics, 285

radio advertising, 190
recognition strategies, 233–4
recruitment, 224–5
recycling, 323–4, 329
registration, 260–1, 350
regulations. *see* laws and regulations
reinforcement theory, of motivation, 246–7
religious protocol, 301–2
revenue sources, 122. *see also* merchandising;
    sponsorship; ticket pricing

risk management
    concept, 142, 145
    handling crises, 150, 154, 335
    incident report forms, 196, 278–80
    policy development for, 153–4
    risk analysis, 40–1, 106, 145–53, 274–5, 287–8
    stages in, 146–53, 274–7
risks, 3–4, 25, 32, 40–1
    analysing impact, 148–9
    bad weather, 25, 71, 142
    concept, 142, 145
    financial, 3–4, 25, 142
    legal, 142
    likelihood and level, 148–52, 275
    mismanagement, 143
    safety and security, 143, 150
    sources, 148tab
    at sporting events, 143–4
    technology-related, 142–3
    types, 142–5
role modelling, 247
run charts, 179, 180–2, 241, 303

safety, 3
    food provision, 260, 317–20
    incident reporting, 278–80
    legislation, 68
    occupational, 269–74
    of venues and sites, 53–4, 277–81
sales promotions, 192–3
sanitary facilities, 329–30
seating plans, 207fig, 300
secondary research, 76, 80–3
security legislation, 67
security services, 262, 267–9
services marketing, 87–9
sets, 209
signage, 191
sites. *see* venues and sites
skills, 34
sound, 208
speakers, briefings for, 300
special effects, 206–7
special events, 5
spectator management planning, 284–7
sponsorship, 95–7, 108–18
    entertaining sponsors, 259fig
    evaluating, 116–18
    motives for, 111–12
    negotiation and implementation, 113–16
    types, 112
sporting events, 5, 8, 262
    bidding for, 164–5
    protocol issues, 304–5
    risks, 143–4
    staging aspects, 210–11